Evidence Based
Coaching Handbook

Evidence Based Coaching Handbook

Putting Best Practices to Work for Your Clients

Dianne R. Stober
and
Anthony M. Grant, Editors

WILEY

John Wiley & Sons, Inc.

Published by John Wiley & Sons, Inc., Hoboken, New Jersey.
Published simultaneously in Canada.

For general information on our other products and services please contact our Customer Care Department within the United States at (800) 762-2974, outside the United States at (317) 572-3993 or fax (317) 572-4002.

Wiley also publishes its books in a variety of electronic formats. Some content that appears in print may not be available in electronic books. For more information about Wiley products, visit our web site at www.wiley.com.

Library of Congress Cataloging-in-Publication Data:

Stober, Dianne R.
    Evidence based coaching handbook : putting best practices to work for your
clients / by Dianne R. Stober and Anthony M. Grant.
        p.   cm.
    Includes bibliographical references.
    ISBN-13: 978-0-471-72086-7 (cloth)
    ISBN-10: 0-471-72086-0 (cloth)
    1. Personal coaching.   2. Executive coaching.   I. Grant, Anthony (Anthony
M.)   II. Title.
    BF637.P36S76   2006
    658.3'124—dc22   2005029366

Printed in the United States of America.
10   9   8   7   6

This book is dedicated to

My parents,
for starting me on a path of knowledge,

to Ben,
for walking it with me,

and to my children,
for taking me down interesting side trails.

(DRS)

My family,
Georgie, Ben, and Toby,

my parents,
Eva and Avi,

my sisters,
Claire and Jane,

and in loving memory of my brother,
David.

I love you all.

(AMG)

Contents

Preface

As an emerging area of study, coaching holds many opportunities to contribute to our bases of knowledge. There is knowledge to be gained in applying coaching to the world as we know it. But before we go too far in that direction, there is also the opportunity to apply existing knowledge to the current practice of coaching. This volume is intended to take some initial steps in that direction with the humble hope that this will prove helpful in grounding coaching practice in a wealth of applicable knowledge. This is not a complete picture of existing theories and bodies of knowledge that can inform the development of coaching but does provide at least a range of perspectives. It is our hope that readers of this book will find information that is useful, stimulating, and maybe even challenging for their own development as coaches.

Putting this book together has been an exciting endeavor for us. From our first conversations at a conference about the need for such a book, we have found ourselves in rousing discussions about what the appropriate models are for coaching, what theoretical foundations are essential, and where the next steps lie in the professionalization of coaching. We have each learned much through this project and hope that others will too.

DIANNE R. STOBER
ANTHONY M. GRANT

April 2006

Acknowledgments

OF COURSE THERE are a number of acknowledgments we would like to make. There are a number of people without whom this project would have never been possible. Most importantly, we would like to acknowledge the contributing authors for their expertise, willingness to share that knowledge in this format, and their hard work in translating all of this into well-written, useful works. Without them, the breadth and depth of this book would not have been possible.

In addition to the contributing authors, a variety of colleagues and friends have given us feedback, support, and encouragement: Shirley Anderson, Michael Cavanagh, Barclay Hudson, Jenny Schwartz, Leni Wildflower, Patrick Williams, Richard Zackon. Thank you all for your contributions that have made this a better book. Our students at Fielding Graduate University and University of Sydney have given us important feedback, asked great questions, and generally pushed our thinking.

Another important source of support we would like to acknowledge involves those at John Wiley & Sons. David Bernstein not only believed in this project, he also provided keen insights, great encouragement, and those all important reality-checks when things were topsy-turvy or looking grim. Ester Mallach was a source of calm, steady support in the midst of infinite details. Micheline Frederick demonstrated her great capabilities of keeping things rolling along smoothly through production of this book (no small feat!). And the staff at Cape Cod Compositors was indispensable in their thoroughness in helping us through the copyediting process.

There are some individuals who were very personally involved in this project: our families. Our spouses, Ben Slocumb and Georgie Grant, not only supported this work but remained enthusiastic and interested even when it meant late dinners, absent-minded partners, and those "It will just be a few more minutes" white lies. And our children, Hannah Slocumb, Eli Slocumb, Ben Grant, and Toby Grant proved to be patient or distracting as our experience required; we hope we were able to do likewise.

And finally, there are clients who contributed to the development of our and the contributors' practice and expertise. Without their willingness to engage with us and to share their lives and experience, there would not be any theories to apply or stories to tell.

Contributors

Geoffrey N. Abbott is an executive coach and researcher. He has been based in El Salvador since 2003, where he is completing his doctoral dissertation under scholarship from the Faculty of Economics and Commerce of the Australian National University. He has been working with expatriate managers and studying how coaching might assist cultural adaptation. Geoff's academic background is in organizational psychology. His related consulting and research interests include the influence of culture and values in the workplace, and—of course—executive coaching. Geoff's coaching clients in Central America, the United States, and Australia are drawn from the commercial, government, development, and academic sectors. His expertise lies particularly with executives who work in cross-cultural or multicultural contexts. Geoff is an associate with the School of Economics and Business (ESEN) in El Salvador. He was formerly Senior Policy Advisor for SBS Australia, a government-funded national television and radio broadcaster specializing in multicultural programming, where he managed strategic planning and cultural research. He has a keen interest in improving his Spanish and golf.

Seth Allcorn, PhD, is an assistant dean and chief financial officer for the Texas Tech Health Sciences Center School of Medicine. Dr. Allcorn has 20 years of experience working with physicians, hospitals, and academic medical centers. He has served as Associate Dean for Fiscal Affairs at the Stritch School of Medicine, Loyola–Chicago, and as the administrator of the departments of medicine at the University of Missouri–Columbia and University of Rochester schools of medicine. He has worked for 20 years as a part-time and full-time organizational consultant specializing in the management of change, strategic planning, and organizational restructuring. Dr. Allcorn is extensively published. He is the author or co-author of 10 books and over 60 papers that have appeared in scholarly and practitioner journals. He is a founding member of the International Society for the Psychoanalytic Study of Organizations.

Dr. Jeffrey E. Auerbach is the founder and president of the College of Executive Coaching, the leader in coach training for professionals with graduate degrees. The College of Executive Coaching is an International Coach Federation Accredited Coach Training Program with courses ongoing worldwide and is based in Pismo Beach, California. Jeffrey is the author of the best-selling *Personal and Executive Coaching: The Complete Guide for Mental Health Professionals* and *Seeing the Light: What Organizations Need to Know—The 2005 State of the Coaching Industry*, the editor of *Building Competence in Personal and Executive Coaching*, and the research director of the 2005 State of the Coaching Industry Project. He is the program committee co-chair of the Tenth International Coach Federation Conference, a steering committee member of the Executive Coaching Summit, on the editorial board of the *International Journal of Coaching in Organizations*, board of directors member of the Association of Coach Training Organizations, steering committee member of the American Psychological Association Healthy Workplace Awards, a consulting psychologist, a certified personal and executive coach, a professional certified coach, and a master personal and executive coach. Dr. Auerbach is available for keynote presentations and consultations to industry groups on the emerging field of executive coaching.

Jennifer Garvey Berger consults and teaches in the areas of adult development, individual differences, and transformational learning. She teaches coaches about complexity of mind and leadership, and how to use advanced listening and questioning techniques to better understand and support their clients. In her writing and her teaching, Jennifer explores the workplace as one of the major centers of learning for adults, and she uses her research and consulting to help adults think about their work and their workplaces in ways that help them make positive changes. An assistant professor at George Mason University, Jennifer has also taught undergraduate, graduate, and professional development courses at Harvard and Georgetown Universities, among others. As a partner with Kenning Associates, Jennifer works with executives in a variety of industries (e.g., BNSF Railroad, Fidelity Investments, McKinsey & Company, SpectraLink) to help people develop the skills and the perspectives that will make their work more effective. She is co-editor of two books, *Acts of Inquiry in Qualitative Research* (Harvard Educational Publishing Group, 2000) and *Executive Coaching: Practices and Perspectives* (Davies-Black, 2002), and is currently writing a book called *Thriving in a Complex World: Twenty-First Century Professional Development* (Elsevier: Butterworth-Heinemann Business Books, scheduled for publication spring, 2007). Jennifer holds a master's degree in teaching and learning and a doctorate in adult development from Harvard University.

Michael Cavanagh, PhD, is both a practicing coaching psychologist and an academic. Michael is the deputy director of the Coaching Psychology Unit at the University of Sydney, where he has been involved in the development of the world's first coaching degree program from its inception to the present day. He is also currently the National Convenor of the Australian Psychological Society's Interest Group in Coaching Psychology (IGCP) with over 650 members across Australia and internationally. As a practitioner, Michael works with senior leaders in a range of multinational and national organizations. Michael's coaching practice and teaching emphasize the use of empirically validated techniques and draw on cognitive-behavioral, systemic, and solution-focused approaches. His areas of special interest include coaching in complex systems, communication and interpersonal skills, solution-focused approaches to goal achievement and problem solving, and working with challenging executives.

Elaine Cox leads the MA in Coaching and Mentoring Practice for the Westminster Institute of Education at Oxford Brookes University, and is also now developing a Professional Doctorate in Coaching and Mentoring for the University. She has a master's degree in continuing education from the University of Warwick and undertook her PhD at Lancaster University exploring the development of mentors in the voluntary sector. In addition, Elaine is editor for the *International Journal of Evidence-Based Coaching and Mentoring* and is a member of the European Mentoring and Coaching Council's Ethics and Standards Committee. In addition to her interests in adult learning and development, Elaine is a regular contributor to academic journals. She is currently researching the use of emotion in coaching and is involved in a collaborative project exploring the coaching interaction and how this engenders change.

Anthony M. Grant, PhD, is a coaching psychologist and the founder and director of the Coaching Psychology Unit at the School of Psychology at the University of Sydney. Anthony has pioneered the evidence-based approach to coaching. Anthony's background is grounded in the realities of the commercial world. Having left school at the age of 15 with no qualifications, he completed his training as a carpenter and ran his own contracting business. Embarking on a second career, he made a successful transition into direct sales and marketing, before beginning tertiary studies in psychology as a mature student and commencing a third career in his 30s. He holds a BA(Hons) in Psychology from the University of Sydney and a Master of Arts in Behavioral Science and PhD from the Department of Psychology at Macquarie University. His PhD thesis is one of the few that explicitly examine the effectiveness of evidence-based coaching. In addition to his academic work, Anthony has many thousands of hours of coach training and coaching experience and works with leaders of national and international organizations as an executive coach. His coaching research and practice have frequently been reported in the national and international media. This is his fifth book on evidence-based approaches to coaching.

Carol Kauffman, PhD, ABPP, an assistant clinical professor at Harvard Medical School, department of psychiatry, runs seminars and offers supervision in positive psychology. She teaches coaching research at the Institute for Life Coach Training, is on the editorial board of the *International Coaching Psychology Review*, and is a reviewer for the *Journal of Positive Psychology* and Routledge Publishing. She holds a Diplomate in Clinical Psychology and is an examiner for the American Board of Professional Psychology. As a performance and personal coach, Dr. Kauffman loves working with people who want to be more effective at work, live their lives purposefully, and become closer with those they love. She specializes in those who have a book, artistic, or research project in their minds and hearts and need help getting it out the door and into the marketplace.

Travis Kemp, PhD, is managing director of The Teleran Group, a registered psychologist and secondary teacher, and a registered member of the Psychotherapists and Counsellors Federation of Australia. He is a founding national committee member of the Australian Psychological Society's Interest Group in Coaching Psychology and is a member and past state chair of the APS College of Organisational Psychologists. He is a fellow of the Australian Human Resources Institute and Australian Institute of Management, a graduate member of the Australian Institute of Company Directors, and member of the Australian College of Educators. In addition to holding the position of adjunct research fellow with the International Graduate School of Business at the University of South Australia, he also holds an appointment as adjunct lecturer at the University of Sydney School of Psychology's Coaching Psychology Unit.

David B. Peterson earned his PhD in counseling and industrial-organizational psychology from the University of Minnesota. He joined Personnel Decisions in 1985, became leader of PDI's worldwide coaching practice in 1990, and was promoted to senior vice president in 1996. David has coached hundreds of senior executives from organizations such as Hewlett-Packard, Shell, Mayo Clinic, 3M, and Target. The models that David developed, such as the Development Pipeline and GAPS Grid, form the foundation of PDI's coaching and leadership development services and products. With co-author Mary Dee Hicks, David has written two best-selling books—*Leader as Coach: Strategies for Coaching and Developing Others* and *Development FIRST: Strategies for Self-Directed Learning*. A pioneer in the field of executive coaching, David has been researching, writing, and training others on the topic for almost 20 years. He has been quoted in the *Wall Street Journal*, *Fortune*, *Time*, *BusinessWeek*, and *USA Today*.

Philippe Rosinski is an expert in executive coaching, team coaching, and global leadership development, sought after by leading international corporations. He is the author of *Coaching Across Cultures* (Nicholas Brealey Publishing/Intercultural Press, 2003) and his pioneering work in bringing the crucial intercultural dimension into the practice of coaching has won him worldwide acclaim. Philippe Rosinski is the first European to have been designated Master Certified Coach by the International Coach Federation. He is principal of Rosinski & Company, a global consulting firm that helps leaders, teams, and organizations unleash their human potential to achieve high performance together with high fulfillment. Previously, he was the Director of Custom Programs at the Center for Creative Leadership Europe. He received an electrical and mechanical engineering degree from the Ecole Polytechnique in Brussels, a master of science degree in electrical engineering from Stanford University, and the Cepac postgraduate business degree from the Solvay Business School in Brussels.

Dianne R. Stober, PhD, is on the faculty of the Organizational Management and Development master's program at Fielding Graduate University. She also teaches in Fielding's Evidence-Based Coaching Certificate Program. As a contributor to the development of coaching as a profession, she has presented and published her work in a variety of scholarly and professional venues such as the American Psychological Association, the International Coach Federation, the Professional Coach and Mentor Association, the Australian Evidence-Based Coaching Conference, and the *International Journal of Coaching in Organizations*. In addition, Dianne maintains an active coaching practice working with a diverse range of individuals and organizations. She has found coaching to be a fruitful application of her longstanding interests in leveraging people's strengths, capitalizing on our many differences, and developing people's inherent potentials. Dianne received her PhD in clinical psychology from Georgia State University, completed her internship at the University of Colorado Health Sciences Center, and received a postdoctoral fellowship at Emory University.

Introduction

ANTHONY M. GRANT AND DIANNE R. STOBER

CHANGE IS A constant. So, too, is the search for better, more effective ways to create and sustain change. This handbook is about articulating theoretically grounded, evidence-based approaches to executive, workplace, and personal coaching. Our hope is that this book will further contribute to the maturation and evolution of the emerging discipline of professional coaching, through making explicit the wide range of theoretical perspectives that can form the foundations of an evidence-based approach.

One of the conflicts in the maturation of a profession of coaching has been the value of open discourse, which is essential for the building of bases of knowledge, compared to business models of intellectual property, which often restrict access to information. It is essential for the coaching community to find ways to balance these needs in a way that allows for models of coaching to be tested and knowledge to be developed and shared. This book seeks to support the move toward discourse in the public domain regarding different theoretical formulations and the evidence behind them as applied to coaching practice.

Coaching is still in the process of establishing its credibility as an effective means for change and growth. Linking coaching practice with existing, applicable bases of knowledge of science and practice is an important step in enhancing credibility and in shifting from focusing primarily on techniques and skills to a broader and deeper understanding of relevant knowledge in coach education.

Recognizing the importance of addressing these issues, an increasing number of coaches from a wide range of disciplines have developed coaching methodologies that are explicitly grounded in the broader academic knowledge base. Indeed, coaching has become an increasingly accepted cross-disciplinary methodology, and people from a wide variety of professional backgrounds are working as coaches. These backgrounds include the behavioral and social sciences, organizational change and development, psychoanalytical therapy, cognitive and behavioral psychology, adult education, as well as business and economic science. Each of these has its own theoretical frameworks and practices, and each has qualities and strengths useful in coaching. As these, and other, bodies of knowledge are brought to bear on coach education and practice, the credibility of coaching as an emerging profession versus a potential fad is enhanced.

Drawing on these considerations, this handbook presents a range of theoretical frameworks. Each chapter details a specific theoretical framework, and then discusses how coaching would be conducted from this framework, using two standard case studies as examples. Each chapter emphasizes different aspects of the coaching process. We designed this format in the hope that it will be helpful both to experienced professional coaches who are looking to enrich their own existing theoretical frameworks and practices and also to students of coaching who are in the process of identifying their preferred or personal framework for understanding and working with human behavior.

THE NATURE OF COACHING

Before discussing the range of theoretical approaches to coaching presented in this book, it may be useful to briefly discuss the nature of coaching, and then examine what constitutes an evidence-based approach.

The aim of executive or life coaching is sustained cognitive, emotional, and behavioral changes that facilitate goal attainment and performance enhancement, either in one's work or in one's personal life (Douglas & McCauley, 1999). In addition, executive or personal coaching is focused on nonclinical populations who do not have clinically significant mental health problems or diagnoses. There has been considerable media interest in coaching (Garman, Whiston, & Zlatoper, 2000), and coaching in the workplace dates back to at least Gorby (1937). However, there is still some lack of clarity as to what coaching actually is.

Definitions of the coaching process vary considerably in their degree of clarity and succinctness, and also the extent to which they emphasize teaching or direct instruction as opposed to the facilitation of self-directed learning. Emphasizing an instructional approach, Parsloe (1995, p. 18) proposes that coaching is "directly concerned with the immediate improvement of performance and development of skills by a form of tutoring or instruction." Also emphasizing instruction, Druckman and Bjork (1991, p. 61) propose that:

> Coaching consists of observing students and offering hints, feedback, reminders, [or] new tasks, or redirecting a student's attention to a salient feature—all with the goal of making the student's performance approximate the expert's performance as closely as possible.

In contrast to the emphasis on imparting information through tutoring or instruction seen in Parsloe's (1995) and Druckman and Bjork's (1991) approaches, Whitmore (1992, p. 8) proposes that "coaching is unlocking a person's potential to maximise their own performance. It is helping them to learn rather than teaching them." The theme of facilitation rather than instruction is echoed by Hudson (1999), who defines the process of coaching as occurring when "a coach helps a client see options for becoming a more effective human being" (p. xix). Hudson (1999, p. 6) proposes that:

> A coach is a person who facilitates experiential learning that results in future-oriented abilities. . . . [A coach] refers to a person who is a trusted role model, adviser, wise person, friend, mensch, steward, or guide—a person who works with emerging human and organizational forces to tap new energy and purpose, to shape new vision and plans, and to generate desired results. A coach is someone trained and devoted to guiding others into increased competence, commitment, and confidence.

Focusing on executive coaching, Kilburg (2000, p. 65) proposes that:

> Executive coaching is defined as a helping relationship formed between a client who has managerial authority and responsibility in an organization and a consultant who uses a wide variety of behavioral techniques and methods to assist the client to achieve a mutually identified set of goals to improve his or her professional performance and personal satisfaction and consequently to improve the effectiveness of the client's organization within a formally defined coaching agreement.

As can be seen, there has been considerable work done attempting to define coaching. Although each contributor to the debate offers different nuances, there are common core themes (Brennan and Prior, 2005). These include a collaborative and egalitarian rather than authoritarian relationship between coach and coachee; a focus on constructing solutions and goal attainment processes, rather than solely analyzing problems; the assumption that clients do not have clinically significant mental health problems; an emphasis on collaborative goal setting; and the recognition that although coaches have expertise in facilitating learning through coaching, they do not necessarily need high levels of domain-specific expertise in the coachee's chosen area of learning. Further, the coaching process is seen as being a systematic process, and is typically directed at fostering the ongoing self-directed learning and personal growth of the coachee.

Thus it is clear that coaching is more about asking the right questions than telling people what to do, and it is not necessarily concerned with subject-matter expertise or advice giving. Underpinning the coaching process are the principles guiding effective adult learning. These include the recognition that adult learners are autonomous, have a foundation of life experiences and knowledge from which they are able to generalize, have a readiness to learn and engage in reflective practice, and wish to be treated with respect (Dailey, 1984).

We also believe that professional coaching should be explicitly linked to the broader knowledge base, should be conducted in an informed-practitioner model, and should be evidence-based.

TOWARD AN INFORMED-PRACTITIONER MODEL OF PROFESSIONAL COACHING

The concept of an informed-practioner model of professional coaching draws on, and further develops, the reflective-practitioner and the scientist-practitioner models established in the behavioral and medical sciences. Within the reflective-practitioner and the scientist-practitioner frameworks, practitioners are trained to have a working understanding of research principles and methodologies. This understanding then enables them to apply informed critical thought to the evaluation of their practices. In addition, such informed practitioners can draw on relevant academic literature to design and implement evidence-based interventions with their own clients (Haring-Hidore & Vacc, 1988) and to evaluate client progress while adhering to ethical practice (Barnett, 1988).

Informed practioners are not expected to be significant producers of research (Parker & Detterman, 1988). Rather they are positioned as educated consumers of research who can utilize related research and critical thinking skills to improve their practices and intellectual understanding of coaching. While the scientist-practitioner model in the behavioral sciences has its critics (O'Gorman, 2001), it has nevertheless been central to the professionalization of the behavioral sciences (Shapiro, 2002).

Movement toward an informed-practitioner model requires that professional coach training programs explicitly address the theoretical and empirical foundations of coaching, provide training in sound research methodologies, develop basic statistical and data analysis skills, and foster informed critical thinking skills in student coaches. Such an approach forms the basis of an evidence-based coaching paradigm.

WHAT IS EVIDENCE-BASED COACHING?

The term *evidence-based coaching* was coined by Grant (2003) to distinguish between professional coaching that is explicitly grounded in the broader empirical and theoretical knowledge base and coaching that was developed from the "pop psychology" personal development genre.

Adapted from its use in medical and social services, evidence-based coaching means far more than simply producing evidence that a specific coaching intervention is effective or being able to demonstrate return on investment. The evidence-based approach is not merely about the use of double-blind, randomized controlled trials or the use of manualized interventions. It is a broader view based on the underlying assumption that translating research evidence into practice can optimize outcomes (Wampold & Bhati, 2004). How that is done is where the controversy begins.

Central to the original idea of evidence-based practice in the medical and social sciences is that research methodologies can be evaluated and classified into "good" and "bad" research. In medicine, and to a great extent in psychology, sitting at the top of the hierarchy, and the accepted gold standard, are meta-analyses—systematic reviews of a large number of randomized controlled trials (RCTs). At the next level are the RCTs themselves, which are studies where individuals have been randomly allocated to a treatment or a control group. Double-blind RCTs, where both the researcher and the participant are not informed as to which group they are in, clearly provide a useful methodology for the testing of medical pharmaceutical interventions.

On the next level in this hierarchy are controlled studies without randomization, which in turn sit above quasi-experimental studies, followed by nonexperimental studies (descriptive, correlational, or case studies), followed by expert opinions and clinical experience. Critics of evidence-based practice have argued that the gold standard drives toward an unrealistic perfectionism and cannot, in fact, deliver certainty (Nord, 2002). While this may be true, double-blind RCTs, despite their limitations, are often the most rigorous scientific approach to determine the effectiveness of an intervention.

However, the key issue here is that coaching engagements are not medical interventions that follow prescribed or manualized treatment regimes, and much coaching does not lend itself to evaluation within a medical model. Indeed, given the nonclinical, nonmedical context of coaching, the medical model may be an entirely inappropriate framework from which to understand, teach, and evaluate coaching—as has also been argued for psychotherapy (Wampold, 2001). However, adopting the view that applying evidence to practice allows for improved practice and understanding is a valuable aim in the development of coaching as a discipline. The different avenues for generating research evidence in coaching remain to be discussed.

Hence, we prefer to take a more sophisticated understanding of the term *evidence-based* and refer to the intelligent and conscientious use of *best current knowledge* integrated with *practitioner expertise* in making decisions about how to deliver coaching to *individual coaching clients* and in designing and teaching coach training programs (adapted from Sackett, Haynes, Guyatt, & Tugwell, 1996). This volume is primarily concerned with elucidating available knowledge.

Best current knowledge can be understood as up-to-date information from relevant, valid research, theory, and practice. Because there is at present a somewhat limited academic coach-specific literature, best current knowledge can often be found in the established literature in related fields of evidence, theory, and practice. Informed-practitioner coaches need to be able to draw on such existing knowledge, adapt and apply this knowledge, and in the light of their own reflective practice, develop grounded frameworks that further inform their work with their clients.

The strength of the informed-practitioner model lies not in developing scientifically tenacious prescriptive intervention models to be applied with unquestioning confidence. Rather, its strength is that it provides theoretical frameworks, information, critical thinking, and methodological rigor that the practitioner can use to navigate the ever-changing waters of the coaching intervention.

Evidence-based professional coaching has the very real potential to become a powerful methodology for individual, organizational, social, and systemic change. The use of theoretically based, empirically grounded coaching is increasing. Ten years ago there was very little coaching-related research or there were few theories for coaches to draw on. This paucity of previously developed interventions has had the benefit of forcing professional coaches to go back to basic principles and re-examine the wider body of academic knowledge in order to create coaching interventions that meet the real needs of coaching clients. This approach means that professional coaches are increasingly able to draw on and contribute to informed and intelligent coach-specific literature.

Coaching still has a long way to go. We argue that an evidence-based foundation for professional coaching that moves away from the prescriptive linear approach too often associated with the medical model, and toward contextually relevant coaching methodologies that incorporate both rigor and the lived experience of practitioners and clients, will result in a comprehensive, flexible, and strong model of coaching.

OVERVIEW OF CHAPTERS

In the following chapters, readers will find a broad range of approaches in coaching. In Part I, contributors examine single theories that have direct application in coaching. In Chapter 1, Dianne Stober proposes that the humanistic perspective is an underlying philosophical foundation of coaching today and links humanistic concepts and evidence to coaching practice. David Peterson discusses the behavioral perspective's contributions to coaching and provides a model for building clients' capacities for effective behavior in Chapter 2. Next, in Chapter 3, Jennifer Garvey Berger outlines constructive-developmental theories in adult development, provides a model of different forms of understanding that affect how we view and interact with the world, and then goes on to discuss how coaches can work with people in these different forms. Jeffrey Auerbach, in Chapter 4, delineates the cognitive perspective as it applies to coaching and demonstrates its use in practice. And in Chapter 5, Seth Allcorn links psychoanalytic theory to organizational and executive behavior and discusses how coaches can effect change by understanding and working with these dynamics.

Part II showcases approaches that are either integrative or cross-disciplinary in nature. Starting us off in Chapter 6, Anthony Grant weaves together theory and evidence regarding goal setting, self-determination, and personality into an integrated goal-focused approach to coaching. Elaine Cox describes a number of important concepts from adult learning theories that undergird coaching approaches, and provides a model that capitalizes on these principles in Chapter 7. In Chapter 8, Carol Kauffman discusses evidence from positive psychology and relates a number of exercises and assessments that can be applied to coaching. In Chapter 9, Philippe Rosinski and Geoffrey Abbott lay out theory regarding cross-cultural issues and provide a model of applying this knowledge effectively in any coaching situation. In Chapter 10, Travis Kemp discusses the use of an experiential, psycho-educative approach to coaching and provides a number of tools and techniques for individual and group learning. Systems and complexity theories are related to coaching practice by Michael Cavanagh in Chapter 11. Finally, to bring things together in summary, Dianne Stober and Anthony Grant propose the utility of a contextual model of coaching that can link all of the approaches together in a model of the principles of coaching.

TWO CASE STUDIES

In addition to the evidence and theory provided in the chapters, each chapter also discusses that particular approach to the same two case studies. It is our hope that readers will gain a sense of not only what the various approaches entail, but also how they are applied. Readers will get an outlook on different angles of approach and at the same time will get a sense of where overlap and similarities exist among these various viewpoints. Descriptions of coaching from each perspective are contained at the end of each chapter.

The Case of Bob

Bob is a 58-year-old Caucasian man who is the CEO of a multinational corporation in industrial development, AMM, Inc. He has been the CEO for eight years and has overseen the corporation's growth from a medium-sized organization to one that has rapidly expanded and acquired other companies. AMM has recently bought out one of its main competitors, XYZ, and Bob is faced with the challenge of merging XYZ into AMM. This acquisition is based in South Korea and the workforce is made up of a combination of European expatriate and South Korean personnel.

In terms of personal style, Bob can be extremely charming and is fun to be around. He is a fast thinker who likes to tell jokes and keep people entertained. He likes to have a high profile and enjoys being the center of attention. He values people who give him positive feedback. Although he enjoys social interacting, he has a tendency to talk more than he listens. Bob values success, both in his personal life and in his work, and although he talks a lot about the importance of social values and giving a hand to those "lower down the ladder" he really prizes winning and winners. In his personal life he enjoys socializing with successful people; he prefers to lead an interesting life and sees himself as someone who likes to play hard as well as work hard. He expects his family and friends to do the same.

Bob is good at showing concern for the problems of others, and will appear deeply interested and focused while he is talking to a person about some personal problem they may have. However, he is not good at following up on his initial comments, and will rarely refer back to an emotionally focused conversation or inquire about the other person's well-being in later conversation with that person. In his personal life this has not been a problem, because his wife Carol enjoys social networking. However, in the workplace Bob is seen as good at talking the talk, but somewhat superficial and not really interested in the well-being of others. This obvious difference between his espoused interest in the well-being of others and his actual actions has contributed to a feeling in the workplace that Bob is rather superficial, and really cares only about results, not people.

He can also be rather volatile, and his tendency toward emotional displays when under pressure, combined with his perceived superficiality, has in the past undermined his credibility with his team. Furthermore, although energetic and adventurous, he tends to ignore his own mistakes (and justifies or rationalizes them), but is very quick to pick up on other people's.

In terms of leadership and management style, Bob uses his considerable personal charisma in laying out a clear vision. He sees AMM as a corporation that leads the world in the development of industrial infrastructure, the design and construction of manufacturing plants and systems. With that, Bob has recognized that infrastructure needs to be customized for different environments, nations, and cultures but he often struggles with how to customize the human interactions needed to make that happen. He is very self-assured of his vision and can be very persuasive in laying out that vision for his board of directors and others. Bob has achieved his current position by persuading others that his way of doing things is right. When someone is not following his plan, Bob generally has seen them as "not getting it" and has often then sought to either get them on board or see to it that they do not have much effect on derailing his plan. For example, when Bob was hired as CEO by AMM, one of the vice presidents, Jerry, did not share Bob's vision of how to integrate the management team from a corporation AMM had acquired. Bob had no compunction about covertly engineering Jerry's transfer from the home office in Chicago to managing their small Southern U.S. office in Texas.

In terms of his background, Bob was raised in the Midwestern United States in an upper-middle-class family. He followed a fairly traditional path through university, an MBA program, and his first job was as a project manager in a large construction firm. Bob prides himself on his ability to win people over to his views and has been viewed by his superiors over the years as someone who can be "pushy" but "gets things done." Initially, his job changes occurred through promotions, but after reaching a senior manager level, he was recruited by other corporations for his ability to make things happen and his desire for achievement. Bob has not generally developed strong friendships in his work life but rather tends to socialize with people who can also have utility in helping him accomplish projects he has in front of him.

Bob has been married to Carol for 32 years and their three children, Katherine, Thomas, and Jake, are all grown and on their own. Carol is very supportive of her husband and arranges many social functions for colleagues of Bob's. She is active in a number of charitable organizations, which gives Bob a feeling of satisfaction that not only is he contributing to the growth and development of business, but through his family he also contributes to the community at large. Bob describes his marriage as a partnership where Carol's activities support his career and he supports her civic endeavors as his time allows. Bob is looking forward to the birth of his first grandchild this next year and describes a sense of achievement and satisfaction in having raised his children to be productive, achieving adults. When asked about his connection with them, Bob describes family get-togethers and holidays as his main way to communicate, although Carol "does her job in keeping me informed about what everyone is up to."

Bob met Carol through a mutual friend at the end of college. As they were dating, he found that not only was Carol an attractive and fun person but she was also someone who liked to get people together and helped him meet others and develop relationships. In describing Carol, he was fond of saying that she was the "glue" sticking people together and he was the "gloss" keeping others entertained. Toward the end of his MBA studies, he asked Carol to marry him and found himself looking forward to having her at his side as he set out to make a name for himself. As they had children and he began to move up the corporate ladder, Bob was proud that he had chosen a partner who kept his family life running smoothly, was loving, and also was someone he could bounce ideas off away from work. He liked to think that he was someone who contributed to Carol's happiness, too.

Bob has been intrigued in the past few years by the notion of coaching as a way to leverage his own thoughts and goals more effectively. He has encouraged direct reports to use coaching in the past and has been impressed with how coaching has increased productivity for some of his executives. As he has contemplated using a coach himself, he has not seen a need for the "soft side" of coaching in terms of balancing his work life or developing his ability to relate to others. Rather his focus is on strategic and managerial issues and getting some help in negotiating a productive merger between AMM and XYZ.

Bob has also begun thinking about his eventual retirement in the next 10 years or so and has recognized having a strong desire to "leave the business running perfectly." While this was not true earlier in his life, his focus at this point is not so much about money; it is more around ending his career just right. And this new acquisition feels like a potential obstacle to a perfect ending.

He presents for coaching with an expressed goal of getting the business running perfectly and leaving on a high note.

Summary of Bob's Case

Bob is a reactive/remedial coaching client. He is a CEO in transition, and his organization is merging with an organization it bought out. His leadership style is highly autocratic with a top-down model of management. While he is self-assured and has a big vision for organization, he does not trust others to implement it with his individualistic view of the world. He is charismatic, but people do not stick with him over time. He tends toward an instrumental way of viewing and using human capital, with a high need for achievement and power. He is self-made, high in persistence, and has been around a long time.

The Case of Bonita

Bonita is a 38-year-old African-American woman who has recently been promoted to the position of vice president of human resources (HR) in a medium-sized Internet service provider company. Bonita is excited to take on this new leadership role, while at the same time she feels some apprehension and worry about her performance and abilities. Her immediate supervisor, Ken, a senior vice president of HR, has been in the company since its inception and has the reputation of being paternalistic and quick-tempered. Bonita has generally gotten along with Ken, albeit from a distance, in the past. However, since beginning her new position, Bonita has found herself at times chagrined by his way of speaking with her, as she feels that he talks down to her, but she has been unable to confront him.

In the past, Bonita has found conflict difficult. She would prefer to avoid unpleasant conversations and often deals with this by trying to influence the other person's view of the situation. For example, when an employee, Rick, kept making sarcastic comments during team meetings, Bonita struggled with confronting him about his behavior. Instead she tried everything she could think of to convince him they were headed in the right direction. In her mind, she was "heading him off at the pass," and she recognized that she was working very hard to get him on board. Her strategy was only somewhat effective. Other team members eventually called him on his rude comments. With her new position and directly reporting to Ken, Bonita is anxious about how to improve her skills and confidence regarding conflict.

In terms of personal style and communication, Bonita exhibits a preference for collaboration and is proactive in generating communication between herself and team members. She states that she "does her best thinking out loud" in team meetings. When undertaking a project, Bonita tends to seek out the opinions of colleagues as she formulates her plans. And before she moves ahead on a plan, she feels more confident in her ideas if she has included others in discussing them and knows she has a sense of how others will react. For example, in her previous position, she was the team leader for educating employees about the new benefits package, which was a major restructuring. While Bonita had a sense of what many of the concerns and issues might be regarding the change, she invited her team to brainstorm what the concerns would be rather than handing them a list and asking for responses to specific items. Bonita continued with this leadership style as they developed their program.

Her supervisor, Rita, whose position Bonita now holds, was known for picking apart new initiatives. Bonita's team privately assumed that Rita would do the same to their work. Bonita had experienced Rita's combativeness before, and moved to include Rita early on during Bonita's weekly report meeting with her. By getting Rita's input early in the process, Bonita buffered her team from Rita's criticism, and Bonita felt that she was able to engage Rita positively. And Bonita's team was pleasantly surprised to find Rita approving their proposed program with minor adjustments.

When Rita recently retired, there were several candidates within the company for her position. Bonita's success with the implementation of the new employee benefits package and other projects had earned her the notice of the president of HR and the CEO, who both endorsed her promotion. Ken, however, had initially pushed for another HR manager, Bill, who had one year less experience than Bonita but was known for his take-charge, forge-ahead leadership style. When the president and CEO both put forward Bonita's name, Ken quickly withdrew Bill's name and Bonita was selected for promotion. While Ken had not actively opposed Bonita's promotion, he had let it be known that "Bonita has some proving to do" in his eyes.

Bonita is married to Martin and has two school-age children, Nicole (12 years old) and Will (8 years old). Martin is an assistant district attorney. They live in a large city in the Southeastern United States with a number of extended family in the area. Bonita struggles at times with the number of hours required for her work and being involved with her children and husband. In her past position in the company she had a fair bit of flexibility, which allowed her to attend her children's school functions. Bonita is concerned about how she will manage this in her new position.

Bonita was the first person in her family to graduate from college and, while she is very involved with her family of origin, she often feels somewhat like an outsider because of her different lifestyle and expectations of life. She was seen as the "smart one" of her family but also felt that she had to work extra hard to succeed. Growing up African-American in a large urban city in a working-class neighborhood, her early education was in an underprivileged school. As her abilities were noticed by her parents, her father took a second job so she could attend a better school. Bonita talks about this sacrifice as "both a blessing and a responsibility" for which she has always been grateful but for which she also has felt pressure to "make my parents proud." Bonita's family members often comment on her success in moving up in the company and into a white-collar world, which results in her feeling proud but also a little uncomfortable.

Bonita met Martin in college at a large public university. They dated through the last half of college and were married soon after graduation. Martin had been accepted to law school, and although Bonita had some initial interest in attending graduate school, she went to work while Martin began his studies in law. Bonita found that working in human resources met her desire to "work with people" and "use my smarts for solving problems." While over the years she has toyed with the idea of returning for a master's degree, she has not felt that lack of a graduate degree has hindered her career thus far.

Bonita and Martin live in a suburban neighborhood that is primarily white, although there are several other African-American and Asian families. This was a difficult decision for them, as they would have preferred in some ways to stay in a neighborhood with more African-Americans; however, they also felt it was very important to be in a neighborhood with high-achieving schools. They make a concerted effort to connect their children to their extended family and make other cultural traditions available to their children through activities such as involvement in the church in which Bonita grew up.

Martin and Bonita had their first child as Martin graduated from law school. Bonita took some maternity leave, but with Martin starting a clerkship with a State Supreme Court judge, they could not afford for Bonita to stay at home. Bonita states that she felt some ambivalence at the time, but with her mother able to care for the baby Nicole, she went back to work without a huge amount of distress. By the time their second child came along, Bonita was fully engaged in her career and, with the support from Martin and continued help from her mother and other extended family, was committed to continuing to work full-time. Bonita and Martin have felt that with both of them working, they are able to provide opportunities to their children that neither of them had growing up, and Bonita also likes the idea that her children, particularly Nicole, see Mommy as having a professional career path in addition to Daddy.

Regarding the juggle between raising young children and work, Bonita states she sometimes questions how well it all works. While she has a lot of trust in her mother's handling of the children, she also wants to be there herself in many ways. Missing out on different milestones in her children's development was hard when they were young, but once they entered school, "it became easier since things like the first day of school or graduating from elementary school are scheduled, not like that first step or first word." Bonita has some worries about how this new position will work in trying to attend as many of the children's functions as possible. She knows that stating clear boundaries with work has been hard at times, and as she is aware of needing to "prove myself" she expects this to be a challenge for her.

In terms of her present situation, the company has offered coaching to all new executives, and Bonita has stated that she would like to participate. Another senior vice president, Holly, is responsible for the executive coaching program. When she interviewed Bonita regarding coaching, Bonita was clearly eager to see what coaching could offer in helping her learn more about herself and how she might achieve success in her new position.

Bonita presents for coaching with an expressed goal of developing her leadership skills, dealing with conflict, and improving work-life balance.

Summary of Bonita's Case

Bonita is a proactive/growth coaching client. She is a collaborative, inclusive person, who tends toward an underassertive and overaffiliative leadership style. She is also a relativity inexperienced leader who is in transition, having been recently promoted to executive level. This has presented challenges for her in balancing the demands of her work and personal life. She has a high need for achievement, is open-minded and curious, and is willing to try new ways of doing things. She is highly intuitive about other people's thoughts and feelings, but far less insightful about her own. However, while she shies away from conflict and prefers to avoid confrontation, she does value learning as a way to self-development.

REFERENCES

Barnett, D. W. (1988). Professional judgment: A critical appraisal. *School Psychology Review, 17*(4), 658–672.

Brennan, D., & Prior, D. M. (2005). *The future of coaching as a profession: The next five years 2005–2010.* Lexington, KY: International Coach Federation.

Dailey, N. (1984). Adult learning and organizations. *Training & Development Journal, 38*(12), 64–68.

Douglas, C. A., & McCauley, C. D. (1999). Formal developmental relationships: A survey of organizational practices. *Human Resource Development Quarterly, 10*(3), 203–220.

Druckman, D., & Bjork, R. A. (1991). *In the mind's eye: Enhancing human performance.* Washington, DC: National Academy Press.

Garman, A. N., Whiston, D. L., & Zlatoper, K. W. (2000). Media perceptions of executive coaching and the formal preparation of coaches. *Consulting Psychology Journal: Practice & Research, 52,* 203–205.

Gorby, C. B. (1937). Everyone gets a share of the profits. *Factory Management & Maintenance, 95,* 82–83.

Grant, A. M. (2003). What is evidence-based executive, workplace, and life coaching? Keynote address presented at the First Evidence-Based Coaching Conference, University of Sydney, Australia, July 2003.

Haring-Hidore, M., & Vacc, N. A. (1988). The scientist-practitioner model in training entry-level counselors. *Journal of Counseling & Development, 66*(6), 286–288.

Hudson, F. M. (1999). *The handbook of coaching*. San Francisco: Jossey-Bass.

Kilburg, R. R. (2000). *Executive coaching: Developing managerial wisdom in a world of chaos*. Washington, DC: American Psychological Association.

Nord, E. (2002). Evidence-based medicine: Excessive attraction to efficiency and certainty? *Health Care Analysis, 10*(3), 299–307.

O'Gorman, J. G. (2001). The scientist-practitioner model and its critics. *Australian Psychologist, 36*(2), 164–169.

Parker, L. E., & Detterman, D. K. (1988). The balance between clinical and research interests among Boulder Model graduate students. *Professional Psychology—Research & Practice, 19*(3), 342–344.

Parsloe, E. (1995). *Coaching, mentoring, and assessing: A practical guide to developing competence*. New York: Kogan Page.

Sackett, D. L., Haynes, R. B., Guyatt, G. H., & Tugwell, P. (1996). Evidenced based medicine: What it is and what is isn't. *British Medical Journal, 13*, 71–72.

Shapiro, D. (2002). Renewing the scientist-practitioner model. *Psychologist, 15*(5), 232–234.

Wampold, B. E. (2001). Contextualizing psychotherapy as a healing practice: Culture, history, and methods. *Applied & Preventive Psychology, 10*(2), 69–86.

Wampold, B. E., & Bhati, K. S. (2004). Attending to the omissions: A historical examination of evidence-based practice movements. *Professional Psychology: Research and Practice, 35*(6), 563–570.

Whitmore, J. (1992). *Coaching for performance*. London: Nicholas Brealey.

PART I

Single-Theory Perspectives

CHAPTER 1

Coaching from the
Humanistic Perspective

DIANNE R. STOBER

COACHING IS ABOVE all about human growth and change. And in recognizing its roots in traditions and disciplines that strive for supporting growth,
coaching would miss a substantial source of knowledge if we overlooked
the contributions of humanistic psychology. In this chapter, I propose that
this perspective is a philosophical foundation for coaching in terms of values and assumptions. As Hedman (2001) notes after drawing parallels between Carl Rogers' humanistic, person-centered approach and literature
on the ingredients of executive coaching, "it should be obvious that
Rogerian principles are central to the success of an executive coaching
program" (p. 73).

The person-centered model is but one of a number of approaches,
mainly to psychotherapy, that fall under the humanistic label. Others
include Gestalt therapy, experiential therapies, and existential therapies. There are many books detailing the intricacies of concepts and
techniques contained in these approaches, and the interested reader
may choose to seek these out. I limit the discussion in this chapter to the
general concepts and assumptions in humanistic approaches that directly apply to coaching.

Translation is necessary, however, in applying these therapeutic theories and practices to coaching. Where much of therapy is focused on resolving deficits and weaknesses in the direction of restoring a person to
functioning, coaching is a process focused on working with a person's
needs, wants, goals, or vision for where they want to go, and then designing steps for getting there. What humanistic therapies and coaching
share is the idea that positive change is a driving force for clients in ei-

17

ther modality. I would argue that both share some basic philosophical assumptions. In particular, the humanistic theory of self-actualization is a foundational assumption for coaching with its focus on enhancing growth rather than ameliorating dysfunction. In fact, the assumption of self-actualization is a significant influence in placing coaching into the realm of a *growth process* compared to general encouragement and advice giving. Whether coaches are engaged in personal development, performance, or executive coaching with their clients, the belief in the potential for positive growth as a driving force is required. I would also like to take this opportunity to note that the term *growth* in this discussion is not limited to a grand, overarching view of actualizing one's potential (which encompasses the whole journey of one's life) but rather runs the gamut from self-actualization to small positive changes that are individual steps in our daily lives.

While some might argue that a large portion, if not majority, of coaching is less about general growth and more about the small steps of finding solutions, developing specific skills, or goal attainment, holding a broader framework of helping people make positive change, such as the humanistic view, can enable the coach to handle the full range of initial matters of interest that clients bring to coaching. This humanistic approach to coaching implies that whether the client comes requesting help with getting more organized, improving interpersonal interactions at work, finding a new career, or starting a business, the client is coming to engage in a process of moving forward and making positive changes, and thus is using a process of self-growth, even if that's not "what they came for." And the humanistic approach provides a context and the ingredients necessary to make those positive changes, whether clients keep a narrow, specific focus or move to a broader view of their potential for growth.

In differentiating humanistic therapeutic approaches from a humanistic approach to coaching, there are several key distinctions. An important one is the difference in the *goal* of the process: Humanistic therapy is aimed at helping clients gain a more *functional* life while coaching usually seeks to help clients move a generally functional life to a more *full* life, whether that is related to a particular issue or area, like being a better leader or changing one's career, or is more broadly defined by the client. Another distinction is between the general *focus* of the process: Humanistic therapy is often tilted toward working with the client's *feelings* (as they are often less processed compared to thinking functions), whereas coaching often focuses more specifically on *actions* the client can take to meet their overall goals for the coaching. Both humanistic therapy and coaching aim to increase clients' awareness of their experience; however, what *purpose* the awareness serves differs. For therapy, the purpose of awareness is seen as an end in itself; that is, by processing one's full experience, one becomes more whole. It is assumed that the main *result*, awareness, will produce changes in behavior. For coaching, the purpose of gaining clarity and fuller awareness (of thoughts, feelings, and sensations in addition to what is in the client's environment) is an initial step toward the desired result of action. So the assumption is that awareness is an *ingredient* for successful action and that the coaching process will harness that in the service of actively making change. These distinctions will show up in how the shared assumptions between coaching and therapy translate to different ways of working with clients.

Returning to these philosophical assumptions shared by coaching and humanistic psychology, Cain (2002) calls the view of the person as self-actualizing "the foundational premise on which humanistic therapies are built" (p. 6). There are several other defining characteristics in humanistic approaches that can be extended to coaching: (1) a relational emphasis as the fundamental source of change, (2) a holistic view of the person as a unique being, and (3) a belief in the possibility of freedom of choice with accompanying responsibility (Cain, 2002). The following section discusses these characteristics, the concepts and theories associated with them, and how they can be applied to our understanding of coaching.

KEY CONCEPTS FROM HUMANISTIC APPROACHES

As we explore the application of humanistic perspectives to the practice of coaching, there are a number of key concepts that bear further elaboration and discussion. Some cut across the different humanistic approaches, and some are more heavily concentrated in one particular system. While these concepts were originally developed for therapists' use in psychotherapy, they are easily extrapolated for relationships such as coaching. I describe each concept as it exists in humanistic therapy and then discuss how it is translated into coaching practice.

GROWTH-ORIENTED VIEW OF THE PERSON

The humanistic approach is founded on an optimistic view of the person. This is not to say that humanistic therapists deny that dysfunction exists; rather, it is a belief that individuals have the capacity to use their experiences and resources to move forward and grow. Within this view, it is assumed that given the right environment (more on this later), people have an internal mechanism, called the self-actualizing tendency, by which growth can occur.

Self-Actualization

Probably the most fundamental proposition of the humanistic view of personality and behavior is the underlying tendency of organisms to self-actualize (Combs, 1999; Maslow, 1970; Rogers, 1951, 1959). Rogers (1951) proposed that human development is directional (forward) and that within the individual framework of the person, people have a basic striving to reach their full capacity. This was a radical notion compared to the formulations given by the psychodynamic and behavioral theorists of the day. Maslow (1970) furthered humanistic theory by studying self-actualizing individuals and describing their achievements and evolution. Both stated that when the context allows, people will choose what is good for them because they then experience satisfaction or pleasure, which results in continuing efforts to evolve and grow. So for humanistic practitioners, developing a contextual climate that supports and nurtures self-actualization is the linchpin for helping clients grow into their potential. This assumption also has a direct implication for how to work with clients: Practitioners are there to *facilitate* the client's *own natural potential* for growth. This view is aptly stated by Cain (2002): "Their faith in the client's potential results in humanistic therapists' disinclination to be directive, but rather to act in ways that free clients to find their own directions, solve their own problems, and evolve in ways that are congruent to them" (p. 6).

TRANSLATION TO COACHING   For coaches, then, this foundational assumption of self-actualization and its implications guides a major distinction between coaching and related activities such as consulting or mentoring: The coach's role is that of facilitator, rather than subject matter expert or more experienced guide. Coaches need to be experts at the *process* of coaching but recognize their clients are the experts on the *content* of their own experience. This is not to say that coaches do not provide any information, but rather that by assuming that individuals have an innate capacity for growth, any information provided by the coach should be in the service of the client's unique potential.

PRACTITIONER-CLIENT RELATIONSHIP

Humanistic approaches were on the forefront of describing the fundamental importance of the relationship between practitioner and client as a source of change in psychotherapy. It is through the relationship and the environment set by the practitioner that clients are able to explore their own experience and choose directions for the future. There are several key qualities to building a productive relationship from the humanistic perspective: collaboration between client and practitioner, and empathy, unconditional positive regard, and authenticity on the part of the practitioner. We will discuss each of these as they relate to a process of growth for the client.

Collaboration in the Practitioner-Client Relationship

Consistent with premises of the self-actualizing tendency, humanistic theorists see collaboration between practitioner and client as a required aspect of a helping relationship. When practitioners approach their clients with the belief that they are inherently capable of positive growth, a natural implication arises of working *with* the client, rather than working *on* the client. This requires an active engagement of the practitioner in facilitating the client's own awareness of how they experience themselves, their situation, what it means, and where they want to go with it. It is a fundamental value in humanistic therapy to approach this engagement by honoring the client's direction (Combs, 1989; Elliott & Greenberg, 2002; Greenberg & Paivio, 1997). So the relationship becomes one of approaching the client as someone to work with in tapping into the client's own sense of unfolding growth and potential.

TRANSLATION TO COACHING The humanistic therapy approach of a collaborative stance with the client translates very directly to coaching. Whether a client is seeking coaching for improved performance in the workplace, work-life balance, or other reasons, a hallmark of coaching is working with the client to construct meaningful choices and actions for the client's specific situation.

Directiveness

As an outgrowth of the collaboration between practitioner and client, the question occurs regarding the degree to which the practitioner directs the process and content of interactions. As is discussed further later, because the client is seen as the expert on his or her own experience, directing *content* is generally not consistent with a humanistic approach. Rather, the practitioner can facilitate the client's growth by engaging the client through the process of the interaction. In Gestalt therapy (Strümpfel & Goldman, 2002); process-experiential therapy (Elliott & Greenberg, 2002); client-centered therapy (Watson, 2002); and other humanistic approaches, the practitioner is highly involved in directing the client toward greater awareness of experience and choice by using particular techniques developed to help clients explore their "growing edges."

TRANSLATION FOR COACHING   For current coaching practice, there is generally an acceptance of the spirit of this concept of process directiveness as opposed to content directiveness from the humanistic tradition, although the balance may vary. In more personal coaching, the aim is often to help clients flesh out their vision of their ideal existence and then develop and enact steps toward that ideal. But it is not up to the coach to direct the content of that ideal; rather, the coach is there to help the client fully describe it and design steps to take them toward it. In executive, organizational, or performance coaching, the balance of directiveness may be somewhat different, depending on the structure of the coaching contract. There are times that the organizational needs or context require the coach to focus on a specific area with the client; however, coaches still will come down on the side of process directiveness in collaborating with the client about what particular actions are best suited for this particular client. When coaching for skills, the line between content and process directiveness may become a bit fuzzy, as often there is particular content the coach provides (e.g., information about listening skills) in the process of facilitating the client's skills development.

The Practitioner's Qualities

For Rogers (1980), it is through an optimal climate (empathy, positive regard, genuineness), in the relationship and provided by the practitioner, that the client's capacity for self-growth is accessed. Likewise, Gestalt therapists have emphasized the importance of genuine contact and warmth between a therapist who does not claim a superior or interpretive position above the client and the client who is actively engaged as an equal expert in his or her own experience (Greenberg & Rice, 1997; Yontef & Simkin, 1989).

One of the greatest strengths of the humanistic perspective, and particularly Rogers' person-centered approach, is the emphasis on a warm, positive relationship between the practitioner and the client. Outcome research and research on the therapeutic, or working, alliance in psychotherapy have all but unanimously shown that the therapist-patient relationship is an essential ingredient to positive growth (see the next main section, on evidence).

EMPATHY   Empathy is one of the most basic capacities required for understanding one another (Bohart & Greenberg, 1997; Rogers, 1975). It goes beyond an intellectual or cognitive understanding of another's experience or viewpoint; empathy includes an understanding of their experience on an emotional level. It is by trying to accurately understand

and communicate the client's full reality without adding, subtracting, or changing information that the practitioner demonstrates understanding at both a cognitive and an affective level. This requires practitioners to maintain a stance of hypothesis, always checking with their clients to ascertain whether they have accurately understood the essence of the client's experience. In order to achieve accurate empathy, practitioners must set aside their own feelings, reactions, and thoughts in order to sense the client's world as if it were their own.

In addition, by demonstrating empathy the practitioner is performing several important tasks: allowing clients to become more fully aware of their own construction of reality, demonstrating positive regard for the self of the client, and building trust in the relationship. When this understanding is communicated, clients can then gain another's view to their own experience, which often is then felt as a deeply rewarding sense of being known and at the same time can allow clients to know themselves more fully, too. Empathy builds trust that the practitioner seeks to understand and that this relationship is one in which the client's experience holds the ingredients for future growth.

Unfortunately, accurate empathy has often been taught as a simple reflection of the client's feelings ("You are angry that your boss criticized you in front of others.") when in fact it is a demanding process of trying to enter the private world of the client and accurately capture meaning and experience (Watson, 2002). As one can well imagine, this is a tall order. Accurate empathy entails both emotional and cognitive processes: Understanding another's frame of reference is a cognitive process that is not possible without also attending to the emotional experience of the other (Duan & Hill, 1996; Rogers, 1975; Watson, 2002).

UNCONDITIONAL POSITIVE REGARD   In order to engage in the process of empathy, it is necessary to also maintain a stance of unconditional positive regard, or acceptance or "prizing" (Rogers, 1951, 1975). It is an acceptance and valuing of the client for who they are. This acceptance does not mean that the practitioner must agree with or endorse everything the client says or does; rather, it means the practitioner is able to maintain an attitude of refraining from judgment (Rogers, 1959). It would be difficult, if not impossible, to be accurately empathic if a practitioner negatively views his or her client. Unconditional positive regard means the practitioner cultivates a sense of continually "being in the client's corner" without imposing his or her agenda or values on the client.

AUTHENTICITY/GENUINENESS/CONGRUENCE   Across different humanistic approaches, there is a recognition that while understanding and accepting clients for who they are is vital, the person and experience of the practitioner in the moment is also important. A number of terms have been used to describe the awareness of practitioners of their own thoughts, feelings, and sensations in the moment of contact: authenticity and genuineness or congruence. By genuineness, or congruence, person-centered approaches mean that the therapist, or practitioner, is able to accurately note his or her experience regarding the client in the present and thus "be himself or herself" therapeutically with the client (Rogers, 1957; Sachse & Elliott, 2002). Authenticity, likewise, in the existentialist tradition, means being open and true to the experience during therapy (Bugental, 1987; Walsh & McElwain, 2002).

This does not mean, however, that the practitioner should be brutally honest in a misguided attempt to be genuine with the client. In fact, there is some suggestion that "excessive genuineness" on the part of the practitioner could be linked to negative outcomes (Sachse & Elliott, 2002). Rather, when authenticity is combined with empathy and unconditional positive regard, clients have a unique opportunity to gain clarity for themselves by hearing another's genuine experience with them given in a context of caring and understanding.

TRANSLATION FOR COACHING   As coaches, then, we have the opportunity at the outset of the development of coaching theory, research, and practice to learn from the psychotherapy literature and maintain the importance of focusing on the development and understanding of a trusting relationship between coach and client. Rogers' emphasis on the importance of accurate empathy and unconditional positive regard, along with his and other humanistic theorists' stress on authenticity both between practitioner and client and within each are critical guides for effective coaching practice. Within coaching, as in psychotherapy, there is recognition that without the client feeling understood and accepted, the chances for coach and client to work together for change are pretty slim. Likewise, failure to give any feedback in coaching conversations regarding what the coach experiences in the interaction is withholding an important source of information to the client. The main difference in how these qualities are demonstrated by the coach is that the coach employs them in the service of building rapport such that clients can actively engage in making choices about the actions they will take in their growth. This contrasts with the therapeutic aim of these qualities, providing a context for increasing awareness in the service of healing.

HOLISTIC VIEW OF THE PERSON

Another defining characteristic of the humanistic perspective is the emphasis on viewing people holistically. There is a rejection of a split between mind and body; rather there is an emphasis on the individual as a dynamic whole. Humanistic theorists would liken descriptions of parts (e.g., cognitive functions, emotional states or traits, etc.) as helpful in understanding the full person like anatomical study is helpful in understanding a living, moving body: It can give a particular view but is not adequate in understanding the whole. When we are functioning at our best, we generally describe this state as feeling "whole," "integrated," or in "flow" (Csikszentmihalyi, 1990).

Range of Human Experience

Most humanistic theorists explicitly state that in order to reach full potential, individuals must value the full range of human experience: our physical, cognitive, and affective, or emotional, realities (Cain, 2002). And since there is often an overreliance on intellectual, cognitive processing, many humanistic approaches stress the importance of emotional and physical processing (e.g, Elliott & Greenberg, 2002; Gendlin, 1996; Mahrer, 1996; Rice, 1974). Overall, humanistic approaches share the view that if attention is not paid to all of our experience, growth is interrupted.

TRANSLATION TO COACHING   For application in coaching, this view is extended to the idea that we cannot see our clients unidimensionally; rather, we tend to look at all areas of our clients' experience. Where humanistic therapists may focus on micro-level experiences, such as "What are you aware of in this very moment?" in order to access immediate experience, the coach may focus on a more macro view of the client's experience and, as needed, inquire about internal states as they impact the broader picture. Thus coaches attempt to understand the client's experience of self (e.g., values, personality, goals, health, etc.); of self-in-relation (e.g., important relationships, interpersonal style, sense of community, networks, etc.); and of environment (e.g., work/career environment, financial situation, physical surroundings, etc.); and each in relation to the other. By approaching our clients in this way, we communicate to our clients that their whole experience is of interest, is important, and is worthy of attention. Of course, this requires the caveat that the focus in coaching also is dependent on what is part of the coaching contract. The aim of coaching may be broader in a personal coaching relationship, while in a performance coaching scenario the focus may be more circumscribed (or not!).

Uniqueness of the Individual

If we accept that we construct reality from our perceptions and make sense of our perceptions in individual ways, then each person is a unique individual. Humanistic interventions share the view that in order to understand another, practitioners must attempt to understand the phenomenological experience of the other. This requires the practitioner to engage in developing a specific, personalized understanding of the client. It also points to an atmosphere of "hypothesis testing" on the part of the therapist in formulating that understanding: as practitioners draw conclusions or construct a view of the client, they must check out their understanding with the client. This applies not only to understanding the client's experience but also to understanding the choices the client makes regarding intentions, goals, and actions.

So if the client is a unique individual, then the relationship between practitioner and client must also be customized (Cain, 1989; Duncan & Miller, 2000; Hubble, Duncan, & Miller, 1999). There is no one-size-fits-all approach in the humanistic perspective. By recognizing the client as the expert on his or her experience and utilizing their own expertise in facilitating awareness and choice, the practitioner and client together can formulate new understanding and directions for growth. This approach underscores the importance of collaboration and the resulting individuality of each therapeutic relationship. Indeed, this is the spirit of an evidence-based approach: the use of the best available knowledge integrated with the practitioner's expertise in the service of the client's experience and context (Sackett et al., 1996).

TRANSLATION TO COACHING   While many coaches generally note that the coaching relationship needs to be tailored to the client (e.g., Dotlich & Cairo, 1999; O'Neill, 2000; Skiffington & Zeus, 2003; Whitworth, Kimsey-House, & Sandahl, 1998; Williams & Davis, 2002), the humanistic approach points out an underlying philosophy of why. This concept of the uniqueness of each individual also plays out in coaching in recognizing that designing action plans and so on must be jointly constructed for the best chance of success. What will work for one client may not for another. By asking clients to not only help design their "homework" but also assess what is likely to get in the way, what supports and resources are available, and how they will recognize success, the coach communicates a customized method as the process.

CHOICE AND RESPONSIBILITY

In the humanistic view, people are seen as having choice in how they respond to their environment. This freedom of choice is not a simplistic notion of complete autonomy; instead it is making choices within each individual's particular context. It is important to note that exercising choice does not mean that we have ultimate power over any situation; rather "there are always both given and chosen aspects of any particular moment" (Walsh & McElwain, 2002, p. 255).

Availability of Choice

Some humanistic theorists, particularly the existentialists, argue that we are unable to avoid making choices that have a bearing on our current and future selves (Frankl, 1967; Yalom, 1989). So while the idea of choice implies a certain freedom, it comes with a responsibility to recognize that in any moment a choice is being made, whether we are aware of it or not. By cultivating awareness of choice being available, we have power to make choices and responsibility for the choices made rather than viewing our situations and reactions as inevitable or immutable. This gives humanistic practitioners a particular avenue to pursue in helping their clients harness the self-actualization tendency.

TRANSLATION TO COACHING   In coaching, there is a basic assumption that change is possible, and that we as human beings have choice both in terms of action and in terms of meaning making. Again, I would argue that these assumptions place coaching in the philosophical tradition of humanistic thought. Many coaches will recognize this humanistic value in the common technique of asking, "Who do you want to be in this situation?" and "What do you want to accomplish in this?" and "How do you want to make that happen?" across many models of coaching (e.g., Goodman, 2002; Peterson & Millier, 2005; Skiffington & Zeus, 2003; Whitworth, Kimsey-House, & Sandahl, 1998). In asking our clients to make clear and conscious choices, we ask them to become active architects of their growth. By holding them accountable for those choices, we underscore the responsibility that comes with choice.

EVIDENCE FROM RESEARCH
ON HUMANISTIC APPROACHES

Conducting empirical research to better understand the utility and outcome of humanistic psychotherapy has a long tradition, primarily dating back to Rogers' initial investigations (1957) and willingness to submit his theories to research. Rogers held that understanding outcomes and processes that influence client success (or failure) is an important task facing those who would propose theory. However, much of this research has not been acknowledged in psychology's rush toward trying to establish one approach's superiority over another in the past few decades (Elliott, 2002). Contributing to the perception that humanistic therapies have little data to support their effectiveness is the position traditionally held by some existential and Gestalt therapists who saw objective, nomothetic research methods as flawed approaches given the subjective, ideographic essence of human experience. More recent developments in advancing the utility of qualitative methods have given new directions to exploring humanistic approaches while maintaining the philosophical assumptions regarding the uniqueness of individual experience (Rennie, 2002).

So what evidence is there for the effectiveness of humanistic approaches to human growth and change? Elliott's (2002) most recent meta-analysis of 86 studies looked at humanistic approaches ranging from client-centered therapy to process-experiential therapy, emotion-focused therapy, Gestalt therapy, and focusing-oriented therapies. He concluded that there is substantial evidence that humanistic therapies are effective based on findings that clients generally show large amounts of change over time; they evidence stable gains after therapy (both in early follow-up posttherapy and after 12 months); clients show substantially more change than comparable control (untreated) clients in randomized clinical trials; and when researcher allegiance to a particular therapy approach is controlled for, clients receiving humanistic therapy generally exhibit similar amounts of change as clients in non-humanistic therapies.

In another avenue of research, when the factors involved in successful change in psychotherapy are investigated, evidence substantiates much of the theory on conditions for growth from humanistic approaches. Orlinsky, Grawe, and Parkes (1994) and Sachse and Elliott (2002) reviewed the research on the process of psychotherapy and found evidence for the positive influence on outcome of a number of variables: empathic understanding; unconditional positive regard/acceptance/affirmation; therapist engagement and a collaborative stance with the client in constructing a positive working relationship; and process directiveness by the therapist (directing the process as compared to directing the content). Genuineness on the part of the therapist was more equivocal, and the research points to the need for more research regarding other factors that likely influence whether this quality is helpful (Sachse & Elliott, 2002).

While there is a substantial amount of evidence that humanistic approaches are effective in psychotherapy and that techniques based on humanistic theories and assumptions are related to positive change, research evidence is lacking on their application specifically to coaching. At this point in the emergence of coaching as a distinct discipline, our best available knowledge comes primarily from extrapolating from related areas, which gives us some clear directions for future development. One of the areas for growth in coaching lies in the investigation of relevant models to coaching and their use as theoretical and research foundations.

HUMANISTIC APPLICATIONS IN COACHING

Some of the key concepts in the humanistic approaches to psychotherapy that directly apply to coaching have been discussed. Now we turn to how they have influenced, both explicitly and indirectly, current thought in coaching and how they can be applied to coaching practice.

INFLUENCE OF HUMANISTIC MODELS ON COACHING

While the warm acceptance of clients for who they are, understanding them as unique individuals, and being authentic in relationship with them seem to be obvious ingredients for successful coaching, it is important to note where these widely held views originated. Rogers was revolutionary in his writings about the centrality of the context and relationship between practitioner and client for helping clients to tap into their own capacity for growth. Many coaching models underscore the importance of a trusting relationship based on empathy and empowering the client (e.g., Diedrich, 1996; Peterson, 1996; Sperry, 1996; Whitworth, Kimsey-House, & Sandahl, 1998; Williams & Davis, 2002). The fact that these factors are often taken as self-evident by coaches is a testament to the acceptance of Rogers' thinking by many.

Likewise, the assumption that individuals have a natural bent to self-actualize and move toward growth is shared among many models of coaching, from executive and business to personal and life coaching. This assumption is demonstrated by the focus on unlocking potential or facilitating growth (e.g., Hargrove, 2003; Hudson, 1999; Whitmore, 1996; Whitworth, Kimsey-House, & Sandahl, 1998; Williams & Davis, 2002; Witherspoon, 2000). Skiffington and Zeus (2003) acknowledge the humanistic philosophical influence by noting that "coaching is humanistic in that it views the human being as the ultimate measure of all things and recognizes that every individual has a capacity, even yearning, for growth and fulfillment" (p. 17).

HUMANISTIC STANCE AS A FOUNDATION FOR COACHING

Given the influences from humanistic perspectives that are evident in current coaching models, I would propose that these values and assumptions are foundational characteristics of coaching. It is hard to imagine a method of coaching that does not contain the values of a warm working relationship, the uniqueness of each individual, choice and responsibility, and the inherent capacity for growth. So regardless of additional techniques or theoretical approaches, the humanistic stance is a shared orientation in coaching. If one considers the evidence from research on humanistic approaches and common factors in therapeutic relationships as pointing to necessary (although not universally sufficient) conditions for processes of human change, then it is essential to build these concepts into any coherent model of coaching.

THE HUMANISTIC GUIDE TO COACHING

In applying the humanistic approach to the process of coaching, there are several guiding principles that provide a framework for the context of coaching: (1) the nature of the coaching relationship is essential; (2) the client is the source and director of change; (3) the client is whole and unique; and (4) the coach is the facilitator of the client's growth. Each of the principles has associated tasks for the coach that will be discussed shortly. In addition, a model of a cycle of change from the humanistic perspective can be described as Awareness-Choice-Execution (ACE) to help clients learn to move through this process themselves.

GUIDING PRINCIPLE 1: THE NATURE OF THE COACHING RELATIONSHIP IS ESSENTIAL

In coaching from a humanistic stance, it is essential to develop a trusting, collaborative relationship between coach and client. What we know from evidence and theory is that the coach must approach and engage the client with empathy, acceptance, and authenticity in the coaching conversation. By communicating these attitudes and behaviors to the client, the coach provides the platform for safety, trust, and collaborative interaction.

Coaching Tasks

1. *Listen for understanding.* A key task for the coach is to develop active listening skills that allow the coach to "walk in the client's shoes" and see the world from his or her internal frame of reference. To develop accurate empathy, one must spend the time and energy to listen to the client's experience, asking for clarification, summarizing the essence of the client's experience, and then checking out that understanding with the client. A related task is communicating that understanding to the client. These steps are essential to building a relationship that relies on an accurate picture of the client and ex-

hibits trust that the coach "gets" the client. Approaching the client in this way not only enables the coach to understand the client better but it also affords the client the opportunity to reflect on and consciously process more of his or her experience.

2. *Cultivate acceptance and look for positive points of connection.* While a constant state of complete acceptance, or unconditional positive regard, might be reserved for saints, yogis, and other self-actualized beings, it is important for the coach to cultivate this way of viewing others. By actively searching for positive aspects of each client with which the coach resonates, the coach can further develop a prizing and acceptance of clients for who they are as human beings. This requires the coach to look for the positive points of connection as the point of entry and to refrain from an attitude of judgment. As Rogers (1951) notes, it is all but impossible to be accurately empathic if the practitioner cannot find a warm acceptance of the person with whom he or she is working. Another way of saying this is: If you can't find something you love about your clients, then you won't be able to understand them. By focusing on the importance of acceptance of the client as a valued person, the coach also has a decision point: If the coach cannot find a comfortable level of positive feeling and warmth toward the client, the coach would best serve the client and himself or herself by disengaging from a coaching relationship and referring the client on to another who is a better match.

3. *Give honest feedback in the moment.* The concept of authenticity, or genuineness/congruence, in humanistic approaches is an essential aspect of the practitioner-client relationship. For the coach, this means being aware of one's thoughts, feelings, and sensations in interactions with the client and being able to communicate these when helpful in an honest, caring way. In all forms of coaching, this involves expressing support and affirmation, but it also means communicating information that may at times be uncomfortable, disagreeable, or not what the client wants to hear. However, if a coach is to serve as a source of truthful information and as a sounding board for his or her clients, being genuine is vital. Being able to warmly communicate both positive and negative information signals to the client that the coaching relationship is a safe place to deal with the total reality of their experience.

4. *Establish collaboration as the process of the coaching relationship.* Because the client is seen as having the capacity for self-growth, coaching is not something done *to* the client but rather *with* the client. The coach must actively engage the client to participate in

his or her own growth process as a full partner rather than a passive recipient of the coach's wisdom. This is true whether the growth process is "becoming the best person I can be" or "improving my persistence and task focus in my work." This can be done at the outset of coaching when the coach is describing his or her approach, philosophy, and expectations for the process, and then should be carried throughout coaching.

GUIDING PRINCIPLE 2: THE CLIENT IS THE SOURCE AND DIRECTOR OF CHANGE

A second guiding principle in the humanistic approach to coaching is the recognition that clients are the source of their own experience and inclination toward growth. Given that they are the experts on their experience, in facilitating a focus toward growth the coach also allows the client to choose the specific direction of the coaching. This is not to say that the coach has no input (remember the coach's task of authenticity); rather the coach's input should be in the service of the client's goals rather than the coach's goals for the client. The coach needs to meet clients where they are and lead from there. In this way the coach not only signals trust in the client's capacities, but also keeps the choice and responsibility for those choices squarely with the client. By doing so, the coach is also reinforcing the client's experience of self-efficacy and self-direction with the day the coaching relationship ends in mind.

Coaching Tasks
1. *Facilitate the client setting the agenda, goals, and direction.* After the coach has gathered sufficient data regarding the person of the client, the coach and client together can engage in fleshing out the client's vision for plans and goals. Setting personally meaningful goals increases the chances that the client will be able to enact and maintain change. Questions like "Where do you want to start?" and "What do you want out of this process?" can help clients in starting out on their own path with the coach right alongside.
2. *Use the self-subject matter expertise of the client as the point of connection.* Remembering that clients are experts on their own experience frees the coach from having to know it all. Familiarity with the context that the client is in is helpful in building the trust of the client but it can sometimes get in the way as there is the potential for coaches to jump ahead to what they see as most important. It is also imperative that coaches maintain an attitude of hypothesis regarding their understanding of the client. It is up to the coach to be

open to, and in fact invite, the client to correct, refine, and elaborate on the coach's understanding and facilitation of the process.

GUIDING PRINCIPLE 3: THE CLIENT IS WHOLE AND UNIQUE

A third guiding principle in coaching from the humanistic perspective is that each client is a unique individual who needs to be understood as a complex whole. The client is not only Sue the manager but she is also Sue the wife and mother, Sue the people person, Sue the marathon runner, and many other Sues. And to understand Sue and help her grow, the coach must come to know Sue as a whole person with many interconnected pieces. The coach must also recognize that because Sue is unique, the coach must tailor his or her approach, interactions, and techniques to fit Sue. There are no cookie-cutter clients, nor is there a one-size-fits-all way to coach.

Coaching Tasks

1. *Assess thoroughly and check for accuracy.* In order to coach at more than a rudimentary, surface level, the coach must take the time to construct a full picture of the client. Even when the coach is working in a fairly circumscribed manner, such as sometimes happens in organizational or skills coaching, it is important to understand who the client is as a whole rather than just gathering data about their career and job-related experiences. In addition, any assessments used can be most effective if they are chosen in conjunction with the preferences and needs of the client. And finally, it is essential that the coach not assume that he or she has understood the client accurately but rather ask for feedback from the client.
2. *Look for interconnections.* In developing a rich picture of the client, the coach must also look for how different areas of the client's life and experience connect with each other. Are there important influences from one area of the client's experience to another? From the humanistic viewpoint, integrating experience such that we are aware of multiple facets of our individual reality is one way we all grow and develop. In coaching, this means that the coach can point out instances where multiple aspects of the client are involved, ask questions about how they are linked, and encourage the client to pay attention to their full range of experience.
3. *Facilitate integrating/aligning.* As the coach highlights interconnections between various parts of the client's life, the coach can also ask questions of the client regarding how aligned the different aspects are or how they may be in contradiction. For example, if

Jacob tells his coach that he is excited to take on an ambitious new project at work and also is talking about his frustration that he missed his son's first step, the coach can facilitate Jacob's awareness of the trade-offs involved and his conscious choice of how he will handle these potentially competing interests.

GUIDING PRINCIPLE 4: THE COACH IS THE FACILITATOR OF THE CLIENT'S GROWTH

Distinct from the role of healer (e.g., psychotherapist), wise elder (e.g., mentor), or outside expert (e.g., consultant), the coach's role is one of facilitation. By building a strong working relationship that is based on a rich understanding of the client and is collaborative in nature, the coach can use the coaching conversation as a means for the client to explore and plan their own direction. Rather than leading the client in any one direction, the coach is a partner and advocate of the client's choices and plans. This also means that the coach can hold the client accountable for the actions the client has chosen to undertake and in so doing provides an honest assessment of the client's growth.

Coaching Tasks

1. *Direct the process, not the content.* If the role for the coach is that of facilitator of the client's internal affinity toward growth, then it is essential that the coach engage actively at the level of assisting the process of identifying and then acting on the client's growing edges. This means that the coach is an active participant, even a leader or catalyst, in using techniques such as active listening, asking open-ended questions, and role-playing or imagining outcomes to help clients expand their experience and potential choices of action. However, if clients are the experts on their experience and can tap into their self-actualizing propensities, then in general it is the client's role to supply the content of the coaching. The exception to this is when the focus of the coaching has already been determined—for example, when a need for learning better communication skills has been identified for a manager. Coaching has its best opportunities for success when the client is the designer of the focus; and even when others have determined some of it, the specific content and the particular solutions or goals should be primarily the conception of the client if they are to fit that particular client's needs and context best.

2. *Maintain an attitude of exploration.* The coach can act as a facilitator also by promoting an attitude of jointly searching for understand-

ing, clarity, and potential answers. By reinforcing openness to experience, the coach models holding options open, recognizing the complexity of people and contexts, and not leaping prematurely to solutions. One way coaches can demonstrate this is by framing their observations of the client and their situation as hypotheses to be tested.

3. *Expand the client's awareness of strengths, resources, challenges.* In facilitating the client's own growth through the coaching relationship, it is an important task for the coach to direct the client to take stock of what qualities, resources, abilities, and so on the client possesses that can support growth and development. It is a strengthening process for clients to consciously assess what they have at their disposal in meeting the reality of their lives (see also Chapter 8 for the contributions of positive psychology in this task). It is also part of increasing awareness of clients to assess what challenges they face. Given that most clients come to coaching with something they want to accomplish, gaining a full picture of the challenges involved is an important task. By focusing attention on what clients bring and what they face, necessary information is processed by the client for the next task, making choices.

4. *Point out choices and help the client make conscious choices.* As the existentialists indicate, as humans we have a certain amount of choice in our moment-to-moment existence. By relating in a warm, accepting, and authentic manner with the client, the coach gains a footing for reflecting choices that are available to the client. By asking open-ended questions and exploring with the client, the coach also provides a context in which the client can take the time, space, and energy to focus on possible choices for themselves. Rather than always reacting to their experience of their context, clients have the opportunity through the coaching conversation to make a conscious choice of action. One framework for exploring choices is using the idea of an experiment. When clients are making new choices about their actions or meanings they are making of events, they are trying out new ways of being. Since these are not proven, well-trod paths, cultivating a sense of trying something out, observing the outcomes (both internally and externally), and then evaluating the new choice for satisfaction or positive change can help make the choice less absolute and more of a trial run.

5. *Facilitate goal-setting and accountability.* In helping clients move forward in their development, the coach can serve the function of facilitator of goal attainment (for a very thorough discussion of goal setting in coaching, see Chapter 6). As clients increase their aware-

ness of their resources, strengths, options, and challenges, and feel both supported by and known by the coach, they can use the coaching relationship as a context for choosing their direction for actions and "playing a big game." The coach can be very active in inviting clients to declare what they want for themselves and to plan how to get there. The coach also reinforces the idea that the client has access to potential directions and the steps needed internally rather than increasing the client's dependence on the coach for the answer. And by maintaining an ongoing relationship and an environment of responsibility for choices made, the coach reinforces the idea of accountability for choices made by the client.

These principles are guideposts to use in navigating the client's world and where the client wants to go. In humanistic coaching, there is no one right way; rather, growth and positive change are an outcome of constructing one's path from the resources and experiences of the client. The coach aids the client in this construction by following these principles and facilitating the client's conscious choices.

THE ACE CYCLE OF CHANGE

The model of Awareness-Choice-Execution (ACE), shown in Figure 1.1, is a tool for the coach to use the principles and tasks just described and to teach clients how to harness their own growth process. In directing the process of coaching for change, the coach can ensure that the client integrates *being* (and awareness of that) with *doing* such that the client comes away with real results.

Awareness

In the humanistic view of change, before one can make a conscious choice, one must be aware. To be fully aware, one must have a view of what has occurred in the past and who one has been. A coaching question might be, "What have you done in the past about X?" But that is only part of the information one must bring into consciousness. It is vitally important to focus on awareness of the present, too. Awareness of the present involves not just what clients think, but also what they feel and physically sense. Full awareness does not come without paying attention to all internal sources of information. Here the coach might ask something like "What do you feel right now as you talk about this?" or "What thoughts are going through your head?" Full awareness in preparation of making choices also means some attention to what the client envisions in the future in terms of hopes, fears, and likely out-

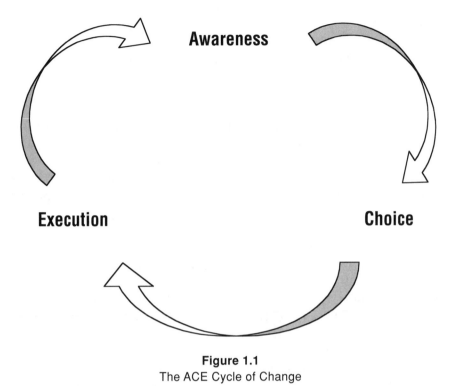

Figure 1.1
The ACE Cycle of Change

comes. So the coach would use the step of Awareness to facilitate clients gaining clarity about the full picture of their experience related to whatever the particular topic might be.

Choice

As we have discussed before, an essential concept in humanistic thought is that of the freedom of choice. In the cycle of change, after the client has engaged in the initial data-gathering phase of Awareness, the client is at the point of the availability of conscious choice. Given the client's awareness of the context, desires, and options that are available, it is time for facilitating the client's decision about what action to take. For example, a client has become aware of a conflict between her current job situation and what is truly fulfilling for her. After developing as full a picture as possible with her coach, the coach might ask something along the lines of "So now that we have a working framework for your situation and what you want and need, what do you want to do about it?" The coach is directing the process of intentional choice but is leaving the actual choice itself solidly with the client. Once the client has decided on a course of action, the coach and client can collaborate on detailing the steps involved and often return briefly to awareness in developing a picture of what challenges might exist, what resources they will bring to bear, and so forth.

Execution

Once the client has made a choice, the next step in the cycle is to execute the plan. Enacting choice is the point in which the client moves from being to doing, which is an essential step in coaching. Facilitating awareness alone does not necessarily propel our client forward, but rather by helping clients detail a plan and then follow through, we have the opportunity to witness the full cycle of growth and change.

Recycling

Moving through each step will help a client use the experience to consciously make choices and take action, but to close the circle, the coach should also direct the client to feed the results of the action back into their awareness. It is this reflective action that allows for further refinement and choice. And by discussing the ACE cycle with the client, the coach also fosters the skills clients can use on their own. Coaching from the humanistic perspective follows the metaphor of "give someone a fish and they'll eat for a day, but teach them to fish and they can eat for life."

CASE STUDIES FROM THE HUMANISTIC PERSPECTIVE

Now to illustrate how the principles and tasks of coaching in this way are implemented, I will discuss a humanistic approach to the cases of Bob and Bonita. In the tradition started by Rogers (1942) and his adherents in recording, studying, and publishing transcripts of humanistic interventions, I would like to discuss the two case studies of Bonita and Bob using transcriptions and descriptions of an early coaching session with Bonita and a session in the midst of the coaching relationship with Bob. While the dialogue related here is hypothetical, it is representative of actual coaching conversations. Comments on the dialogue between client and coach delineate how the humanistic concepts and guiding principles and tasks in coaching are applied.

The Case of Bonita

In starting the coaching conversation, I, and most coaches regardless of orientation, would ask Bonita what brings her to coaching and what she wants out of it. In the very first conversation, we would get a sketch of her awareness of the challenges she faces, what her experience has been thus far, and at this point, what she wants to focus on in the coaching context. My goals in that session are for her to leave feeling like I understand her and her situation, that she has gained some clarity about what she wants, and that we will collaborate in a process that will help. Given the material in the case studies, let us assume that when asked, Bonita has identified a number of goals for herself in coaching: increased comfort and skill in dealing with conflict, a better sense of herself as a leader and player in the organization, and improvement in her abilities to balance the requirements of her new position with those in her personal life. To get to these goals, Bonita will have shared a certain amount of background information, which would also afford me the opportunity to begin the process of building rapport. Along the way, we would have highlighted readily apparent resources and strengths Bonita has: a bright intellect; curiosity and a willingness to try new things; a collaborative, team leader style; the ability to move between different contexts/environments; and strong family support. One other topic I would contribute to the initial conversation would be the ACE cycle of change and how we will use it to help Bonita focus on her goals. Here is a dialogue transcript that follows a likely conversation in a session shortly after our initial meeting.

Coach: It's good to see you, Bonita. How's life been since we last met?

Bonita: It's been pretty good. I felt great after that first meeting with you. When I walked out I thought, "Well, here's someone I can really talk to and who has an idea of how to help me focus on what I can do to be successful."

Coach: I'm glad. Sounds like you walked out feeling like you have a partner to help in drilling down to what you want and how to get it. Since we talked, what have you noticed?

Bonita: Well, that ACE cycle has already helped. I was thinking about how I was going to set up this new program in training help desk personnel. In the past as a program manager I would usually think about what would work, or maybe bring it up in a meeting with my staff and we'd all work on the structure. But now it's not *my* project, it's my project manager's. So my task has changed to leading rather than designing. That ACE thing helped me realize that with the change in position, I need to make some more choices.

Coach: So this ACE thing seems like a good fit for you in how to approach some of your goals, huh?

Bonita: Yes.

Coach: That's great. Now in terms of our time today, do you want to go on with this issue of how to make the transition from designing to leading that came up since last time? It certainly fits with one of your goals of becoming a better leader. Or is there something else that you want to make sure we take time for? This is one of those choice points we've talked about.

Bonita: Hmm. (*Pause*) I think I have some ideas about this particular project, but something that I *really* want to talk about today is dealing with Ken's outbursts.

Coach: Okay. Let's talk about dealing with Ken. We can check in again at some point about how things have gone with your leadership of your project manager, or you can call or e-mail between our meetings if you get stuck anywhere in working through the ACE cycle. So let's focus on what you're aware of when you think about Ken and his scenes.

In this interchange, I am letting Bonita relate her experience since our last session in her own way, without asking for any specific initial direction. This leaves the content direction with Bonita and communicates to her that I am going to meet her wherever she is (Principle 2, Tasks 1 and 2). Bonita notes that she felt understood and valued, indicating that we have built rapport and an initial working relationship (Principle 1). Bonita relates some change in how she's viewing her experience and starting to expand awareness and recognize the possibility of choice (Principle 4, Tasks 3 and 4). I go on to direct the process by asking Bonita to make a conscious choice about the direction of the conversation (Principle 2, Task 1). When Bonita chooses to head in another direction, I follow but mark the topic of leadership as something to return to in the future (Principle 4, Task 5).

Bonita: Well, last time we identified a goal for me is to get more comfortable with conflict and how to handle it. You know, one of the people I have the biggest issue with in this is Ken. When someone like Ken jumps in my face or questions what I said, I just automatically shut down. I'd like to do something different than that. It's like he has all the control with his scary way, but I'd like to have some, too—only in my own way.

Coach: I almost get this image of Pinocchio becoming a real, live boy instead of the puppet he'd been.

Bonita: Oohh, that's a good one! Sometimes when Ken's being his difficult self with me, I feel like I'm being jerked around, just like a puppet on a string. I hate that.

Coach: So what would becoming a real, live person mean in dealing with Ken?

Here I am using my own internal experience in an authentic way to further Bonita's awareness of moving from reaction to choice. This interaction also demonstrates an empathic evocation of Bonita's experience by expanding the picture of her interactions with Ken. The tasks of demonstrating empathy and acceptance while giving authentic responses serve to strengthen the relationship (Principle 1, Tasks 1–3) while also serving to leverage my role as facilitator in exploring Bonita's experience (Principle 4, Task 3). In the ACE cycle, we're still in the Awareness step, trying to get a rich enough picture of what Bonita's experience has been so we can then start looking at choices she might have.

Bonita: (*Sigh*) I'm not sure. I can think more of what it doesn't mean than what it does. It means not being wimpy and just avoiding him. But I also know that getting mad and yelling back is just the other end of reacting.

Coach: It sounds to me like you know that the challenge with Ken is not getting stuck in following his behavior, but the picture isn't so clear yet about who you want to be in dealing with him.

Bonita: You got it. That's were it starts getting fuzzy.

Coach: Are you game to work our way through to coming up with an action plan?

Bonita: You bet.

Coach: So I've heard you say that you feel jerked around, and in the past you've just shut down. And you're aware of not wanting to avoid him or responding just like he does. Is this about right? What else is there?

Bonita: (*Nodding*) I know that others also don't like that behavior from him and would be glad if someone confronted him. I'd like to think that if someone did, the rest of us would stand behind them. But I'm not sure.

Coach: So there is a resource here in terms of potential support. But you don't know if you can count on them.

Bonita: Right.

Coach: Has anyone confronted him before?

Bonita: Well, before I was promoted, I heard about what happened when Pam, who's no longer here (*eyebrows raised*), yelled back. Ken basically put her back in her place and then within a year she was gone. I didn't know her well, but I think she was just sick of some of the politics. Other people said they wished they could have yelled back, but they saw what happened.

Coach: So Pam's choice didn't work so well, huh? Even though others have the fantasy of doing the same thing, they recognized it backfired?

Bonita: Right, so I can learn from that! It has to be something constructive, I think, but also something that I could actually do.

Coach: So for you, the choice of joining him in his game isn't attractive, which is great, because you're right: Going the constructive route is more likely to get you what you want. And it needs to be something you can see yourself doing. So what does that look like?

Bonita comes up with a fair amount of experience that gives a pretty good picture of the situation and Bonita's experience in the past. I have used active listening, feedback skills, and a collaborative stance (Principle 1, Tasks 1, 3, 4), and have facilitated Bonita's gaining clarity and expanded awareness (Principle 4, Tasks 2, 3) as I move Bonita toward identifying choices.

Bonita: Being strong, cool, and not flustered.

Coach: Now there's an image. When we first met, you talked some about how you struggle with trying to keep people from being angry by pleasing them. Bonita the Strong, Bonita the Cool, Bonita the Unflappable is a pretty different person! As the Cool Bonita have you ever dealt with someone who's mad?

Bonita: Hmm. (*Thinking*) About the only time I can think that I've done that is with my kids. Now my son, Will, he could throw a temper tantrum with the best of them when he was younger! (*Laughs*) But seriously, it was a real test of my patience, keeping my cool, and not playing into it.

Coach: How did you do it?

Bonita: I would just breathe, remember that giving him any attention would just encourage him, and pretty soon he saw that it wasn't going to work. Okay (smiling), I think I see some possibilities here!

I am asking Bonita to use the whole of her experience in looking for choices (Principle 3). There are interconnections between her experience as a mother and her situation at work, and compartmentalizing the different aspects of herself would limit her available knowledge and choices. While bringing awareness of her whole self into play, Bonita can capitalize on her life experience. She's now moved from Awareness to Choice in the ACE cycle.

Coach: Got some choices in mind?

Bonita: First, remember to breathe! And then, I am going to have to remove myself from the game Ken plays.

Coach: How?

Bonita: What about saying I'll come back later when it's a better time? I used to use that with Will. I'd just walk away with him yelling and screaming.

Coach: Sounds like a good possibility for the one-on-one situation.

Bonita: You bet. It's going to take a lot of practice for me!

Coach: How do you want to get some practice?

Bonita: Maybe we could practice here? Or maybe I can also practice at home with Martin. He knows the whole deal with Ken. Or heck, Nicole and Will try to get me into power struggles or talk back plenty. I can practice how to stay out of it and have a strong but respectful way to talk with them!

Coach: So you have plenty of ideas of how to get a little practice in before confronting Ken. Want to make a commitment to any of them?

Bonita: Hmm. Maybe we could do a role-play—and I can put it into practice on my own with the kids, too.

Coach: (*Smiling*) Way to multitask, Bonita—you might as well get two for the price of one! Seriously, you've made some important connections between Ken's behavior and some of what you face as a parent, so why not tackle both? Now, how about we set up the situation to practice here. . . .

I ask Bonita to now explore the action plan she's come up with. Bonita comes up with her own next step in Execution. Note that I am nondirective in telling Bonita what to do, that remains her responsibility and choice (Principle 2, Task 1 and 2).

This coaching conversation would go on to use role-play as a way to try out new ways of interacting and practicing these behaviors. While many approaches might use role-plays for practice, I would point out that from a humanistic perspective, there would be a substantial amount of energy also put into expanding awareness in the moment ("What thoughts, feelings, or sensations are you aware of as you tell me that you will come back when we can talk productively?"), reflecting on the specific choices being made and whether there are more to be explored ("Are there any other strengths you want to bring into play here?" or "Do you have any other ways you want to say this?"), and giving feedback ("When you said that to me, I felt stopped in my tracks and kind of stunned."). And we would also discuss how to feed back this information into the next cycle of ACE as she refines her comfort and skill in dealing with conflict. Bonita would also leave this coaching session with some specific actions to take that we have designed together along with the homework to note outcomes, thoughts, feelings, and so on to further process her experience in this area.

As the coaching progresses, I would continue to ask Bonita to drive the direction of our work. This reinforces her ability to make conscious choices and her responsibility to do so. By having established her goals from the start of coaching, and by continuing to check in with Bonita about their continued utility and whether there are additional goals, I would also underscore Bonita's accountability to herself and to our coaching.

I would anticipate that with Bonita's willingness to explore and learn, we would find at the end of our formal coaching relationship that she had made substantial progress on her goals. And given her ability and experience in moving from one environment, such as her blue-collar family background, to another, such as a white-collar career and environment, Bonita can be expected to leverage the coaching context to facilitate her transition to an executive position. I would leave the door open for future collaboration and might anticipate occasional recontact for specific issues or another round of coaching should she face another major challenge such as this transition in her career.

The Case of Bob

Bob comes with a broad focus for coaching: the issue of legacy. And while Bob has seen the results of coaching with others, he has not used it for himself. So in the initial conversation with Bob, I would make sure that in addition to gathering information about Bob and his goals for the coaching, I would ask him to articulate his assumptions about coaching and give him a very clear statement about my framework and style of coaching. My aim for that first meeting is to get enough information from Bob about who he is and what he wants so that we both have a clear articulation of what the focus and territory of the coaching will be. As with all my clients, I would want to make sure that Bob leaves feeling understood and accepted, and that he can trust me to give him straight feedback. Given the material from the case studies, we will assume that the following goals were determined: using the coaching as an opportunity to reflect on and refine his strategy for merging XYZ into AMM effectively; leverage his strengths of vision, charisma, and recruiting others to his vision to the merger task; and laying out a plan for his eventual retirement, including succession planning.

One of the challenges in working from a humanistic model with Bob would likely be the focus on awareness. From information in the case study background, feedback from others indicates that Bob does not currently reflect on his experience much and tends to stay on the surface of issues. That said, by meeting Bob in his element in terms of language and staying true to the principle of allowing the client to lead in terms of content and designing his own solutions, I would anticipate that it is possible to work with Bob in moving toward his goals. It would also be crucial for the coach to use feedback in an empathetic but very straightforward manner to give Bob a reflection of his experience and an accurate picture of his effect on others.

One of the strengths of the humanistic approach that would be important to rely on in working with Bob is trying to work from *within* Bob's frame of reference as a starting point. This is in contrast to the coach deciding where Bob needs to go. The first approach would capitalize on Bob's own, self-defined growth process rather than trying to use the coach's to influence Bob. The challenge of this approach is to find those points of connection where the coach can really appreciate Bob (acceptance and positive regard) without yielding to the temptation to want to "fix" Bob.

As a collaborative relationship is built and I reinforce the concept that Bob is the driver for where change takes him and what that looks like in relation to his specific goals, a number of particular topics might likely arise. Bob has seen coaching as primarily a strategic tool for him and has noted that he does not see a need for the "soft side" of coaching. However, when filling out the picture of his goals, it is likely that interactions with others will become a part of his assessment of either the resources or the challenges involved. And his skills and style of interacting will become part of his increasing awareness.

A likely scenario for the issue of Bob's people skills is in discussing his plans for integrating XYZ with his company. In persuading others to support his vision, something Bob prides himself on, it is quite likely that Bob will describe his executives in fairly strategic terms, rather than as real people. A possible opening for feedback and further exploration for me as his coach might be a statement like "When you describe your people, I get the feeling of something like cogs in the wheel of your plan. I wonder if they ever feel this way?" This opens the door for Bob to explore both the strengths (e.g., his approach moves things along) and the challenges (e.g., people might feel they are not valued as people) of his interpersonal style. These types of exploration of awareness bring Bob the opportunity to see more possible conscious choices of action.

As with Bonita, I would use the mnemonic of the ACE cycle to give Bob a tool for reflecting as broadly as possible on his experience and use that awareness to identify choices and plan the steps to implement them. For Bob, exploring his experience widely is not his general style, so asking him if he has a full enough picture is likely to be an essential process-directive aspect of coaching Bob. The following dialogue illustrates how directing the development of a fuller awareness can be successful with a client such as Bob:

> *Coach:* It's good to see you again, Bob. How are you?
> *Bob:* Fine. It's been busy as ever around here.
> *Coach:* So where would you like to start today?
> *Bob:* I guess I'd like to update you on what's been up since last time we talked and then get down to business. So first item, I've brought in one of my best VPs to liaise with the executives over at XYZ. He's a smart cookie and he gets what I'm trying to do in linking up AMM's manufacturing lines with what XYZ has done. And he's one of those guys who can get to the heart of the matter with anyone, no matter where they're from. So like we talked about last time, I put Jim in position to do the relationship building with XYZ along with our strategy goals.

Coach: Sounds like you're feeling pretty comfortable with that situation now. How'd you decide between Jim and Terry?

Bob: Both of them have great strategy and mission skills, but last time we talked, I got clear that one thing I was missing was someone who can really pull two different sets of people together. Jim is great at that back and forth between people stuff and with him there I can leave that to him. He'll give me the language I need to use to lay out the vision with the XYZ folks.

Coach: So you're well on your way in your plans about merging the two leadership teams. That must feel good.

Bob: Yep. It feels good to know I'm getting my bases covered. So that's where I am with the merger. It's one more piece to put together to have this place shipshape before I'm ready to step away.

> *Here I ask Bob to generate the agenda for the session (Principle 2, Task 1) and am also continuing to build the relationship through listening and feedback (Principle 1, Tasks 1 and 3). Next I ask Bob to connect his experience of dealing with the merger to his plans for succession (Principle 3, Task 2) and expand his awareness (Principle 4, Tasks 2 and 3).*

Coach: So what other pieces to do you need to fit into the puzzle?

Bob: Hmm. Well, obviously I need to see this merger gel. Now that I have my full team together, I'm feeling better about it. But will it hold in the long run, especially once I'm gone?

Coach: Sounds like you're not sure about AMM's stability without you.

Bob: Well, I have been the one to rally the troops for each challenge. It sounds kind of arrogant like that, but I guess it's hard for me to imagine anyone else doing it.

Coach: It must be pretty hard to contemplate leaving something that you've worked at for so long and trust someone else to take over. So what would have to be there for you to feel good about handing AMM over?

Bob: (*Pause*) That's a hard one. I'd have to know that whoever it is gets the business we're in and can motivate all these people to keep moving ahead. It's going to take someone who can make everyone else want to succeed as badly as he does.

Coach: So I hear someone with experience in the business, a motivator, and someone who's hungry. Does that bring anyone to mind?

Bob: Yeah, me. (*Grins*) But I can see the day when I'm not as hungry anymore. And that will be the day to start getting out.

Coach: So you have a pretty good idea about what signals that the time has come. That's important. What else?

Bob: When it's time, I want to already know who I'll be handing things over to. I don't like leaving things up in the air for something that important.

Coach: So another vital piece is having someone already in the wings so you'll feel as comfortable as you can.

> *Throughout this set of interchanges, I am directing Bob to further develop his conscious awareness of his eventual retirement and his desire to leave the*

company in good hands (Principle 4, Tasks 1–3). While I am not using the terms "awareness" and "exploration," but rather am matching Bob's language style, the process is still firmly rooted in the Awareness step in the ACE cycle.

Bob: Yeah. Now Jim, he could be a real possibility. What do you think?

Coach: Hmm . . . could be, but do you want to make your choice right now? (*Smiles*)

Bob: (*Chuckles*) Caught me. Sometimes I can jump so fast. I like to think I have a good gut instinct.

Coach: Good instincts are important to have. But part of my job as your coach is to help you flesh out the whole picture whenever possible. Do you have the requirements clear enough to start making choices?

While it is important to allow Bob to direct the content (Principle 2, Tasks 1 and 2), the coach's role is to direct the process (Principle 4, Task 1). So I bring Bob back to the process of expanding his awareness around what qualities his successor will need before Bob jumps to the Choice step of the ACE cycle.

Bob: Probably not. So I guess it's time to sit down and make a list.

Coach: Sounds good. So what do we add to experience, motivating, hungry?

Bob: High energy. Someone who wants results and knows how to get them. Now that we've added XYZ, the next CEO has to be comfortable internationally, especially with Asian cultures.

Coach: Okay, let's add those to the list. Any more?

Bob: Yeah, they have to be able to build a team and then let them do their job. No micromanagers. And ultimately, they have to be able to sell their vision. That's about it right now.

Coach: All right. I'm guessing more will come, so I'm going to leave some more space here. And as we work on refining this picture, we can add some more. This project will take a few iterations before we get to implementation. We have an emerging picture of who your successor needs to be, but now I'd like to shift your focus to another aspect of succession—who are you in this process?

I am pointing out that there is likely more here to assess while acknowledging that Bob feels fairly complete at the moment. So I shift to looking for related areas of experience for Bob, such as his role in succession planning (Principle 3, Task 2), and will move the process toward integrating and aligning these different pieces (Principle 3, Task 3). All of these remain in the Awareness step and will be used by Bob and the coach to design choices.

Bob: Okay. I want to be the one to identify who'll take over, so first I'd say I'm the evaluator of potential candidates. And after I settle on one, I'd say I'm their mentor.

Coach: So you have two roles to fill: evaluator and mentor. Which one do you want to focus on now?

Bob: Well, the mentor side of it will be the longer haul. How about we start there. . . .

We would go on to as fully as possible, flesh out what it means to Bob to be a mentor: what he sees as necessary for success; what experiences he has had both being mentored and mentoring others (it is likely that more conversation will arise here regarding his interpersonal style); what resources he has for this role; what challenges exist; and what steps he needs to take to become a successful mentor for his successor. Again, for me as a humanistic coach, it is Bob who is supplying the content while I focus on directing his exploration of his experience and facilitate his design of actions he will take.

In addition to discussing Bob's role in grooming a successor, another topic likely to come up in pursuit of his goal of "leaving on a high note" is what he envisions for himself after he retires. This is an expansion of his initially more focused goal of leaving AMM running "perfectly," and reflects the likely outcome of Bob engaging in the reflective act of focusing on his own experience and awareness of that.

In summary, Bob's interpersonal style might challenge me as a coach to refrain from trying to convince him of the need for the "soft side." But by meeting Bob where he is and facilitating his own pattern of growth, I would anticipate that our chances of Bob experiencing success in coaching would be increased as we found positive changes that fit his unique person. I would anticipate that many of Bob's choices of action might reflect his more strategic view of life, but using coaching as a springboard, Bob would likely expand his abilities to incorporate more of his experience. As we moved toward terminating our formal coaching engagement, I would talk with Bob about how he will carry on the processes he has learned in our work together.

CONCLUSION

In summarizing the contributions to coaching from the humanistic psychotherapy tradition, I would like to underscore that the values of a belief in people's inherent capacity for growth, the importance of a collaborative relationship, the appreciation of the whole person, and a belief in the possibility of choice are values that are consonant with the practice of coaching as it is today. These humanistic philosophical assumptions are generally in operation for coaches, regardless of specific orientation or techniques.

I hope that in the course of this discussion despite the criticisms of the humanistic approach as wishy-washy in terms of "leaving it all up to the client," readers come away with a sense of how a humanistic stance involves a deep involvement and active engagement with the client to facilitate growth. And by leaving the direction of the course and content of change to the client, the coach increases the likelihood of facilitating growth and actions that will actually stick for that particular client. And finally, even if a coach is operating from a different theoretical framework, the evidence from humanistic research on the necessary ingredients for an effective relationship and the common values on human growth are takeaways to be used.

REFERENCES

Bohart, A., & Greenberg, L. S. (1997). *Empathy reconsidered*. Washington, DC: American Psychological Association.

Bugental, J. F. T. (1987). *The art of the psychotherapist*. New York: W. W. Norton.

Cain, D. J. (1989). The paradox of nondirectiveness and client-centered therapy. *Person-Centered Review, 4*, 123–131.

Cain, D. J. (2002). Defining characteristics, history, and evolution of humanistic psychotherapies. In D. J. Cain & J. Seeman (Eds.), *Humanistic psychotherapies: Handbook of research and practice* (pp. 3–54). Washington, DC: American Psychological Association.

Combs, A. W. (1989). *A theory of therapy*. Newbury Park, CA: Sage.

Combs, A. W. (1999). *Being and becoming*. New York: Springer.

Csikszentmihalyi, M. (1990). *Flow: The psychology of optimal experience*. New York: Harper & Row.

Diedrich, R. (1996). An iterative approach to executive coaching. *Consulting Psychology Journal: Practice & Research, 48*, 61–66.

Dotlich, D. L., & Cairo, P. C. (1999). *Action coaching: How to leverage individual performance for company success*. San Francisco: Jossey-Bass.

Duan, C., & Hill, C. E. (1996). The current state of empathy research. *Journal of Counseling Psychology, 43*, 261–274.

Duncan, B. L., & Miller, S. D. (2000). *The heroic client: Doing client-directed, outcome-informed therapy*. San Francisco: Jossey-Bass.

Elliott, R. (2002). The effectiveness of humanistic therapies: A meta-analysis. In D. J. Cain & J. Seeman (Eds.), *Humanistic psychotherapies: Handbook of research and practice* (pp. 57–81). Washington, DC: American Psychological Association.

Elliott, R. & Greenberg, L. S. (2002). Process-experiential psychotherapy. In D. J. Cain & J. Seeman (Eds.), *Humanistic psychotherapies: Handbook of research and practice* (pp. 279–306). Washington, DC: American Psychological Association.

Frankl, V. E. (1967). *Psychotherapy and existentialism*. New York: Clarion.

Gendlin, E. T. (1996). *Focusing-oriented psychotherapy: A manual of the experiential method*. New York: Guilford Press.

Goodman, R. G. (2002). Coaching senior executives for effective business leadership. In C. Fitzgerald & J. G. Berger (Eds.), *Executive coaching: Practices & Perspectives* (pp. 135–153). Palo Alto, CA: Davies-Black.

Greenberg, L. S., & Paivio, S. C. (1997). *Working with emotions in psychotherapy*. New York: Guilford Press.

Greenberg, L. S., & Rice, L. N. (1997). Humanistic approaches to psychotherapy. In P. L. Wachtel & S. B. Messer (Eds.), *Theories of psychotherapy: Origins and evolution* (pp. 97–129). Washington, DC: American Psychological Association.

Hargrove, R. (2003). *Masterful coaching* (Rev. ed). San Francisco: Jossey-Bass.

Hedman, A. (2001). The person-centered approach. In B. Peltier, *The psychology of executive coaching: Theory and application* (pp. 66–80). New York: Taylor & Francis.

Hubble, M. A., Duncan, B. L., & Miller, S. D. (1999). Directing attention to what works. In M. A. Hubble, B. L. Duncan, & S. D. Miller (Eds.), *The heart and soul of change* (pp. 407–447). Washington, DC: American Psychological Association.

Hudson, F. M. (1999). *The handbook of coaching: A comprehensive resource guide for managers, executives, consultants, and human resource professionals.* San Francisco: Jossey-Bass.

Mahrer, A. R. (1996). *A complete guide to experiential psychotherapy.* New York: Wiley.

Maslow, A. H. (1970). *Motivation and personality.* New York: Harper & Row.

O'Neill, M. B. (2000). *Executive coaching with backbone and heart: A systems approach to engaging leaders with their challenges.* San Francisco: Jossey-Bass.

Orlinsky, D. E., Grawe, K., & Parkes, B. K. (1994). Process and outcome in psychotherapy. In A. E. Bergin & S. L. Garfield (Eds.), *Handbook of psychotherapy and behavior change* (4th ed., pp. 270–376). New York: Wiley.

Peterson, D. B. (1996). Executive coaching at work: The art of one-on-one change. *Consulting Psychology Journal: Practice & Research, 48,* 78-86.

Peterson, D.B., & Millier, J. (2005). The alchemy of coaching: "You're good, Jennifer, but you could be *really* good." *Consulting Psychology Journal: Practice & Research, 57,* 14–40.

Rennie, D. L. (2002). Experiencing psychotherapy: Grounded theory studies. In D. J. Cain & J. Seeman (Eds.), *Humanistic psychotherapies: Handbook of research and practice* (pp. 117–144). Washington, DC: American Psychological Association.

Rice, L. N. (1974). The evocative function of the therapist. In D. A. Wexler & L. N. Rice (Eds.), *Innovations in client-centered therapy* (pp. 289–311). New York: Wiley.

Rogers, C. R. (1942). *Counseling and psychotherapy: Newer concepts in practice.* Boston: Houghton Mifflin.

Rogers, C. R. (1951). *Client-centered therapy: Its current practice, implications, and theory.* Boston: Houghton Mifflin.

Rogers, C. R. (1957). The necessary and sufficient conditions of therapeutic personality change. *Journal of Consultative Psychology, 21,* 95–103.

Rogers, C. R. (1959). A theory of therapy, personality and interpersonal relationships. In S. Koch (Ed.), *Psychology: A study of a science* (pp. 184–256). New York: McGraw-Hill.

Rogers, C. R. (1975). Empathic: An unappreciated way of being. *The Counseling Psychologist, 5,* 2–10.

Rogers, C. R. (1980). *A way of being.* Boston: Houghton Mifflin.

Sachse, R., & Elliott, R. (2002). Process-outcome research on humanistic therapy variables. In D. J. Cain & J. Seeman (Eds.), *Humanistic psychotherapies: Handbook of research and practice* (pp. 83–115). Washington, DC: American Psychological Association.

Sackett, D. L., Haynes, R. B., Guyatt, G. H., & Tugwell, P. (1996). Evidence based medicine: What it is and what it isn't. *British Medical Journal, 13,* 71–72.

Skiffington, S., & Zeus, P. (2003). *Behavioral coaching: How to build sustainable personal and organizational strength.* Sydney, Australia: McGraw-Hill Australia.

Sperry, L. (1996). *Corporate therapy and consulting.* New York: Brunner/Mazel.

Strümpfel, U., & Goldman, R. (2002). Contacting Gestalt therapy. In D. J. Cain & J. Seeman (Eds.), *Humanistic psychotherapies: Handbook of research and practice* (pp. 189–219). Washington, DC: American Psychological Association.

Walsh, R. A., & McElwain, B. (2002). Existential psychotherapies. In D. J. Cain & J. Seeman (Eds.), *Humanistic psychotherapies: Handbook of research and practice* (pp. 253–278). Washington, DC: American Psychological Association.

Watson, J. C. (2002). Re-visioning empathy. In D. J. Cain & J. Seeman (Eds.), *Humanistic psychotherapies: Handbook of research and practice* (pp. 445–472). Washington, DC: American Psychological Association.

Whitmore, J. (1996). *Coaching for performance* (2nd ed.). London: Nicholas Brealey.

Whitworth, L., Kimsey-House, H., & Sandahl, P. (1998). *Co-active coaching: New skills for coaching people toward success in work and life.* Palo Alto, CA: Davies-Black.

Williams, P., & Davis, D. C. (2002). *Therapist as life coach: Transforming your practice.* New York: W. W. Norton.

Witherspoon, R. (2000). Starting smart: Clarifying coaching goals and roles. In M. Goldsmith, L. Lyons, & A. Freas (Eds.), *Coaching for leadership: How the world's greatest coaches help leaders learn* (pp. 165–185). San Francisco: Jossey-Bass.

Yalom, I. (1989). Love's executioner. New York: Basic Books.

Yontef, G. M., & Simkin, J. S. (1989). Gestalt therapy. In R. J. Corsini & D. Wedding (Eds.), *Current psychotherapies* (4th ed., pp. 323–361). New York: Peacock.

CHAPTER 2

People Are Complex and the World Is Messy: A Behavior-Based Approach to Executive Coaching

DAVID B. PETERSON

I HAVE A simple yet fundamental assumption about coaching: The purpose is to change behavior. The core of my coaching boils down to one equally simple yet provocative question for the participant: What are you going to do differently? Implicit in that question is a focus on action and a focus on the future (rather than the past). This chapter outlines a rich set of models, tools, and techniques designed to help people answer that question and then follow through to take the actions that lead to lasting change, better results, and greater satisfaction.

A second assumption is that people are complex and multifaceted. Therefore, behavioral approaches that reduce complex human behavior to mechanistic stimulus-and-response chains will not succeed. Human behavior flows from a combination of affective, cognitive, behavioral, and even spiritual elements. So while the focus of this approach is on behavior,

Author note: Every time I write I am reminded of how much I owe my former colleague, Mary Dee Hicks, whose thumbprint is all over this chapter. Many others have contributed to the thinking represented here, including Marc Sokol, Elyse Sutherland, Susan Mecca, my coaching clients, and the participants who have attended workshops and presentations where these ideas have been explored, tested, and refined. I would also like to express my gratitude to Lowell Hellervik, Cindy Marsh, and Dave Heine at Personnel Decisions International for providing the environment and the support for writing. Few consulting organizations have been so generous.

the whole person must be addressed in the process. Behavior is about far more than just the observable behavior; it's the result of a whole person with a rich, multifaceted life—past, present, and future—interacting with the people and the world around the individual. Failure to address the whole person in coaching will yield inadequate or temporary results.

A third assumption is that the world is messy. Although certain elements are simple and predictable, our lives and our interactions with others contain complicated, ambiguous, and unpredictable variables that may change over time. This assumption has significant implications for coaching, especially in how we help people sustain changes in their lives. If the same behavior might produce radically different results in different settings, then coaches must help the people they coach become effective learners, capable of translating their lessons into new settings, even after the coaching has ended. Therefore, in addition to changing behavior, a second purpose of coaching is to enable people to be better learners. Enhancing self-guided learning is so important it is embedded in the following definition of coaching: "Coaching is the process of equipping people with the tools, knowledge, and opportunities they need to develop themselves and become more effective" (Peterson & Hicks, 1996, p. 14).

A fourth assumption is that what happens in the coaching session matters less than what happens on the job, at home, or in whatever settings are important to the person. The more people I coach, the less I rely on breakthroughs in insight that generate excitement in our conversations. Instead, I focus on facilitating the steady progress that leads to long-term sustainable changes in behavior outside the coaching conversation.

In their analysis of the learning techniques that actually improve performance, Druckman and Bjork (1991) reinforce this assumption: "The crux of the problem is that learning and performance are not the same. . . . Procedures that enhance performance during training may or may not enhance long-term retention and transfer to altered contexts; conversely, procedures that introduce difficulties for the learner and impair performance during training may foster durable and flexible post-training skills" (pp. 24–25). To translate this to coaching, what contributes to better learning within the coaching session may in fact interfere with effective use of the learning outside of the session. Conversely, the types of experiences that lead to tangible long-term changes in behavior may feel like slogging through mud in the coaching session. A familiar example is that massed practice (e.g., cramming the night before a test) produces better immediate learning, whereas spaced practice (e.g., studying the same topic regularly over an entire semester) produces better retention and better long-term performance. Effective coaches use the principle of spaced practice by helping their clients practice new behaviors across multiple sessions; the participant may learn more slowly, but the results last longer. Other examples are included later in this chapter, but due to space limitations readers are encouraged to read Druckman and Bjork's (1991) third chapter, "Optimizing Long-Term Retention and Transfer."

A fifth assumption is that caring about the people we coach is a vital part of the process. Coaches need to demonstrate (behaviorally!) that they are interested in their clients and are committed to helping them accomplish meaningful goals. The techniques that follow are inevitably hollow if they are not used in the context of a positive, caring, warm, and respectful relationship.

KEY CONCEPTS

Practitioners and researchers describe a range of behavioral and cognitive-behavioral techniques that are useful in coaching (Ducharme, 2004; Grant, 2001; Kampa & White, 2002; Moore & Highstein, 2005; Peltier, 2001) and in improving work-related performance in general (e.g., Andrasik, 1989; Baldwin & Baldwin, 2001; Braksick, 2000; Daniels & Daniels, 2004; Dickinson, 2000). Critics often oversimplify behavioral approaches as mechanical, unsophisticated, narrow, or manipulative (Ducharme, 2004; Peltier, 2001). However, even advocates recognize that purely behavioral techniques are not sufficient for coaching people to deal with the complex and messy realities of life.

This section includes brief overviews of classic behavioral techniques, including modeling (Rosenthal & Steffek, 1991); feedback (Kluger & DeNisi, 1996); shaping and successive approximation (Baldwin & Baldwin, 2001); self-management (Kanfer & Gaelick-Buys, 1991); rewards and reinforcers (Peltier, 2001); and behavioral practice (Druckman & Bjork, 1991). These topics are embedded in a discussion of four frameworks that are intended to expand the traditional picture of a behavioral methodology. Even though the frameworks are holistic in nature, including cognitive and affective components as well as behavioral, the focus of their use in coaching is still behavioral. For example, when discussing motivation, the coach's purpose is not to change a person's motivations or to increase the person's insight into their origin, but to see how the person being coached can most effectively use these motivations to guide, shape, and reinforce desired behavior. Thus the coach is far more likely to ask "What would you like to do about it?" than such insight-oriented questions as "Why do you think that is?" or "Where do you think that came from?," or an affect-oriented question such as "How do you feel about that?" The latter types of questions may be useful in building an effective working relationship, but they are not, strictly speaking, a necessary aspect of coaching.

THE DEVELOPMENT PIPELINE

If, as stated previously, the purpose of coaching is to change behavior, then it seems essential that coaches have an understanding of the "active ingredients" required for such change to occur. The Development Pipeline describes the necessary and sufficient conditions for change and serves as a guide to where coaching can provide the greatest value for a given individual (Hicks & Peterson, 1999; Peterson, 2002). The five necessary conditions (see Figure 2.1) are:

1. *Insight.* The extent to which the person understands what areas need to be developed in order to be more effective (Elliott et al., 1994; Kluger & DeNisi, 1996; Prochaska, DiClemente, & Norcross, 1992; Prochaska, Norcross, & DiClemente, 1994).
2. *Motivation.* The degree to which the person is willing to invest the time and energy it takes to develop oneself (Dweck, 1986, 2000; Miller & Rollnick, 2002).
3. *Capabilities.* The extent to which the person has the skills and knowledge that are needed (Druckman & Bjork, 1991; Rogers, 2004).
4. *Real-world practice.* The extent to which the person has opportunities to try new skills at work (Druckman & Bjork, 1991; Holton & Baldwin, 2003).
5. *Accountability.* The extent to which there are internal and external mechanisms for paying attention to change and providing meaningful consequences (Cameron & Pierce, 1994; Holton & Baldwin, 2003; Prochaska, DiClemente, & Norcross, 1992; Prochaska, Norcross, & DiClemente, 1994; Rogers, 2004).

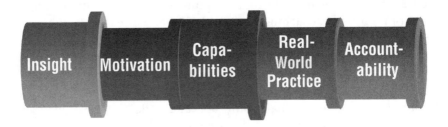

Figure 2.1
The Development Pipeline

The pipeline metaphor highlights that this is a constraint model (Goldratt & Cox, 1992): The amount of change a person can make is constrained by where the pipeline is most narrow. That is, a limitation in any one of the five conditions serves as a bottleneck that sets the upper limit on how much change can actually occur. For example, one person might want to be more strategic (high Insight, Motivation) but might lack the basic skills (low Capabilities) and not even have an opportunity to use them in their current job (low Real-World Practice, Accountability). Attending the best-designed workshop on strategic thinking might increase their capabilities, but still not produce meaningful behavior change. Only when the additional constraints of Real-World Practice and Accountability are addressed in tandem with Capabilities will change ensue for this person.

It is not necessary to get a precise measure of the various conditions; a coach only has to have a working hypothesis as to what is most constrained. In the case study of Bonita, for example, her insight about her interpersonal relationships and leadership style seems to be reasonable. Her motivation to address conflict, however, appears to be relatively low, and it appears that her capabilities are constrained in this area as well. Given some of the difficult relationships around her, opportunities for real-world practice appear to be sufficient. The level of accountability is not clear from the case study. A working hypothesis of her Development Pipeline for addressing conflict is presented in Figure 2.2. This picture suggests, for example, that giving her additional feedback would have little impact on her behavior, because Insight is not constrained.

High Insight and low Motivation is a relatively common profile: "I know I should get better at addressing conflict, but I don't want to come across as pushy or aggressive"; "I know I should spend more time net-

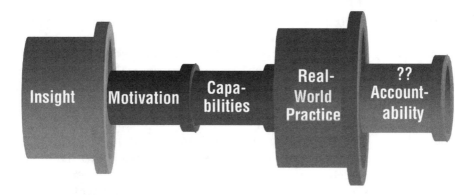

Figure 2.2
Bonita's Development Pipeline for Conflict Management at Work

working, but I just never find the time"; "My boss keeps telling me to take more risks, but it's just not worth it." A combination of high Insight and low Capabilities is also common: "I want to be more strategic but I just don't know what exactly I'm supposed to do."

Using the Development Pipeline as a diagnostic is a way to ensure that coaching uses the person's time effectively and efficiently. If Insight is high, a thorough assessment with detailed feedback doesn't add as much value as it does when Insight is low. If the Capabilities condition is the most constrained, coaching will probably have the greatest immediate impact by proceeding directly to skills training and practice. Then, as capabilities increase, the coach can shift the focus to whatever condition is then most constrained. Coaching is a cyclical process, shifting as needed from one area to the next and back again, always addressing the source of the major constraint.

Working with each person where the Development Pipeline is most constrained is one of the keys to truly customizing coaching (Peterson, 2002). Coaching programs that prescribe the same process for everyone (e.g., beginning with obligatory 360-degree or multirater feedback) end up wasting time for at least some of the participants. Although few actually take the opportunity, coaches have the luxury of being able to continue gathering assessment data throughout the entire process, rather than having to do it all up front. Similarly, coaches can think strategically about when insight needs to be increased and by how much, and then find the most effective way to do that.

GAPS GRID

The second framework, the GAPS Grid, expands the first two conditions from the Development Pipeline to outline the types of information that people need for Insight and Motivation (Peterson & Hicks, 1996). Many coaches (and others responsible for development experiences) seem to focus narrowly on feedback and thus lose sight of the big picture. The two-by-two GAPS Grid (see Table 2.1) examines where the person is now (left-hand column) and what matters most (right-hand column). Both issues are considered from the person's perspective (top row) and from the perspective of any significant others, such as boss, senior management, direct reports, peers, the coach, and family (bottom row).

Goals and Values refers to what matters to the person and what motivates his or her behavior. This includes values such as power, wealth, altruism, learning, security, status, affiliation, variety, and achievement. Changes in behavior will last only if they are reinforced at some level by the person's existing motivations.

Table 2.1

GAPS Grid with Representative Questions

	WHERE THE PERSON IS	WHAT MATTERS
The Person's View	**Abilities** *How They See Themselves*	**Goals and Values** *What Matters to the Person*
	• How does this person see his or her own major strengths? • Where do they see their weaknesses or areas they would like to get better at? • What abilities do they feel will serve them best at accomplishing what matters? • What aspects of their skills or style will get in the way of accomplishing what matters? • What skills do they think have contributed to their success so far? • What additional skills would have been helpful for them?	• What are the person's most important goals, values, and interests? • What motivates them? • What is most demotivating to them? • What do they find most rewarding? • What really inspires them to do their best? • What kinds of activities do they enjoy? • What would make work more fulfilling for them? • What do they care most about in life? • What gives them the greatest sense of satisfaction?
Views from Other Perspectives	**Perceptions** *How Others See the Person*	**Success Factors** *What Matters to Others*
e.g., boss, coach, colleagues, senior management, family, friends, social networks	• How do others perceive them? • What do other people say about them? • How do others view the person's strengths, weaknesses, style, and impact? • To what do other people attribute this person's successes and failures?	• What is necessary for this person to be successful in his or her current role? How are those factors changing? • What types of people and what skills are most valued in this organization? Why? • What does their boss (and other senior managers) expect of someone in this role? • What kinds of people are most successful in this organization? Least successful? • What can be learned from looking at relevant competency models, job descriptions, and performance metrics? • What social norms and organizational values are people expected to follow?

Abilities refers to the person's view of their own skills, abilities, and style.

Perceptions refers to how others (e.g., boss, colleagues, direct reports, coach, family) see the person. Separating Abilities and Perceptions makes it explicit that the purpose of exploring GAPS information is not to get agreement on feedback, but to understand it from multiple perspectives. It is assumed that the person's view of their abilities will differ in important ways from other people's perceptions. In addition, other people are likely to have different, even conflicting, perceptions of the person. These discrepancies are not contradictions to be resolved, but information to be understood.

Success Factors refers to the expectations of others regarding what it takes to be successful in various roles, such as the person's current or desired job, or social role as team member, leader, or even family member. Success Factors on the job may be found in job descriptions, annual goal setting and objectives, competency models, organizational and cultural values, and informal analysis of who is and is not successful, as well as in the implicit assumptions and unspoken social norms for behavior. Research by the Gallup Organization finds that clear expectations are one of the essential conditions for high performance (Buckingham & Clifton, 2001; Buckingham & Coffman, 1999).

Because the Success Factors serve as criteria for evaluating how well a person fits, or might potentially fit, a given role, they shape people's perceptions of others. In the case study of Bonita, for example, her boss apparently views a take-charge, assertive style as one of the Success Factors. Because he did not see Bonita in that way, he did not see her as a great fit for her new role.

If a person's Insight or Motivation is constrained (in terms of the Development Pipeline), then a GAPS conversation is useful. Although it is common to begin with feedback (e.g., multirater surveys, assessments, or organizational interviews), it is more productive to begin with the right-hand column of the GAPS Grid, where the deepest and most useful insights arise. The first step is to get a clear picture of the person's own Goals and Values. Surprisingly, relatively few people take the time to reflect deeply on what is most important to them. Through strategic questioning a coach can help the person articulate what is most meaningful to them. Second, build a clear picture of what is expected by others—the Success Factors. What does the person's manager expect? The boss's boss? Other important players in the organization?

Feedback (i.e., Perceptions data) will be taken seriously only when it is seen as relevant to what matters. If the connection is not clear, the coach might as well be telling people their calculus skills or their ability to speak ancient Greek are weak. It may be true, but it will not inspire much change. Indeed, once the Success Factors are clear to people, they may see the need to change even without feedback from others. For example, if someone understands that the criteria for getting a sought-after promotion include demonstrating strategic thinking and team leadership skills, they may search for opportunities to acquire and/or demonstrate those skills.

Coaches can facilitate exploration of Goals and Values and Success Factors, and may even share their own perspective on what matters. Greater value comes, however, when the coach teaches the person how to reflect on what matters to them and gather information about what is important to others. Another skill critical for long-term development is the ability to get feedback from others. Therefore, rather than seeing the coach's role as primarily to help increase the person's motivation and insight, a more powerful role for the coach is to facilitate an understanding of what kinds of information are necessary and how to obtain them. This may come about through modeling the behaviors, teaching and practicing feedback-seeking skills, and shaping feedback-seeking behavior through success approximation and reinforcement. Although feedback from the coach can be an important tool, it generally represents the kind of dilemma portrayed by Druckman and Bjork's principle of learning versus transfer. The more the coach provides clear, explicit feedback in the session, the faster the person gains new insights. However, the person's ability to take those insights and apply them in future settings can be minimal. In contrast, when the coach teaches the person how to generate one's own feedback (Druckman & Bjork, 1991), initial learning may be slower, but the impact is more lasting and the person acquires a skill to be used in future settings, independent of the coach's presence.

CLEAR GOALS, CONSCIOUS CHOICE, AND EFFECTIVE ACTION

The third framework—clear goals, conscious choice, and effective action (Peterson & Millier, 2005; Peterson & Sokol, 2005; Peterson & Sutherland, 2003)—forms the foundation of most coaching conversations and helps answer the core question, "What are you going to do differently?" After a brief overview, an example will demonstrate what such a conversation might look like.

Clear Goals

This is similar to the Goals and Values of the GAPS Grid, but tends to be used in coaching at a more tactical level, as seen in questions such as:

"What do you want to accomplish in this meeting?" "What are you try-ing to accomplish with your team?" "What is the purpose of your strategic plan?" Two basic types of questions are used to help the per-son clarify their goals for a specific situation: The first asks directly about goals (e.g., "What are you trying to accomplish?") and the second explores barriers and constraints (e.g., "Where are you stuck?" "Why isn't that happening now?") Note again that this follows a constraint-based methodology. If the person is clear on what they want and there is nothing in their way, things would be going fine. So either they are not clear or something is impeding their progress.

Part of the complexity inherent in the human condition is that there are always multiple goals in play. In one situation, for example, a person may be motivated by a desire to get results, get things done reasonably quickly, have fun, and feel valued. Sometimes the motivations are easier to see by looking at what people want to avoid: I don't want to waste time, offend others unnecessarily, look foolish, or damage my career.

Conscious Choice

Once the person is clear on what they are trying to accomplish, those goals become the criteria by which various options are generated (e.g., through brainstorming) and then evaluated. Evaluation can often be as simple as asking the person, "In light of all your criteria, which of these options do you think is going to be most effective?" If the choice is diffi-cult, evaluation might take the form of reviewing the most viable op-tions against each of the stated goals.

Effective Action

Once an option is chosen, it is important to make sure that it can be im-plemented effectively. If the action is relatively simple, merely walking through the plan verbally might suffice. For more complicated tasks, ef-fective action might involve repeated behavioral practice, reflection and feedback, and learning new skills.

CASE STUDY—BONITA

To use this approach, one of the first steps is to find a specific situation to work on. This stems from an assumption that behavior can most effectively be changed through concrete, behavioral examples, not through abstract principles or aware-ness. Drawing again on the Bonita case study, here is a hypothetical conversa-tion—starting with clear goals—halfway through an early coaching meeting.

Coach: You also mentioned that you wanted to talk about conflict management. Where is that an issue for you?

Bonita: Some people are so aggressive, and I just prefer to keep things harmonious. We all have to work together. I think we can come up with good answers through open discussion. My way might work slower sometimes, but we build a stronger team.

Coach: So is there a specific situation coming up where you anticipate conflict?

Bonita: Things can be uncomfortable with Ken sometimes. He talks down to me. Like I was saying earlier, I don't think he respects me.

Coach: So where is the conflict?

Bonita: I'd like to be able to talk to him about that—to tell him what I feel.

Coach: And that will generate some conflict?

Bonita: I think so. I think Ken will tell me if I can't stand the heat, get out of the kitchen.

Coach: So if you were in a conversation with Ken, to tell him how you feel, what would be your goal?

Bonita: Just to tell him. If he knew how I felt, he might treat me better.

Coach: What else would you like to accomplish?

Bonita: I just want to let him know.

Coach: Earlier it sounded like you hope that he would change how he talks to you. Is that another goal for the conversation?

Bonita: I'd like to see that. But I'm not sure it's realistic.

Coach: What else would you like to see in this conversation?

In a more insight-oriented approach, the coach might explore Bonita's doubts about what is realistic. In this behavior-based approach, the goals will be explored through testing them behaviorally to see what works and what doesn't.

Bonita: Well, if we're going to get into it, I'd like to find out what he really thinks about me—find out if he respects me or not.

Coach: What else?

Bonita: You know, I'd like him to see that I have a lot to offer. I'd like to get him to see that even though my style is different from his, I can be a good leader.

Coach: What else?

Bonita: That would be pretty good. I'm not sure what I'd actually say, but that's what I'd like to see.

Coach: So given all that we've talked about so far, how would you summarize what you would like to accomplish in the meeting?

Bonita: Just what I said. I'd like him to see that I have a lot to offer.

Coach: That sounds very different from what you started with, where you said you just wanted to tell him how you feel.

Bonita: Yes, but I think this is what really needs to happen. We have to talk this through.

Note how the coach gently persists to help Bonita think through what she really wanted to accomplish. Sometimes a person might say, "I just want to tell you what

I think" or "I just want to hear your side of the story," when in fact she wants to solve a problem. The discrepancy can actually escalate the conflict because the other person might think he has met the person's goals: "Okay, I hear what you're saying. Thank you." Then, when the person in Bonita's position persists—because what she really wants is not what she put on the table—tensions flare.

Undoubtedly, Bonita has other goals in this conversation, but the chief goal is now clear enough to proceed. This is a cyclical process and it does not all have to come out at once.

> *Coach:* So let's look at some different ways that you could approach the conversation. How would you like to begin? (*Conscious choice*)
> *Bonita:* By laying it on the line. That's not my style, but that's what I need to do.
> *Coach:* Okay, so how would you do that? What exactly would you say?
> *Bonita:* Ken, I'd like to talk to you about how we get along. I really want us to have a good working relationship, so it would be helpful to figure out what we both can do to make that happen.
> *Coach:* (*Speaking as Ken*) I think our relationship is fine.
> *Bonita:* Well, Ken, I'm not sure I do. . . . (*Pause*) I'm not sure what to say next.

Here the coach shifts into behavioral practice that is based not on an artificial role-play, but on actually rehearsing what Bonita needs to say. Although such practice conversations tend to proceed in small segments, they are otherwise as realistic as the coach can make them. The more realistic the practice, the greater the likelihood of skill transfer and long-term retention of learning (Druckman & Bjork, 1991).

> *Coach:* Okay, let's debrief what just happened. You said you wanted to lay it on the line. How well did you do that? (*Effective action*)
> *Bonita:* Pretty good. But I didn't expect his response.
> *Coach:* Let's go back a bit: How exactly did you state the purpose of the conversation?
> *Bonita:* That I wanted to have a good working relationship.
> *Coach:* So how is that laying it on the line? Talking about wanting a good relationship sounds pretty safe and innocuous to me.
> *Bonita:* I'd get there eventually. I don't want to just drop a bomb on him.
> *Coach:* Okay, so what do you want to do: lay it on the line or get to it eventually? (*Clear goals*)
> *Bonita:* I'm afraid that if I don't lay it on the line right away, I'll soften what I want to say too much. He intimidates me.
> *Coach:* Okay, so what's a way you could tell him what you want that won't blast him? Because it sounds like you want to be direct but you also want to treat him with respect. (*Clear goals again*)
> *Bonita:* Yes, that's important.
> *Coach:* So what could you say? (*Conscious choice*)
> *Bonita:* Ken, I really want to have a good working relationship with you, but there are some things that I just don't feel good about.
> *Coach:* (*Speaking as Ken*) Like what?

Bonita: Sometimes when you talk to me, I'm not sure that you respect me. You talk down to me sometimes.

Coach: Okay, so how well did that work for you? Was that respectful and direct?

Bonita: Yeah, pretty good. (*Effective action, measured in terms of how well it helped accomplish her goals*)

Coach: Okay, let's keep going. (*Speaking as Ken*) Bonita, I don't think you should take everything so personally. You're a senior manager now—you have to act like one.

Bonita: See, that's exactly what Ken would do! Talk down to me like that. . . .

Through a continuous process of clarifying her goals, making a conscious choice, practicing the action, and then cycling through again, Bonita learns how to handle this conversation more effectively. The insights come from trying a behavior and reflecting on how well it accomplished the desired goal. In the role play, when her initial comment to Ken did not work well, it helped Bonita clarify that she had an additional goal that she had not mentioned—to treat Ken with respect. So in a very behavioral example, she began to learn both new behaviors and new insights. As Bonita and her coach continue to work through the conversation, Bonita will continue to learn new ways to handle surprises. One of the chief benefits is the increase in self-confidence she will feel when she sees that she is able to handle a variety of challenges.

COACHING STRATEGIES

The fourth framework for coaching is the five coaching strategies that address the most common challenges coaches face (Peterson & Hicks, 1996):

1. *Forge a partnership:* Build trust and understanding so people want to work with you.
2. *Inspire commitment:* Build insight and motivation so people focus their energy on development goals that matter.
3. *Grow skills:* Build capabilities so people can do what is required.
4. *Promote persistence:* Build stamina and discipline to make sure learning lasts on the job.
5. *Shape the environment:* Build organizational support to reward learning and remove barriers.

Strategies 2 to 4 explicitly address the necessary conditions in the Development Pipeline:

- *Inspire commitment: Insight and Motivation.* This strategy is primarily implemented through GAPS and clear goals, conscious choice conversations.

- *Grow skills: Capabilities.* This and the following strategy are discussed later in this section.
- *Promote persistence: Real-world Practice and Accountability.*

The strategies highlight two other important responsibilities that the coach has. First, in order to even have the opportunity to help the person change, the coach must establish an effective working relationship of trust and understanding. One of the most consistent findings in the therapy literature is that the relationship itself is often a significant factor in helping people grow (Hill, 2001; Lambert, 2004; Mahoney, 1991). In coaching, whether or not the relationship itself can facilitate change, an effective working relationship is still a prerequisite for the conversations and the work that needs to be done together.

The term *partnership* was chosen deliberately to capture a sense of two equals co-designing the process. It contrasts vividly with the common term *coachee*, which reflects, intentionally or otherwise, a passive state of receiving what the coach offers. Coaching requires a commitment from the coach to care about engaging the person as a partner in figuring out what they will do together.

Second, the coach has an opportunity to look beyond the one-to-one conversations with the person and help shape the environment. At a minimum, this involves coaching the person on what can be done to enlist the support of others, anticipate and manage how other people might react, find appropriate sources of feedback and encouragement, and anticipate other obstacles and challenges. It might also involve coaching the person's boss or sponsor on how they can support the coaching process, or even consulting to the organization on how the culture (e.g., norms, values, role models) and various systems (e.g., goal setting, compensation, performance management) might better support coaching and development.

CASE STUDY—BONITA REVISITED

Continuing the hypothetical conversation with Bonita from the last section will highlight several behavioral techniques important to the third and fourth strategies: growing skills and promoting persistence. We left off with Bonita commenting, as part of the practice conversation, that Ken is likely to talk down to her even if she brings this point up to him. (For the sake of brevity the following conversation is edited to highlight the relevant techniques. An actual coaching conversation would involve even more attempts to draw out the ideas of the person being coached.)

Coach: So how would you like to respond to Ken if he talks down to you during this conversation?

Bonita: Point it out to him right when it happens.

Coach: What would you say?

Bonita: It's tempting to say, "See? You're doing it right now!" But that probably won't be very helpful. I guess I could say, "Ken, I'm feeling like you're talking down to me right now."

Coach: (*Speaking as Ken*) No, I'm not. You just take everything too personally. You have to learn to play in the big leagues now.

Bonita: Yes, so he's still doing it. Now I don't know what to do again.

Coach: Okay, let me teach you two techniques—one for introducing the topic and another for dealing with it if he continues talking that way.

At this point, the coach explains the two techniques and demonstrates simple examples of what Bonita might say. Then, rather than having her practice the new skills in isolation, which would facilitate rapid learning, the coach asks her to try out the new skills as part of the conversation. That way, Bonita has to learn to use the skill in the context of a real-life conversation, where there are no cues and no pauses to think.

Coach: Do you have an idea of how you might use this with Ken?

Bonita: Sort of. . . .

Coach: (*Speaking as Ken*) Okay, so what did you want to talk about today?

Bonita: Ken, sometimes when we talk I feel like you're talking down to me. I'd like to explain my perspective a bit more for you, then take some time to make sure I understand how you see me and our conversations, and then figure out how you and I can work together without me feeling like you're talking down to me.

Coach: (*As Ken*) I think you're just taking things too personally, Bonita. I'm sure if you just spend a little more time . . .

Bonita: Ken, I'm very interested in hearing your reactions, but I'd like to make sure you understand my perspective first. Let me explain. . . .

Coach: Let's stop for a second here: How is this going so far?

Bonita: I feel nervous. But I got the message out and stuck with it.

Coach: (*As Ken*) I know where you're coming from, Bonita. You're just too sensitive and you need to be tougher.

Bonita: As I said, I'd like to explain my perspective. Even if you think you already know, I'd like to make sure.

Coach: (*As Ken*) Look, Bonita, I don't have time for this. This is not a touchy-feely kind of place and if you can't cut it maybe you should reconsider working here.

Bonita: Ken would never say that.

Coach: Perhaps not. But I want you to be prepared for whatever he says, even if it's something you don't expect. Because you're doing fairly well sticking to your message, I'm going to raise the stakes a bit. I'll keep coming at you with different thoughts, and as I was just doing, even acting irritated and frustrated with you. Even if it's not exactly what Ken might say, the purpose is for you to practice these new skills no matter what happens.

Bonita: Okay. That makes sense.

Here the coach is demonstrating two other learning principles from Druckman and Bjork (1991), providing contextual interference and increasing variability and variety in practice. These techniques help replicate the messy world that people live in, where other agendas and emotions interfere with the person's goals and where unpredictable things happen. If time allows in this session, the coach will practice at least one more conflict conversation with Bonita, giving her exposure to even greater variability and variety. Throughout the conversation, the coach is also using the techniques of shaping and successive approximation to gradually guide Bonita to more effective conflict management skills.

After additional practice, moving through several conversations step-by-step so that Bonita has the opportunity to practice all elements of her new techniques, the coach shifts gears to debrief.

Coach: So what have you learned so far?

Bonita: Mostly that I can do this. It isn't as hard as I thought.

Coach: What else did you learn?

Bonita: That I really have to be clear on what I want. If I'm not totally clear, I lose focus and back down. When I know exactly what I'm trying to do, I can stay anchored on that.

Coach: What else?

Bonita: I can be very direct and still treat people with respect. I never understood how to do that before. But staying clear on my purpose and just sticking to the process seems to work.

Coach: What else?

Bonita: I already knew this, but I understand better that the conversation has two sides—me listening to them and them listening to me. I need to keep that distinction really clear—about when I'm talking and when I'm listening. I'm usually too quick to just stop talking anytime the other person interrupts.

Coach: What else?

Bonita: That's quite a bit, don't you think?

Coach: It works for me. So let's talk about what you're going to do differently now. Based on what you learned today, what exactly will you do differently?

Bonita: I'm going to schedule a time to go talk to Ken. I'll take some time to write down my goals and exactly what I want to say so I remember it.

Note how persistent the coach is in asking for the lessons Bonita has learned. This requires that she actively process the experience, including the subtle lessons as well as the obvious ones, which facilitates retention (Druckman & Bjork, 1991). A useful guideline is to make sure the person feels like they are working at it. The coach asks "What else?" with an open mind, not searching for any particular answer, merely assuming that there is more if the person reflects on it. Then, the coach poses the ultimate question: What are you going to do differently? This marks the transition from thinking about the session to thinking about what happens next, which is the heart of coaching. In addition to Druckman and Bjork's principles, which combine learning and transfer, the technique known as bulletproof action steps (Peterson & Millier, 2005; Peterson & Sutherland, 2003) is also useful in promoting persistence.

> *Coach:* When will you schedule the meeting with Ken?
> *Bonita:* As soon as I get back to the office.
> *Coach:* Will that be the first thing you do?
> *Bonita:* I'll probably check my e-mail and voice-mail first.
> *Coach:* So you'll schedule the meeting after you go over e-mail and voice-mail?
> *Bonita:* Yes.
> *Coach:* How long will that take?
> *Bonita:* Anywhere from 10 minutes to an hour.
> *Coach:* How will you remember to schedule it?
> *Bonita:* I'll just do it.
> *Coach:* What might get in your way?
> *Bonita:* If there's a crisis or something. Or if someone stops by to talk. We've got a couple of big projects and there's a lot going on right now.
> *Coach:* And if you get distracted, when will you schedule the meeting?
> *Bonita:* Before I leave work.
> *Coach:* Okay. When will you write down your goals and what you want to say?
> *Bonita:* Probably this weekend when I get some time to think.
> *Coach:* What's your best guess on when and where you'll do it?

The coach continues with a series of practical, behavioral questions designed to help Bonita come up with a workable plan: How long do you think it will take? How can you make sure you don't get interrupted? What else might make it difficult to finish writing it this weekend? What will you do with the piece of paper you've written your goals on? How will you make sure you have it with you to review right before the meeting with Ken? And so on.

These questions may seem extremely basic, or even micromanaging, but part of the purpose of such painstaking detail is to help people visualize exactly what will happen, anticipate obstacles, and develop contingency plans. It also teaches them a process they can use to begin to make conscious choices to change their own habits.

There are two more aspects to the fourth strategy, promoting persistence (i.e., addressing Real-World Practice and Accountability). First is the assumption that positive reinforcement is necessary in order for Bonita to persist with her new skills. Although reinforcement is not explicitly applied, it is integral to the approach described here. That is one reason so much time is spent clarifying the person's goals—to make sure that they are important and clearly articulated. That helps to ensure that effective action directed toward achieving those goals will produce a positive outcome. Even if, for example, Bonita is not totally successful in her conversation with Ken, if she feels that she accomplished some of her goals or made tangible progress toward those goals, or even just learned something useful, she should feel positively reinforced. For that reason, the coach needs to make sure that early attempts to use the skill are likely to be reasonably rewarding. In this case, Bonita demonstrated quick learning and was adept at handling the various challenges offered by her coach. If she had not been so skillful, the coach would have focused on helping her find simpler places to engage in Real-World Practice before attempting the conversation with Ken, such as a minor disagreement with a colleague with whom she has a good working relationship.

The last tactic for promoting persistence is demonstrated by the following questions from Bonita's coach, designed to help her reflect after she engages in Real-World Practice.

> *Coach:* After you have the conversation with Ken, I'd like you to take two minutes to think through three questions: "What worked well? What didn't work? What would I like to do differently next time I face a similar situation?" How does that sound?
>
> *Bonita:* It makes sense.
>
> *Coach:* How would you state those questions in your own words?
>
> *Bonita:* What worked, what didn't, what do I want to do next time?
>
> *Coach:* What will it take for you to remember those questions and remember to ask them after you talk to Ken?
>
> *Bonita:* (*Smiling*) I can see where this is going. . . . I'll write it in on the same sheet of paper that I write the goals on. In fact, maybe I'll write the questions down right now so I don't forget.
>
> *Coach:* (*Also smiling*) Sounds good, Bonita. What else would be helpful for you?

EVIDENCE FOR EFFECTIVENESS

There is substantial evidence that the individual techniques mentioned so far can produce some degree of behavior change as part of a therapeutic intervention (Druckman & Bjork, 1991; Kanfer & Goldstein, 1991; Lambert, 2004). There is less empirical evidence that these techniques are effective in coaching (Kampa & White, 2002). However, Peterson (1993; see also Peterson & Kraiger, 2004) studied 370 managers who participated in an intensive coaching process based on similar behavioral principles. Many of the techniques were the same, but the models and principles were not as explicitly defined at that time. Participants were rated at three points in time: at the beginning of coaching, at the end of coaching (6 to 12 months later), and at least one year following the completion of coaching. Ratings were from three perspectives—self, boss, and coach—and addressed specific learning objectives as well as global outcomes such as overall job performance. Based on the boss ratings alone (arguably the most objective of the three rater perspectives), the average effect size, reflecting how much people improved on their individual coaching objectives, was 1.56 standard deviation units, approximately the equivalent of moving from the 50th to the 93rd percentile of performance. These gains were still evident in the follow-up ratings over a year later. A control group of items showed no change at the end of coaching or at follow-up.

PUTTING IT INTO PRACTICE

Coaching Bonita

Now that the basic principles and tools of this behavior-based approach to coaching have been laid out, here is a picture of how they apply to the two case studies, starting with Bonita.

When working with new coaching clients, I typically begin by asking three sets of questions that parallel the GAPS categories of Goals and Values, Success Factors, and Perceptions:

1. What would you like to get from your coaching? What would you like from me as your coach? (I take clients' goals, values, and expectations very seriously, and find that understanding and valuing what matters to them builds trust and strengthens the relationship.)
2. Tell me a little about your job: What do you do, what are the biggest challenges, and what does your organization expect of you?
3. What do you think other people want you to get out of your coaching? Who are the key players and how do they see you?

Depending on the range of issues they are interested in working on, I may briefly explore a topic in more detail to form a preliminary hypothesis on the Development Pipeline constraints. With Bonita, for example, I see her primary constraints on conflict management as Motivation and Capabilities. The preceding sections outlined the methods I would use to work with her on these two areas. Motivation would be addressed through clarifying her goals as well as by building her capabilities and providing a gradually escalating series of challenges to increase her sense of confidence and self-efficacy. In subsequent meetings, we would continue to practice different conflict situations and I would most likely teach her additional skills as well. She would leave each meeting with specific action steps, based on what she learned in that meeting. When she returns for the next meeting, I would ask what worked, what didn't, and what she learned from her experiences. Then we would identify new situations to practice, until she is comfortable that she can handle conflict as well as she needs to.

I typically work with my clients in four half-day sessions, about four to six weeks apart, although the specific arrangements are always individualized. Holding longer sessions allows us time to practice a range of situations in depth when we meet. The spacing in between provides sufficient time for clients to experiment with the new skills and behaviors. I am also available by phone and e-mail at any time clients would like to talk.

Bonita also indicates an interest in exploring work-life balance. I often find that people view work-life balance in terms of the hours available to do the things that are important, and there are never enough available hours to satisfy them. So I focus the coaching on helping them clarify their goals and values to get at what matters most to them. I'd ask Bonita, "What would you hope to accomplish if you had more time? With what aspects of work and family are you not satisfied, and what would you like to change?" Our work on clear goals would continue with prioritizing which goals are most important. Then we would shift to conscious choice, with questions like, "When you have time at home (and at work), what are the highest priorities you want to focus on?" "What do you want to do with the time that you have at home (and at work)?" Being conscious about what she does will help her use the available time on the highest priorities. Finally, effective action means that we might talk about how efficient she is at handling certain tasks (e.g., e-mail, voice-mail, meetings) and search for useful time management techniques. I imagine we would get into conflict management in this area as well, working on how to set clear boundaries with people at work, including negotiating expectations and agreements on what she takes on. We would discuss the advantages and disadvantages of her inclusive, collaborative style and search for ways to balance multiple goals: How can she be participative and efficient at the same time? How can she treat people with respect and still meet her own needs?

As we proceed with our coaching, we might also discover additional topics to work on. In addition, when I work with people who are new in their role, I help them explore five different topics, which might also lead to other areas for us to address.

1. *Business agenda.* What are the business priorities you need to accomplish to be successful?
2. *Leadership agenda.* Who do you want to be as a leader, and how will your actions reflect that?
3. *Relationship agenda.* How will you establish and manage positive working relationships with important stakeholders?
4. *Personal agenda.* How will you manage your time and your priorities in the face of multiple demands and expectations?
5. *Learning agenda.* How will you learn from your experience and build new and better capabilities?

Clearly, we are already addressing some of these topics, although each of the agendas has a more detailed set of questions that we would explore. For example, on the relationship agenda I might ask Bonita to list the key stakeholders, what her relationship is like with each one, their major motivators (i.e., Goals and Values), and her best sense of what they want from her (i.e., Success Factors).

Finally, I would want to make sure Bonita is enlisting the help of others at work. We would talk about whom she can go to for feedback and advice, and we might even practice how she could ask people for constructive feedback to make sure that she gets thoughtful and honest input.

So far I have not mentioned my communication with the organization. Organizational desire for input and knowledge of the coaching relationship ranges from situations where the person is the sole owner of the coaching to situations where the organization expects to know everything that transpires. My position is that, first and foremost, the expectations need to be clear and agreed to by all parties. Second, even if the program is confidential to Bonita, I will encourage her to keep open communication channels to her sponsors, telling them what we're working on, what she's learned, and what feedback and support she would like from them. My role as coach is temporary, and it is important to leave Bonita with the skills and relationships in place for ongoing development.

If Bonita is like most of my clients, at some point I will ask for the hundredth time, "What else would you like to work on?" and she will say, "Actually, things are going pretty well right now." If she has been implementing her action steps, reflecting on what she's tried, getting feedback from others, and then cycling through the process again and again (Peterson & Hicks, 1995), she will likely have made the progress she was seeking and it is the appropriate time to explore bringing a close to the coaching relationship.

Coaching Bob

Bob and I would begin with the same set of questions I ask all clients (see page 69). He would talk about wanting to leave the business running perfectly and I would ask him what he needed to do to achieve that. After we explored his views in detail, I would ask him what it would take from other people's perspective to achieve that (i.e., Success Factors). I can imagine him dismissing the views of at least some of the possible stakeholders. I do not see it as my job, as his coach, to convince him that he needs to change his leadership style based on feedback from others. However, I see it as my job to make sure he has all the necessary information, based on what is important to him (e.g., legacy, reputation), to decide if he wants to make some additional changes. So I would strongly urge him to work with me on exploring GAPS information.

Our coaching would probably proceed down two paths. One path is exactly what Bob is asking for. Using the method of clear goals, conscious choice, and effective action, we would practice how he negotiates deals, handles challenging leadership situations, and works more strategically. The most likely Development Pipeline for Bob in these areas is high Insight, Motivation, and Real-World Practice, moderate Accountability, and moderately low Capabilities. So the best approach is just to help him acquire the necessary skills.

The second path is to explore other potential development needs. For this second set of issues, Bob's pipeline is actually quite different compared to the first set. Feedback from others indicates that in areas such as credibility, relationship-building, coaching and mentoring, his Development Pipeline shows significant constraints on Insight, Motivation, and Accountability. To zero in on the Insight and Motivation conditions, I would strongly encourage Bob to do a systematic GAPS Grid analysis. Given that several of his Goals and Values hinge on others, not the least being his desire to leave things running perfectly, it seems imperative that he have all the information to understand what that means to others as well as what that means to him.

One possible outcome is that he simply refuses to solicit input from others. However, I suspect that several of his own motivations could be used to persuade him of the necessity of doing so. Table 2.2 presents a hypothetical GAPS analysis for Bob. Knowing what he values, I would simply ask him, "If status, reputation,

Table 2.2
Hypothetical GAPS Grid for Bob

	WHERE BOB IS	WHAT MATTERS
Bob's View	**Abilities**	**Goals and Values**
	• Driven, persistent • Smart, logical • Dynamic leader • Self-made leader • Business savvy • Knows the business • Visionary, intuitive • Talented • Warm, friendly, sociable • Charming, engaging, entertaining • Persuasive • Not touchy-feely • Needs to get better at strategic thinking, managing mergers	• Achievement, success, winning at all costs • Status, prestige, visibility, getting positive attention from others, especially those who are successful • Power • Independence, autonomy • Results • Efficiency • Image, reputation • Legacy • Fun, adventure • Family (primarily as a symbol of success and happiness) • Contributing to others
Views from Other Perspectives	**Perceptions**	**Success Factors**
e.g., colleagues, coach	• Smart • Confident • Powerful • Articulate • Charismatic, entertaining • Cares only about results, not genuinely interested in others • Autocratic • Impatient • Critical of others, not very trusting • Superficial • Volatile, emotional under pressure • Low credibility, inconsistent follow-through • Manipulative	• Strategic • Visionary • Leadership • Industry knowledge • Business and financial savvy • Engaging and inspiring others • Listening • Building a team • Building relationships • Coaching and developing other leaders • Trustworthy, credible • Customer-focused • Aligning the organization

and legacy are so important to you, don't you think it's worth finding out how people see you? You don't even have to do anything about it, but wouldn't you at least want to know?" Another type of question to hook his interest would be "Given that you want to leave a perfectly running organization behind you, you'll need a strong team of people in place. How will you make sure that you have the right people with the right intentions, so that you can hand it over with confidence?" Both of these types of questions lead to an exploration of what is important to other people and how they see Bob (i.e., Success Factors and Perceptions). Other points based on simple logic also help build the case. For example, I might ask Bob to describe the ideal candidate to take over the CEO role when he leaves. There is a good chance he would describe someone with capabilities and style similar to his own. So I would then ask how he would feel if he had to work for someone like himself. How will Bob convince someone else, as talented and motivated as he is, to work for him for 10 more years? Bob might see the need to treat at least some of his more talented leaders differently.

There is a good chance that the result of a coach-facilitated GAPS exploration for Bob is that he would begin to see other areas he needs to change, simply to ensure that his own goals are met. For example, if people do not trust him, they will be less likely to follow his visionary ideas. If people think he is superficial and insensitive, they will say things that tarnish his reputation and personal legacy. If people think a perfectly running organization requires a leader who coaches and develops others, builds strong teams, and motivates and inspires the organization—even if Bob doesn't believe such things—no one else will be impressed with the organization that Bob leaves behind. Showing him that his own personal success hinges on other people's expectations and perceptions is the method for increasing his Insight and Motivation. That information can then be gathered directly by Bob holding conversations with a variety of people (of course, only after we've practiced skills for listening, building trust, expressing interest in others, etc.). I might also interview people about Bob's leadership strengths and weaknesses as a way to help Bob get a better perspective of how others view him. Bob might not fully understand how intimidating it can be for certain employees to talk openly with an authoritative CEO. Once the Insight and Motivation are there, Bob and I would discuss what other behaviors he might want to change, if any. Bob, like anyone else, will be motivated to change only when he sees how it is in his own self-interest. For someone like Bob, other people's perceptions may not have much value in themselves, but if he sees how other people's perceptions of him impede him getting what he wants, he will probably decide to try another approach.

CONCLUSION

To expand on the comment that opened this chapter, the purpose of coaching is to help other people learn how to change their own behavior in order to more effectively accomplish what matters to them and to others. There are many coaching methods and philosophies that can help people accomplish that. However, an approach focused on people's actual behaviors ("What are you going to do differently?") is the most direct and efficient way to get there.

A behavior-based approach can be just as warm, nurturing, and supportive as any other method, even though stereotypes of the cold, detached style of old-school behaviorism persist. The behavioral approach presented here demonstrates a deep desire to help people find ways to get more meaning and a greater sense of fulfillment out of their work and their lives. It starts with finding clarity around what really matters to people, and then helps them get there. Because of the emphasis on learning how to learn, this approach can have an impact that persists long after the coaching is finished.

REFERENCES

Andrasik, F. (1989). Organizational behavior modification in business settings: A methodological and content review. *Journal of Organizational Behavior Management, 10*(1), 59–77.

Baldwin, J. D., & Baldwin, J. I. (2001). *Behavior principles in everyday life* (4th ed.). Upper Saddle River, NJ: Prentice Hall.

Braksick, L. W. (2000). *Unlock behavior, unleash profits.* New York: McGraw-Hill.

Buckingham, M., & Clifton, D. O. (2001). *Now, discover your strengths.* New York: Free Press.

Buckingham, M., & Coffman, C. (1999). *First, break all the rules.* New York: Simon & Schuster.

Cameron, J., & Pierce, W. D. (1994). Reinforcement, reward, and intrinsic motivation: A meta-analysis. *Review of Educational Research, 64*(3), 363–423.

Daniels, A. C., & Daniels, J. E. (2004). *Performance management: Changing behavior that drives organizational effectiveness* (4th ed.). Atlanta, GA: Performance Management Publications.

Dickinson, A. (2000). The organizational behavior management culture: Its origin and future directions. *Journal of Organizational Behavior Management, 20*(3/4), 9–58.

Druckman, D., & Bjork, R. A. (1991). *In the mind's eye: Enhancing human performance.* Washington, DC: National Academy Press.

Ducharme, M. J. (2004). The cognitive-behavioral approach to executive coaching. *Consulting Psychology Journal, 56*(4), 214–224.

Dweck, C. S. (1986). Motivational processes affecting learning. *American Psychologist, 41*, 1040–1048.

Dweck, C. S. (2000). *Self-theories: Their role in motivation, personality, and development.* Philadelphia: Psychology Press.

Elliott, R., Shapiro, D. A., Firth-Cozens, J., Stiles, W. B., Hardy, G. E., Llewelyn, S. P., & Margison, F. R. (1994). Comprehensive process analysis of insight events in cognitive-behavioral and psychodynamic-interpersonal psychotherapies. *Journal of Counseling Psychology, 41,* 449–463.

Goldratt, E. M., & Cox, J. (1992). *The goal: A process of ongoing improvement* (2nd rev. ed.). Great Barrington, MA: North River Press.

Grant, A. M. (2001). Coaching for enhanced performance: Comparing cognitive and behavioral approaches to coaching. Presented at the Third International Spearman Seminar, *Extending Intelligence: Enhancement and New Constructs,* Sydney, Australia.

Hicks, M. D., & Peterson, D. B. (1999). The development pipeline: How people really learn. *Knowledge Management Review, 9,* 30–33.

Hill, C. E. (Ed.). (2001). *Helping skills: The empirical foundation.* Washington, DC: American Psychological Association.

Holton, E. F., & Baldwin, T. T. (Eds.). (2003). *Improving learning transfer in organizations.* San Francisco: Jossey-Bass.

Kampa, S., & White, R. P. (2002). The effectiveness of executive coaching: What we know and what we still need to know. In R. L. Lowman (Ed.), *Handbook of organizational consulting psychology* (pp. 139–158). San Francisco: Jossey-Bass.

Kanfer, F. H., & Gaelick-Buys, L. (1991). Self-management methods. In F. H. Kanfer & A. P. Goldstein (Eds.), *Helping people change: A textbook of methods.* Boston: Allyn & Bacon.

Kanfer, F. H., & Goldstein, A. P. (Eds.). (1991). *Helping people change: A textbook of methods.* Boston: Allyn & Bacon.

Kluger, A., & DeNisi, A. (1996). The effects of feedback interventions on performance: A historical review, meta-analysis and preliminary feedback theory. *Psychological Bulletin, 119,* 254–285.

Lambert, M. J. (Ed.). (2004). *Bergin and Garfield's handbook of psychotherapy and behavior change* (5th ed.). New York: Wiley.

Mahoney, M. J. (1991). *Human change processes: The scientific foundations of psychotherapy.* New York: Basic Books.

Miller, W. R., & Rollnick, S. (2002). *Motivational interviewing: Preparing people for change.* New York: Guilford Press.

Moore, M., & Highstein, G. (2005). Principles of behavioral psychology in wellness coaching. In I. F. Stein, F. Campone, & L. J. Page (Eds.), *Proceedings of the second ICF coaching research symposium.* Washington, DC: International Coach Federation.

Peltier, B. (2001). *The psychology of executive coaching.* New York: Brunner-Routledge.

Peterson, D. B. (1993). Skill learning and behavior change in an individually tailored management coaching program. Unpublished doctoral dissertation. University of Minnesota, Minneapolis, MN.

Peterson, D. B. (2002). Management development: Coaching and mentoring programs. In K. Kraiger (Ed.), *Creating, implementing, and managing effective training and development.* San Francisco: Jossey-Bass.

Peterson, D. B., & Hicks, M. D. (1995). *Development FIRST: Strategies for self-development.* Minneapolis, MN: Personnel Decisions International.

Peterson, D. B., & Hicks, M. D. (1996). *Leader as coach: Strategies for coaching and developing others.* Minneapolis, MN: Personnel Decisions International.

Peterson, D. B., & Kraiger, K. (2004). A practical guide to evaluating coaching: Translating state-of-the-art techniques to the real world. In J. E. Edwards, J. C. Scott, & N. S. Raju (Eds.), *The human resources program evaluation handbook.* Thousand Oaks, CA: Sage.

Peterson, D. B., & Millier, J. (2005). The alchemy of coaching: "You're good, Jennifer, but you could be *really* good." *Consulting Psychology Journal, 57*(1), 14–40.

Peterson, D. B., & Sokol, M. B. (2005, April). *Coaching leaders around critical choices.* Master tutorial presented at the annual conference of the Society for Industrial and Organizational Psychology, Los Angeles, CA.

Peterson, D. B., & Sutherland, E. (2003, April). *Advanced coaching: Accelerating the transition from good to great.* Preconference workshop at the annual conference of the Society for Industrial and Organizational Psychology, Orlando, FL.

Prochaska, J. O., DiClemente, C. C., & Norcross, J. C. (1992). In search of how people change: Applications to addictive behaviors. *American Psychologist, 47,* 1102–1114.

Prochaska, J. O., Norcross, J. C., & DiClemente, C. C. (1994). *Changing for good.* New York: William Morrow.

Rogers, R. W. (2004). *Realizing the promise of performance management.* Bridgeville, PA: DDI Press.

Rosenthal, T. L., & Steffek, B. D. (1991). Modeling methods. In F. H. Kanfer & A. P. Goldstein (Eds.), *Helping people change: A textbook of methods.* Boston: Allyn & Bacon.

CHAPTER 3

Adult Development Theory and Executive Coaching Practice

Jennifer Garvey Berger

PERHAPS ONE OF the most exciting elements of coaching is that it allows one person (the coach) to specifically and individually target professional development opportunities for one other person (the client). Coaching is perhaps the most customized way possible of working to help improve the achievement and satisfaction of another person at work. Its success and worth depend on a variety of factors—most particularly, on the relationship between the coach and the client and on the ways the coach is able to ask questions, offer insights, and help the client develop new skills, perspectives, and understandings. One of our biggest challenges as coaches, then, is to keep our focus firmly on the experience of our clients—and to understand the current situations as our clients understand them, in addition to the way we understand them. It is this combination—of holding our own perspective while we hold the perspective of our clients—that makes coaching so powerful. It is also one of the things that makes coaching so challenging.

To ameliorate some of that difficulty, there are myriad theories we can draw on to help us understand other people while holding on to our own perspective. Theories of individual difference give us a way to make sense of the different meaning making of another person. Theories of personality, race, class, gender, or cultural difference (e.g., Gilligan, 1993; Heath, 1983; Jacobi, 1973; Lewis & Jacobs, 1995; Myers, 1993) are just as important to our work as a strong understanding of business

Thanks to Joan Wofford, Catherine Fitzgerald, Brian Emerson, and Michael Berger for reading and commenting on earlier drafts of this paper.

models, systems theories, and so on (e.g., Senge, 1994). Another key factor, and perhaps the one most often overlooked, is the development of our clients.

The notion that adults grow and change over time hardly comes as a surprise. Lived experience suggests that some people are "farther along"; some have what we think of as "wisdom," or are "more mature" than others. Still, few people have more than a gut-level sense of this idea of maturity, so it can be hard or impossible to know what to do about an "immature" client. How do you help someone with a narrow perspective? Are all forms of immaturity helped by the same interventions? How can we target our interventions to the particular place of the client? Theories of adult development offer insight into these questions.

CONSTRUCTIVE-DEVELOPMENTAL THEORIES OF ADULT DEVELOPMENT

Early theories of adult development were most often connected to age or phase of life (e.g., early 30s as a time to settle into young family life) (e.g., Erikson, 1980; Levinson, 1978, 1996). In contrast, *constructive-developmental* theories (e.g., Basseches, 1986; Baxter Magolda, 1992; Belenky, Clinchy, Goldberger, & Tarule, 1997; Fisher, Rooke, & Torbert, 2000; Kegan, 1982, 1994; Kitchener, 1986; Perry, 1968) are centered on the particular meaning making of each individual person rather than on age or phase of life. They are *constructive* because they are concerned with the way each person creates her world by living it (rather than believing, as some theories do, that the world is outside us with some kind of objective truth to be discovered). They are *developmental* because they are concerned with the way that construction changes over time to become more complex and multifaceted. Unlike the age/phase theories, these theories do not assume that years lived and life stages completed necessarily mean anything developmental at all. There are a wide variety of constructive-developmental theories—all with overwhelming similarities in their orientation to development, and all describing quite similar trajectories. The theory with which I am most familiar—and the one upon which this chapter is primarily based—is Robert Kegan's (1982, 1994) theory of adult development.

Constructive-developmental theories tend to focus on development in particular and specific ways. They look at issues of authority, responsibility, and ability to tolerate complexity and ambiguity. The easiest way to understand them is as they relate to perspective taking and relationship to authority. As people develop, they become more and more able to understand and take into account the perspectives of others while, at the same time, becoming more aware of their own responsibility for their emotions, life events, and so on. As people develop, the *content* of their ideas may not necessarily change (e.g., someone might retain a belief he developed in his MBA program that a good leader maintains open lines of communication with his direct reports), but the *form* of their understanding is likely to change (e.g., what "open communication" means may be revised and expanded).

Of course, every theory has its limits. Constructive-developmental theories focus on complexity and perspective taking; thus they do *not* focus on many other aspects that make humans interesting and unique—nor do they focus on group or system interactions (although there is much to be learned about groups and systems from paying attention to the meaning making of individuals). These theories don't claim that perspective taking is the most important part of an individual; they just attempt to understand (and sometimes measure) this one facet of human experience.

What does any of this have to do with coaching? Coaches are human, and it is the human tendency to assume that others see the world the way we do—at least if they see it *right*. Even coaches with sophisticated understandings about their clients' differences are unlikely to fully understand the qualitatively different developmental forms of understanding adults have and the profoundly different worlds they construct as a result. An understanding of these differences allows us to be more careful listeners, to make connections we would not otherwise have made, and to suggest interventions that can lead to clients' heightened success and development. The following section describes the rhythm of development and sketches out the four most common developmental forms of adulthood: Prince/Princess, Journeyman, CEO, and Elder.

FORMS AND TRANSFORMATION

From our earliest days, each of us has been engaged in an ongoing journey to learn and to grow. These two human forces are often connected, but they are not the same. Learning can be about acquiring a new skill or knowledge base. If I master PowerPoint in order to put together a slide show for a client, I've clearly learned something. I have new information in my head. But have I really *grown*? From a developmental perspective, real growth requires some qualitative shift, not just in knowledge, but in perspective or way of thinking. Growing is when the *form* of our understanding changes; we often call this "transformation." Learning might be about increasing our stores of knowledge in the form of our thinking that already exists (in-form-ation), but growing means we need to actually change the form itself (trans-form-ation). Each moment of our development, then, is a potentially temporary form of understanding that, with the right support, can change to become more expansive (more on support later). As we grow, the previous form is overtaken by the new form, leaving traces of the less mature form behind like rings in a tree trunk.

The rhythm of this movement is about increasing our ability to see more complexity in the world. When we are young, we have very simple ways of understanding the world (the earliest form of understanding mostly just makes the distinction between "Mother" and "Not-mother"). We grow to see and understand more and more fine gradations in the world, and as we do this, we begin to question assumptions we had made before (perhaps there are differences among those beings formerly considered to be "Not-mother"). Many developmental theorists (e.g., Kegan, 1982, 1994; Piaget & Inhelder, 2000) name this as the distinction between *subject* (that which you cannot yet see) and *object* (that which you can see and make decisions about). As elements of understanding move from subject to object, our worldview becomes more complex, and constructive-developmental theorists would say we have developed. This can happen when we discover a choice where we once saw only one option, when we discover multiple perspectives where we once saw only through a single lens. Each small shift from subject to object increases our scope, but enough incremental changes actually add up to qualitatively different ways of seeing the world, to transformation, the creation of different forms of understanding.

According to constructive-developmental theorists, there is a recognizable pattern of those forms of understanding. These forms generally fall into identifiable, qualitatively different ways of making sense of the world in adulthood (as well as many identifiable in-between places where a person will have parts of one form and parts of another).[1] In the descriptions that follow, I offer metaphorical names for these different forms of understanding. These names are meant to be evocative, to give you an initial sense of what characterizes these different forms of understanding. They are not meant in any way to suggest that the metaphorical name offered is representative of actual people who might hold the position named (see Table 3.1 for a comparison of relationship to authority and perspective-taking across all the forms of understanding).

---

[1]Kegan (1982, 1994) and Belenky et al. (1997) parse adulthood into four large meaning-making worlds; Fisher, Rooke, and Torbert (2000) offer seven, and Perry (1968) suggests nine. I follow Kegan's distinctions because they make the most logical sense to me.

Table 3.1

Comparison of Orientation to Authority and Perspective
Taking across the Adult Forms of Understanding

Form	Perspective Taking	Authority
Prince/ Princess	The only perspective the Prince understands is his own. All others are mysterious.	Authority is found in rules and regulations. When two external authorities disagree, it is frustrating but not internally problematic.
Journeyman	The Journeyman can take—and become embedded in—the perspectives of other people, theories, and so on. When he sees the world, he sees it through these other perspectives, judging right and wrong, good and bad, from the perspectives of others.	Authority is in an internalized value/principle/role that comes from outside himself. When those important values, principles, or roles conflict (as when his religion disagrees with an important value from his partner), he feels an internal tearing, as though parts of himself were pitted against one another.
CEO	The CEO can take multiple perspectives while maintaining his own. He can understand the views and opinions of others and often uses those views or opinions to strengthen his own argument or set of principles.	Authority is found in the self. The self-authored system determines the individual's rules and regulations for himself. When others disagree, this can be inconvenient or unpleasant, but is not internally wrenching.
Elder	The Elder sees and understands the perspectives of others and uses those perspectives to continuously transform his own system, becoming more expansive and more inclusive. He does not use the perspectives of others to fine-tune his own argument or principles like the CEO does; rather, he puts the entire system at risk for change with each interaction with others.	Authority is fluid and shared, and is not located in any particular person or job. Rather, authority comes from the combination of the situation and the people in the situation. A new situation (or different players) may shift where authority is located.

Prince/Princess Form

This form of understanding in adults is marked by the combination of a sense of self-centeredness and a focus on what *I* want (much like our visions of spoiled imperial youth). More common in teenagers and young adults, the Prince/Princess form is nonetheless sometimes seen in adults in their 40s, 50s, and beyond. Princes/Princesses cannot yet take the perspective of others, so the thinking and feeling of those around them is generally mysterious. Authority lies outside them, and is marked by both the formal authority of a title and also power over them in some way. Because of this, they appreciate (and obey) rules because of the direct consequences of the rules; they are unlikely to be motivated by mysteriously abstract factors like loyalty or a commitment to the relationship.

It is often easy for us to imagine a child or teenager having this form of understanding (and in fact that's where you'll find most Princes/ Princesses), but harder to picture an adult. As a quick example, let's look at Michelle.[2] Michelle was a supervisor for a clothing manufacturing company. She had dropped out of school when she was 16 to work on this shop floor herself, and now, at 41, was managing 20 shop floor workers. Married with three children, Michelle thought she was doing pretty well in the world—she had worked up through the ranks, her people listened to her and did what she said, she rarely got in trouble with the higher-ups, and she was making an excellent salary. Understanding the world through the Princess form, Michelle knew that her job was to follow the rules and keep her people in line. As long as she didn't rock the boat, the higher-ups would leave her alone and she could make her own way with her people. She had an understanding with those who worked under her; they knew that this was a world of give-and-take, of you-scratch-my-back-and-I'll-scratch-yours. She knew that she could cut her people some slack and that they'd return the favor, but she also knew that she needed to use her power to keep folks in line. She was enormously frustrated with the managers who asked her to do something outside her job responsibility "for the sake of the team." She felt great about this company and had worked there her whole life, but her job was her job—she knew it well, and if they wanted something done outside the parameters of the job, they'd better pay her outside the parameters of her job. Michelle had the most possi-

---

[2]All case studies in this section are compilations of people I have worked with as a researcher, coach, or consultant. No case is drawn from a single example, and thus all names, identifying features, etc., are obscured.

ble supervisees in a line position, and she knew that if she was going to get promoted, it would be off the shop floor and into a cube somewhere. Without direct connection to the people who were making the products, Michelle figured she'd be unhappy. She didn't know what the higher-ups did, and she didn't much care as long as they stayed out of her way. Michelle was happy staying right where she was.

In short, the Prince/Princess form of understanding has important strengths, weaknesses, and areas for growth that a developmentally aware coach can see.

KEY STRENGTHS   When a straightforward job is important, a Princess is in her element. She is great when there are clear images of right and wrong, good and bad that can be reinforced through external rules and rewards. Princesses see a direct connection between external rewards and external results—for this leader, linking salary to productivity is likely to be a key incentive.

KEY BLIND SPOTS   The Princess is unable to take on the perspectives of other people or be influenced by abstractions. She does not have an orientation to her own inner psychological world—or anyone else's—and so isn't able to understand the subtleties of human interaction. In fact, she can rarely see subtleties at all, and she lives in a world with only two choices for every decision—us and them, right and wrong, what I want and what everyone else wants. Her clarity about such things as right and wrong tends to be oriented around her own well-being (because she cannot yet take the perspectives of others or be oriented to abstract ideas and therefore isn't influenced by these things). Because of this, the Princess is likely to follow the rules of the organization to the extent that following such rules is in her own best interests. She is unlikely to follow rules or regulations because of abstract concepts such as loyalty or duty because she is not personally influenced by such abstractions.

AREAS OF GROWTH   The central issue for growth in the move from Princess to Journeyman, the next form of understanding, is for Michelle to learn to understand—and internalize—the perspectives of others. This happens gradually as, for example, she first realizes that she has the best interests of the organization at heart because she and the organization rely on one another (in a kind of a tit-for-tat way) and then that she feels a kind of loyalty to the organization that goes beyond her own best interests (when, for example, she supports reduction in pay or benefits that makes the organization more sound but at the same time reduces her own salary).

TARGETED COACHING INTERVENTIONS[3]   A coach can be a wonderful help to a Princess, supporting her to grasp the central idea that other people have perspectives of their own—different from hers, but ultimately comprehensible. Developmental activities include asking the Princess to have informal conversations with colleagues she finds mysterious and then reporting to the coach the colleague's perspective. Having the Princess notice—and record—her growing understanding of the perspectives, theories, and ideas of other people will support her on her journey toward becoming a Journeyman. Questions like "How do you think he sees his actions?" or "How do you think that seemingly-stupid decision makes sense to her?" will anchor her perspective taking in the concrete, observable actions that are comfortable for Princesses.

CENTRAL COACHING PITFALL   Buy-in may be especially hard with these clients, and they are likely to need prodding with some concrete consequences directly tied to their changed performance. Another issue is the coach's own potential frustration with the client—Prince/Princesses can seem self-centered and shortsighted, and since their perspectives are not at all psychological, these clients can seem to have little or no curiosity about others. Knowing this is a developmental place that every person travels through—instead of a character trait that is more permanent—will help the coach develop appropriate goals and interventions.

Journeyman Form

The metaphorical step from Prince or Princess is not to King or Queen, but to Journeyman. In the Journeyman form of understanding, the formerly imperial Prince or Princess begins to see other perspectives and understand authority in a new way. No longer trapped inside their own perspectives, Journeymen now internalize the perspectives of others. It is at this stage that they can begin to become devoted to something larger than themselves and become loyal to—and embedded in—some larger system/theory/relationship. This larger system, however, is not the Journeyman's to make decisions about. Rather, like an apprentice working with a particular master craftsperson, the job is to become as much like the master craftsperson as possible, to see with his eyes, to carve with his hands; the hands of the Journeyman become *the same* as the hands of the master. And so it is with development. As the Princess grows to take a new Journeyman perspective, she now sees through that

---

[3]Each of these targeted coaching interventions I offer is designed to help a coach support a client to develop. Development for its own sake is not a good coaching goal, however. Development for a particular end (e.g., for improved job performance in a job that is too complex for the client's current form of understanding) is the reason to pursue these activities.

new perspective, becoming fused with it. It is as if she has left the solitary confinement of her own mind and welcomed new members into her perspective and decision-making process. Like a young executive looking for guidance beyond herself, she has created an internal board of directors to help her see the world and make decisions. This metaphorical board may be made up of important theories, relationships, or ideas. However, the Journeyman is not the chairperson of this internal board, leaving room for disagreements or power struggles among board members.

This image is familiar to us when we think about teenagers who can seem to rely on friends—or, more largely, on popular culture—for their opinions about everything. Research done with constructive-developmental theories, however, shows that this form of understanding is far more typical in adults than anyone might assume. In fact, studies done using the Subject-Object Interview (SOI) (Lahey, Souvaine, Kegan, Goodman, & Felix, 1988), the measure of Robert Kegan's theory of development, show that 13 percent of the population studied is in the Prince/Princess form of understanding (or on the way to the Journeyman form), 46 percent is at the Journeyman form or on the way to the CEO form, and 41 percent is fully at the CEO form or on the way to the Elder form (0 percent of the population is fully at the Elder form) (Kegan, 1994).[4] As you see from these figures, it is likely that many executives and managers understand the world through the Journeyman form of understanding. (It is also likely that many executive coaches also see the world from this form of understanding; more on this later.)

What does the Journeyman form of understanding look like? Take Timothy as an example. Timothy had worked his way through the ranks of the pharmaceutical company and was now a vice president with five unit managers reporting to him. As a new vice president, he had faltered at first, and morale—and productivity—had briefly plummeted. The executive vice president (EVP) had stepped in, taken Timothy and the other VPs on a management retreat that offered a clear and coherent company theory of leadership, and given him access to the company's best coaches and consultants to support his enacting of that theory. That intervention had turned things around for Timothy—he was a smart man and a fast learner. Now there was a serious sense of "our way" in Timothy's division, and his loyalty to the EVP knew no bounds; Timothy's highest compliment was for someone to say that he and the EVP

---

[4]In the group of studies Kegan reports, the age range (of those studies that report age) is from 19 to 55, with most studies focused on participants 25 or older. The population as a whole is also quite highly educated, with many holding graduate degrees.

were "of the same mind." As long as Timothy could rely on the guidelines they had come up with together, he handled his job and his people with a consistency and kindness that won him accolades and respect. As the pharmaceutical business began to change—with increased pressure from global markets that did things quite differently—Timothy felt at sea. He doggedly pursued his former strategy—even when faced with data that showed that it wasn't working—because he felt that it was "the company way." With his Journeyman form of understanding, he could not create a new way from the new information.

The Journeyman, which is perhaps the most common form of understanding of adulthood, is vital for coaches to understand.

KEY STRENGTHS   The Journeyman's strength is his ability to take on others' expectations for good performance. He can be reflective about the issues involved and perhaps name and value the perspectives of others. He is loyal to the idea, group, or organization with whom he identifies—so loyal that he subordinates his own interests to the interests of that group.

KEY BLIND SPOTS   The Journeyman lacks the ability to untangle divergent perspectives or resolve conflicting viewpoints; he cannot mediate between the perspectives of important others. Similarly, a Journeyman cannot yet mediate between his own internal competing identifications, so that when his role as good father conflicts with his role as good employee, he is likely to feel stuck and unable to find an appropriate course of action.

AREAS OF GROWTH   In the move from Journeyman to CEO, this person will benefit from opportunities to move away from external theories or rules and to reflect on overarching principles and values that can help him resolve the conflicting perspectives of others. He can grow to see that no one theory, group, or organization is infallible, and he can develop a more personal and nuanced set of beliefs and loyalties.

TARGETED COACHING INTERVENTIONS   The Journeyman needs support to separate his own voice from the voices of important other people or theories. This can take the form of a journal—or even the careful ear of a coach to point out the voice as the coach hears it. Training on very careful, reflective listening (e.g., Jentz & Wofford, 2004; Patterson, Grenny, McMillan, & Switzler, 2002; Stone, Patton, & Heen, 1999), too, can help a Journeyman who has already started this journey (but will be very difficult for those not already on the path toward the CEO form). The Journeyman also needs reassurance that this separation is not an end to those important beliefs and relationships, but rather a deepening. For psychologically oriented clients, a little information about adult development can help smooth their paths; they can see that others have traveled this path before without ruining their personal lives or allegiances. For others, the coach can offer evidence that this new voice is not a failing of loyalty or relationship, but rather a new way to be in relationship with others.

POTENTIAL COACHING PITFALL   Depending on the coach, there are two central coaching dangers for the Journeyman's coach. Both concern the Journeyman's potential to become embedded in the coach's perspective. For some coaches, this will feel gratifying—look how helpful I'm being! For others, this will feel discouraging—can't my client think for himself *at all*? In either case, the coach's job is to keep the client's developmental journey in mind and to remember that becoming the authority *on behalf* of the Journeyman's own developing self-authority is the coach's place.

CEO Form

In a modern, global world, the Journeyman is likely to begin, eventually, to bump up against conflicting ideas and perspectives of which his form of understanding can not make sense. When this happens, he needs to find some mediating force to help him decide among the different—and reasonable—options. To continue an earlier metaphor, as his board of directors begins to disagree (or not keep up with the times), he needs some way to break the tie or add new information. He needs, in short, a chairman of the board to mediate among the different ideas, relationships, and theories that formed his internal board. When he himself becomes the chairman of the board, he has developed a new form of understanding.

This CEO form of understanding looks most familiar to us as what adults are *supposed* to look like. CEOs are those (at, of course, any level of an organization) who own their own work, make their own decisions, and mediate among different perspectives with relative ease. While Journeymen embedded in a particularly robust surround might look as though they own their own work (as Timothy likely did earlier), that tendency comes from the circular direction of someone else telling them to own their own work. CEOs, by contrast, do not need (and generally do not particularly welcome) people to tell them what to do or how to do it. They are likely to have opinions about things they know well, and are likely to form opinions about things they don't know well. CEOs may be frustrated by Journeyman employees (Why are they always asking for permission for everything?) and enraged by or discouraged about Journeyman bosses. Since Journeymen are more common in the population than CEOs, there is likely to be an ample store of these frustrations.

Samantha, who saw the world through her CEO form of understanding, was a middle manager in a small financial services company. She was hired by a manager she thought was wonderful, and he and Samantha had been very collaborative together. They didn't always agree—as she often said, she saw things her way and he saw things his way—but they always worked through their differences in ways that arrived at the best outcomes. After a company reorganization, though, Samantha found herself with a manager whom she found overly rule-bound. Instead of encouraging her to have different opinions and work through the differences together as she had done in her previous position, Samantha's new manager, a Journeyman, wanted them to think alike from the very beginning and seemed frustrated if her opinion was different from his. He seemed to think that if she were thinking about things in the right way (which equaled his way) then she would come to the same conclusions he had.

Samantha's employees mostly valued her enormously; they thought she had a coherent vision for the group and that she could keep track of the day-to-day details it took to implement that vision. Part of that vision was about letting her employees have lots of control over their own work—as long as they were contributing to the overall shared mission of the division. Some of her employees, though, seemed at sea when Samantha asked them to think of her as a resource and not as a boss. "But you *are* our boss!" they told her. "How can we be sure we're on the right track if you won't tell us how you want us to do things?" Samantha tried to reassure them by explaining that she trusted them to find their own particular path toward the end goal they all shared, but they continued to want her input in ways that felt too dependent to her. With her needy (Journeyman) employees and her controlling (Journeyman) boss, Samantha, once a star performer, became less and less effective and began searching for a new position.

While CEOs have the form of understanding most stereotypically associated with adults, there is still much to be learned from developmental theory about their strengths and weaknesses—and about how to help them grow.

KEY STRENGTHS   CEOs are likely to have a clear sense of personal mission that can be extended to the organizational realm—a vision that takes into account various stakeholders without becoming overly influenced by any one voice. Similarly, they have the ability to hold on to many different perspectives and make an informed decision that takes competing perspectives into account but is driven by their own sense of mission or values.

KEY BLIND SPOTS   CEOs can have an attachment to their own mission that can become inflexible. They may also have trouble dealing with the most complex situations, such as cross-cultural or cross-functional leadership, or any tasks that require them to examine their own system of values or principles and call them into question.

AREAS OF GROWTH   CEOs benefit from seeing the way their own personal theories and practices of leadership are limited and from expanding their images to include other—even competing—theories and practices.

TARGETED COACHING INTERVENTIONS   In the move from CEO to Elder, the CEO needs the opportunity to bump up against especially complex situations. A coach can help the CEO see new perspectives, but perhaps more helpful is to encourage the CEO to take on job assignments that offer the chance to understand and interact with very different paradigms. Helping CEOs increase their curiosity about other systems of understanding may also help them challenge their own system—not with the hope of *refining* the system, but with the hope of *transcending* it. *Note:* Because most organizational work does not demand the Elder form of understanding, a coach will have to be certain that developmental goals are where the client wants to invest his or her energy.

POTENTIAL COACHING PITFALLS   To support a CEO to grow to be an Elder is complex and difficult work, and may make a special developmental demand on the coach. If this sophisticated client outstrips the coach, the coach has to be willing (and able) to work with a client whose understanding of the world feels unfamiliar and (sometimes overly) complex. Often instead of urging additional complexity (which might be extremely difficult if the client has a more complex form of understanding than the coach), a coach can "mirror the complexity" of the client (Fitzgerald, 2000). This takes sophisticated thinking and high-level skills on the part of the coach.

Elder Form

As we have seen earlier, when a Journeyman questions the infallibility of her external guides, she begins to develop the internal guide that is the hallmark of the CEO form of understanding. Similarly, when the CEO begins to question the infallibility of his internally driven self-authoring system, he begins to take steps toward becoming an Elder. This move toward Elder has never been seen before midlife, and it is seen rarely even then. Still, because the world today may make demands on leaders for capacities even beyond the CEO form, the Elder form is an important one to begin to understand.

Elders are tuned in to all the various constituencies around them. They see multiple layers of every issue and can understand multiple perspectives. Unlike those making meaning from the CEO form of understanding, an Elder is likely to be less ideological, less easy to pin down about a particular opinion or idea. This is because the Elder is more oriented to the *process* of leadership than to any single product or outcome. This can make things disconcerting for her direct reports, and, as we see in the following example, can even make things disconcerting for the leader herself as she grows in this direction.

José, an EVP at an oil company, was widely respected because of his intelligence, his ability to manage people effectively, and his clear vision about what he wanted the world to be like. Through the years, he had felt that vision becoming clearer and had worked to find staff members who could share and add to that vision. A few years ago, though, José had begun to notice what seemed to him to be his own inability to believe in his single-minded goals any longer. He found that instead of advocating strongly for a single position, he began to see the validity in all the positions around the table. And it wasn't just that his convictions were weakening; instead, it was as though the distinctions between his goals and other people's goals had dissolved; even when their goals were quite different, he had a harder and harder time knowing which one he believed in most strongly. He found himself questioning his assumptions about the way the world worked, noticing what assumptions others were making, and understanding the ways those assumptions shaped their ideas about right and wrong. As he noticed these connections, he began reshaping his own assumptions to make them more inclusive.

As he developed, people began to be drawn to him in different ways. Instead of having only his division employees come to him to be told what to do, people all over the organization seemed to be coming to him for guidance or help in other ways—to get his perspective on an issue, to have him help them see where others were coming from. José really liked the new ways he and his colleagues were interacting, and he found himself less tied to organizational structures and opinions than ever before. He was also finding that he was less troubled by the daily irritations that used to bother him. Now when he felt irritated, he looked to himself to see where the problem lay, and he found that he was becoming more and more interested in the various reactions—even negative ones—that he found himself having. Even his negative reactions seemed a sign of his interest and vitality, and he began to appreciate his quick angry response (because he still had the temper that had troubled him throughout his career) as a key that there was some important assumption or value that was being challenged.

Still, with all that was good in his position and all the increased inter-action with colleagues throughout the organization, José was finding himself more lonely than he had felt before. While he was able to offer help to colleagues throughout the organization, he found that there were few people in whom he could really confide, and while he con-stantly tried to unearth and question his own assumptions and the assumptions of others, there wasn't anyone who helped him do that work. A bigger issue, though, was that José was noticing a major change in the boundaries around the persona he'd bring to work and the differ-ent persona that he thought of as his home self. He was feeling like those boundaries—which he once fought hard to create and maintain—were detrimental to his work in some way. Somehow it felt as though he was bringing only part of himself to his job, and that meant that he couldn't really be with his work in the way that he'd most like to. He felt as if his whole sense of the work world more generally was shifting and he was not quite sure what was going to take the place of his old images. Now, when José was at the top of his career, he couldn't find a place for himself anywhere. Although this was distressing, some-times it felt very exciting. José found it amazingly liberating to be able to escape from the world he used to know and to forge his own path to a new place.

If Albert Einstein was right when he claimed, "The significant prob-lems we face cannot be solved at the same level of thinking we were at when we created them," the need for Elders in organizations is clear. As the world becomes increasingly complex, the complexity of the Elder is going to be pivotal inside organizations. Given the tiny percentage of the population who has even begun to enter into the Elder stage, it is unlikely that any organization will have many people at this form of understanding. This is a particular problem because as the world gets increasingly complex, supporting leaders who can manage the com-plexity and ambiguity around them will be increasingly important; or-ganizations need these leaders more than ever. From this perspective, the good news is that the aging of the baby boomer population and the longer productive work lives people are having now mean that perhaps our chances of supporting Elders are becoming more and more likely.

We are likely to coach far fewer people with the Elder form of under-standing than any other, but keeping an eye on the possible trajectory of all clients may help them see how far it is possible for them to develop. And the opportunity to be good company for an Elder (especially for those of us who do not see the world through that form of understand-ing ourselves) requires an intentional look at their strengths and their needed support.

KEY STRENGTHS The Elder's strength is her ability to see connections everywhere. She is able to look at an issue from multiple sides and see the ways that the different perspectives overlap.

KEY BLIND SPOTS Because we do not yet know of a form of understanding beyond the Elder's, it is hard to know what her particular developmental blind spots might be. What is clear, however, is that because this order of mind is so rare, Elders have few peers who make meaning in similar ways. It also may be difficult for those who see the world through other forms of understanding to fully understand the perspective of the Elder, so her ideas may feel overwhelming, confusing, or just wrong (as, for example, someone making meaning at the dichotomous Prince/Princess form may resist a CEO's explanation that there aren't really clear right and wrong answers).

AREAS OF GROWTH One of Robert Kegan's (1994) names for those with this order of mind is "self-transformational." Those at this level are constantly working to grow, to question their own assumptions, to understand and cope with greater and greater amounts of complexity. Because of this, the world is a constant source of growth for the Elder.

TARGETED COACHING INTERVENTIONS Because most organizations are likely peopled with leaders who are mostly Journeymen and CEOs, Elders often outgrow their organizational roles (because development rarely goes hand in hand with a promotion). As they become Elders, they find that their organizational roles require them to act in ways that seem more and more narrow, and their colleagues do not understand this difference. This may lead to their leaving organizations and finding new outlets for their complexity. A superb and sophisticated executive coach—especially one who understands development—can offer an Elder a place to be known in the fullness of her complexity and can help smooth what can be a challenging transition from the certainty of a CEO to the openness of the Elder. For those in the transition toward the Elder form of understanding, reading about developmental trajectories can be enormously useful. Emerging Elders can gain a context and a new perspective on themselves and see some models of what a fuller Elder form of understanding looks like—models that are mostly missing from popular culture. Often, simply knowing that a coach can support their paradoxical thinking (or at least hang in with it) can help the Elder feel better understood.

POTENTIAL COACHING PITFALLS The Elder becomes very good at ratcheting down her complexity and showing only pieces of her understanding; that is often a coping mechanism for dealing with other perspectives (generally, she does not do this in a condescending way). If a coach seems unable to grasp (or at least be present to) her sophisticated understanding, the Elder will simply not offer it, which makes the coaching enterprise much less useful.

In between the Forms

It can take years—even decades—to move fully from one form of understanding to the next. Most of this time is spent in between the forms of understanding, relying sometimes on one form, sometimes on the next. For example, Journeymen who begin to grow into CEOs will find themselves torn, at times, between what their guiding theory/relationship/culture might indicate and what their new emerging self-authored self believes. An executive coach who is knowledgeable about developmental paths can recognize these in-between places and help provide the support and challenge a client needs in order to grow to the next form of understanding.

USING DEVELOPMENTAL THEORIES IN EXECUTIVE COACHING

Using developmental theories in coaching seems to me as important as using any other theory of individual difference—and with the same cautions. As with our use of any theory of difference, we have to avoid caricature, oversimplification, or even over-reliance on any one theory (or family of theories) as we think about the complexity of another human being. William Perry, one of the earliest constructive-developmental theorists, urged people to remember, "The first characteristic of any theory is that it is wrong in any particular case."

Also, like other theories of individual difference, developmental theories help us understand ourselves better—which is key if we are to get out of the way during the coaching process and not project ourselves onto our clients. We have to remember, though, not to impose the theory on the client, either; theories are useful lenses only if we can take them off—they become blinders if we are fused with them and cannot gain distance from them.

There are two major differences between developmental theories and other theories of individual difference. The first major difference between a theory about development and a theory about personality or gender is that development is hard to see initially, and even once you have a handle on it, it moves and changes; personality and gender (and other pieces of individual difference) tend to be easier to identify in the beginning, and, once identified, are likely to be more constant. The second major difference is that inherent in a developmental perspective is the sense that there is a higher place—and we tend to have a belief that if higher is better (more complex, more able to take perspectives), lower is less good. These two differences are both important in and of themselves, and also point to some particular ethical issues that are central to working with adult development theories.

DEVELOPMENT IS INVISIBLE—AND IT CHANGES

A coach who comes from an initial meeting with a client is likely to know many things about the client. Race, gender—even things like Myers-Briggs personality type—are all potential handholds for the coach's understanding of the client. Developmental level is unlikely to be as easy to uncover. It might take several conversations—or the use of a specific developmental assessment (discussed shortly) in order to determine with any accuracy the developmental form of understanding of a client. Once you've discovered this form, however, you can target your coaching interventions, questions, suggestions, and so on more specifically to the meaning making of your client's form of understanding. As you offer these specific interventions, you're likely to discover that your client's frame of understanding may grow or shift, that you may find him or her trying out new places that are farther along, or, during particularly stressful times, falling back on less-sophisticated forms of understanding. Development is about motion, and while understanding developmental theories will help you understand the motion, they don't prevent occasional dizziness when faced with unexpected starts and stops.

HIGHER IS BETTER

Perhaps the most serious criticism of developmental theories is that they are necessarily judgmental and that they privilege some things over others. This concern is important because it is true. Developmental theories are hierarchical, and they do have the internal belief that as you move along your developmental path, you have *more* of some things than you had before (and, necessarily, more of some things than others who are not yet as far as you). Developmental theories do also privilege some things; constructive-developmental theories privilege ability to take multiple perspectives and see many shades of gray. Both of these serious critiques are accurate.

I believe that while these are true, they are not inherently problematic. We all have judgments inside us about our clients (and our partners and our families and ourselves). Developmental theories don't create such judgments, they shape them and offer a framework for making good decisions about them. The difference between "I'm frustrated with my client because he can't ever make up his mind for himself" and "I'm frustrated about what to do with my client because he hasn't yet developed the capacity to make up his mind for himself" is enormous. While both sentences point to the same issue, the second sentence—aided by a developmental perspective—points to a time in the future when the client may be able to do that which he cannot yet do and also hints at some practical ideas to support him before he gets there. Similarly, we all make decisions about more and less (we may have clients who are "really smart" or "incredibly high on emotional intelligence" or "really in need of people skills"). Development is just another way of categorizing our judgments so that we can test them and decide whether they're worth holding on to—and worth helping our client work on.

ETHICS

What both these issues point to, however, is another layer of ethical awareness. Developmental theories are tools, and like any tool, they can be used to help or used to cudgel. Because developmental theories are difficult to understand, it is necessary that the coach gets a good background in the theory before making use of them—especially before using any assessments. Because developmental theories can look relatively simple (i.e., higher = better), coaches have to be very careful about what they do with such information. Badly interpreted or explained developmental data leads to a shallow understanding that can potentially be used against a client (or by a client against someone else). Finally, because developmental theories point to areas of strength and areas of weakness, they offer coaches some useful ways for bringing clients to vulnerable places; on the edge of their form of understanding, clients are likely to feel uncomfortable and sometimes even afraid (see Berger, 2004, for more). Coaches have to be sure to use these theories *on behalf of the journey the client wants to take* and not on behalf of the quest for development for the sake of development. In many cases, a situation can be resolved and the client can move forward toward greater success without changing his or her form of understanding at all. In other cases, the situation will never be resolved until the client has a more sophisticated form of understanding. It's vital for coaches to know the difference between these different coaching scenarios.

ASSESSMENT

As useful as they are, developmental theories are not particularly user-friendly. Constructive-developmental theory is challenging to learn about and also difficult to measure. My argument in this chapter is that simply understanding developmental trajectories leaves coaches far better equipped to understand the diverse needs of their clients; actually going as far as measuring clients' particular developmental space is less necessary. If you decide to go the extra step and attempt to measure the current development of your client, a variety of developmental measures are available—none of which is perfect (e.g., Baxter Magolda, 1992; Kegan, 1982, 1994; Lahey et al., 1988; Loevinger & Wessler, 1970; Perry, 1968; Torbert & Cook-Greuter, 2005). The measure I prefer above the others I have used and/or studied is the Subject-Object Interview (SOI) (Lahey et al., 1988), the measure of development that follows Robert Kegan's theory of adult development. This is a 60-to-90-minute semi-clinical interview that explores the meaning making of the interviewee. It was developed by Kegan and his colleagues at Harvard, and has been shown to be a valid and reliable instrument in a very wide variety of settings, populations, and ages. It involves searching not for *what* someone believes about the world, but for *how* someone believes about the world. For example, it does not matter to the instrument whether a client's beliefs about participative leadership are favorable or unfavorable. What does matter is how those beliefs were formed, what is most important about those beliefs, and what is most at risk about failing to live out those beliefs.

I prefer the SOI because it is very client-friendly (people generally enjoy being interviewed), it deepens the relationship, and it offers a great deal of information to the coach about what is currently at the front of a client's experience—and what is on the cutting edge.

The limitations of the SOI are all practical. It is very difficult to administer (and requires a huge amount of practice, study, and support), and it is time-consuming (and therefore expensive) as it is a 60-to-90-minute interview that then needs to be transcribed and scored. That said, I have found that the work of becoming a trained and reliable scorer of the SOI has profoundly changed the way I listen and the store of good questions I might ask—more than any other single thing I have learned about coaching, people, and so on. For that reason, it has seemed well worth the investment of my time. It may be that learning any developmental measure fully would offer some of these benefits, but the particular ways of listening, asking questions, and moving someone to the edge of his understanding that the SOI requires makes this a rich and valuable resource.

CASE STUDIES

The use of developmental theories does not begin with answers but with questions. While there are some conclusions we can often draw about clients, it is more my experience that developmental theories help me question my own assumptions rather than cause me to make more of them. In this section, I use the two common case studies to show how developmental theories can lead to new questions—and also how our conclusions can lead to targeted interventions. This means that any application of developmental theory is likely to involve first asking a variety of careful questions before making any assumptions; one of the great gifts of developmental theories is that they show us how often our assumptions are misplaced.

For example, Bonita has difficulty with conflict, a difficulty any coach would want to help her overcome. Developmental theory, unlike many other theories, does not first ask, *Why does she have this difficulty?* and *What can we do about it?* Instead, developmental theory first asks, *What does conflict mean to Bonita?* and *How does conflict have meaning to Bonita?* First a developmentalist can determine what we might reasonably assume about Bonita's development by virtue of the information we have thus far. It seems unlikely that she makes sense in the Princess form of understanding; there is too much about her that is focused on understanding the perspectives of others. Similarly, it seems unlikely that Bonita is an Elder. One definitional element of the Elder form of understanding is that they do not see conflict as negative; to the contrary, conflict is life-affirming and helpful for an Elder.

This means that, given the minimal information we have about Bonita, we could begin by testing an early assumption that she is making meaning either from a Journeyman form of understanding or from a CEO form. Finding out which is more likely is pivotal to the kind of support she needs in order to be more skilled at conflict management (see Table 3.2 for a summary of these differences).

It might be that Bonita holds her conflict as a Journeyman. For a Journeyman, conflict can be wrenching, because conflict can tear at her own sense of herself. Because Journeymen do not yet have a self-authored system, their understanding is made up by the theories, ideas, opinions of important others. If an important other believes that Bonita is incompetent, or if two important others disagree, Bonita is likely to feel torn about her own competence, or about what to do next. Similarly, if she is a Journeyman, Bonita is likely to be embedded, to a certain degree, in her surroundings. If conflict is generally regarded as unpleasant in her work culture (as it is in many places), Bonita may feel the need to protect her team from the conflict as much as possible (even when, from a larger perspective, that is not a good idea).

If Bonita currently has a Journeyman form of understanding, a coach has several concurrent jobs: to convince her that good leaders engage in productive conflict (thus, if she wants to embody the role of good leader, she will have to do this, too); to provide some format Bonita can use to protect herself from becoming too embedded in the conflict itself; and also to give her the skills to handle the conflict well.

Table 3.2

Summary of Developmentally Appropriate Coaching Interventions for Bonita

	Journeyman	CEO
Conflict avoidance is about	• The tearing inside Bonita herself that comes from having conflict outside her. • Images she has of other important leaders who seem not to engage in conflict themselves.	• An aversion to conflict because it's unpleasant. • A part of Bonita's self-authored system that suggests that conflict is always negative or problematic. • A blindness to conflict more generally such that she doesn't even know it is around her.
Biggest hurdle to overcome	• The sense that she might be torn apart by the conflict—that it might hurt the foundation of who she is.	• Whatever belief is operating that means that avoiding conflict is logical.
Possible coaching strategies	• Offering her evidence from authorities in whom she trusts (maybe you, her coach) that shows that conflict can be productive. • Helping her acquire new skills around handling conflict well.	• Persuading her that conflict is sometimes a help in a situation. • Having her track this in her own situation. • Helping her acquire new skills around handling conflict well.

It might be, on the other hand, that Bonita sees her world through a CEO form of understanding. In that case, she may have decided that conflict is divisive or uninteresting, and/or she may not have skills to deal with it effectively. A coach can help Bonita uncover examples from her own experience where conflict assisted in a positive outcome, and can help her remember times when not addressing conflict was more problematic for a leader. A coach can also support Bonita to learn more about theories of conflict (thus helping her tweak her self-authored system). If Bonita is on her way to the Elder form, a coach can help her uncover some of the paradoxes of conflict (i.e., that it feels disruptive to relationships but can actually deepen them).

No matter what her form of understanding, Bonita is likely to also need some new skills around dealing with conflict because someone who avoids conflict is unlikely to become good at facing it simply because she has changed her mind about its benefit.

Notice that in neither of these cases was the coaching focused on helping Bonita *develop*; rather, the interventions were designed to meet Bonita at her current form of understanding. A developmental perspective can be helpful even if development (i.e., transformation to a more complex form of understanding) is not a goal. In fact, one of the benefits of a developmental theory is that it is easier to ascertain whether development is necessary to meet the current coaching goals. If Bonita can achieve success in her position without changing her form of understanding, that would be a wonderful outcome. Indeed, since developmental growth is always associated with some losses (because to acquire a new perspective necessarily means giving up an old one), helping a client make developmental gains is only one of a variety of possible positive outcomes.

Sometimes, however, development is a goal. For example, while the case study does not provide enough information to be certain, Bob's story is quite consistent with a CEO frame of understanding.[5] A developmentally-oriented coach would first check this assumption about Bob, testing for the possible Journeyman frame of understanding and the far less possible (given what we know about Bob's lack of interest in other perspectives) Elder form of understanding.[6] The key markers for his CEO form would be to find out whether his clear and enduring vision is of Bob's own creation (as a self-authoring CEO would be) or is a vision he has adopted and internalized from some external source (as a Journeyman).

For the purposes of this chapter, though, let us assume that the coach has asked those questions and has discovered, indeed, that Bob is making meaning at the CEO form of understanding. With a client at this form, the coach's own authority is likely not to get her very far; neither is a glowing recommendation from someone Bob knows well. Instead, she needs to show her competence. In this case, it may be particularly difficult to get Bob on board; a developmentally-oriented coach will have to explain to Bob that his stated coaching goals may well require some of the "soft side" work he initially has excluded if he is to succeed in the ways he most desires. While a coach can begin with Bob's stated goals and

---

[5]Bob's case is a little too close to the stereotype for a CEO, so I want to remind readers that the CEO form outlined here can be quite affiliative (as Bonita's is, if she is at the CEO form of understanding) and inclusive, and that those at the CEO form can have excellent relational and interpersonal skills.

[6]Bob's case does not rule out a potential Prince form of understanding; however, it would be highly unlikely to see the Prince form of understanding at Bob's age and Bob's level in the organization. It would be wise to check occasionally to see how concrete and material Bob's motivations really are.

wishes, she will have to help him understand that it is important for him to have a more complex set of goals. From a developmental perspective, a coach will see that (1) Bob's current, CEO form of understanding may not be enough to keep up with the complexities in this boundary-spanning post-merger world, and (2) Bob is systematically hampering his own development by pushing his vision to the exclusion of all other perspectives.

For Bob to really thrive in this new cross-cultural work, he needs to loosen his hold on his own vision and begin to understand the perspectives, cultures, and ideas of others, not just to hold them up against his own thinking, but to really understand them as important and powerful—if different—perspectives/cultures. To do this Bob needs to grow toward the Elder form of understanding. A sophisticated coach may begin this process by simply looking for times when Bob's current system is not complex enough to help him meet his challenges—and pointing that out to Bob. Similarly, a coach can look for times when Bob admires the thinking or perspective of someone else, and help him think about how to use that other perspective to escape his own.

It may be that introducing a developmental framework might eventually be an appropriate—and compelling—piece of information for a coach to share with Bob; it might help him understand that his goals are aligned with some development work on his part in a variety of ways, and that development is not simply a help on the "soft side" for which he seems to have little patience. It might be helpful to actually use a developmental measure with Bob so that he can understand his own growth trajectory and begin to outline the ways an Elder might be more suited to the central work of managing cross-culturally and also leaving a legacy behind. Any of these might become the "disorienting dilemma" that many theorists think is the key to helping someone see a new perspective (e.g., Mezirow, 2000, p. 22).

Once Bob has begun to see his own development as a goal, there are a variety of exercises he can do in order to begin to transcend his CEO form of understanding. The first is simply about listening well. Learning to listen well (and really begin to understand fully the perspective of another person *as that person understands it*) is a developmental activity for people at almost any form of understanding. Bob needs the company of a coach to understand that different perspectives can have their own wisdom and that there are often pieces of truth in opposite points. At the same time, to help Bob develop requires that he begin to understand the fallibility of his own internal system. Providing 360-degree feedback may help begin that understanding. An equally important piece of data will be Bob's own search for ways his vision is partial. If he can begin to note (perhaps in a journal or by the use of any other record-keeping device) any way that his vision is not absolutely perfect, he may begin to understand the key Elder perspective that any vision, no matter how excellent and thoughtful, is necessarily partial. As Bob loosens his hold on his own vision, he may become more confused and less clear-headed; again, this is where the company of a developmentally knowledgeable coach is pivotal. Developmental theories make a rough map of paths taken by others, and even if Bob's journey is quite different, the journeys of others can inform his journey and help him have patience for those times when the path is difficult.

USING ADULT DEVELOPMENTAL THEORIES FOR SELF-ASSESSMENT AND SELF-DEVELOPMENT

I do not want to close this chapter without some recognition that developmental theories—while useful in our work with others—are also very helpful in our work on/with ourselves. Whenever I teach or consult about developmental theory, even if the focus is on helping others, questions inevitably arise about what this means for the coach as he walks his own developmental path. It is unlikely that there are many coaches who make meaning from the Prince/Princess form of understanding; coaching requires a perspective-taking ability and an orientation to the complexities of the inner life and the individual in relationships that is invisible to the Prince/Princess. It is quite likely, however, that there are many coaches who are Journeymen and CEOs (and far fewer who are Elders). Learning about your own development—and witnessing and supporting the development of your clients—is in itself a developmental activity. While developmental theories can be humbling (because it would be lovely—but unlikely—to think of ourselves at the pinnacle), they are also very hopeful. As you intentionally map your own developmental path, you can contribute to creation and growth of developmental theories generally. And as we pay attention to our own development and the development of our clients, we may all find what Bertrand Russell promises: "The universe is full of magical things patiently waiting for our wits to grow sharper."

REFERENCES:

Basseches, M. (1986). Dialectical thinking and young adult cognitive development. In R. A. Mines & K. S. Kitchener (Eds.), *Adult cognitive development: Methods and models* (pp. 33–56). New York: Praeger.

Baxter Magolda, M. B. (1992). *Knowing and reasoning in college : Gender-related patterns in students' intellectual development.* San Francisco: Jossey-Bass.

Belenky, M. F., Clinchy, B. M., Goldberger, N. R., & Tarule, J. M. (1997). *Women's ways of knowing: The development of self, voice, and mind.* New York: Basic Books.

Berger, J. G. (2004). Dancing on the threshold of meaning: Recognizing and understanding the growing edge. *Journal of Transformative Education, 2,* 336–351.

Erikson, E. H. (1980). *Identity and the life cycle.* New York: W. W. Norton.

Fisher, D., Rooke, D., & Torbert, B. (2000). *Personal and organisational transformations: Through action inquiry.* Boston: Edge/Work Press.

Fitzgerald, C. R. (2000). *Transformative coaching for executives at midlife.* Paper presented at the Linkage coaching and mentoring conference, Chicago.

Gilligan, C. (1993). *In a different voice: Psychological theory and women's development.* Cambridge, MA: Harvard University Press.

Heath, S. B. (1983). *Ways with words: Language, life, and work in communities and classrooms.* New York: Cambridge University Press.

Jacobi, J. (1973). *The psychology of C. G. Jung.* New Haven, CT: Yale University Press.

Jentz, B., & Wofford, J. (2004). *Communicating to lead and learn.* Atlanta, GA: Kenning Associates.

Kegan, R. (1982). *The evolving self: Problem and process in human development.* Cambridge, MA: Harvard University Press.

Kegan, R. (1994). *In over our heads: The mental demands of modern life.* Cambridge, MA: Harvard University Press.

Kitchener, K. S. (1986). The reflective judgment model: Characteristics, evidence, and measurement. In R. A. Mines & K. S. Kitchener (Eds.), *Adult cognitive development: Methods and models* (pp. 76–91). New York: Praeger.

Lahey, L., Souvaine, E., Kegan, R., Goodman, R., & Felix, S. (1988). *A guide to the subject-object interview: Its administration and interpretation.* Cambridge, MA: Harvard University, Graduate School of Education, Laboratory of Human Development.

Levinson, D. J. (1978). *The seasons of a man's life.* New York: Ballantine Books.

Levinson, D. J. (1996). *The seasons of a woman's life.* New York: Alfred A. Knopf.

Lewis, P., & Jacobs, T. O. (1995). Individual differences in strategic leadership capacity. In J. G. Hunt & R. L. Phillips (Eds.), *Strategic leadership.* New York: Quorum Books.

Loevinger, J., & Wessler, R. (1970). *Measuring ego development.* San Francisco: Jossey-Bass.

Mezirow, J. (2000). Learning to think like an adult: Core concepts of transformation theory. In J. Mezirow (Ed.), *Learning as transformation: Critical perspectives on a theory in progress* (pp. 3–34). San Francisco: Jossey-Bass.

Myers, I. B. (1993). *Gifts differing: Understanding personality type.* Palo Alto, CA: CPP Books.

Patterson, K., Grenny, J., McMillan, R., & Switzler, A. (2002). *Crucial conversations: Tools for talking when stakes are high.* New York: McGraw-Hill.

Perry, W. G. (1968). *Forms of intellectual and ethical development in the college years.* Cambridge, MA: Bureau of Study Counsel, Harvard University.

Piaget, J., & Inhelder, B. (2000). *The psychology of the child.* New York: Basic Books.

Senge, P. M. (1994). *The fifth discipline: The art and practice of the learning organization.* New York: Doubleday/Currency.

Stone, D., Patton, B., & Heen, S. (1999). *Difficult conversations: How to discuss what matters most.* New York: Viking.

Torbert, B., & Cook-Greuter, S. (n.d.) *Leadership development profile.* Retrieved from www.harthill.co.uk/ldf.html January 10, 2005.

CHAPTER 4

Cognitive Coaching

JEFFREY E. AUERBACH

As A COACH, I'm a thought partner. As a thought partner, I help my clients think with more depth, greater clarity, and less distortion—a cognitive process. Coaching is largely a cognitive method. Cognitive coaching tools, like the ones described in this chapter, are the foundations of many coaches' toolboxes.

However, there is more to coaching than a set of methods—cognitive methods or any other. Coaching without the humanistic side of a caring, trustworthy coach won't get off the ground. A coach who neglects the emotional side of the client completely will be shutting out a critical element. Students of emotional intelligence know that feelings are to be attended to as potential sources of useful information. Emotional self-awareness is a foundation for success in life (Stein & Book, 2000). Even the coach who uses largely cognitive approaches must incorporate emotional knowledge. As this chapter emphasizes, emotions are linked to cognition.

My own style of coaching is holistic, values-based, action coaching (Auerbach, 2001) emphasizing the whole person, moving toward their most important goals, congruent with their vital values. I use many tools from many fields—but for the purpose of this chapter I focus on cognitive coaching tools that stem from the emerging cognitive coaching theory. As my research of over one hundred organizations that utilize coaching shows, not only has coaching had an incredible increase in utilization over the last five years, but coaches who are well trained, experienced, and who can employ a variety of coaching tools, are the most sought after practitioners in this emerging field (Auerbach, 2005a; Auerbach

Acknowledgments: I would like to gratefully acknowledge Jeanne Auerbach and Todd Kettner for their assistance with this project.

2005b). Cognitive coaching tools are practical, are learnable, and bring clear value to your coaching clients.

BACKGROUND ON COGNITIVE THERAPY

As a cognitive coaching theory begins to be developed, it is natural to examine the empirically based related field of cognitive therapy. The first principle of cognitive therapy is that your moods are strongly related to and often triggered by your cognitions, or thoughts. A cognition refers to the way you look at things—your perceptions, mental attitudes, and beliefs. A cognition includes the way you interpret things—what you say about something or someone to yourself. Burns (1980) stated, "You feel the way you do right now because of the thoughts you are thinking at this moment."

Cognitive therapy is easily distinguished by what it is not. Cognitive therapy does not follow the path of the Freudian, who attempts to help the client by uncovering repressed ideas and wishes and aiding in the translation of conscious thoughts into their symbolic meanings. Nor does the cognitive therapist operate as a behaviorist, affecting behavior by rewards and punishments or gradual exposure to anxiety-provoking events. Rather the cognitive therapist assists clients in identifying errors in their thinking and aiding them in adopting more accurate, useful cognitions. Moreover, the cognitive therapist may identify whether there is an absence of accurate, useful cognitions, even if particular thinking errors are not identified.

Burns's (1980) research documents that negative thoughts that cause emotional turmoil usually contain gross distortions. Although the "automatic thoughts" that one has appear valid initially, there is often an irrational element, and this twisted thinking can cause anxiety and depression, and block people from adopting new, more useful behavior. The primary principle of cognitive therapy is that by pinpointing and eliminating the mental distortions that cause upset, mood can be improved. Coaches believe that eliminating thinking errors that contribute to poor relationships with people will lead to better relationships with others and improved decision making—which leads to higher performance.

Albert Ellis (1979) developed the ABC rational-emotive therapy (RET) approach emphasizing that people become unhappy or develop self-defeating habits because of unrealistic or faulty beliefs. In Ellis's model the "A" stands for an activating experience, which the individual believes causes "C," the emotional consequence. For example, an employee enters his office building on Monday morning and his manager walks by without saying hello (activating experience); the employee feels a wave of gloom and anger wash over him (consequence). RET helps the employee realize that the cause of the gloom and anger is not that the manager did not acknowledge him, but rather it is in-between—the "B" for beliefs about the activating experience. It was the employee's faulty belief that he "must be approved by almost everyone at all times" that prevented him from considering other options, such as, "Maybe he didn't see me because he was talking to someone else as he walked in." RET emphasizes that it is beliefs that cause feelings—not events.

Aaron Beck (1976) stated:

> Psychological problems are not necessarily the product of mysterious, impenetrable forces but may result from commonplace processes such as faulty learning, making incorrect inferences on the basis of inadequate or incorrect information, and not distinguishing adequately between imagination and reality. Moreover, thinking can be unrealistic because it is derived from erroneous premises; behavior can be self-defeating because it is based on unreasonable attitudes. Thus, psychological problems can be mastered by sharpening discriminations, correcting misconceptions, and learning more adaptive attitudes. Since introspection, insight, reality testing, and learning are basically cognitive processes, this approach to the neuroses has been labeled cognitive therapy.

The cognitive therapist helps the client unravel distortions in thinking and learn alternative, more realistic ways to approach the world. The essential concept that errors in thinking create problems is catalogued by Ellis's list of "irrational ideas" and Burns's list of 10 "cognitive distortions."

Here are 10 common cognitive distortions that are adapted for coaching from Burns's popular best-selling book, *Feeling Good* (1980):

Definitions of Cognitive Distortions Seen in Coaching

1. *All-or-nothing thinking.* You see things as either black or white. When your performance is not perfect, you conclude you are a total failure. The sales professional makes four sales in a row, and loses the fifth, but concludes, "I can't do this!"
2. *Overgeneralization.* You see a single negative outcome as a continuous pattern of defeat. The sales professional loses a sale to the competition, even though he makes most sales, and views the situation as yet another failure of many and therefore concludes that he is a failure.
3. *Mental filter.* You pick out a sole negative detail and cannot seem to see anything else to help you put things in perspective. An employee is irritated with her manager and goes over the ways she has been mistreated and does not see the many ways the manager is trying to improve their working relationship.

4. *Disqualifying the positive.* You reject positive experiences by thinking they are unimportant or have ulterior motives attached. An executive wants to reward a manager with a choice new assignment but the manager discounts the opportunity and sees it as "He's just trying to give his work to me."

5. *Mind reading.* You conclude that someone is thinking something negative about you even though there are no facts that convincingly support your conclusion. An employee who has a new manager concludes, "She doesn't like me," but other knowledgeable and reasonable observers say that they can't see any evidence of that.

6. *The fortune teller error.* You believe that things will turn out badly before there are reasonable facts to support that opinion. The consultant concludes that she cannot land a particular contract when she has no way of knowing that for certain.

7. *Catastrophizing.* You exaggerate the importance of a minor event; other reasonable people may not see the event as an issue at all, but you seem obsessed with it. A dentist's front office person resigns and the dentist concludes that a disaster has occurred, that there is no chance of finding anyone new who is even half as good. The dentist makes the conclusion that she will lose half her patients.

8. *Emotional reasoning.* You believe that your negative emotions are facts that should be acted on. The manager feels suspicious of an employee and concludes, "If I feel this way he must guilty."

9. *"Should" statements.* You believe things must be done a certain way and you communicate this in your own self-talk and to others. The employee feels angry when her co-workers do not do things the way she thinks they should even though very few people could live up to her expectations.

10. *Labeling.* This is a powerful form of overgeneralization; instead of describing a specific behavior, you attach a negative label to yourself or the other person. Rather than discuss the specifics of a behavior, the person uses a global label that generally can be disputed because the person does not always fit the label (although their behavior might temporarily). Labeling is name-calling. The manager thinks, "I'm a loser" or "They are jerks."

Adapted from D. D. Burns, *Feeling Good: The New Mood Therapy* (New York: William Morrow, 1980).

THE SCHEMA CONSTRUCT IN TERMS
OF COGNITIVE COACHING

Schema therapy is also rooted in cognitive-behavioral therapy theory but also integrates other elements such as childhood and adolescent origins of psychological problems, emotive techniques, the therapist-client relationship, and maladaptive coping styles (Young, 2003, p. 5).

A schema is a blueprint imposed on experience that helps individuals interpret an experience and guides their responses. A schema is an abstract representation of the elements of an event. Within cognitive psychology, a schema is an abstract plan that guides an individual's thinking and responses. In terms of cognitive coaching, a schema is a broad mental guideline for interpreting a situation and how to respond to the situation. A schema may be adaptive or not. In psychotherapy, and in coaching, some schemas can be identified as old, outdated, and bringing about maladaptive or unintended consequences. Some schemas may be appropriate in early life but inappropriate later. For example, a child's schema might be "I can't do that without asking permission." For a young child this would be appropriate, but for a manager, this schema, taken too far too often, will have the impact of the manager appearing indecisive, lacking independence, and devoid of initiative.

Schemas lead to sets of behaviors that are coping styles. Our client's coping styles may or may not be productive. To avoid the clinicalization of coaching, in coaching we may call these coping styles behavior patterns or common practices.

For the psychologically minded coach an understanding of the concept that our clients have underlying schemas, or complex mental models (beliefs that affect behavior), can help us understand the clients' behaviors. We can help our clients ultimately examine their mental models to aid them in choosing behaviors that are productive rather than old response sets that interfere with their current needs and goals.

Although most coaches view coaching as an activity we engage in with clients who do not have clinically significant DSM-IV disorders, some clients not only will have limiting mental models, but may also have maladaptive coping styles where they are responding to situations as if they are a threat rather than an opportunity. Coaches do need to know when to refer a coaching client to a therapist for treatment of mental disorders. Some more psychologically oriented coaches may find an understanding of maladaptive coping styles as helpful to them in analyzing the client's situation and in guiding some of the coaching approaches chosen. This is true even if they never speak with the client about the concept of maladaptive coping styles and choose instead to use language that is positive such as "This is an opportunity for development" rather than "This is a maladaptive coping style."

Another relevant concept from schema therapy is the schema mode model and the four mode categories. Three of the four mode categories are maladaptive by definition, but the fourth category is especially relevant for coaching—the healthy adult mode. According to schema theory, the overarching goal is for clients to further strengthen their healthy adult mode. The healthy adult mode is the "executive style" that nurtures, affirms, and protects the more vulnerable parts of oneself; limits angry outbursts and assists with impulse control in accordance with the principles of reciprocity and self-discipline; and talks back to unhelpful parts of one's personality (Young, 2003, p. 278).

An updated, abbreviated version of schema work as it applies to cognitive coaching is to:

1. Assist the client in identifying and labeling unhelpful mental models and behavior patterns.
2. Assist the client in learning where unhelpful mental models contribute to current difficulties or limit options.
3. Discuss the benefits of altering mental models.
4. Engage the higher-order component of the client's personality to adopt mental models that are congruent with the client's values and goals, and then plan action steps to realize the benefits sought.
5. Utilize an accountability process to increase the likelihood that desired outcomes are achieved.

Next we will examine another similar version of this concept of cognitive coaching.

COGNITIVE COACHING FOR SCHOOL ADMINISTRATORS

The term *cognitive coaching*, which is used in an expanded manner in this chapter, is believed to have been first used in the mid-1980s by Costa and Garmston with educators (Costa & Garmston, 2002). Their version of cognitive coaching was utilized as a supervision model that principals could use with teachers in order to positively impact teacher thought processes and ultimately improve classroom instruction. Although cognitive approaches in personal and executive coaching are ubiquitous, their model is well developed, has been taught to many professionals, and has had published studies documenting outcomes, so an overview is valuable to the student of coaching.

The goal of cognitive coaching with educators was to produce self-directed individuals who demonstrate high performance, both individually and as community members. The authors saw cognitive coaching as based on many fields of study, including, but not limited to, linguistics, individuation, constructivism, mediation, cognitive theory, humanistic psychology, systems thinking, and clinical supervision. Costa and Garmston (2002) state that the goal of their version of cognitive coaching is not to teach people new skills and capabilities but to be a mediator of people's thinking. They contend that cognitive coaching enhances the ability of the person being coached to examine their patterns of thinking and behavior, and to reconsider the underlying assumptions that precede actions.

The cognitive coaching process for educators relies on a trusting relationship and utilizes tools such as rapport, pausing, paraphrasing, probing, and identifying inner resources. Further, throughout the coaching conversations they emphasize that the person being coached is in the process of developing the five states of mind, which they define as efficacy, flexibility, consciousness, craftsmanship, and interdependence.

Another component of their version of cognitive coaching is that the coach practices the four "capabilities of a mediator" which are described as (1) knowing one's intentions and choosing congruent behaviors; (2) setting aside unproductive patterns of listening, responding, and inquiring; (3) adjusting one's own style preferences; and (4) navigating through the three coaching maps. The three coaching maps are described next.

The three mental maps the coach uses are (1) the planning conversation, (2) the reflecting conversation, and (3) the problem-resolving conversation. The planning conversation includes the coach helping the person coached with goal clarification, identification of success indicators, planning approaches, establishment of a learning focus, and an awareness of the coaching process. During the reflecting conversation, the coach asks the person to summarize their impressions of their experience, analyze causal factors and determine cause-and-effect relationships, make meaning from their analysis, develop insights, and commit to use this learning in the future in multiple areas. If the person receiving the coaching is "stuck," the cognitive coach may use the problem-resolving conversation to help the person move from the existing, undesired state to the desired state by using the tools of pacing and leading, and helping the person identify resources and learning to help them move toward the desired state. This approach borrows heavily from Milton Erickson's (1989) philosophy that the individual already has a vast storehouse of learning, memories, and resources that the coach can facilitate the individual to utilize.

This cognitive coaching approach for educators has an outcome study research base with positive effects obtained from the students whose teachers had gone through the cognitive coaching program, including significant improvement compared to control groups on the Iowa Test of Basic Skills, reading scores, and math scores (Costa & Garmston, 2002).

Outcome studies also indicated that after teachers had participated in the cognitive coaching program they improved their teaching methods, including teaching more thinking skills to their students (Edwards & Newton, 1994). They also increased their use of standards-based education, made fewer referrals of their students to special education and focused more of their time on student learning compared to control groups, (Garmston, Linder, & Whitaker, 1993). As an added benefit, the teachers themselves became more satisfied with teaching as their profession (Edwards & Newton, 1995).

ACTION SCIENCE, MENTAL MODELS, AND THE LADDER OF INFERENCE

Chris Argyris, Professor of Education and Organizational Behavior at Harvard University, is credited with creating the field of action science (Argyris, 1990), which is a strategy for designing situations that foster effective stewardship in any type of organization. To help individuals in groups learn how to become ready to make changes and overcome barriers to organizational change, action science does not simply focus on improving the participants' problem-solving or decision-making skills. Action science focuses on looking inward, reflecting on our thoughts, learning new frameworks, and establishing new thinking routines.

Senge (1990) popularized many of Argyris's ideas and describes how errors in thinking can also plague entire organizations. He calls these errors "organizational learning disabilities." Senge describes seven organizational learning disabilities (adapted from Senge, 1990).

1. *I am my position.* Individuals identify with the title of their position more than the purpose of their position, hence they tend to see their responsibilities limited to the immediate boundaries of their specific job. As American car companies struggled to improve productivity in their assembly plants compared to Japanese imports, they disassembled a Japanese car and found that all the bolts that held the engine block in place were the same, whereas in the American car there were many different-sized bolts holding the engine on. With the American car there were several different engineers

responsible for different elements of the engine and engine block; each thought they were doing their job well, but the end result was a much slower assembly—different wrenches were required for the different-sized bolts, and more inventory had to be managed. The Japanese had one group of engineers who oversaw more of the process, and this lack of tunnel vision made for more efficiency and higher quality.

2. *The enemy is out there.* People often have a propensity to find someone else to blame if something goes wrong—this occurs with individuals and also develops very easily in teams. For example, the politician who loses an election may say, "The media never gave me fair coverage"; the marketing department may blame its lackluster sales on the engineering department for being too slow in getting out the desired product, whereas the engineering department is frustrated that the marketing department promises products that engineering cannot yet produce. Blaming others reduces the chances that people will do all they can to create improvements.

3. *The illusion of taking charge.* In general, being proactive is considered positive. However, sometimes being proactive—acting in anticipation—comes down to being aggressive without having thought through impacts. In other words, sometimes when people think they are being proactive they are actually being reactive. Senge points out, "True proactiveness comes from seeing how we contribute to our own problems."

4. *Fixation on events.* Our lives are so busy that we are usually involved in highly pressing activities—everything feels urgent. Our businesses are focused on events that are impacting us or will impact us soon. We need to be focused, of course, on what needs to be done now, but this makes it difficult for us to keep our eyes on the big picture. Serious threats are not always immediate occurrences but often are gradually evolving situations that are not a single, sudden event—global warming, environmental degradation, and an overall decline in education are examples.

5. *The parable of the boiled frog.* Organizations often don't see changes coming until it is too late—just like a frog will immediately try to hop out of a pot of boiling water but will float contently in a pot if the water starts out lukewarm and is gradually heated to boiling. Similarly in failed marriages, marriage therapists say that often people wait too long to try to get help with their relationships. The U.S. auto industry fell victim to the same learning disability when it let its market share fall from 96 percent to 60 percent from 1967

to 1989 because the slip in market share came gradually. Senge says the solution is to slow down and notice the gradual processes, which can cause the largest difficulties.

6. *The delusion of learning from experience.* We learn best from experience. Think about how you learned to walk, talk, ride a bike, type at a keyboard, or drive a car. In these situations our learning is fast because the feedback from our trial-and-error learning is immediate. But what happens if the feedback won't be available for years? Learning is disrupted. When decisions have consequences beyond the horizon it is most difficult to learn from experience. Most organizations tackle these difficult situations by forming groups to focus on a smaller chunk of the challenge. But those groups often become fiefdoms—hence the rise in cross-functional teams to attempt to decrease the impact of this problem by reducing thinking in isolation.

7. *The myth of the management team.* Argyris (1990) says management teams are often full of people who demonstrate "skilled incompetence"—teams of people who are proficient at missing the learning that could be had by careful inquiry and observation of events, forces, trends, and people around them. Instead, many teams spend time protecting turf, maintaining the appearance of cohesion, and avoiding true inquiry into the thoughts of others who disagree with them.

The coach who is familiar with Senge's organizational learning disabilities can help the client identify them and has a vocabulary enabling a discussion with the client on the challenges the disabilities have for effective performance.

COGNITIVE THERAPY AND ACTION SCIENCE CONTRIBUTE TO COACHING

Insightful coaches will be able to observe elements of Beck's "cognitive distortions," Ellis's "irrational ideas," or Senge's "organizational learning disabilities" in their clients. Next, coaches need a general strategy of how to help their clients learn to mange their thoughts in a more effective manner.

Coaches usually work with clients who want to be more effective in their careers or develop more fulfilling lives, but have no significant, diagnosable mental illness. The coach will often use a coaching conversation approach to help clients see themselves accurately, evaluate their situations and their options, examine their assumptions and thought processes, and utilize introspection and insight to achieve their goals. Since these are essentially cognitive processes, many of the techniques utilized by coaches are called by this author "cognitive coaching techniques." Furthermore, the coach employing cognitive techniques helps the client observe assumptions, erroneous conclusions, mental models, unproductive schemas, and maladaptive self-talk, and learn and execute alternative ways of viewing situations. This leads to the coaching client being able to develop more constructive methods of inner communication that underpin more effective behavior, successful outcomes, and, ultimately, higher life satisfaction.

Some coaches subscribe fully to the philosophy that clients always have all the answers within them so the coach's role is only to ask questions and never give advice. Utilizing a Rogerian (Rogers, 1995) style, some coaches may do fairly good work in some situations by relying on establishing a trusting relationship, communicating a sense of positive regard, and asking thoughtful, powerful questions. However, competent coaches are well advised to also have in their coach's toolbox a number of varied exercises, approaches, strategies, and tools to be able to think on their feet and have a more diverse set of approaches that will be deemed helpful. Cognitive coaching techniques will fill that toolbox.

MENTAL MODELS

Our mental models are our beliefs about how the world works and how people work. Mental models can be useful, or they can get in our way. Mental models usually limit us to familiar ways of thinking and behaving. Examples of mental models are "People cannot be trusted"; "Early to bed, early to rise makes a man healthy, wealthy, and wise"; "In this company if you don't have an engineering background you will never be taken seriously"; "If I get a good education I will have better job prospects." Mental models are not inherently good or bad, but they are active—they do shape our behavior (Senge, 1990). Relevant to this point, Albert Einstein is frequently quoted as having said: "No problem can be solved from the same consciousness that created it."

Senge (1990) postulates:

> These mental models that hinder the acceptance of new insight are deeply ingrained internal images that managers working in a given organization tend to internalize unconsciously and often fail to adjust even though they are no longer relevant in a rapidly changing business environment. Thus, there exists an imperative need to study the discipline of mental model management,

which basically involves the conscious monitoring, testing, and improvement of the internal images that can greatly influence the manner that an organization's managers perceive the business environment in which they operate.

Coaches can make a strong impact by integrating a discussion of mental models into the coaching conversation. A key method that sophisticated coaches can use to assist their clients is to help their clients:

- Recognize their mental models.
- Grasp how much unexamined mental models affect their decision making and behavior.
- Learn how to slow down and reflect on their mental models.
- Learn how to have conversations that encourage an open discussion of mental models, assumptions, and inferences.

LADDER OF INFERENCE

If we, and our clients, don't have a method to become aware of our thought processes and our mental models, we will be unable to change recurrent patterns of poor thinking and the resultant disappointing outcomes. The ladder of inference (Argyris, Putnam, & Smith, 1985; Senge, Kleiner, Roberts, Ross, & Smith, 1994), also called the assumption ladder (Nadler, 2006), is a tool you can use to help your clients see how they make subjective interpretations or inferences from an observation that leads to a particular conclusion and/or behavior. By utilizing the ladder of inference in your coaching, you will help your clients have greater awareness of their thought processes and help them catch erroneous assumptions and other thinking errors.

Although the original ladder model included seven steps, many authors, consultants, and coaches are now referring to five steps of the ladder.

The five steps are:

1. At the first or bottom rung of the ladder, we are exposed to images, words, and other sensory data.
2. At the second rung, we select certain data and focus on it.
3. At the third rung, we make assumptions about the data we selected.
4. At the fourth rung, we draw conclusions.
5. At the fifth rung, we take actions based on our conclusions.

As people quickly climb up the ladder—usually unaware that they are unconsciously going through this process—their attitudes and beliefs are also limiting what data they pay attention to. In practice, people usually believe that their beliefs are the truth and that their truth is obvious. (An example of using the ladder in a coaching conversation is presented later in this chapter.)

An excellent use of the ladder of inference is to teach the model to your clients so they can educate the people around them about this communication tool. In this way a common vocabulary is formed that serves the group in obtaining higher-quality results.

APPLYING COGNITIVE COACHING TO THE CASE OF BOB

Bob is a successful executive used to being in charge, used to giving orders, and satisfied when everything is moving along well—he likes action. It is no surprise that due to his bottom-line-results orientation he would have found coaching attractive for his managers. What is wonderful is that he has been seriously contemplating working with a coach for several years.

Bob's Motivation for Coaching

Bob is seeking coaching now for five reasons: (1) he has his most difficult merger yet to manage—integrating a largely South Korean (and European expatriate) operation with an American operation; (2) his self-image is largely linked to his professional success, and he wants this merger to be successful—he sees it as a chance to demonstrate a shining jewel of accomplishment as he prepares to retire; (3) he is smart and recognizes this is tougher than other acquisitions that he has made so he hopes to find a coach who will be a consultant to him and has specific knowledge about successfully managing this type of merger; (4) the stated goal is to leave "on a high note" which represents a most important theme—he wants to leave a well-run, profitable company as his personal legacy; and (5) he knows he wants to retire within 10 years, so in the back of his mind he would like someone to talk to about retirement. At a certain level he realizes his whole adult life has been about career success, climbing, and building—and although this has not been a focus previously, with the right coach he will want to talk about what's next.

Perspectives on Coaching Bob

Bob will want a highly experienced coach who has status and is recognized as an excellent coach. He will expect the coach to be prepared, competent, and straightforward. He will want his coach to be logical and goal oriented.

When the coach steers the conversation in a particular direction, Bob will want clear evidence of the benefits for the time he spends in coaching (Kise & Krebs Hirsh, 2000). Bob won't likely be interested in development unless he is convinced it will help him get the results that he wants.

Bob is immensely successful in his mind, so if the coach suggests he should do something differently he will need to know why. He is so goal-focused that he rarely considers the impact of his own actions on others. Part of the coaching process will eventually be to help him see that people get things done and often work harder if their needs are considered.

An interesting question for Bob is whether he would get more loyalty if he acknowledged and rewarded the contributions of others. He might think he is doing that already. He might not really know what others really think of him—and he is not likely to want the coach to do a formal multirater evaluation.

Bob faces a major challenge in dealing with both the South Korean and European business cultures. The South Korean cultural challenge will be formidable for Bob. He may very likely derail here unless he learns a new way of interacting with his South Korean leaders. If he does not learn to understand the cultural differences and expects his South Korean counterparts to act as he does, he will lose credibility with key leaders in the acquired company. If this happens, all of Bob's other strengths will likely not be able to override this negative impact.

The coach will need to be able to find some small ways that Bob can begin to understand which cultural differences would be important to acknowledge because they could interfere with his success. The coach can start in small ways and work to increase openness and attentiveness to others under the premise of helping him best manage the merger.

An element of coaching to use with Bob will be the thought partner role that helps him use strength identification, challenge and goal definition, cognition identification, cognitive restructuring, reframing, brainstorming, and scenario planning before rushing to act. Over the course of the coaching, cognitive coaching techniques can be utilized to skillfully challenge Bob to examine how his thoughts are leading to behaviors and whether those behaviors are getting results he wants. If not, what thoughts would be helpful to alter that would lead to behaviors that best achieve the results he seeks, and success in this transition he faces?

Cultural Issues with Bob's Management Style and Acquisition of XYZ

Bob has engineered the acquisition of a company made up of European expatriate and South Korean personnel. Both business cultures are different from a U.S. business culture, but for the purposes of this chapter, I focus on the issue of interacting with his new South Korean executives since this will represent more of a culture clash than with the European executives.

Bob's strengths in dealing with his new executives are that he can be extremely charming, entertaining, hardworking, intelligent, verbal, poised, and humorous. Some of his opportunities for development that are especially relevant for interacting with his South Korean managers are that he likes to talk more than listen, is often seen as superficial, and doesn't spend much time on the nuances of relationships.

Although the coach does not need to be a content expert in either Bob's business issues or the cultural issues, the coach will be a great asset in a critical area if he or she can help Bob open his mind to the seriousness of the cultural issues he faces with his new South Korean team.

Bob will need to learn the various protocols that are part of South Korean business relationships. Most importantly, he needs to learn about how important the development and maintenance of proper interpersonal relationships are to South Korean businesspeople. His South Korean executives will be highly sensitive to interpersonal relationships, and they will be sensitive to Bob's spirit and how he presents himself. Several factors, notably, of course, being the CEO, but also his age, past business success, and education will be impressive to the South Koreans, as they will look at these as a way to measure him and to determine the degree of respect they will pay him. The fact that he is an educated CEO approaching 60 will mean that in a Confucian society he will automatically be granted some honor and respect that is associated with that status and position. Bob is bright, social, and motivated. The coach who can convincingly begin to provide this cognitive education on the cultural issues so relevant to his business objectives will be seen as knowledgeable due to this just-in-time learning. Bob will likely grasp that in this case he needs to adjust his style as a practical approach to get the outcome he wants, even though his first reaction will be "I'm the CEO—they need to get with my program or they are out of there."

Excerpt of Coaching Session with Bob

This would be a case where the coach would: (1) use some of his or her content expertise to establish credibility, (2) get the client to think more carefully about what his goals are, (3) identify how Bob's normal patterns of thinking will help or hinder the outcomes he is seeking, (4) get a clearer picture of his mental models, (5) identify his options for learning and thinking, and (6) potentially help Bob revise mental models and cognitions to help him achieve his goals.

> *Bob:* I'm going to Seoul next week to meet with my execs over there.
> *Coach:* I know you've been looking forward to getting the process going and also wondering how to make it get off to a good start.
> *Bob:* I think we have a lot in place already. My staff has been on the ball, and the people there are going to roll out the red carpet for me. It should be fun.
> *Coach:* What are some elements of the trip that you want to talk about in our meeting today?
> *Bob:* Well, I mainly want to know how quickly they can get the integration completed. My staff has been asking for more information, but they are slow to respond. I want to get some answers. We've got to take advantage of the economies of scale. To recoup the investment as fast as possible we have to evaluate if there are any of their business units that are underproductive, and then we need to fix them or get rid of 'em. I need some details on it and I want them as soon as possible. I want them to speed things up.
> *Coach:* You are not satisfied with the pace?
> *Bob:* No. I'm their new CEO—they need to learn my style if we are going to get along. I wouldn't have bought them if I didn't know they are a great company—but now I need to light a fire under them so they realize that I'm serious about folding their company into AMM.

Coach: You mentioned you need to light a fire under them. Tell me a little more about why you said that.

Bob: I've had my VPs ask their president for some reports and I haven't gotten them yet. Either they are not cooperating or they don't understand my schedule.

Coach: Could there be other explanations?

Bob: What? What do you mean?

Coach: Could there be other explanations for why you haven't got what you asked for?

Bob: I don't like it when you beat around the bush. What do you think the explanation is?

Coach: We talked about the ladder of inference last week. It sounds to me that you are looking at a piece of the data—you didn't get some reports you asked for and you are concluding you need to light a fire under them. I'm just wondering if there could be other reasons that you haven't gotten what you asked for.

Bob: Well, there might be. I just bought their company. They're nervous. They don't know what I will do. They are probably worried about their jobs.

Coach: Yes, I think you are right. I wonder if there are some other big elements to this, too.

Bob: Like what?

Coach: What impact do you think it is having that you are trying to merge an American business culture, a European business culture, and a Korean business culture?

Bob: Well, I'm sure it has an impact, but basically I'm the CEO so they need to do what I say. After all, I thought with their emphasis on respecting elders this would be an easier merger than many others.

Coach: You might be minimizing there, Bob. I have a feeling it could be a much larger impact. I worked with some other companies beginning to work in South Korea and they said the cultural issues were large. Have you heard of *nunchi?*

Bob: What?

Coach: Nunchi. Koreans like to read your "spirit." They want to meet you in person and read your face; they feel it helps to really understand you. They call it *nunchi.* It means looking in a person's eyes and getting a nonverbal reaction and sensing what you are really about. In my work in South Korea, I found that they would try to get a read on you as early as they can. My understanding is that you are right—as a Confucian society, your position is very important to them; but how you handle the details of your relationships with your key leaders over there is also critical.

Bob: Hmmm. . . . Really!

Coach: Yes. So do you think this is an area where you have strengths?

Bob: Yeah, I'm pretty good with people.

Coach: My impression is that you are comfortable with people and being in front of people, but I think you are minimizing the importance of this. I think you are overlooking the importance of the subtleties of relationships to gain their loyalty. You are obviously exceedingly smart and have more business savvy than pretty much anyone I know but I don't sense that this emphasis on relationships is rising onto your radar screen. I have a hunch that you are—I hate to say it, but you are oversimplifying what it will take personally to pull this off.

Bob: Why?

Coach: You are leading a company halfway around the world—you need them to be loyal to you, and they have to feel you are loyal to them. You know, I like to help my clients focus on and leverage their strengths but this is an area where frankly you may have some liabilities, too. We didn't do a formal multirater evaluation, but do you remember we did an informal assessment of what some of your managers and execs thought were strengths and areas where you could become stronger? What was the hardest-hitting feedback you remember getting?

Bob: Well, some people thought I acted kind of superficial.

Coach: Right, and that is exactly what your South Korean executives will likely be sensitive to.

Bob: So, this is strange because I have lots of confidence in working with people. I get a kick out of entertaining and telling jokes and, you know, being the center of attention. You don't think that will work, huh. . . . Well, what do you think I should do?

Coach: Learn more about working with the South Koreans and examine your attitudes about working with others.

Bob: Okay, I can see merit to that. What would be good to do?

Coach: What are your beliefs about the best way to work with people?

Bob: I like to get people excited, entertain them, cheer them up, get them motivated—then tell them what they need to do to make great things happen.

Coach: How well has that been working for you?

Bob: Well, my board thinks it has been working well. I got a hefty bonus this past year for the huge growth we've made. I admit, though, it may not be the only style to use in this new situation.

Coach: I think you are right. Perhaps some leadership style flexibility might be needed in this situation. What do you think are some new elements of a leadership style that will help you with the merger?

Bob: I guess I need to make more personal connections with them. Get to know them more—ask about their families.

Coach: How else will you make personal connections with them?

Bob: Figure out what makes them tick—what motivates them.

Coach: Maybe. Other ideas?

Bob: I'm not sure.

Coach: There must be other execs facing the same challenges of merging with Korean companies, and dealing with building relationships for business success. What do you think they might do?

Bob: There are probably articles on this—I could do a Web search.

Coach: Sounds good. Anyone else you could talk to about this?

Bob: I could ask my team what they think we could all do to work on this relationship-building thing. I guess we should do this right away as part of the preparations for the trip.

Coach: So what are all the things you are going to do, and when are you going to do them?

Bob: I'm going to ask Mary to do a Web search on doing business in South Korea—especially on the relationship stuff. I'll have her set up a conference call for my team tomorrow to see if anyone else has any ideas about this. I'll ask if anyone knows some South Korean execs that we can ask for advice on this, too.

Coach: I have something else I want to ask you.

Bob: What?

Coach: This impression of acting rather superficial to some people—it might have hurt to hear that.

Bob: Well, I'd say I was surprised. I always thought of myself as very good with people. I don't think I'm a superficial person.

Coach: Right, that would be labeling you in a global way. That would be overgeneralizing the feedback. I think what people mean is that there are some behaviors some people see you do sometimes that create an impression that you act superficially. I think we should take this seriously because of the importance of building deep loyalty with your Korean team.

Bob: That's pretty strong.

Coach: I know this is important to you—making this merger work. I think you could learn what thoughts and behaviors you might have that lead some people to think this. Maybe you have some mental models that contribute to some behaviors that people take the wrong way.

Bob: Okay. What should we do?

Coach: What would lead a person to conclude that one is acting in a superficial way?

Bob: Not really caring; acting like you are listening when you aren't, and maybe saying you will do something and then forgetting about it.

Coach: Okay, were there times today when you did any of those things?

Bob: Yeah—honestly, I often probably act like I'm listening but I'm really thinking about something else.

Coach: What are you thinking when you are pretending to be listening but aren't?

Bob: That I've got more important things to do.

Coach: So is that one of your general beliefs—what I would call a mental model—that sometimes you have more important things to do than to listen to other people?

Bob: Well, honestly, yes.

Coach: Does that cause any negative impacts?

Bob: Well, probably. I think some people can tell and get pissed off. They don't say anything, of course, because I'm their boss.

Coach: Do you feel it would be helpful to you to change this in some ways—especially in light of what we have been talking about with your South Korean contingent? What ways could you adjust this?

Bob: I guess I could track how frequently I really am ignoring people because I think I have something more important to be thinking about.

Coach: That sounds good. Is there something more you could do?

Bob: I might play around with your "mental model" idea and see if there is another one that might help me more with the merger.

In this vignette the coach used informally, in a conversational manner, the principles of the ladder of inference, thinking errors, mental models, behavior log, and a coaching homework assignment to help a rather egocentric coaching client evaluate whether his mental models, thinking, and behavior are going to get him the results he wants. The coach used content expertise to establish credibility with a status-conscious client, challenged the client to consider an underexamined area—cultural issues and their impact on business—and held back from prescribing solutions but let the client identify steps he could take to learn a more helpful mental model that will impact thinking, behavior, and hopefully results in line with the client's goals.

UNDERSTANDING BONITA THROUGH THE EYES OF THE COACH

Bonita is trying to do it all. She is a values-oriented person who enjoys using her strengths in pulling people together to accomplish tasks of value while keeping everyone happy. She is an African-American woman, first to graduate from college in her family, first to get a white-collar job, and first to move her family into a more affluent neighborhood. There is a strong family story of how her father worked a second job to give her extra opportunities and she feels a responsibility to live up to other people's expectations. Bonita has three initial driving forces that make her especially interested in beginning coaching: (1) she is in a transition to a new position where she wants to be successful; (2) she wants to be able to spend time with her children's activities, but her boss has publicly stated she needs to prove herself and she is worried about whether she will be able to have the flexibility in her work she desires; and (3) her boss has a quick temper and she is distinctly uncomfortable with conflict. Bonita is open and eager to begin the coaching relationship.

Perspectives on Coaching Bonita

Bonita's style is to be an enthusiastic, collaborative leader—she wants to work with others and help others. Bonita comes across as a caring, cooperative person who has in her heart the best interests of others. She will be able to speak in a way that others hear her easily—without offending or alienating others. She is concerned about the mission of her group's work and places importance on people's values being met, people being included, and arriving at group consensus. Bonita is clearly supportive of others and generally has optimistic feelings about people. She believes in being committed and loyal to people and organizations—she is a team player. She comes across as warm but also practical, and she seems to have talents in keeping things running harmoniously. Bonita is a natural facilitative leader, leading by helping others plan and cooperate to meet goals and build consensus. She uses her interesting mix of a thoughtful style and a people-oriented style to her advantage to influence and pull people together.

She will feel especially stressed if she receives excessive criticism or if her values are interfered with. If she gets in a phase of being overly collaborative and not moving onto the action stage it is a clue she is feeling overwhelmed. She has to watch out for taking on too many responsibilities and thereby using up all her energy, leaving her feeling exhausted and frustrated. She feels uncomfortable in contentious situations and is irritated by people who are belittling and patronizing of themselves or others. She may go overboard in pursuing harmony.

Bonita is undergoing a stressful transition and is struggling internally with her thoughts and feelings about work and family issues. To deal with the stress she will benefit from more rest, self-care, and reflection, turning over some responsibilities after prioritizing them objectively. She will like reviewing stressful situations with an impartial person—her coach. When she does make time for it, she will enjoy relaxing and having social time with her family.

Bonita will connect most easily with a coach who is insightful, supportive, communicative, inspiring, and friendly and who will help her focus on her specific developmental needs. She will enjoy working with a coach who will be collaborative with her on developing learning strategies, who will spend time flushing out ideas, and who she feels has an understanding of the many issues she is facing.

Coaching Vignettes with Bonita

There are many areas that can be explored and analyzed in the case of Bonita, but for the purposes of this chapter I will focus on cultural issues, mental models, and her concerns about handling conflict.

Focus on Cultural Issues

To improve understanding of my client and to build rapport it will be important for me to ask, in some manner, the following type of question:

Coach: Bonita, I don't really know what it is like to be an African-American woman. I'm thinking that since you are, and you are the first in your family who graduated from college, to have achieved such a high-level professional position, and moved your family away from your extended family, that these have been major steps in your life in some way. Will you tell me what would be important for me to have more understanding on about these cultural issues? I think it will help me in coaching with you if you let me know more about how all this fits together. I am curious.

Exploring Mental Models

In this next vignette the coach explores a mental model with Bonita.

Coach: How should we focus our time together, Bonita?

Bonita: I love working with my team, but Ken, my boss, is another story. He's so judgmental and brusque. I've got to find a way to make it work better with him.

Coach: You want your working relationship with him to improve.

Bonita: Yes. You know how much I value getting everyone to work together. But with my manager I don't feel we are doing that. Well, I feel I'm trying but he's not satisfied—I don't think he thinks I'm up to the role.

Coach: You said you don't think he's satisfied. You remember last week we went over the ladder of inference tool. How about we use that concept here and walk up the ladder together?

Bonita: Okay.

Coach: Are there some data or facts that are related to you saying he's not satisfied or he's thinking you're not up to the role? I think it would be a good idea to look at this to see if you are doing any mind reading.

Bonita: He tells me what to do, he acts impatient, he interrupts, he laughed at what I said yesterday, and he said I'm too collaborative.

Coach: What stands out to you from that?

Bonita: Well, when he acts impatient and says, "You're too collaborative," I think he is saying to me, in essence, "You're doing this job wrong and you're disappointing me."

Coach: Could you be making some assumptions here? Just out of curiosity, are there some other ways to interpret what he's saying or doing?

Bonita: Well, I think he acts impatient with almost everyone. Maybe that is just how he is. Maybe even if he believed I was doing a good job he would still act impatient when I ask lots of questions. I know I ask more questions than most people do.

Coach: Could it be that there are other explanations, too? Other thoughts? Other explanations?

Bonita: Well, when he says I'm being too collaborative maybe he doesn't mean I'm doing everything wrong—maybe he just means that sometimes I should make my own decisions quicker.

Coach: What can you do to test this new conclusion?

Bonita: I could ask him.

Bonita is open to this style of "educative coaching." She enjoys the coach bringing in concepts and dialoguing with her about how she can use them. The coach asks questions that help her identify assumptions that are linked to her mental model of "I must not disappoint people." The coach could go down the road of linking this mental model to her feelings about not letting down her parents or her extended family, which most therapists would do, but the coach does not see a compelling need to do so—at least at this time. Note that her solution of asking Ken, which ostensibly seems like a reasonable approach—get some data to verify if her assumption is correct—is another collaborative approach. This may be an excellent next step, but the coach makes a mental note that at some point it would be helpful to facilitate her taking a look at how when she asks some people questions they may feel annoyed, interrogated, or impatient. This is a potential unintended impact of what in many ways is a positive, useful, collaborative style. The coach makes a note that a multirater evaluation could be useful for Bonita to help her increase her own self-awareness and accurate self-assessment.

Exploring Thought Processes about Conflict and Adapting Useful, Realistic Thoughts

In this vignette the coach explores with Bonita any assumptions and "automatic thoughts" she has about dealing with conflict.

Bonita: I mentioned to Ken that I'd have my cell phone with me but I was going to have to miss a cross-functional team meeting that he wanted me to go to because I was going to have to take my daughter Nicole to a dress rehearsal since my husband is out of town for business. Ken just looked at me and said, "I hope you are up for the realities of this job," and walked away. I thought that was so rude!

Coach: He just said that and walked away?

Bonita: Yes. I felt scared and angry—like he was threatening my position. He really has no clue how he affects other people.

Coach: That must have hurt. What happened next?

Bonita: I thought of calling after him and saying I wanted to talk to him about that, but I didn't. Then I thought of phoning him, because I don't want that kind of thing to go on, but I don't think it would help. I don't know. I wanted to talk to you about it.

Coach: I'm curious—you said you don't think it would help to talk to him? What leads you to say that?

Bonita: That's just the way he is. I'm his employee—he talks that way to other people he manages, too. If I try to talk to him about it, it might turn into an argument. Maybe he is right. This job and my being a mom do have some conflicts. You know I never feel comfortable if there is conflict.

Coach: I know you have said that and that you wanted to work on managing conflict in our coaching work. As much as I'm sorry he said that, which I agree sounds very insensitive, this gives us something concrete to work on in terms of dealing with conflict. What thoughts were going on in your mind right after he said, "I hope you are up for the realities of this job"?

Bonita: I thought: "What a jerk! I can't believe he said that!" It is no use talking to him—he just won't change.

Coach: What else?

Bonita: This might turn into a big argument. And I might get teary-eyed if we get into it.

Coach: What would be the worst thing that might happen?

Bonita: He might get madder at me if I try to talk to him about it, and because I get so uncomfortable with conflict I might get all teary-eyed.

Coach: Have you gotten all teary-eyed in a conflict with someone at work before?

Bonita: Not for a long time.

Coach: When you did, were there dire consequences?

Bonita: Well, I felt embarrassed.

Coach: Would you say the risk of feeling embarrassed is worth the benefit of standing up for yourself a little more?

Bonita: Well, I wouldn't like it, that's for sure, but yes.

Coach: Remember that we talked a couple of weeks ago about some automatic unhelpful thoughts that you sometimes have? I think in this situation you have some magnification going on—you know, exaggerating the risks of letting Ken know how you feel after he makes a particular remark. Have you seen anyone else constructively talk to Ken about this kind of thing before?

Bonita: Yes.

Coach: What happened?

Bonita: I think Ken basically got what the person was saying. He did apologize and looked a little chagrined, but he took it okay. I thought it was pretty tense, but I guess it was good the person said something.

Coach: Yes. I think you might be magnifying the negative impact of becoming a little teary-eyed if you have to confront him a little. I don't like to have to confront people when they are insensitive to my feelings, either. What I hear from my clients is that the feeling often is "Why don't they just get it? Why do I have to go through this?" But your self-care is important, isn't it? You have yourself to take care of, in part so you can be there fully for other people you care about outside work, too—your kids and your husband. How helpful is it for you when you have that thought, "I'd better not speak up—I might get all teary-eyed and then be embarrassed"?

Bonita: I don't think it is very helpful, actually. But it is what I think and it is a concern I have.

Coach: If you were to substitute a helpful thought for "I might get teary-eyed and embarrassed," what would it be?

Bonita: I could think instead, "I can control myself—I have to take care of myself, so speaking up is a good idea."

Discussion

Here the coach draws upon the coaching conversation from a previous session and helps the client link some automatic thoughts to unhelpful outcomes. The coach uses a slight bit of self-disclosure to keep the relationship strong as a particularly sensitive and difficult issue for the client is worked with. The client identifies for herself what would be a useful thought to substitute, and the next step is that the coach would help the client come up with a specific plan to track her automatic thoughts. She would then note the impact of the thoughts and make a specific plan to begin substituting more helpful thoughts—and track the positive impact of that adjustment.

CONCLUSION

Careful thinking is critical to effective coaching. Although there are many useful coaching approaches, the cognitive coaching approach of identification of mental models, unhelpful thoughts, and the addition of realistic, helpful thoughts, combined with practical tools—like the ladder of inference—are solid coaching techniques that can be some of the most frequently utilized tools in the coach's toolbox.

REFERENCES

Argyris, C. (1990). *Overcoming organizational defenses.* New York: Prentice-Hall.

Argyris, C., Putnam, R., & Smith, D. (1982). *Reasoning, learning and action.* San Francisco: Jossey-Bass.

Auerbach, J. E. (2001). *Personal and executive coaching: The complete guide for mental health professionals.* Pismo Beach, CA: Executive College Press.

Auerbach, J. E. (Ed.). (2005a). *Proceedings of the First College of Executive Coaching Conference: Vol. I. Building competence in personal and executive coaching.* Pismo Beach, CA: Executive College Press.

Auerbach, J. E. (Ed.). (2005b). *Seeing the light: What organizations need to know about executive coaching—The 2005 state of the coaching industry report.* Pismo Beach, CA: Executive College Press.

Beck, A. (1976). *Cognitive therapy and the emotional disorders.* New York: New American Library.

Burns, D. D. (1980). *Feeling good: The new mood therapy.* New York: William Morrow.

Costa, A. L., & Garmston, R. J. (1996). Cognitive coaching: A foundation for renaissance schools—syllabus. *The Art of Coaching Foundation Seminar.* Sacramento, CA: Institute for Intelligent Behavior.

Costa, A. L., & Garmston, R. J. (2002). *Cognitive coaching: A foundation for renaissance schools.* Norwood, MA: Christopher-Gordon Publishers.

Edwards, J. L., & Newton, R. R. (1994, October). *Qualitative assessment of the effects of cognitive coaching training as evidenced through teacher portfolios and journals.* (Research Rep. No. 1994-3). Evergreen, CO: Authors.

Edwards, J. L., & Newton, R. R. (1995). *The effects of cognitive coaching on teacher efficacy and empowerment.* Paper presented at the annual meeting of the American Educational Research Association, San Francisco, CA.

Ellis, A. (1979). The practice of rational-emotive therapy. In A. Ellis & J. Whiteley (Eds.), *Theoretical and empirical foundations of rational-emotive therapy.* Monterey, CA: Brooks/Cole.

Erickson, M. (1989). *The collected papers of Milton H. Erickson on hypnosis: Volume I. The nature of hypnosis and suggestion.* E. Rossi (Ed.) New York: Irvington Publishing.

Garmston, R., Linder, C., & Whitaker, J. (1993, October). Reflections on cognitive coaching. *Educational Leadership, 51*(2), 57–61.

Kise, J. A. G., & Krebs Hirsh, S. (2000). *Introduction to type and coaching: A dynamic guide for individual development.* Palo Alto, CA: Consulting Psychology Press.

Nadler, R. (2006). *Leaders' playbook. How to apply emotional intelligence: Keys to great leadership.* Santa Barbara, CA: Psyccess Press.

Rogers, C. (1995). *On becoming a person: A therapist's view of psychotherapy.* New York: Mariner Books.

Senge, P. M. (1990). *The fifth discipline: The art and practice of the learning organization.* New York: Bantam Doubleday Dell Publishing Group.

Senge, P., Kleiner, A., Roberts, C., Ross, R., & Smith, B. (1994). *The fifth discipline fieldbook: Strategies and tools for building a learning organization.* New York: Doubleday.

Stein, S., & Book, H. (2000). *The EQ edge: Emotional intelligence and your success.* Toronto: Stoddart Publishing Company.

Young, J., Klosko, J., & Weishaar, M. (2003). *Schema therapy: A practitioner's guide.* New York: Guilford Press.

CHAPTER 5

Psychoanalytically Informed Executive Coaching

SETH ALLCORN

EXECUTIVE COACHING IS, if anything, an intensely personal dyadic relationship between the executive and the coach. Unlike coaching a team of individuals, executive coaching has as its singular focus aiding the executive to perform better. This appreciation directs our attention to the interpersonal nature of this transaction and, like all relationships, it is the subjective, out-of-awareness, unconscious, and very often hard-to-discuss aspects of the relationship that count. Understanding these dimensions of the interpersonal world requires a theory such as psychoanalytic theory that provides in-depth insight into human nature. This insight yields a form of executive coaching that encourages understanding the executive's inherently complex sense of self and that of the coach as well. Sensing the executive by using oneself as an instrument of knowing requires the development of reflective insight that permits locating and interpreting self-experience generated within the coaching context as well as within daily life.

Psychoanalytically informed executive coaching requires context setting. A psychodynamic approach to executive coaching is a collaborative process between the coach and the executive. The approach attends to the executive's unconscious attachments and emotional investments relative to the organization, its workers, and the coach who assists the client in seeing more clearly how his or her internal world affects the

Acknowledgment: The contributions of Michael Diamond to this chapter are important to acknowledge. He provided a considerable amount of the theory and content to make this chapter possible.

organization and its members. Exploring an executive's individual leadership style, psychological defenses, relational patterns, and transference and countertransference dynamics must, therefore, be grounded in a good understanding of the organization's culture, history, and operating challenges.

This is a challenging context to explore. I will begin by discussing two related conceptual frameworks: organizational diagnosis and the interpretation of organizational text. These frameworks are critical to our *contextualizing* the work of executive coaching. I then discuss three ways psychology and psychoanalytic theory inform coaching—psychological defense mechanisms, the interpersonal world of object relations, and the intrapersonal worlds of transference and countertransference. These are most often seamlessly interwoven to create a mutually reinforcing psychological structure that unconsciously contributes to behavior and who the executive is. This is illustrated in the concluding case examples of executive coaching.

I also want to add two provisos. The psychologically informed approach discussed blends traditional aspects of organizational consulting with executive coaching. A seamless continuum exists between knowing the organization and knowing the executive. Each affects the other in a continuous interplay of organization, social, interpersonal, and individual dynamics. Exploring one of these elements to the exclusion of the other is inconsistent with psychoanalytically informed coaching. To be appreciated is that this challenge leads to understanding that coaching and consulting are variations on a theme—organizational intervention.

The second proviso addresses the paradoxical nature of this approach to coaching. Psychological defensiveness frequently, but not invariably, introduces into the workplace problematic performance issues. Some defenses are adaptive to deal with the high-stress world of executives. A corollary is that coaching using this approach should not be confused with therapy in any form. To be avoided is diagnostically labeling the executive. This not only blocks knowing the executive's humanity; it might also be the case that this is a self-serving defensive act on the part of the coach to feel in control relative to the executive.

CONCEPTUAL FRAMEWORK FOR PSYCHOANALYTICALLY INFORMED COACHING

CEOs, senior executives, and their colleagues in middle management continually shape and reshape their organization. What the organization is and how it operates are an extension of this shaping that is influenced by unconscious, hard-to-discuss interpersonal and group dynamics. Executive coaching is inextricably linked to understanding the organization in order to understand the executive.

ORGANIZATIONAL DIAGNOSIS AND EXECUTIVE COACHING

Understanding an executive independent of the workplace is not really possible. The executive's effects upon the organization and its members offer insights that may be used in coaching. Just as important is the effect of those with whom the executive works (superiors, subordinates, and employees) upon the executive. No executive is an island. He or she is always impacted by others, organizational history, and events. Understanding these bidirectional influences is aided by a thorough organizational diagnosis.

Levinson (1972, 2002) offers a model for psychoanalytically informed organizational assessments in *Organizational Diagnosis* that incorporates various levels of data collection and describes a psychodynamic process for engaging organizations and leaders by immersing consultants in the organization's dynamics. These levels of data collection include (1) genetic and historical data, (2) structural and process data, and (3) interpretive or narrative data. His approach to organizational diagnosis integrates data from "objective reality" and "psychological reality," thereby illustrating the importance of analyzing the unconscious meaning behind supposed concrete and rational organizational dynamics.

Organizational diagnoses such as this create context for executive coaching. Coaches who articulate issues and challenges by providing concrete stories about how leaders engage the organization and its members create a reflective learning context. Reflecting these stories back to the executive also often draws out relational patterns and intrapersonal conflicts that typically stem from childhood. In particular, well-established defensive coping strategies that deal with anxieties pertaining to uncertainty, loss, rejection, and persecution are surfaced. Also to be discerned are instances of transference and countertransference that provide insights into better understanding the subjective meaning of individual and collective actions and experience within organizations. Psychoanalytically informed organizational diagnosis may be understood to be informed by the hermeneutic and narrative scholarly tradition (Ricoeur, 1970; Schafer, 1983; Spence, 1982). The tradition emphasizes the importance of understanding the text and subtext of organizational narratives.

ORGANIZATIONAL TEXT AND EXECUTIVE COACHING

In their article, "Interpreting Organizational Texts," Kets de Vries and Miller (1987) propose a number of "rules of interpretation" that are consistent with Levinson's (1972) diagnostic attention to "patterning" and "integration." Following the collection of varied data, the organizational narrative is constructed by shaping "the different observations into an interconnected, cohesive unit" through the rule of *thematic unity* (p. 245). The method of thematic unity becomes crucial to making sense out of the dense nature and sheer volume of narrative and observational data.

Next, it is important to look for a fit between present-day events and earlier incidents in the history of an individual or organization based on the rule of *pattern matching*. Pattern matching reveals repetition or what Kets de Vries and Miller (1987) call the tendency to become "entangled in 'displacements in time'" (p. 245). The relevance of these displacements (transferences) as a tool for introspection and the surfacing of pattern matching are further discussed later. The notion of pattern matching, however, like that of thematic unity, provides a theoretical context that guides organizational consultants in categorizing seemingly chaotic masses of narrative data into a coherent organizational story.

Next, and in contrast to a strict hermeneutic approach, the principal rule of *psychological urgency* includes the assumption that somewhere in the text it is possible to identify the most pressing problems. "It is important, then, to pay attention to the persistence, enthusiasm, regularity, pervasiveness, and emotion surrounding decisions, interactions, and pronouncements" (p. 246). Members may repeatedly mention common or similar overriding barriers to organizational change and progress. They revisit the same organizational myths or stories in their narratives as a way of reenacting them to master painful organizational experiences. These narrative data, however, require interpretation, in order to be able to appreciate the associated unconscious dynamics. In other words, it is often the case that some of the more critical issues of the organization are disowned, disavowed, and displaced by members onto more superficial concerns.

Finally, Kets de Vries and Miller call attention to the rule of *multiple functions*. "Depending on the psychological urgency at hand, a part of the text can have more than one meaning and can be looked at from many different points of view" (p. 246). They continue: "It is thus necessary to seek out meaning at multiple levels, to determine the individual as well as the organizational roots and consequences of actions and decisions" (p. 246). The rule of multiple functions stresses the need to seek validation and confirmation of meaning with organizational participants.

In sum, organizational consultants and coaches who pay attention to the nuances of unconsciously shared thoughts, feelings, and experiences in the workplace gain a deeper, multidimensional understanding of the workplace that permits unpacking the text. "Its usefulness resides in its reminding us that psychoanalytic explanation depends on our knowing what an event, action, or object means to the subject; it is the specifically psychoanalytic alternative to descriptive classification by a behavioristic observer" (Schafer, 1983, p. 89). This implies that the coach who understands what organizational artifacts, events, and experiences unconsciously signify to organization leaders and members possesses important knowledge that may be brought to the coaching process.

Psychoanalytically informed organizational diagnosis, it may be concluded, presents the coach a challenging context in which to function. Not only must commonplace organizational artifacts, events, and history be taken into consideration, so must the subjective experience of organizational participants. Paying attention to the organizational story that unfolds as organizational data are collected most often reveals these experiences. Making conscious the story and many of its fantastic qualities is enabled by paying attention to individual and group defenses, the quality of the interpersonal world, and transference and countertransference dynamics. In particular, the self becomes an instrument of observation and data collection, thereby revealing the subjective and intersubjective world of work. I now turn to a discussion of psychological defensiveness in the workplace (Allcorn & Diamond, 1991).

USE OF PSYCHOANALYTIC THEORY IN EXECUTIVE COACHING

Individual and group psychological defenses abound in the workplace. They may take as many forms as the diversity of human nature has to offer. Some are, however, more prevalent and/or have a greater impact in the workplace. Before I discuss these defenses, the context in which they arise must be described.

PSYCHOLOGICAL REGRESSION AT WORK

Psychological regression represents an unwitting endeavor of organization participants to manage their anxieties. Regression is defined here as the metaphoric return to earlier modes of object relations where stage appropriate conflicts reemerge in the present. To put it simply, adults come to rely on familiar, yet unconscious childhood defenses to combat anxieties at work in the present. Regression is most often accompanied by the interplay of various types of psychological defenses aimed at allaying the distressing experience of anxiety.

Many have observed that group and organizational membership entails an intrapersonal compromise between individual demands for dependency and autonomy. These are dilemmas of human development rooted in the psychodynamics of separation and individuation. The mere presence of a group, Bion (1959) observed, presumes a defensive state of psychological regression among participants. Referencing Freud (1921), Bion wrote: "Substance is given to the phantasy that the group exists by the fact that the regression involves the individual in a loss of his 'individual distinctiveness' (1921, p. 9). . . . It follows that if the observer judges a group to be in existence the individuals composing it must have experienced this regression" (Bion, 1959, p. 142). For Freud and Bion, psychological regression coincides with group and institutional membership.

Workers with limited freedoms and a sense of powerlessness may engage in psychologically regressive behavior. Relations between divisions become contentious and riddled with conflict. Otherwise mature adults find themselves thinking in primitive categories of good or bad, all or nothing, enemy or ally, characteristic of an active fantasy life fueled by psychologically defensive processes. And, finally, there is always the danger that bureaucratic, silolike organizations might foster regression into more homogenized and conformist, authoritarian organizations (Diamond, Stein, & Allcorn, 2002). Shared individual anxieties of group and organizational membership generate a vicious cycle of regressive and defensive responses.

Kernberg (1998) recently explored several dimensions of psychological regression in organizations and organizational leaders. According to Kernberg, workplace regression stems from "a breakdown of the task systems of organizations when their primary tasks become irrelevant or overwhelming or are paralyzed by unforeseen, undiagnosed, or mishandled constraints; the activation of regressive group processes under conditions of institutional malfunctioning; and the latent predisposition to paranoid regression that is a universal characteristic of individual psychology" (pp. 125–126). Kernberg, consistent with Bion, views dysfunctional group and organizational structures and their ineffective leaders as unwittingly fostering psychological regression.

There are many forms of organizational malfunctioning and regression. Inordinate power at the top exaggerates the impact of personality deficits throughout the organization, negatively affecting organizational culture and climate. Organizational leaders may create an atmosphere of vicious competition, win-lose dynamics, mistrust, and secrecy. Defensive strategies, structures, and cultures may further produce oppressive policies and constraints that limit autonomy and suppress creativity and free-flowing ideas among workers, thereby fostering further retreat toward psychological regression.

In sum, rather than effectively managing participant anxieties, the destructive pull of psychological regression in groups and organizations perpetuates members' anxieties. These anxieties, then, provoke psychological defensiveness and splitting and projection that may be experienced by coaches via countertransference. In addition, these dynamics promote additional confusion in the form of strong emotions and anxiety, thereby reinforcing the process of psychological regression (Person, 1995). As a result, these psychodynamics become self-sealing, repetitive, compulsive processes embedded in people and their organizational systems.

I now turn to a discussion of psychologically defensive practices that may be observed to be characterological in nature (Horney, 1950). They are also so often observed to be present in the workplace that they are seldom called into question.

ARROGANCE AND VINDICTIVENESS

Arrogance on the part of executives produces some of the most extreme organizational outcomes as evidenced by WorldCom and Enron. Arrogance may take many forms such as the normal rules of fair play and civility not applying to the individual. Willful behavior that includes a reckless disregard for accurate reality testing and shared decision making may abound. Those who cross this individual do so at their peril. Injuries to this individual's arrogant pride must be vindicated by punishing the victimizer and discrediting his or her point of view.

This outcome, it may be appreciated, is largely a reaction formation to former self-experience of not being loved or powerful and in control. Challenging this defensive response to most often oppressive and unsupportive childhood experience requires an appreciation of the unconscious properties of this reaction formation. In this instance, the child fought back by developing an overdetermined and hard-to-defend sense of self-worth. Fighting back against parental figures and others to defend and vindicate this false sense of pride, it was understood by the child, would not result in the further loss of love and affection since little was available to the child anyway. A coach who approaches this executive in a direct, matter-of-fact manner will predictably evoke responses to defend the arrogant self, possibly by ignoring or dismissing the coach. This appreciation encourages coaches, upon recognizing these character traits, to approach the executive in a gradual manner that encourages reflection on behavioral patterns as compared to defensiveness.

NARCISSISM IN THE CORNER OFFICE

A closely related and frequently encountered psychologically defensive response to early life experience is the pursuit of admiration, love, and respect where none was offered in childhood. The executive may be observed to avoid making tough decisions where someone's ox gets gored. Doing so risks losing admiration, love, and respect. Organizational resources and promotions may be wielded in such a manner as to create these outcomes often resulting in an intensely loyal, unquestioning, and supportive group of individuals who have as their tacit job "pumping up the executive's ego."

The coach who confronts this dynamic may encounter an equally intense defense of this individual's preoccupation with external sources of approval and self-gratification. Every effort may be made to seduce the coach out of role by offering to expand income generation, inclusion in special occasions, and long, rambling discussions aimed at interpersonal bonding to convert the coach to membership in the band of loyal and devoted supporters. Challenging these dynamics not only is difficult, it is potentially threatening to the coach who may regrettably have to be let go as a result of just not "getting it."

Once again, gradualism is most likely to succeed, although this individual does want to please others, including you the coach. A collaborative and reflective working relationship may be developed with time.

ABSENT WITHOUT LEAVE (AWOL)

A third, not uncommon, coaching challenge is the executive who, when confronted with a challenging leadership opportunity, consistently looks to others to handle it or who may neither handle it nor look to others to deal with it. Not responding to a crisis may be an option. Many organization stories and their subtext may point to a willingness to follow if led, a lack of clear direction and leadership, and the blocking of those who could lead from doing so. Employees and midlevel managers may be bitterly frustrated and hope for change is largely absent save for the replacement of the executive and perhaps his or her (non)leadership team.

The executive coach is once again faced with a challenge. Executives who possess these attributes respond by avoidance and dependency ("What should I do?"). Expectations of their changing their behavior are felt to be threatening and coercive. Once again these responses are associated with deeply ingrained defenses evoked in childhood by parenting that either stripped them of self-worth and feelings of self-efficacy ("I can't do it. I can't lead.") or overwhelmed them with demands regarding their behavior that were experienced as excessive, invasive, and coercive, leading to a defensive response of avoidance of the expectations of others ("Just leave me alone."). In some ways this is the most problematic of the three defensive character traits encountered in coaching opportunities. Resistance and passive aggression may be hard to overcome. Little progress may be made, and meetings may be frequently canceled or cut short. Reflection and listening to feedback may be steadfastly avoided, leaving the coach to feel marginalized, incompetent, and unsuccessful—just like many others in the organization.

These commonly found coaching opportunities are supported by many other types of psychological defenses such as rationalization, denial, intellectualization, and displacement of anger and aggression on to safe others who will not strike back (Allcorn & Diamond, 1997). Many manipulative behaviors may also be in evidence such as guilt trips, the assumption of victim status, various forms of seductive behavior, gamesmanship and dominating, threatening and controlling actions (e.g., "The best defense is a good offense."). The psychoanalytically informed coach must, therefore, be prepared to deal with many forms of individual, group, and organizational defensiveness that diminish organization performance. The diversity of the possible problems faced precludes providing a 10-step program on how to deal with them. Rather, self-reflection and self-directed research are indicated.

I now turn to a discussion of the interpersonal world that not only includes these defensive patterns but also relationships of the executive to subordinates, employees, customers, vendors, and the organization, as well as his or her coach.

INTERPERSONAL WORLD OF OBJECT RELATIONS

Some scholars have argued Sigmund Freud was preoccupied with exploring intrapsychic processes to the exclusion of the interpersonal world. Others have argued that Freud implicitly or explicitly addressed the interpersonal world. Those that followed Freud did intensely examine the interpersonal world to create a new field of theorizing—that of object relations. It is not possible here to review all the theoretical perspectives associated with this school of thought. I narrow the discussion to the examination of three informative concepts: denial and splitting, projection, and projective identification. These concepts illuminate the richness of this arena of theorizing and some of the true complexity of understanding interpersonal relations.

DENIAL AND SPLITTING

Objects (others in one's mind) are invariably experienced as neither all good nor all bad. Relationships with others may, at times, be loving (rewarding) or filled with hate (not rewarding). We, in fact, often try to ignore or deny one or the other of these experiences. A leader may be idealized by all as near perfection in achieving high return on investment. Some leaders may also be almost universally despised and hated. In each of these cases the leaders possess weaknesses or strengths that, while present, are essentially unknown to others. These unacceptable attributes have been denied to exist and split off from the individual, leaving a purified remainder (all good or all bad). An executive may be spoken of throughout the organization as outstanding and "walking on water" or, conversely, thought of as incompetent, mean, threatening, arrogant, and detracting from organizational performance.

PROJECTION

Denial and splitting lead to projection. An executive who wishes to be seen as all-powerful, knowing, and worthy of admiration and loyalty locates within himself or herself personal qualities, thoughts, and feelings inconsistent with these self-images. Upon recognition they are denied to exist. This permits them to be split off, leaving a powerful and admirable self-residue. However, the dynamic does not end there. The executive projects these disposed-of parts of self onto others as mental objects, thereby providing some measure of control of these objects in fantasy. This outcome inevitably leaks into the interpersonal world. Staff and employees are then, with near absolute certainty, known by the executive to be weak, helpless, uninformed, lacking leadership skills, and unworthy of being admired because they are worthless. This results in an executive who has exceptional self-confidence and a staff and employees who are thought of as helpless and requiring the leadership, and most often micromanagement, of the faultless executive. In sum, the interpersonal world is split into the all-good executive and largely all-bad group of organization members.

PROJECTIVE IDENTIFICATION

The projection of dispossessed parts of the executive and of the employees as a group leads to the possibility of coming to know oneself as the object of the projections in a manner consistent with the projections. Others may treat executives as "godlike" or "satanic" consistent with the projected content. This constant interpersonal press encourages unconscious introjective identification of the projected content by the executive. "I must be this way since everyone thinks so" (Tansey & Burke, 1989, p. 45). The executive is at least in part self-transformed into "all good" or "all bad" with the accompanying self-experience. The executive comes to feel superior or perhaps inferior—a people person or a hard-hearted number cruncher.

The converse holds true as well. The executive may deny and split off weaknesses, limitations, and incompetencies and locate them in the employee group, who are then treated accordingly and encouraged to experience themselves as weak, limited, and incompetent. In response, they feel the need for their near-perfect leader to save them from themselves. Unlike projection, which is an intrapsychic process or fantasy, in both of these instances projective identification is distinctly interpersonal.

OBJECT RELATIONS AND COACHING

Thus far not examined is how these aspects of object relations theory inform coaching and, just as important, the coach. You, the coach, are subject to your own processes of denial, splitting, projection, and projective identification. This is not merely a problematic outcome. It must be embraced as a certainty. An idealized senior executive encourages the coach to join in this shared group fantasy (e.g., identification with and introjection of an inferior status). What would a lowly, marginally competent coach have to contribute to this great person's ability to lead and manage? Certainly, consistent with the psychologically defensive process already discussed, confronting this bigger-than-life figure with his or her feet of clay may not feel like a survivable encounter or even an encounter that can be contemplated without considerable anxiety.

An individual fulfilling a coaching and consultative role is just as vulnerable as everyone else to engaging in self-denial, splitting, and projection and perhaps more so as a result of being seen as an expert on human behavior in the workplace (i.e., psychological regression). In this case one might expect to find within the coach a self-image devoid of limitations, skill gaps, and even psychological processes and emotions. It is the executive who is known to need help with these aspects of human nature, not the coach. It is in this realm that the personally disorganized coach serves more as an instrument of disorganization for those who are coached. Avoiding an outcome such as this is important. The ability of executive coaches to stay in touch with thoughts and feelings and maintain a reflective stance is essential. I now turn to the third leg of our intellectual stool—transference and countertransference.

SIGNIFICANCE OF TRANSFERENCE AND COUNTERTRANSFERENCE IN UNDERSTANDING THE WORKPLACE

Transference and countertransference are key conceptual tools for the psychoanalytic study of organizations (Baum, 1994; Czander, 1993; Diamond,

1993, 1998; Kets de Vries & Miller, 1984; Levinson, 1972; Schwartz, 1991; Stapley, 1996; Stein, 1994). According to Hunt (1989), psychoanalytic approaches to fieldwork take three assumptions into account in their examination of researcher-subject relations. First, they assume unconscious processes exist in which "much thought and activity takes place outside of conscious awareness" (p. 25). Second, "the unconscious meanings which mediate everyday life are linked to complex webs of significance which can ultimately be traced to childhood experiences" (ibid.). That is, "the psychoanalytic perspective assumes that *transferences*, defined as the imposition of archaic (childhood) images onto present day objects, are a routine feature of most relationships," one that has clear bearing on the executive coaching endeavor (ibid.). Hunt goes on to argue that transference, whether positive or negative, "structures social relationships in particular ways" (ibid.). And, thirdly, she assumes that "psychoanalysis is a theory of intrapsychic conflict" (ibid.).

Participants' conscious desires and wishes may contradict unconscious fears and anxieties stemming from childhood. These internal conflicts then affect workplace experience and performance, and often shape the nuances of roles and relationships in organizations. Hence, we study organizations, in part, by paying attention to the sometimes conflicted and contradictory ways in which the subjects (e.g., organizational members) engage us as consultants as well as our own responses to them. In particular, the interpretation of transference, whether in the nature of the attachment to the organization, superordinates, or subordinates, or to the coach, provides a deeper understanding of individual and organizational dynamics and greater insight into the meaning of organizational membership (Allcorn & Diamond, 1997; Baum, 1994).

To summarize, psychoanalytically informed organizational diagnoses provide a means of knowing the psychological reality of the workplace. In particular the inevitability of transference and countertransference in the workplace among organization members and relative to outsiders such as coaches and consultants provides context for knowing and understanding the workplace. Before discussing transference and countertransference as ways of understanding the psychological reality of the workplace, defining these terms is important.

TRANSFERENCE AND COUNTERTRANSFERENCE DEFINED

Psychoanalytic terms are often used in idiosyncratic ways that may be thought of as placing a new spin on a term or that may be borrowed from a previous idiosyncratic application. There are also instances where the terms are simply described differently. These considerations make it important to provide a definition of these two psychoanalytic concepts.

Transference

According to Moore and Fine (1990), transference is "the displacement of patterns of feelings, thoughts, and behavior, originally experienced in relation to significant figures during childhood, onto a person involved in a current interpersonal relationship" (p. 196). This process is largely unconscious and therefore outside the awareness of the subject. Transference occurs as a result of the nature of the here-and-now object relations (self and other) that trigger familiar assumptions and archaic feelings rooted in previous attachments. It is the case within organizations that structural hierarchy and roles of power and authority frequently provide a context for transference and countertransference reminiscent of childhood and family experience. It is typically the case in organizational consultation that, despite our psychoanalytic orientation, we know little of the childhood experiences of those with whom we consult. Nonetheless, we can assume that organizational members bring to the workplace their history of internalized object relations and that this affects working relationships via transference and counter-transference dynamics. Numerous opportunities in the consultation process will therefore occur to observe and experience repetitive patterns of object relationships that provide our clients insights into organizational culture and their performance. Thus, the displacement of patterns of thinking, feeling, and action from the past onto the present in the workplace does occur and can be expected to be prevalent where issues of power and authority are present.

Countertransference

Countertransference is narrowly defined as a specific reaction to the client's transference. Countertransference works much the same as transference. It arises out of a context where the coach's feelings and attitudes toward a client are influenced by the client's transference onto the consultant. In addition to these feelings and attitudes, elements of the coach's life are also displaced onto the client, which then influences the coach's analytic understanding. Countertransference, therefore, reflects the consultant's own unconscious response to the client, though some aspects may become conscious. Acknowledgment of countertransference dynamics in the consultation process is problematic, making working in teams crucial to the processing and constructive utilization of countertransference data. I now turn to the theoretical implications of using transference and countertransference to understand the psychological reality of the workplace.

Nature of Transference and Countertransference in the Workplace

To begin, although each aspect of the concepts is separately discussed, it is important to appreciate that these potentialities coexist, thereby creating hard-to-understand and chaotic experiences on the part of the coach. It is this appreciation that leads to a deep respect for the complexities that any endeavor to know the psychological reality of the workplace will encounter. The executive coach is faced with an exceptional challenge, that of locating the overarching organizational text from this stew of experience and unconscious organizational dynamics.

Organizational life is rich with a stockpile of transference dynamics between employees and executives, executives and employees, individuals and their organizations, and clients and coaches. Executives may evoke positive transference from some employees and negative transference from others, depending on the quality and vicissitudes of internalized authority relations and their childhood experiences. Employees may evoke positive or negative transference on the part of executives, depending on how responsive they are to receiving direction. The perception of employee resistance may be unconsciously associated with a distant echo of a past relationship with a parent who stubbornly resisted the efforts of the child to have an effect on the parent. It is also the case that groups and divisions within an organization end up transferring historical experience onto the groups and divisions that surround them within the organizational milieu. And last, these same processes of transference are frequently evoked by the presence of consultants and coaches who inadvertently may trigger anxiety and regression.

In conclusion, the analysis of transference and countertransference dynamics supplies insight into the nature of coach-client relations and the aims and fantasies of organizational members regarding their working affiliation with the organization and its leadership and members. The analysis inevitably reveals psychologically defensive responses to anxiety-ridden aspects of the workplace. These anxieties are often unconsciously and automatically responded to by familiar means worked out during childhood and are referred to as psychological regression.

A Note on Kleinian Theory—The Linking of Object Relations to Transferential Outcomes

Klein's (1959, 1975) conception of the paranoid-schizoid and depressive positions further informs our inquiry. The pre-Oedipal paranoid-schizoid position is driven by persecutory anxieties and fears characterized by psychological splitting of self and others into good or bad, caring or rejecting, nurturing or withholding, black or white objects.

This position is primarily one of experiencing the other as an object held in one's mind as split and fragmented into polarized part-objects. Psychological splitting is then combined with projective identification as an unconscious effort to manipulate and coerce the object by projecting undesirable self-experience into the other. Also to be noted is that, in contrast to an internal and external world of fragmented relationships, the Kleinian depressive position is characterized by the self-experience of objects as whole and thereby comprised of good and bad dimensions—the so-called gray area of psychological reality is mournfully acknowledged.

Klein's corresponding view of transference and countertransference encourages attention to be paid by the coach to the other (the executive) in the form of attending to self-experience fueled by the executive's efforts at projective identification and the coach's unconscious introjective identification with the projected content. At this point knowing oneself is much the same as knowing the other. Introjective identification may, if identified, be safely returned to the executive by speaking of one's own experience. I now turn to the underlying complexity associated with using transference and countertransference with case examples of organizational intervention.

CREATING CHANGE—USING TRANSFERENCE AND COUNTERTRANSFERENCE AS THE BASIS FOR ORGANIZATIONAL INTERVENTIONS

Thus far suggested is that organizational life is filled with unconscious processes that are hard to locate and understand but which, nonetheless, influence organizational dynamics and executive performance. Transference and countertransference dynamics between coaches and organizational participants (those coached) represent a psychoanalytically unique stance and frame of reference. It is within the context of these relationships that we can observe and experience underlying organizational dynamics peculiar to a particular organizational culture and its group of members. Transference and countertransference transport members' anxieties and their concomitant defensive and regressive actions (such as splitting and projection) into workplace roles and relationships that shape the intersubjective structure and meaning of organizational experience. It is, therefore, essential in this context that the coach is able to retain a self-reflective (observing ego) stance in which subjective (and intersubjective) experience is accessible for examination and reflection. Therefore, the capacity by psychoanalytically informed coaches to contain anxiety-filled workplace experience enables organizational clients to engage in reflective learning for change and minimize regression. However, at the same time, the likelihood of a regressive pull toward introjecting positive (idealizing) transference onto the coach or consultant is increased and may indeed be unavoidable.

Transference dynamics that develop toward the coach, that he or she is aware of despite their regressive nature, enables the coach to establish a reflective alliance with the executive. An essential component of this alliance is the capacity for "containment" and "holding" where the coach stands at the interpersonal and organizational boundary with one foot inside and one foot outside the institution. Trust is an essential component of this relationship that comes about as a result of fair and unbiased listening and observing on the part of the coach to all the organizational data collected. The commitment to listen while withholding judgment and asking for clarification of communications of affect, experience, and perceptions is viewed positively by executives (Stein, 1994). These aspects of a successful organizational and coaching intervention are highlighted in the following case examples.

CASE STUDIES

The Case of Bob: Psychoanalytically Informed Case Notes

Bob appears to possess many of the narcissistic, arrogant, and vindictive character traits described earlier. These traits encourage the individual to seek the admiration and love of others. Bob possesses charismatic qualities that, when combined with intelligence, experience, and considerable personal drive, make him a good candidate for admiration on the part of others. His loving wife, who takes care of informing him of his children, is loyal and devoted, traits he no doubts expects from others around him. This observation is reinforced by his vindictive triumph over a colleague who "did not get it" and was transferred out and by his volatility when confronted with problems. He presents those around him a paradox. He is willing to elicit emotion-filled conversations that are not subsequently revisited. Although he portrays himself as a caring people person, his primary focus is win-lose achievement and the utilitarian use of others. As he approaches the end of his career he has been presented a difficulty in the form of a merger that threatens to derail his fantasy of getting the business to run perfectly before he leaves.

There are also indications that his interpersonal world contains aspects of denial, splitting, and projection. Those lower down the ladder need his helping hand. He sees himself as superior to others. Less clear in terms of its meaning is what appears to be his denial and rationalization of his efforts to develop authentic attachment to others as compared to their being human resources.

Psychoanalytically Informed Coaching

The following description of work contains content which is not in the original case. This is essential since psychoanalytically informed coaching must address the self-experience of the coach not present in the cases. The following is therefore a fiction created to illustrate psychoanalytically informed coaching.

The coaching process began with Bob initially agreeing to two two-hour sessions per week for an eight-week period. From the start, however, he was resistant to committing the time to the sessions. The first session was devoted to reflecting back many of the diagnostic findings about his organization, his staff and employees, and the challenges that lay ahead. This proved to be a time-consuming process as Bob frequently wanted to revisit his past, including explaining and defending himself, others, his decisions, and discuss his aspirations of leaving the company in perfect condition when he retires.

Efforts to engage him in a self-reflective process (the "soft side" of coaching) were refocused by Bob on making him more effective at the merger work. He was steadfast in this pursuit despite receiving considerable feedback to the contrary from the organizational diagnosis data. In particular he did not perceive a gap between his espoused theory and how he actually performed his work. Neither did he perceive a problem with how he related to others. Examples of how he alienated others by his win-lose and manipulative behavior when approached discreetly were not heard, and when approached more directly he dismissed them, redirecting discussion to how to make the merger successful. Despite the "soft side" having an instrumental underlying role in the problems he was having with the merger, he continued to avoid dealing with these issues. As the merger difficulties unfolded he also began to describe the dynamics in black-and-white polarized ways, especially regarding the new organization's leadership team whom he described as resistant to his direction and "not getting it." Progress on the merger was falling short of Bob's expectations

The coach recognized elements of narcissism and arrogance as well as the polarizing world of split object relations. He also, after a few sessions, began to feel angry, anxious, marginalized, and somewhat incompetent to effect change although the working relationship with Bob was quite friendly. The conclusion he gradually drew was that his feelings were a good indicator of Bob's feelings and self-experience regarding his work, the merger, and his pursuit of what seemed like an impossible-to-achieve task to set the stage for his retirement. In fact, despite his best efforts, things were headed in the wrong direction.

Starting with the fourth session, the coach approached Bob by sharing some insights drawn from his experience of Bob's story and its themes. The articulation of feelings he might have in Bob's role—feelings of anger, frustration, even fear of not meeting perfectionistic self-expectations for the merger—were initially greeted with silence and a few repositionings by Bob in his chair. The intervening silence was allowed to accumulate until Bob could locate a response. Bob gradually acknowledged that he also had many of these feelings and that his ever more highly energized efforts to get control of the merger were not working. To be noted is that this approach translates the coach's self-awareness of feeling angry and frustrated into understanding Bob in his role.

This session, based on the reflecting back of the coach's self-experience (his interpretation of countertransferential material), was validated by Bob's response. It permitted a shift to a more reflective stance. In a sense Bob knew the coach "got it" and that if the coach could speak of these emotions and self-experience, so could Bob. Thereafter, the coach's work with Bob led not only to more self-insights but also to better insight into interpersonal, group, and organizational dynamics. The coach gradually explored black-and-white imagery as it arose as well as some of Bob's win-lose behavior, resulting in some success at working through the merger by the last two sessions. This permitted revisiting Bob's feelings and self-experience in a reflective mode as to what had changed and how it affected him and his work. During the eighth session Bob expressed satisfaction with his progress and asked for the work to continue at the rate of one session per week.

Where to from Here?

Bob's developing ability to learn from self-reflection combined with new insights provided by the coach as to how to better understand interpersonal, group, and organizational dynamics will require ongoing nurturing. In particular, at key points high stress may evoke regression to the old ways of coping. The need for longitudinal follow-up is clear in order to establish reflectivity as a way of doing business.

The Case of Bonita: Psychoanalytically Informed Case Notes

Bonita is an upwardly mobile mother of two who is also African-American. She wants to achieve good performance but also has a self-identified weakness that leads her to avoid conflict and confrontation. When presented with a difficult situation, doing nothing is often an option. At other times, she compensates by trying to avoid confrontation through building consensus with others. She does not appear to be preoccupied with wanting to be liked or admired so much as to simply avoid feeling anxious. She wants to try to deal with her avoidance and dependency on others when dealing with stressful and conflicted situations, which means dealing with the origins of her distressing experience of anxiety (transference). Also to be noted is that there are present feelings of guilt related to abandoning the care of her children to her mother. In some ways she is not good enough at work and not good enough at being a mother.

Psychoanalytically Informed Coaching

The coaching process began with Bonita agreeing to meet weekly for two hours for two months. Coaching commitments with a number of other executives at the same company also encouraged the coach to further explore the nature of this high-tech organization. In particular, those in senior leadership positions who contributed to creating a culture that valued innovation but also combativeness and interpersonal competition needed to be better understood (e.g., an organizational diagnosis).

Bonita consistently said that she was eager to receive help. However, while articulating a desire to learn more about herself, she proved to be defensive and resistant to exploring her thoughts and feelings that led her to avoidance and dependency on others in the face of conflict. She preferred to focus on developing specific skills that would help her deal with conflict and become a better leader.

Efforts to confront her were consistently avoided by Bonita, who tried to convince the coach that all she needed were skill sets and helpful hints on how to use them.

The experience of this avoidance led the coach to feel frustrated and, at times, aggressive toward Bonita. "Why doesn't she listen?" This self-experience led to an appreciation of why others had a tendency to aggress and confront Bonita, thereby evoking her regression toward compulsive avoidance (an interpretation of countertransference). During the fifth session, the coach finally offered his feelings as a way for Bonita to understand her resistant and avoidant but ever pleasant behavior. If he was feeling frustrated and as though he should confront Bonita, might not others feel the same way, creating a self-fulfilling and feared outcome? Bonita listened intently but said little in response. The balance of the session was spent discussing yet another situation that needed resolution.

The next session began slowly by Bonita offering some insight into her being rejected as an action-oriented black woman who took charge. When asked what she speculated would happen if she did act decisively, she was not sure and finally spoke of a world split into approving and disapproving. It was the case that her father was a strong and opinionated man she had learned never to cross. She was making progress locating for herself the origins of her anxieties about taking strong positions. She was getting to know herself better in the process of locating transference dynamics that tended to create crippling anxiety and fear within this otherwise intelligent and capable executive.

By the close of the eighth session she was beginning to explore what would happen if she acted decisively. To her relief, when she did, nothing arose that she was not able to deal with. Her anxiety, fears, and fantasies were being gradually worked through by successful episodes of action-oriented behavior.

Where to from Here?

Bonita's willingness to try new, more decisive behavior that she could forthrightly justify to others had to be encouraged. It was only a matter of time until Ken strongly confronted her, which would be a test of her ability to deal with an authority figure without shrinking away. Telephone consultation was made available as needed for a three-month period to provide her support as she continued to explore her newfound self-authorization.

Summary of Case Studies

The case examples provide much of the content of the recommended organizational diagnosis. The organization's history, culture, and the overarching context for the coaching endeavor are known. The character traits described also contribute to the understanding of the executives to be coached. The dysfunctional nature of the traits is nicely illustrated. To be noted is that these traits are a familiar and heavily relied upon coping response to psychological regression evoked by the distressing experience of anxiety. They contain many elements that first arose in childhood. The cases also provide an opportunity to explore object relations phenomena. Denial, splitting, projection, and projective identification can be located in the cases. In particular, each has elements of black and white polarized thinking.

CONCLUSION

This chapter emphasizes that psychoanalytically informed coaching begins with a carefully developed organizational diagnosis that creates insight into organizational history, narrative, and culture. In particular, the diagnosis informs executive coaches of the problems and issues faced by executives as well as the problematic aspects of their leadership styles and interpersonal world. The case examples illustrate the role psychological defenses, splitting and projection, and transference and countertransference play in facilitating executive learning and change. They also illustrate the significance of the coach as a vessel for projections as well as the receiver of much of the same behavior others have received as illustrated by the diagnostic data. As such, the ability to understand and interpret countertransference is a significant contributor to executive coaching.

REFERENCES

Allcorn, S., & Diamond, M. A. (1991). Managing stress and anxiety in clinical laboratories. *Clinical Laboratory Management Review, 5*(3), 154–165.

Allcorn, S., & Diamond, M. A. (1997). *Managing people during stressful times: The psychologically defensive workplace.* Westport, CT: Quorum Books.

Baum, H. S. (1994). Transference in organizational research. *Administration & Society, 26*(2), 135–157.

Bion, W. R. (1959). *Experiences in groups.* New York: Basic Books.

Czander, W. (1993). *The psychodynamics of work and organizations.* New York: Guilford Press.

Diamond, M. A. (1993). *The unconscious life of organizations.* Westport, CT: Quorum Books.

Diamond, M. A. (1998). The symbiotic lure: Organizations as defective containers. *Administrative Theory and Praxis, 20*(3), 315–325.

Diamond, M. A., Stein, H. F., & Allcorn, S. (2002). Organizational silos: Horizontal fragmentation in organizations. *Journal for the Psychoanalysis of Culture and Society, 7*(2), 280–296.

Freud, S. (1921). *Group psychology and the analysis of the ego.* New York: W. W. Norton.

Horney, K. (1950). *Neurosis and human growth.* New York: W. W. Norton.

Hunt, J. C. (1989). *Psychoanalytic aspects of fieldwork.* London: Sage.

Kernberg, O. (1998). *Ideology, conflict, and leadership in groups and organizations.* New Haven, CT: Yale University Press.

Kets de Vries, M. F. R., & Miller, D. (1984). *The neurotic organization.* San Francisco: Jossey-Bass.

Kets de Vries, M. F. R., & Miller, D. (1987). Interpreting organizational texts. *Journal of Management Studies, 24*(3), 233–247.

Klein, M. (1959). Our adult world and its roots in infancy. *Human Relations, 12,* 291–301.

Klein, M. (1975). *Envy and gratitude and other works, 1946–1963.* New York: Delacorte.

Levinson, H. (1972). *Organizational diagnosis.* Cambridge, MA: Harvard University Press.

Levinson, H. (2002). *Organizational assessment.* Washington, DC: American Psychological Association Press.

Moore, B. E., & Fine, B. D. (1990). *Psychoanalytic terms & concepts.* New Haven, CT: Yale University Press and American Psychoanalytic Association.

Person, E. (1995). *By force of fantasy.* New York: Basic Books.

Ricoeur, P. (1970). *Freud and philosophy.* New Haven, CT: Yale University Press.

Schafer, R. (1983). *The analytic attitude.* New York: Basic Books.

Schwartz, H. S. (1991). *Narcissistic process and corporate decay.* New York: New York University Press.

Spence, D. P. (1982). *Narrative truth and historical truth.* New York: W. W. Norton.

Stapley, L. F. (1996). *The personality of the organization.* London: Free Association Books.

Stein, H. F. (1994). *Listening deeply.* Boulder, CO: Westview Press.

Tansey, M., & Burke, W. (1989). *Understanding countertransference.* Hillsdale, NJ: Analytic Press.

PART II

Integrative and Cross-Theory Approaches

CHAPTER 6

An Integrative Goal-Focused Approach to Executive Coaching

Anthony M. Grant

This chapter draws on the goal-setting, self-determination, and personality literature from the behavioral sciences and presents an evidence-based, integrative goal-focused approach to executive and workplace coaching, and then relates that approach to the two case studies presented in previous chapters. The process of coaching is essentially about helping individuals regulate and direct their interpersonal and intrapersonal resources to better attain their goals. Such self-regulation has a long and well-researched history in psychology (Bandura, 1982; Collier, 1957). Indeed, Carver and Scheier (1998) argue that all human behavior (here behavior is broadly defined to include cognitions, emotions, and actions) is a continual process of moving toward or away from mental goal representations, and that this movement occurs by a process of feedback control.

The core constructs of goal-directed self-regulation are a series of processes in which the individual sets a goal, develops a plan of action, begins action, monitors their performance, evaluates their performance by comparison to a standard, and based on this evaluation changes their actions to further enhance their performance and better reach their goals. In relation to coaching, the coach's role is to facilitate the coachee's movement through the self-regulatory cycle. Figure 6.1 depicts a generic model of self-regulation.

In practice, the steps in the self-regulatory cycle are not discrete, or with clearly separate stages; rather, there is significant overlap between each stage. Coaching in each stage should aim to facilitate the process of the next. For example, goal setting should be done in such a way as to

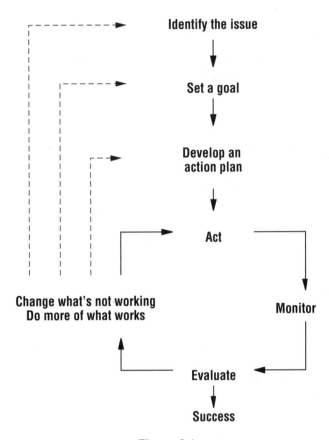

Figure 6.1
Generic Model of Goal-Directed Self-Regulation

facilitate the implementation of an action plan; the action plan should be designed to motivate the individual into action, and should incorporate means of monitoring and evaluating performance in addition to incorporating regular follow-up coaching sessions.

ISSUES RELATED TO BEHAVIORAL SELF-MONITORING

The monitoring and evaluation of actions as the coachee moves through the cycle is a vital part of the coaching process. This may seem like a self-evident point; however, people are often not skilled in the self-reflective process, and are frequently unaware of their behavior or the impact their behavior has on other people (Jordan & Troth, 2002). Thus the coach needs to ensure that action plans focus on observable concrete behaviors that are clearly discernable to the coachee.

The exact means of monitoring will, of course, vary according to the coachee's goal. Some behaviors will be easier to monitor than others. Exercise or activity-based actions can be relatively straightforward to monitor. Interpersonal skills in the workplace may be more difficult, and the coach and coachee may have to be quite creative in devising means of monitoring and evaluating. One technique may be for coachees to self-reflect after a meeting and take some time to rate themselves on their interpersonal skills. Such ratings could include counting the number of open-ended questions they asked during the meeting or rating their awareness of the other person's feelings, and these ratings should be written down. Such self-monitoring is invaluable in coaching.

ISSUES RELATED TO SELF-REFLECTION

Self-monitoring and self-evaluation are metacognitive processes, metacognition being the process of thinking about one's thoughts, feelings, and behaviors. In relation to the self-regulatory cycle, focusing attention on the self allows individuals to better access the internalized mental representations of the standards and reference values by which they evaluate their performance. Indeed, higher levels of self-awareness were found to be related to sales performance for salespersons for whom sales were important (Hollenbeck & Brief, 1987), and Church (1997) found that high-performing managers were significantly more self-aware than low-performing managers.

The development of an individual's self-awareness through coaching may be particularly important when coaching is directed at enhancing interpersonal skills, for example in leadership coaching or sales coaching. This is because the development of leadership skills may well be limited by low self-awareness (Bar-On & Handley, 1999; Goleman, 1995). Further, individuals with high levels of self-awareness appear to hold more functional (i.e., stable and internal) attributions for success than individuals low in self-awareness (Briere & Vallerand, 1990), and they tend to be less negatively affected by negative feedback (Doherty & Schlenker, 1991).

However, high levels of self-awareness may be also associated with psychopathological rumination and depression (Trapnell & Campbell, 1999). Indeed, in evaluating the impact of life coaching on self-reflection and insight, Grant (2003) found that higher levels of self-reflection were inversely related to goal attainment, and suggested that an overemphasis on self-reflection may actually be counterproductive in the coaching process.

Given the importance of these metacognitive processes and their relation to goal attainment, coaches need to be attuned to the coachee's abilities in these areas, and this is particularly the case in developmental coaching that focuses on intra- and interpersonal issues.

A SOLUTIONS FOCUS

Coaching is a goal-oriented, solution-focused process in which the coach works with the coachee to help identify and construct possible solutions, delineate a range of goals and options, and then facilitate the development and enactment of action plans to achieve those goals.

Solution-focused approaches have their roots in Milton H. Erickson's approach to strategic therapy. Solution-focused approaches have been found to be effective in a range of issues including organizational change (Bloor & Pearson, 2004) and life coaching (Grant, 2003).

The emphasis on solution construction in preference to problem analysis, as well as the use of positive, nonpathological language are important in goal-focused coaching. The use of pathology-laden terminology and a clinical medical model can be unhelpful (de Shazer & Lipchik, 1984; Drewery & Winslade, 1997), and may even contribute to the creation and maintenance of problem behaviors (Walter & Peller, 1996).

This is not to say that a solution-focused approach eschews or ignores the existence of problems. To do so may well alienate clients who need to talk about their problems. Having the time and space to talk about distressing or worrisome issues can be a cathartic experience, and in doing so clients often develop clarity and insight. Indeed, as will be discussed, an understanding of the psychosocial dynamics that create or sustain the problem can be invaluable in creating a case conceptualization and then using such information to raise the coachee's awareness of the issues and develop solution-focused action plans.

The coach's skills lie in helping the coachees tell their problem story in a way that reframes the presenting problem as being solvable and highlights the client's resources and ability to define and move toward a solution, while at the same time building a collaborative relationship in which the coach has permission to hold the client accountable for proposed action steps. At its best, the solution-focused approach enables people to access and use the wealth of personal experience, skills, expertise, and intuition that resides within all of us. It allows coachees to find individualized and creative solutions to the issues and concerns that face them.

ATTENTIONAL FOCUS AND LANGUAGE

Central to the solution-focused approach is the coach's ability to help the client purposefully focus attention toward possible solutions. Such mindfulness is frequently effortful for the client. In many respects it is easier to discuss and analyze existing problems than to shift attention toward developing responsibility and personal action.

The inability to purposefully focus on desired goals and action steps is associated with negative outcomes such as procrastination (Ferrari, 2000); anxiety (Mansell, 2000); poor task performance (Norris, Lee, Cea, & Burshteyn, 1998); and hypochondriasis (Cavanagh & Franklin, 2001), whereas a strong metal focus on one's goals is associated with goal attainment and enhanced performance and enjoyment (Lee, Sheldon, & Turban, 2003).

Indeed, as we direct attentional recourses, what we focus on tends to grow increasing salient. We have all experienced lying in bed late at night listening to a dripping tap that seems to grow louder and louder. Similarly, in coaching, if we overly focus on problems we tend to perceive them as increasing in complexity and urgency. Conversely, if we train ourselves to be vigilant and on the lookout for solutions, we tend to find them (Elliot & Harackiewicz, 1996).

Thus, the coach's role is to find ways to direct the coachee's attention toward solutions, and to foster the emergence and development of a solution-focused mind-set. There are two key interrelated factors in this process: (1) *changing the viewing*—that is, helping the coachee to perceive the issues in a new, more useful way, and (2) *changing the doing*—that is, helping the coachee to develop behavioral change.

Changing the viewing involves at least five things: (1) detailing the preferred outcome, (2) identifying exceptions to the problem, (3) amplifying existing resources, (4) building coachee self-efficacy, and (5) acknowledging the progress made so far.

Changing the doing also involves at least five things: (1) acknowledging possibilities by turning presenting problems into platforms for solution construction, (2) asking "how" questions instead of "why" questions, (3) generating client-congruent multiple options, (4) using small specific doable action steps, and (5) finding ways to leverage systems to facilitate individual change.

Central to these notions is the skillful use of language. The coach needs to be able to reflect and reframe the coachee's statements in a way that creates new ways of viewing and doing. Following are some examples of solution-focused language:

- *Language that highlights exceptions.* Coachee: "I really hate what I'm doing." Coach: " I hear what you're saying. . . . Which parts of your job are less unpleasant for you?"
- *Language that acknowledges possibilities.* Coachee: "I just can't connect with those clients." Coach: "So, up till now you haven't found

a point of contact. I wonder what they are really looking for in their dealings with you?"

- *Language that clarifies goals.* Coachee: "I really want to improve my leadership skills." Coach: "So, what does good leadership mean to you?"
- *Language that moves them forward and creates options.* Coachee: "I just don't feel like I'm getting anywhere with this. . . . I feel really lost." Coach: "So, you'd like to get back a sense of direction? What would give you that?"
- *Language that rolls with resistance.* Coachee: "But I couldn't do all of that . . ." Coach: "So which bits could you do?"
- *Language that fosters a systems perspective.* Coachee: "I guess I just am really not up to this." Coach: "I wonder who would be most surprised to hear you say that?"
- *The preferred outcome.* Coach: "Imagine that you went to bed tonight, and when you woke up the problem had somehow magically disappeared, and the solution was present . . . but you didn't know that the solution had arrived. What is the first thing that you'd notice that would tell you that the solution was present?" Alternatively, "If things were going well, what would be different?"

The coach's ability to use such often quite challenging language will be related to the quality of the collaborative nature of the coaching relationship and to the degree to which the coach is able to hold the coachee accountable. These factors are in turn related to the goals of the coaching relationship.

GOAL SETTING: THE "HOW" OF GOALS

Goal setting is the foundation of successful self-regulation and effective coaching. There is a voluminous literature on goal setting that can usefully inform the coaching process (Rawsthorne & Elliot, 1999).

Commitment to goals is critical (Hollenbeck & Brief, 1987), and high commitment is attained when the goal is perceived as being attainable and important, or when the individual participates in determining outcomes. Goal setting is most effective when there is feedback showing progress in relation to the goal, and goals stimulate planning in general. Often the planning quality is higher than that which occurs without goals. Furthermore, the effects of goal setting can be long-lasting. For example, managers' goals for the number of levels of future promotion have been found to be a significant predictor of the number of promotions received over a 25-year time span (Howard & Bray, 1988).

Goal setting is a necessary but not sufficient part of the coaching process—plans must be developed and enacted. Action planning is the process of developing a systematic means of attaining goals. Vande-Walle, Brown, Cron, and Slocum (1999) found that systematic action planning was associated with sales performance, and good action planning is particularly important for individuals who have low self-regulatory skills (Kirschenbaum, Humphrey, & Malett, 1981). The coach's role in the action planning stage is to develop the coachee's ability to create a realistic and workable plan of action.

One key outcome of successful action planning is the facilitation of the coachee's transition from a *deliberative* mind-set to an *implementational* mind-set (Gollwitzer, 1996; Heckhausen & Gollwitzer, 1987). The deliberative mind-set is characterized by a careful weighing of the pros and cons of action and a careful examination of competing goals or courses of action (Carver & Scheier, 1998). The implementational mind-set is engaged once the decision to act has been made. This mind-set has a determined, focused quality, and is biased in favor of thinking about success rather than failure.

The shift from the deliberative to the implementational mind-set is important, not least because individuals in implementation tend to perceive themselves as being in control of their outcomes (Gollwitzer & Kinney, 1989) and experience a positive and optimistic view of their chances of success (Taylor & Gollwitzer, 1996). Such cognitions themselves are associated with higher levels of self-efficacy, self-regulation, and goal attainment (Bandura, 1982).

THE MULTIFACETED NATURE OF GOALS

Goals are not a monolithic construct. In coaching it may be useful to distinguish among different types of goals such as outcome, distal and proximal goals, approach and avoidance goals, performance and learning goals, higher- and lower-order goals, and the actual concrete results that the coachee achieves. These are important distinctions as different types of goals differently impact a coachee's performance and experience of the goal-striving process.

The time framing of goals is an important part of the goal-setting process, and can influence the coachee's perception of the attainability of the goal (Karniol & Ross, 1996). *Distal* goals refer to longer-term goals, and can be understood as being akin to the broad vision statements often referred to in business or management literature. Distal goals, which are experienced as being more abstract, fuzzy visions of the future, rather than concrete goals that are specifically defined, allow for greater flexibility in the development of action planning strategies (Khan & Quaddus, 2004) and can be more motivating than proximal goals. *Proximal* goals are shorter-term than distal goals, can stimulate more detailed planning than distal goals (Manderlink & Harackiewicz, 1984), and are important tools in action planing. In essence, the action steps derived in the coaching session are a series of proximal goals. Combining both distal and proximal goals into the coaching process can lead to enhanced strategy development and better long-term performance (Weldon & Yun, 2000).

Most coaching programs explicitly focus on setting *outcome* goals, which are frequently a straightforward statement of some desired outcome (Hudson, 1999)—for example, "to increase sales of widgets by 15 percent in the next three months." This is a useful approach, because for individuals who are committed and have the necessary ability and knowledge, outcome goals that are difficult and are specifically and explicitly defined allow performance to be precisely regulated, and thus lead to high performance (Locke, 1996). Indeed, many coaching programs focus on the setting of SMART goals (specific and stretching, measurable, achievable or attractive and agreed, realistic, and time framed), and this approach is supported by some of the goal-setting literature (Locke & Latham, 2002).

However, there are times when overly specific goals will actually alienate the coachee, and may lead to a decline in performance (Winters & Latham, 1996). For individuals who are in a highly deliberative mindset or in a contemplation stage of change, it may be more useful to purposefully set more *abstract* or quite vague goals and focus on developing a broad, fuzzy vision, rather than drilling down into specific details and setting more *concrete* goals. For individuals at this point in the change process, vague goals are often perceived as being less threatening and less demanding (Dweck, 1986).

Goals can be considered as being ordered hierarchically, with concrete specific goals being subsumed under *higher-order* and broader, more abstract goals (Chulef, Read, & Walsh, 2001) in a fashion similar to the "Big Five" (openness, conscientiousness, agreeableness, extraversion, and neuroticism) personality traits and the lower order facet scales of actions (for openness), order (for conscientiousness), trust (for agreeableness), and anxiety (for neuroticism) (Costa & McCrae, 1992). Hence, abstract goals such as "to be a great leader" can be understood as being vertically higher than the *lower-order* and more specific goal "to increase business profits by 25 percent in the next quarter," and there is some empirical support for this notion (Chulef, Read, & Walsh, 2001; Oishi, Schimmack, Diener, & Suh, 1998).

Coaches also need to be attuned to the existence of *competing* or *conflicting* goals whereby pursuit of one goal interferes with the pursuit of another goal. Sometimes goal conflict is relatively easy to identify as in the two goals "to spend more time with my family" and "to put more time into work in order to get a promotion." However, the conflict between goals may not always be immediately apparent. For example, the goal "to get my sales force to sell more widgets each week" may be in perceived conflict with the goal "to have a more hands-off and people-centered leadership style," if the coachee finds delegation difficult and is used to a more controlling management style.

In terms of hierarchy, the goal "to have a more hands-off and people centered leadership style" can be considered to be a higher order goal than the goal "to get my sales force to sell more widgets each week". These two goals are also in conflict. The skill of the coach here is to help the coachee find ways to align seemingly conflicting goals both vertically (between higher and lower order goals as in this example), and also horizontally. An example of vertical alignment in this case would be to find a way that the coachee could develop a more hands-off people centered style of a type that motivates the sales force to sell more widgets. Such congruence is important in facilitating both goal attainment and well-being (Sheldon & Kasser, 1995).

Avoidance goals are expressed as a movement away from an undesirable state, for example, "to be less stressed about work." Such a goal does not provide a specific outcome target. There is a wide range of behaviors that might be associated with such a goal. In contrast, an *approach* goal is expressed as a movement toward a specific state or objective—for example, "to enjoy a fulfilling balance between work demands and personal relaxation." Not surprisingly, it appears that there are important differences in self-evaluation and personal well-being that are related to the propensity to set either avoidance or approach goals.

Coats, Janoff-Bulman, and Alpert (1996) found that people who tended to set avoidance goals had higher levels of depression and lower levels of well-being. Other studies have found that the long-term pursuit of avoidance goals is associated with decreases in well-being (Elliot, Sheldon, & Church, 1997), and that approach goals are associated with both higher levels of academic performance and increased well-being (Elliot & McGregor, 2001).

Performance goals focus on the doing. These are often experienced as being competitive, that is, to perform really well on a specific task and to receive a favorable evaluation from others. Such goals tend to focus the coachee on issues of personal ability (Gresham, Evans, & Elliot, 1988). An example of a performance goal in executive or workplace coaching might be "to upgrade the widget sales process to best-practice standards." Performance goals can be very powerful motivators, especially where the individual experiences success early in the goal-attainment process. However, performance goals can actually impede performance, particularly when the task is very complex or the goal is perceived as highly challenging and the individual is not skilled or is low in self-efficacy. Furthermore, in highly competitive situations or when there are very high stakes, performance goals can foster cheating and a reluctance to cooperate with peers (Midgley, Kaplan, & Middleton, 2001).

In such cases *learning* goals may better facilitate task performance (Seijts & Latham, 2001). Learning goals (sometimes referred to as mastery goals) focus on the learning associated with task mastery, rather than the performance of the task. An example of a learning goal in executive or workplace coaching might be "research current best practice in widget sales processes and learn how to implement to best practice standards." Learning goals tend to be associated with a range of positive processes including perception of a complex task as a positive challenge rather than a threat; greater absorption in actual task performance (Deci & Ryan, 2002); and enhanced memory and well-being (Linnenbrink, Ryan, & Pintrich, 1999). Furthermore, individual performance is enhanced in highly complex situations when team goals are framed as being learning goals (Kristof-Brown & Stevens, 2001). One benefit of setting learning goals is that they tend to be associated with higher levels of intrinsic motivation, which in turn is associated with performance (Sarrazin, Vallerand, Guillet, Pelletier, & Cury, 2002).

Although the differences in the articulation of these different types of goals may appear to be minor or merely semantic, in fact the way a goal is expressed is very important (Rawsthorne & Elliot, 1999), and coaches need to be finally attuned to such nuances if they are to work effectively with their clients.

The key issue for coaches is one of informed flexibility in goal setting. For example, in the right circumstances, coupling learning goals with approach and performance goals creates a powerful synergy that can enhance performance, learning, and intrinsic motivation (Pintrich, 2000), and thus lead to both goal attainment and increased well-being.

SELF-CONCORDANT GOALS: THE "WHY" OF GOAL-FOCUSED COACHING

Understanding the why of goal setting is also important in coaching. Goals that are self-congruent and in alignment with the coachee's core personal values or developing interests are more likely to be engaging and associated with a willingness to make greater effort. Self-concordance theory (Sheldon & Elliot, 1998) offers the goal-focused coach a useful framework from which to understand and work with the reasons and motivations underpinning goal selection and goal strivings.

Self-concordance refers to the degree to which a goal is aligned with an individual's enduring intrinsic or identified interests, motivations, and values. This is a simple but very powerful framework for understanding the values related to goal setting. Derived from self-determination theory (Deci & Ryan, 1980), the self-concordance model emphasizes the extent to which individuals perceive their goals as being determined by their authentic selves, rather than compelled by external or introjected forces. Underpinning self-determination theory is the notion that people have psychological needs that arise as a function of the complexity of the human organism. The self is conceptualized as an enduring and relatively stable mental construction that has the ability to direct behavior in such a way as to satisfy such organic needs (Sheldon & Elliot, 1999).

The self-concordance approach delineates the perceived locus of causality (PLOC; see Figure 6.2) as varying on a continuum from controlled (external) factors to internal (autonomous) facets. It is important to note that it is the individual's perception of the locus of causality that is the key issue in determining the extent to which the goals are deemed to be self-integrated and where they sit on the external-internal continuum.

As Sheldon and Kasser (1998) note, external motivation is experienced by the individual as behavior that is caused by factors outside of the self. External motivation is where the individual strives to attain some kind of payoff such as money, awards, or approval from others and would probably not strive for this goal without these kinds of external rewards. Introjected motivations are characterized by anxiety and guilt, with the individuals feeling coerced by their own internal sanctions. Such goals may be talked about by the coachee in terms of "should" or "ought to."

In contrast, internal facets are enduring motivations that are perceived as being internally determined and are experienced as emanating from self-directed choices; coachees feel as if they really "own" the goal and that the goal is personal. Autonomous facets can be either intrinsic or identified.

Intrinsically motivated behavior stems from the individual's core values, and is naturally enjoyable, engaging, and self-integrated. These kinds of goals are pursued "for the love of it," and such goals and the strivings associated with them are highly rewarding in themselves. Identified motivation stems from personal conviction and developing interests; the individual has thought about the goal, and although this

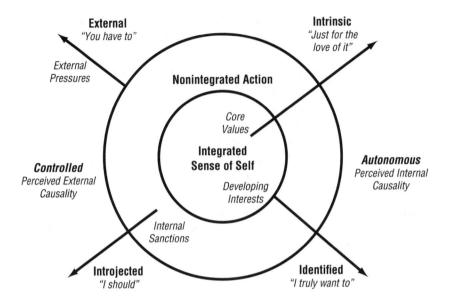

Figure 6.2
Perceived Locus of Causality Model

goal and associated values may have originated from other people, the individual now wholeheartedly agrees with it, endorses it, and personally values it highly.

The fact that the external-internal causal dimension is not objective but is in relation to the coachee's perception is an important point for coaches. The goal "to sell 1,000 widgets this month" may be a goal set by a sales manager and not the coachee. However, if the coachee loves to interact with customers and finds great personal satisfaction in selling widgets, then this goal will be experienced as being congruent with his or her sense of self, and thus would be internal or identified. Conversely, if the coachee's primary reason for striving to reach the goal is some external reward (e.g., financial) or introjected (e.g., shame or guilt), then the perceived causality falls outside of the coachee's sense of self and there is an external perceived locus of causality.

The external-internal dimension has been found to have an important impact on goal striving, effort, well-being, and satisfaction with goal outcomes (Sheldon & Kasser, 1995) Self-concordance correlates with positive concurrent well-being, and also with sustained effort over time; individuals who strive toward self-concordant goals tend to try harder and for a longer period, leading to an increased chance of goal attainment. In addition, self-concordance makes goals more satisfying when they are attained (Sheldon & Elliot, 1999), and this kind of goal-related satisfaction may be an important motivational reference point when the coachee starts striving toward another goal. Furthermore, and of relevance to coaches working in a global context, the relationship between well-being and the pursuit of self-concordance goals is robust cross-culturally (Sheldon et al., 2004).

SELF-CONCORDANT GOAL ALIGNMENT

Given these issues, it is important that coachees' goals are as self-congruent as possible, and in the coaching process coaches may need to play an active role in helping their coachees align goals in order to make them personal and congruent. There are at least four factors that may influence successful goal alignment.

First, coachees need to be able to identify the enduring and authentic from transitory or superficial whims or desires, thereby more effectively focusing their efforts. Second, coachees need to be able to distinguish between goals that represent their own interests and goals that represent the interests of others, what Sheldon (2002) refers to as "me" and "not-me." This requires a high level of personal awareness. Given that levels of self-awareness and insight vary greatly (Church, 1997), this may not be easy for some coachees. Third, the goal content needs to be expressed in a way that facilitates the alignment of the goal with the coachee's internal needs and values. Fourthly, the coach needs to have the ability to recognize when a goal is not self-concordant, and then be able to relanguage and reframe the goal so that it does tap into the coachee's more internal needs and values.

Relanguaging and reframing are core coaching skills. An effective coach needs to be able to reflect and reframe the coachee's responses in order to create different ways of looking at the issues and thus develop different ways of behaving.

In the case of reframing the externally perceived goal "to sell 1,000 widgets this month," the coach first has to recognize that the goal has been perceived by the coachee as external and not self-concordant. The coach then has to raise this issue with the coachee—the principle of awareness. The coach may say something along the lines of "I get the feeling that this is not a really exciting or fun goal for you. It seems as this has been pretty much foisted on you. I wonder if there is some way we could make this really work for you."

The coach then needs to help the coachee identify and articulate what is really important for the individual and then find a way for the coachee to align those authentic intrinsic needs with the goal. The questions coaches would ask of themselves would be "What is this person really looking for here? What are his needs and values? How can we crystallize these into actionable steps?"

The coach might ask the coachee a question along the lines of "Can I ask you a question here . . . what is really important to you? What are the nonnegotiables in your life?" In response the coachee might state that he places great intrinsic value on providing for his family. The coach's task is then to find a way of aligning the sales goal with the coachee's intrinsic motivations. The coach could ask, "If you were to reach this sales goal, what would that give you that you could pass on to your family?," and this might sometimes be effective.

However, the first difficulty in this process is to set up a series of subgoals that bridge the gap between the higher-order intrinsic goal and the lower-order sales goal, and the coach will need to beware of trying to reframe the goal too quickly and stretching the link between higher-order and lower-order goals too much, too soon. If this process is not paced well, rapport will be broken. A better question might be to simply ask the coachee a question such as "I wonder how you could link the sales goal to those things that are really important to you?" and then to help the coachee figure it out.

The second difficulty is to find a way once the link has been made that the coachee can monitor and evaluate progress through subgoals toward the higher-order goal and make those monitoring processes meaningful. The subgoals need to be quite concrete, as overly abstract goals may result in derailment. For example, the coachee could break down the overall sales target into a series of subgoals and relate the attainment of each subgoal to some specific facet of family life. The identification of these factors should be primarily generated by the coachee, as this process can easily sound superficial and trite and in itself become an external or introjected process if there is too much direction from the coach.

The third difficulty is in making the attainment of the subgoals rewarding and enjoyable. Here the coach and coachee need to be creative and brainstorm options.

Finally, the fourth difficulty is helping the coachee stay on track, continue to work toward the main goal, and remain enthused over time. One way to do this is to extend the alignment process to include specific personality traits. Figure 6.3 shows an integrative model of goal-focused coaching.

PERSONALITY STYLE-GOAL ALIGNMENT

The goal alignment process is profoundly personal. In addition to working with the external-internal dimension, an understanding of some key personality dimensions may be useful to the coach in maximizing coachee-goal alignment. Knowledge of common personality traits can be very useful to alerting the coach to possible derailers and frequently can provide a useful point of reference in aligning the goals to the client's needs; this approach is particularly useful in coaching the more challenging client. Hogan and Hogan (2001) draw on established clinical and psychiatric models of personality disorders, and present a dimensional model of personality traits in which personality lies on a continuum from "personality-disordered" to "healthy expressions of personality style."

Each of these personality styles has specific behavioral, emotional, and cognitive traits, and each has some quite specific needs that drive behavior. For each style, there will be a way to frame the goal that will be appealing

Figure 6.3
An Integrative Model of Goals

to the client, and there will be other ways of framing the goal that will alienate or at least be disinteresting to the client. Table 6.1, adapted from Cavanagh (2005), presents some common personality styles and summarizes the types of appeals likely to motivate specific styles.

"Charlie" has many of the traits of a narcissistic or bold leader. He is a stockbroker in his late 40s. He manages a sales team of 20 and he also has his own client base. He is well dressed, extroverted, entertaining, and charming. His clients love him and his sales track record is one of the best in his industry. However, he was recently passed over for promotion, and as part of an organizational leadership development program was assigned a coach. His 360-degree feedback indicates that many of his sales team reported that they felt undervalued and sometimes intimidated by his pacesetting style.

The feedback from his peers indicated that they saw him as being brash, rude, arrogant, and pushy. Charlie was quick to highlight numerous examples of his successes. He gave a wide range of reasons why he should have been promoted. When questioned about the way he managed and developed his team, he stated that he felt deeply for his team and that he would do anything for them, but there was no justification for failing to meet sales targets; after all, "if I can make the figures, so should they." He is sure that he did not get the promotion because the Managing Director and his peers were jealous of and threatened by him.

As can be seen from this brief outline, the key themes of Charlie's narcissistic personality style are a sense of entitlement, grandiosity, a need to be envied and admired, a lack of empathy, a need to be considered special and unique, and a need to be the center of attention.

The broad goal for the coaching engagement was to increase Charlie's ability to develop his direct reports and to build more collegial relationships with his peers. Clearly, this goal is not naturally concordant with Charlie's personality. Thus, in establishing a coaching relationship and setting a frame of reference for working on this broad goal, the coach needs to be mindful of how best to discuss the benefits of working on the goal.

Frames of reference that emphasize empathy for others and a need to acknowledge deficiencies or personal failures are not likely to engage Charlie in the coaching process. Indeed, such an approach may well lead to defensiveness and increased resistance. However, the coach can connect the more adaptive behaviors associated with the goal to the coachee's needs, in this case, increased public profile and personal gain.

Although such pragmatic approaches may be seen as Machiavellian (Berglas, 2002), when used appropriately at the beginning of the coaching relationship, they are invaluable in aligning the goals with the

Table 6.1

Personality Styles, Derailers, and Goal-Alignment Issues
Relevant to the Two Case Studies

Personality Style	Hogan's Typology	Key Need or Motivator	Examples of Appeals Likely to Motivate Engagement in Coaching and Foster Alignment with Goals	Examples of Appeals Not Likely to Motivate Engagement in Coaching	Derailers
Narcissistic	Bold	Need for personal admiration	Enhancement of public profile, opportunities for praise, potential to distinguish oneself, emphasis on uniqueness and being special	Empathy for others, appeals to acknowledge deficiencies/failures, promotion to others' rights or well-being	Arrogance
Antisocial	Mischievous	Need for power and to be the winner	Appeals that emphasize personal gain, challenge, winning, excitement, and risk	Appeals to empathy, social conformity, compromise, and self-sacrifice	Mischievousness
Dependent	Dutiful	Need for affiliation, affection, and approval	Appeals that emphasize belonging, social cohesion, security, and social approval	Appeals that emphasize challenge, winning, excitement, and risk	Eagerness to please
Avoidant	Cautious	Need to avoid negative evaluation	Appeals that address acceptance and security needs, and minimize unpleasant feelings	Appeals that emphasize risk taking, excitement, or public exposure	Excessive caution

Adapted from Cavanagh (2005).

client's needs and facilitate the formation of a collaborative working relationship from which to start the coaching engagement. Over time, during the coaching engagement, the goals can and should be be revisited. Once the coachee is engaged in the coaching process, other frames of reference can be introduced that offer alternative and more challenging ways of understanding (Cavanagh, 2005).

Change is not easy, and despite best attempts at personality-goal alignment, the legwork still has to be done. The coachee still needs to enact the goals and to stay focused on desired outcomes. This is where coaches really do earn their money. Keeping clients focused on the bigger picture and reminding them of the benefits of maintaining action is a central and vital part of the coaching relationship. To do so the coach needs to be aware of the dynamics of change, and be able to match the goal and the coaching process to the coachee's readiness to change.

MODELS OF TRANSITION, CHANGE, AND GOAL-FOCUSED COACHING

Coaching is about fostering directed purposeful change in the pursuit of specific goals. There are three key models of transition and change that can be useful in goal-focused coaching: Bridges' (1986) Transition Model, Schlossberg's (1981) Adaptation to Transitions Model, and Prochaska and DiClemente's (1984) Transtheoretical Model of Change. These models are useful because they give another framework from which to understand the coachee's relationship to the enactment of goals.

BRIDGES' TRANSITION MODEL

Bridges' (1986) model distinguishes between *change* and *transition*, and focuses on the role of emotional reactions to change. Bridges (1986) argues that change is something situational and external. Change happens when something starts or stops. For example, the physical act of moving from one office to another is a change. In contrast, transition is the internal experience of a gradual, psychological reorientation process as we respond and adapt to change. Transition may result from a change, but is often triggered by the news that a change is imminent. In Bridges' (1986) model there are three parts to transitions: ending, neutral zone, and new beginnings.

The model starts with the recognition that transitions start with an ending; one thing must end in order that something else can begin. Hence, the ending phase is one of letting go of the past. There may be a sense of loss, mourning, anger, and/or resentment. Bridges recommends the individuals in the endings phase give themselves enough time to complete the process.

The next stage is the neutral zone, the core of the transition process. This stage is characterized by a sense of confusion and uncertainty about the future. Bridges cautions against prematurely moving out of the neutral zone and suggests that the neutral zone is a place of promise and opportunity, and represents a great chance for creativity and renewal.

The final stage in the model is a new beginning. Here the new vision for the future is developed and enacted. Disorientation and anxieties transform into excitement about new opportunities and actions. Bridges (1991) suggests that individuals in this stage need to maintain a focus on their goals, tune in to their thoughts and feelings, and be open to the need to alter plans in response to unexpected events.

In coaching, this model highlights the place of emotions in the transition process. This is a very useful tool that coaches can use to normalize their clients' emotional responses to transitions.

SCHLOSSBERG'S ADAPTATION TO TRANSITIONS MODEL

Schlossberg's (1981) Adaptation to Transitions Model outlines some of the key psychosocial factors mediating transition through change. Schlossberg (1981) cites three sets of factors that affect a person's adaptation to change:

1. *Characteristics of the transition itself.* These include role change (gain or loss), source (internal or external), timing (gradual or sudden onset), affect, (positive or negative), and duration (permanent, temporary, or uncertain).
2. *Characteristics of the pretransition and posttransition environments.* These include internal support systems, intimate relationships, cohesion of family unit, social networks, institutional supports, and the physical environment.
3. *Characteristics of the individual going through the transition.* These include psychosocial competence, sex and sex-role identification, age and life span, state of health, race/ethnicity, socioeconomic status, value orientation, and previous experience with a transition of a similar nature.

This model is useful for coaches because it provides a framework for analyzing an individual's difficulties with a particular transition, a cognitive map for understanding reactions to life events, and a way for coaches and their clients to analyze the missing links between transition and adoption.

To facilitate movement toward adaptation to change, coaches should work to help clients develop a clearer perception of their overall life goals; facilitate clients in developing a clearer understanding of their present needs; help clients evaluate how they presently manage strain, stress, and decision making; help clients identify and evaluate their present typical response patterns to a new situation; and facilitate clients' acquisition of new skills that will aid in more effective coping with their own objectives.

Such transition models are very helpful in giving a broad framework for understanding the transition process in relation to major life events and to people's goals. However, they do not focus on the psychomechanics involved in the adoption of specific behaviors, nor do they suggest which strategies might be most effective at different points in the change process as clients move toward their goals.

TRANSTHEORETICAL MODEL OF CHANGE

The Transtheoretical Model (TTM; Prochaska & DiClemente, 1984) was originally developed in reference to addictive behaviors such as smoking and drug and alcohol misuse, and is of great use to coaches who need a model of change that is focused on the underlying psychological mechanisms related to the adoption of new behavior.

Over time the model has been successfully applied to a wide range of problem behaviors and health-related behaviors and both individual and organizational change (Levesque, Prochaska, & Prochaska, 1999; Prochaska, 2000).

The model posits that change involves a progressive transition through a series of six identifiable, although somewhat overlapping, stages. Progression through these stages can result in permanent change. However, for most individuals change is a cyclic process, and many individuals relapse into old behavioral patterns before the new behavior is permanently maintained. On average, people will relapse six to eight times before moving into the maintenance stage. The stages of change are:

1. *Precontemplation.* In this stage there is no intention to change in the foreseeable future.
2. *Contemplation.* Individuals in this stage are considering making changes, but have not yet made any changes.
3. *Preparation.* Here individuals have increased their commitment to change, intend to make changes in the near future, and often have started to make small changes.
4. *Action.* Individuals in this stage are engaging in the new behaviors, but have made such changes for only a short period of time (usually less than six months).

5. *Maintenance.* Individuals in this stage have been consistently engaging in the new behavior over a period of time (usually at least six months).
6. *Relapse.* Many attempts at change result in relapse—a return to the old behaviors.

As people move through these stages they experience a number of cognitive and motivational shifts. Decisional balance, developed from Janis and Mann's (1977) gains versus losses model of decision making, suggests that individuals weigh up the pros (perceived benefits) and cons (perceived costs) of making change. For individuals in the precontemplation stage the cons of change will be more salient that the pros, and this decisional balance is gradually reversed as individuals move through the stages.

There are two other core constructs: self-efficacy and habit strength. Self-efficacy is the belief in one's competency to perform a specific task (Bandura, 1977). Self-efficacy plays a central role in behavior change, affecting whether individuals decide to make changes, the amount of effort they put into creating change, and the length of time they persevere in the face of adversity. Self-efficacy increases as individuals move through the stages of change (Marcus, Eaton, Rossi, & Harlow, 1994).

Habit strength refers to the psychological and physiological aspects of the behavior in question (Velicer, Rossi, & Prochaska, 1996). In workplace or executive coaching when coaching for leadership style change, habit strength might be assessed by the ease (or difficulty) with which an individual can enact new behaviors such as reflective listening, question asking (instead of autocratically dispensing opinions), or remaining calm in situations that would normally provoke an emotional outburst.

The TTM has important implications for guiding coaching practice. Prochaska, DiClemente, and Norcross (1998) outline a number of guidelines for facilitating change based on the TTM that have application in coaching practice.

First, avoid treating all individuals as though they were in the action stage. It is a common mistake to assume that because clients have presented for coaching, they are ready to do the work of change. Coaches need to explicitly assess the client's readiness for change.

Such assessment can be conducted by written questionnaire, behavioral observation, or self-report. Individuals in the action stage are likely to achieve better and quicker outcomes than those in contemplation and preparation, and so individuals in the action stage can handle more challenging behavioral-change assignments and more difficult goals than other individuals in earlier stages of change.

Second, facilitate the insight-action crossover. Individuals who are reluctant to make changes are typically in the contemplation or preparation stages (Grimley & Lee, 1997) and spend more time thinking about their problems than actually changing their behavior. For such clients it is important that coaches focus on facilitating a shift from just thinking about problems to actual behavioral change.

Third, anticipate relapse. For most people, relapse—slipping back into old behavior—is a normal part of the change process (Marlatt, 1996). The coach needs to include relapse-prevention strategies, prepare the client for possible setbacks, and minimize guilt and shame if relapse does occur, and help the client move back into action as quickly as possible.

Because there are different factors at play in each of the stages of change, it is important that coaches match intervention strategy to their coachees' stages of change.

Stage-Specific Coaching Strategies

For individuals in the *precontemplation stage* the general principle is to raise awareness, and the key point here is to increase the amount of information available to coachees so that they can move forward into action. There are many ways of raising awareness, including sales or performance data, structured qualitative feedback, or 360-degree feedback. In addition, in this stage the coach should help the coachee identify behaviors that are not problematic.

One conversational coaching technique that can be effective is to ask the "better question": "In what way would this change make things better for you?" or, if necessary, "You'd better change or else. . . ." Clearly, the "You'd better change or else" conversation is one that the coach should carefully prepare for, as this may well be highly challenging. This type of conversation needs to be firm but collaborative.

The key characteristic of the *contemplation stage* is ambivalence, the conjoint holding of two or more conflicting desires, emotions, beliefs, or opinions. The general principle for individuals in the contemplation stage is to continue to raise awareness through self-revelation. Individuals in this stage are engaged in a balancing act, unconsciously trying to manage their ambivalence by balancing the pros and cons of change. It is as if they were standing in the middle of a child's seesaw trying to maintain their balance.

A common mistake here is to rush in and give the coachee specific goals and action steps. However, doing so will usually simply increase resistance, or they fall off the seesaw! Rather than confront resistance, the coach should *roll with the resistance*, take a tactical retreat and try a range of different techniques, including *simple reflection* in which the coach reflects back the coachee's main points. Another technique is *amplified reflection*: "So what you're saying is that you'll *never* change?" The coach can also use *double-sided reflection*. Here the coach reflects back to the coachee both sides of the ambivalence, "So, on the one hand you feel change would be a benefit because of XXX, but on the other hand you feel XXX."

For many people in the contemplation stage such double-sided reflection may be one of the few times they have heard their ambivalence clearly expressed. By articulating the coachee's ambivalence, a coach creates a personal reflective space in which the coachee can explore the ambivalence and begin to see the issues with greater clarity.

Paradoxical techniques can also be very effective. When confronted with the coachee's arguments against change, the coach agrees with them, and then emphasizes the advantages of the dysfunctional attitude or behavior. The point here is to get coachees to present the arguments for change themselves. This approach can make clients aware of the powerful forces that motivate them to remain stuck in the problem. The coach may say something like "Well, given all the advantages of this thought [or attitude or behavior], why should you change? To be frank, I don't think you're ready to change yet." Paradoxical techniques can be very effective, but they require skill and timing.

In the *preparation stage* the coachee is getting ready to enact change. The key principles here are more about fostering commitment, although awareness and self-evaluation are still important. In this stage the coach should be helping the coachee focus on the future, developing a clear vision and making small and consistent action steps toward the goals. It is important for the coach and coachee to monitor progress closely, and to positively reinforce new desired behaviors by acknowledging and celebrating the attainment of small subgoals. It is often important to find ways to structure the environment to support the desired change. For example, if an individual is trying to develop a more inclusive leadership style in team meetings, it might be useful for the person to change the seating arrangements and to have some kind of physical cue in the room that would remind the coachee to listen and let others talk.

In the *action stage* and the *maintenance stage*, the general principle is to increase self-directed change. Here the coachee can be working on more stretching goals and devising strategies to maintain the change.

In the *relapse stage* the general principle is to normalize and move the coachee back into action as soon as possible. Here the coachee can reframe relapse as a normal part of change process, and minimize shame and embarrassment. Look for past successes and build on those, and try something new.

Relapse prevention is an important part of coaching. It is often helpful to inform coachees that they may relapse despite their best attempts at change. This information is best given once coachees have experienced some early success, and when they are feeling good about their progress. To give detailed information about relapse too early in the coaching process is to give coachees an excuse not to change. Addressing the issue of the normality of possible relapse gives the coachees permission to be frank about their progress, and this is particularly important when coaching perfectionist high achievers. Such clients may feel that they have failed if they don't make the changes quickly and exactly according to plan, and the associated shame may lead to disengagement from the coaching process.

Once the coach has addressed the issue of possible relapse, it is necessary to plan to prevent relapse. This can be done through rehearsing how to deal with problem situations, helping the coachee develop coping strategies, or even working out how to avoid situations that might trigger the problem behaviors.

It is clear that the informed goal-focused coach will be drawing on a wide range of evidence-based theories while coaching. These theories and the client's responses help the coach develop an understanding of the psychosocial mechanics of the issues, and thus inform the development of a conceptual model. Such case conceptualization is an essential part of goal-focused coaching.

CASE CONCEPTUALIZATION AND GOALS

Regardless of the coach's theoretical perspective, case conceptualization lies at the heart of evidence-based coaching. A case conceptualization is an overall view or map of the case, which describes and operationalizes the factors that create and maintain the individual's difficulty, and also the factors that may contribute to a solution. The case conceptualization is a working hypothesis that links the presenting issues or potential solutions to the underlying psychological mechanisms (thoughts, feelings, and behaviors) and may also detail the environmental, social, or systemic factors at play.

A case conceptualization is developed collaboratively with the client and is an active and ongoing process that is open to modification. Case conceptualizations are frequently sketched on a whiteboard or paper, and the process of developing a framework from which to understand the presenting issues brings clarity and is often therapeutic in itself.

There are two fine balancing points for the coach in developing case conceptualizations. First, there is a balance to maintain between (1) drawing on expert sociopsychological knowledge and through this knowledge overly influencing the client's understanding, and (2) acting as a facilitator who helps the client create a personalized and relevant case conceptualization.

Second, there is a balance between (1) developing an understanding of the factors that create or maintain any problematic issues and using this understanding as a platform from which to construct solutions, and (2) avoiding getting drawn too deeply into problem analysis and creating analysis paralysis.

In short, a good case conceptualization highlights the important aspects of the client's situation in a way that is understandable to the coach and client, links the issues to the client's stage of change, makes the issues amenable to change, aids choice and implementation of intervention, and helps the client and coach understand the development of new issues and other aspects of the coaching relationship.

CASE STUDIES

The Case of Bob

Overview of Potential Issues

Bob presents with the initial expressed goal of becoming a better leader, getting the business running perfectly, and leaving on a high note. As with many coaching clients, Bob is in a period of transition. His business has grown rapidly and his leadership style has been somewhat successful up to this point. However, his pacesetting and charismatic approach style may not serve him well in dealing with the new challenges, and he will need to develop greater flexibility. On a personal level, he also is beginning the process of disengagement from his working life. Like many leaders in his position he seeks to leave a lasting legacy, and this may be associated with a need to make meaning of his work life. Further, his sense of self will be challenged by the required shifts in leadership style. Finally, his relationship with and his role within his family may change as his moves into a new phase of his life. This case study discussion focuses on his leadership style rather than family issues.

There are several steps for effective process management in executive coaching. Many coaches use a methodology that involves an initial briefing with the person in the organization who will be the "sponsor" and point of reference within the organization. The purpose of this meeting is to assess the organizational context and determine what the organization sees as being the criteria for success. Following this meeting the coach may assess the executive using interview, self-assessment, or 360-degree feedback. This information may then be fed back to the organization and the coachee and a development plan formulated.

Feedback systems will need to be set up so that the coachee will be able to judge his progress during the coaching engagement. The coaching can then begin, and there should be regular reviews of progress and feedback from within the organization. This type of systemic embedding and organizational alignment is a critical foundation for successful executive coaching. A discussion of these issues can be found in Chapter 11 and so will not be discussed here.

Positioning Coaching: The Early Stages

This case is primarily developmental coaching, although some skills coaching would be involved. In the initial meeting with Bob (a meeting held before the coaching process starts) I would take time to discuss the nature of coaching, and I would be careful to position coaching as being different from consulting. This is important, as Bob's focus is on business results, and he may be approaching coaching looking for quick-fix business advice, rather than personal and professional development. These early stages are vital in the formation of a collaborative working alliance, and I would need to get a good sense of Bob's personality style and his needs very early on so that we could discuss his goals in a manner that will be engaging and attractive to him.

The first real coaching session would focus on defining the issues and creating self-concordant and engaging goals, and detailing confidentiality and process management issues. In addition we would establish a time frame for the coaching engagement with sessions held fortnightly over approximately a six- to nine-month period.

Frequently coachees feel a need to tell their stories and give the coach a lot of detail about their lives to that point in time. While this can be useful in cathartic terms, and some clients find that a life review helps them place the coaching in context, my preference in goal-focused coaching is to keep this stage quite short and stay focused on goals and solution construction, rather than delving into the past. I have found that if something is important, then it will come to the surface.

At this early stage of the coaching relationship I would be listening to identify Bob's readiness for change. Although he might well be in the preparation stage in terms of his willingness to start coaching per se, I would expect him to be in contemplation or even precontemplation in relation to the specific behaviors that he really needs to address.

Thus I would be happy to work with quite vaguely expressed higher-order goals in the first instance, and to use these to establish a working relationship. Bob's initial expressed goal for coaching is about being a better leader and getting the business running perfectly and leaving on a high note. We would explore to see if these were the real issues. What does "perfect" mean to him? How would other people see "perfect"? For myself as the coach, this would be the beginning of a case conceptualization process.

In this part of the coaching relationship I would be acting in a psychoeducational role, giving the coachee necessary information and conceptual frameworks (Chapman, Best, & Van Casteren, 2003) and there is a fine balance to be found between the role of expert knowledge giver and facilitator of Bob's personal self-discovery process. An essential part of the coaching process would be to help Bob become more aware of his thinking patterns, and of the relationship between thinking styles and emotional responses.

Bob has many of the characteristics of an alpha male with a strong narcissistic style. He wants to be seen in a positive light, and is likely to become highly defensive and even aggressive if inappropriately challenged. His preference would be for hard facts and measurable data, and he would give credence to coaching interventions based on research that also had been endorsed or shown to be effective by well-known business leaders (Ludeman & Erlandson, 2004). In terms of enhancing his interpersonal style, for example, it might be useful to discuss how day-to-day conversations have an important impact on the quality of the leader-subordinate relationship, and how these in turn have a very real impact on work performance (Howell & Hall-Merenda, 1999).

I'd also spend some time discussing the role of values by exploring the links between transformational leadership styles (Bass, 2002) and the degree of self-concordant goals set by team member engagement (Bono & Judge, 2003). In explaining the concept of self-concordant, I'd talk about raising the "what's in it for me" factor for his employees and the effectiveness of aligning organizational goals with employees' core needs and values (Oishi et al., 1998). The emphasis in the coaching conversation with Bob would have to be on the utility of enhancing workplace relationships in terms of increased performance rather than humanistic factors.

Although there is clearly evidence of some destructive narcissistic behavioral patterns in Bob's relationships with others, my preference would be to leave addressing these directly until the later sessions unless Bob raised those issues earlier himself. However, I would be asking Bob questions designed to raise his awareness of the real issues. For example, "What makes for a truly great leader—business results alone, people skills alone, or both people skills *and* business results?" "What would be different if you had even better leadership skills?" "How do you know what people really think of your leadership style?"

Because of his narcissistic style it might be useful to position the coaching as helping him further develop his reputation as being an outstanding leader, rather than being a remedial or confrontational process. An important personal developmental insight for Bob would be to see that he needs to change the way he relates to this team and be seen to genuinely care about developing other people, and that it would be only through this that he will be able to get the cohesion his organization needs to deal with the merger and be best positioned for future growth.

From this conversation we may well arrive at the conclusion that a great leader is one who can see the merger through while increasing business profits, increasing delegation, developing key members of the team, maintaining control of the process, and also looking good to others. Thus, in the early stages of the coaching relationship the overall goal might be expressed along the lines of *"To develop strategies to take Bob's leadership skills to the next level, consolidate the business, and build a solid foundation for future growth, and the success of this would be evidenced by increased business performance and a leadership style that brought out the best in his management team."*

In terms of goal hierarchies and horizontal and vertical congruence, Bob holds the higher-order goal "to be a better leader," and this may be perceived to be in conflict with the lower-order goals of "seeing the merger through," "increasing business profits," "increasing delegation," "developing key members of the team," "maintaining control of the process," and "looking good to others." Clearly it would take some time and coaching skill to align these goals both horizontally and vertically and find ways that Bob could (for example) increase delegation while not feeling out of control. Figure 6.4 gives an overview of the relationships between these goals and the alignment process.

The Transition Process

It might be useful to give Bob a frame of reference of the transition process. I would sketch out Bridges' model and get Bob to talk about which stage he was at, and together we could mind map the issues on a whiteboard. I would also use Schlossberg's (1981) model to ask questions that would raise Bob's awareness of the characteristics of the transition itself, the characteristics of the pretransition and posttransition environments, and the characteristics of the individual going through the transition. This is a case conceptualization process and would be the beginning of the construction of a shared mental model of the issues.

It is important that the first session finishes with a sense of collaborative engagement and that Bob leaves with a homework action plan that will help him develop his understanding of the real issues and move them forward.

In Bob's case his action steps following the first session could be to explore ways he could get the information he needs. Useful homework might be for him to keep a record of his interactions with others, rating each interaction on a 1 to 10 scale for rapport, his use of questions, emotional content, and how well he paid attention to the other person. In addition, it would be important for him to begin a formal 360-degree feedback process, although frequently coachees at this level have had several 360-degree feedback reports in the past, but have failed to make significant changes.

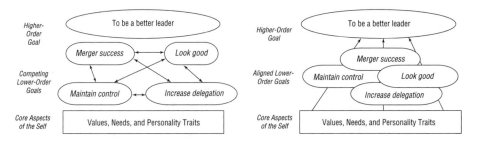

Figure 6.4
Goal Alignment and Higher-Order Goals

Doing the Work of Change

Once the foundations have been established, there is a trusting collaborative relationship, and the 360-degree or other feedback data is in, the real work of change starts. Here we move from contemplation to preparation. Although higher-order "better leadership" goals are useful in the initial stages of coaching, there will come a point where the real issues will need to be addressed in a forthright and direct fashion.

One leverage point might be to highlight discrepancies between his espoused interest in the well-being of others and the perception that he is self-serving and volatile. This will probably not be comfortable for Bob, and I would expect him to be quite defensive and to rationalize and justify his past behavior. It is not unknown for such clients to have temper outbursts or show strong emotions in the coaching session. Rather than being coaching derailers, such displays can be pivotal moments in the coaching relationship, providing powerful learning opportunities for the coachee.

Once the key issues have been identified, behavioral changes need to be designed and action plans developed and monitored. In addition to highlighting Bob's personal resources and his ability to make the required changes, a useful solution-focused approach would be the "letter from the future," a future visioning technique in which the coachees talk, from a future perspective, about how they attained their goals. To guide Bob in this process, I would ask Bob questions, such as, "What objective behaviors do other people need to see from you?" "What mind-set do you need to adopt?" "What needs to change in the organizational systems [organizational structure, e-mails, way that meetings are run, etc.] in order to support you in making these changes?" "What needs to change in the organization's cultural norms and subjective values?"

In addition to this strategic overview, more detailed skills coaching would be useful preparation here, with the coach modeling and then, in turn, Bob rehearsing active listening skills and emotional control techniques. He would receive detailed feedback, so that he leaves the coaching session with a sense of confidence that he can perform the new behaviors when needed.

In terms of between-session action steps, rather than attempt to make large changes to all of Bob's relationships at once, I would encourage him to identify two or three key people in his team to focus on. In selecting those we would look for leverage, identifying those with whom a change in relationship would have impact on other people around them.

The current merger would be an ideal place for Bob to start practicing his new behaviors in his interactions with others. The kinds of external behavioral change we would focus on would include listening to others' opinions without interrupting, remaining calm under pressure, accepting and acting on criticism, following up on promises and previous conversations, and demonstrating a flexibility in leadership style.

The kind of internal change we might use would include a some type of high performance mind-set training program, which would include an attentional training process in which Bob would take a few minutes during the day to sit quietly, listen to his thoughts and feelings, and practice a simple form of mindfulness meditation. This will provide him with tools to enable him to recognize his mood changes and increase his ability to remain centered and calm under pressure.

In order to keep the momentum up, he would need to complete a daily logbook or some other kind of record, coupled with fortnightly coaching sessions, and occasional e-mail contact. In terms of the stages of change, he would be moving from preparation into action stages, and failing to closely monitor and reinforce the behaviors can result in relapse.

Dealing with Relapse

Relapse in an almost inevitable part of any change process. In Bob's case, because we are dealing with traitlike issues, relapse is to be expected. The challenge here would be to keep Bob engaged and focused on the goal. Bob is likely to find relapse quite threatening and is likely to become defensive and even aggressive, would probably blame others, and may even blame the coach for not being effective. This will be a vital point in the coaching engagement. In order to avoid derailment, a purposeful explicit shift to short-term learning goals may be useful here. Rather than Bob trying to be "perfect," I would encourage him to become more reflective, analyzing his interactions with others for insights and making written notes on his key learnings. Relapses now become learning opportunities rather than a failure point, although there is a fine line between framing these as learning opportunities and letting Bob off the hook for unacceptable behavior.

With Bob there may well be a series of successive relapses with each being quite emotive, and over time he might become increasingly disillusioned with the possibility of ever making real change. If this happened it might indicate a need for a shift to a more therapeutic modality such as a referral to a qualified mental health professional.

Termination and Maintenance

Toward the end of the agreed six-to-nine-month time frame, I would start discussing the termination process, and part of this would be to invite Bob to contact me whenever he needed to and to normalize this kind of intermittent support.

Setting the stage for successful maintenance requires that Bob will have made the changes at both an observable behavioral level and also at a deeper, more personal level. Within the six-to-nine-month period we would rerun the 360-degree feedback process, and these results would indicate whether perceived behavioral change had taken place.

Maintenance of change requires that Bob identify potential derailers and develop specific strategies for dealing with these on an ongoing basis. For Bob the potential derailers would include excessive stress and complacency. Bob will need to keep vigilant, and I would suggest that he keep a regular log of how he is feeling and coping with stress. He will need to build his resilience by monitoring his thinking and watch out for unhelpful and highly judgmental thought patterns; the attentional training exercises would be important here.

If Bob continues with his developmental journey, over time his sometimes painful learning through coaching will become simply another part of his broader life story—the process through which he grew as a leader. This kind of sense-making grounded in a realistic self-efficacy will form the foundation for a new sense of self and ongoing development.

The Case of Bonita

Overview of Potential Issues

Bonita presents with the initial expressed goal of developing her leadership skills, dealing with conflict, and improving her work-life balance; in short, she seeks to develop a broader and more flexible range of leadership styles. Like Bob, Bonita is in a period of transition. She is in the relatively early stages of her leadership career, and there are some fundamental emotional and behavioral changes to be made if she is to realize her full potential.

To date her natural preference for an affiliative, participative leadership style has served her well. However, in her new position she will have to manage a greater number of stakeholders and a broader range of personalities than before. She will need to become more assertive and less avoidant. As some of her key needs are for harmony, cohesion, and approval, developing flexibility in leadership style may be personally challenging for her. She has considerable strengths to build on. In addition to being genuinely interested in the coaching process, she has already demonstrated that she can proactively manage potential conflict and she has strong family support.

On a personal level, she faces the challenge of balancing her desire to be more involved with her family and children with her career aspirations. Bonita is lucky in that her extended family are able and willing to be involved with looking after her children. For Bonita, it may be hard for her to accept that she does not have to be the perfect mother. Some of the dominant themes from her family of origin were about sacrificing oneself in the service of others, in that her father worked two jobs so that she could attend a good school. Consequently, she felt under pressure to perform well and to make her parents proud. At the same time, as a child she may well have resented these pressures, and her desire to spend more time with her children may be in part informed by her own childhood experience.

Bonita is in a early stage of leadership development. She is unlikely to have participated in a 360-degree feedback process, and I would consider it very important that we gather feedback and meet with her immediate supervisor Ken to get his support and buy-in for the coaching process and to set up a system so that Bonita can have frank and open discussions with Ken about her leadership style. Ideally, one would like Ken to be acting as a manager/mentor in helping Bonita make these changes. The relationship between Bonita and Ken is collegial, but because Ken has tendency to be paternalistic, judgmental, and quick-tempered and favors a pacesetting style of leadership, it will be important to ensure that expectations of the meeting are clear and that the meeting runs smoothly. I would want this meeting to consist of an open discussion about the issues that Bonita is going to focus on, input in objective behavioral terms from Ken as to what would constitute "success," and an agreement to meet again about halfway into the coaching engagement to jointly review progress.

Positioning Coaching: The Early Stages

Bonita's case is predominantly developmental coaching, with a substantial skills component. In the initial meeting with Bonita, before the actual coaching process commences, I would outline the nature of coaching and spend time arriving at a shared agreement about how the coaching will proceed. Because the coaching game plan involves getting feedback and discussions with Bonita's manager, I would be careful to stress confidentiality issues, and to position myself as *her* coach, rather than an agent of the organization. However, because Bonita is an enthusiastic participant and is people-orientated, I would not expect any objections from her to holding meetings with Ken or in getting 360-degree feedback. Once we have held the meeting with Ken and gotten the feedback, we would start the coaching process.

The first coaching session would focus on the 360-degree feedback and the development of a broad vision and some specific goals. In contrast to Bob, where an early discussion of his problem behaviors may prevent a collaborative coaching relationship from being formed, I would address the problems associated with Bonita's avoidant style very early on in the coaching engagement. It is unlikely that the results of the feedback would be totally unexpected, but Bonita may not be aware of the extent to which her team members would see her as having difficulties in confronting unacceptable behavior.

In this session we would identify the broad goal of the coaching relationship, and I would be looking to find ways to align the organization's goals with Bonita's own needs and values and her stage of change. Bonita has a number of important strengths, and her core values of affiliation and people development would form a useful foundation for framing the objectives of the coaching program. In contrast to Bob's strong narcissistic traits, Bonita's focus is more on the well-being of others, the creation of group harmony, and gaining the approval of other people. Her style could be described as a mixture of the Avoidant/dependent and affiliative styles (Goleman, 2000). She has a tendency to avoid conflict, and she tends to deal with potential conflict by compromise, influencing and accommodating divergent positions rather than taking a stand or direct discussion of difficult issues.

While this can be an effective approach, as an emerging leader an important insight for her would be to learn that conflict is an inevitable part of leadership (Rapisarda, 2003). Her tendency to ignore individual differences in opinion rather than address issues directly leads, in the longer term, to increased dissatisfaction and lack of clarity for team members, and ultimately undermines her own position as leader. Although she is aware of her tendencies in this area, in order to give her a conceptual framework to understand conflict, I may suggest that she complete a conflict assessment measure such as the Thomas-Klimann Conflict Mode Instrument (Thomas & Klimann, 2003). Here I would be again acting in a psychoeducational role, attempting to balance the expert's and facilitator's roles.

Ideally, this discussion would lead Bonita to the realization that her tendency toward an avoidant leadership style is ultimately self-defeating. By not being assertive in proactively managing conflict, she is in fact reducing other people's well-being and not fulfilling her leadership obligations. So, in discussing a potential game plan for the coaching process, I would want to frame the goals as an opportunity to increase belonging and social cohesion. While I would emphasize the benefits of her leadership development for others, Bonita ultimately needs to be making these changes for herself, and a change in focus onto her own development will mark an important developmental shift for her.

Goal Alignment Process

Once we had established that the broad goal of developing effective ways to handle conflict through a more flexible leadership style was self-concordant, we would start to explore the different goals that will need to be aligned. A successful outcome would be for her to demonstrate to Ken that she can be assertive, become comfortable with conflict, further develop the relationship with the president of human resources and the CEO, and remain inclusive and democratic, while improving her team's performance and improving her quality of family life.

In terms of goal hierarchies and horizontal and vertical congruence, Bonita holds the higher-order goal "to develop a broader range of leadership styles," and aligning this with the lower-order goals may present a challenge. However, Bonita has a number of strengths that will help her in this. She already has demonstrated that she can act proactively to deal with potential conflict with Rita, and I would encourage her to talk about her personal strengths in handling this situation. I would also highlight that she already successfully deals with conflicting goals in relation to her family life.

As she may feel like she's not being the "perfect" mother, it might be useful for her to explore some of her beliefs about the nature of motherhood, and to examine whether her aspirations are realistic or idealistic. It would be important for her to arrive at a balanced view of the costs and benefits of being a professional working mother so that she feels comfortable about putting ongoing effort into her future development, and this would be an important part of the goal alignment process.

At some point the issue of her ethnicity would need to be discussed. It is probable that minority group membership has impacted her beliefs about conflict and her sense of belonging. In exploring these issues, it might be useful for her to view her development as, in part, role modeling for other African-American women.

The Transition and Change Process

As with Bob, Bonita is in transition. In many respects she is in the endings phase, and is moving into the neutral zone in terms of Bridges' model. She is leaving behind an aspect of herself that has been with her since childhood, and that is the notion that she needs to be "good": in order to be accepted by others, she needs to make them feel comfortable, and she should not rock the boat or make trouble for others. The aim of coaching will be to support her in this transition process and help her toward her goal of a more flexible leadership style. Central to Bonita's growth as a leader will be the development of a broader systemic view. She will need to learn to read the organizational context and to learn to tailor her style to match specific individuals.

In terms of the Transtheoretical Model of Change, Bonita is in preparation, and in line with this stage, I would be looking for small and specific action steps that will foster her commitment, enhance her self-efficacy, and raise her awareness of her own internal processes. For example, she might draw up a table listing the different people with whom she works. The point of this would be for her to start to take action in proactively managing conflict and disputes, by developing a more in-depth understanding of each of the people she works with. In doing this she is starting to develop a broader range of interpersonal styles and greater flexibility. In this table she could briefly list each person's key characteristics and rate on a scale the degree to which she feels comfortable about being assertive with that person. She could also detail how she typically behaves with each person, and if there is anything about each person that triggers avoidant behaviors for her. This is the beginning of a case conceptualization process, and this will raise her awareness of the underlying issues that trigger avoidance and that foster appropriate assertiveness.

Doing the Work of Change

Once she has identified some key points to focus on, it might be useful for her to purposefully notice when avoidance behaviors get triggered. I would also like her to notice when she is appropriately assertive, and what is different about those times.

In creating change, she will need to set a number of subgoals and focus on each in turn. For example, once we have identified the people with whom she has difficulty in being assertive, we might rehearse person-specific short assertiveness role-plays, and such skills-based approaches are often very helpful (Aspinwall & Taylor, 1997). It will be particularly important for her to develop conflict management skills, identifying problem situations that might trigger avoidance early in the process, before they become problematic. The mastery of these skills will be crucial in her personal development as a leader.

As for her manager Ken, Bonita may find it useful to rehearse the kind of decisive behaviors that he regards as being important in a leader, and to clearly demonstrate these in her meetings with him. However, behavioral change alone is not sufficient to create long-lasting change (Grant, 2001). Bonita will need to spend some time reflecting on her emotional reactions to these activities. Setting learning goals in addition to performance goals will be helpful in fostering self-reflection, and may make the goals less threatening. This kind of double-loop learning deepens and personalizes learning (Argyris, 2002).

Bonita will also need to make some changes in her home life. I would encourage her to take some time off from work to spend with her family. She may be able to take a day off from time to time, or even to schedule a regular half day. Again, I would expect this to be personally challenging, as the tension between work and family commitments can be considered to be competing goals. One way that might be useful for her to align these goals would be to explore ways in which spending extra time with her family actually helps her workplace performance. For example, time spent with her family may refresh her and give her a new perspective on work problems. She may be able to do some work from home, and framing these activities as learning goals may be helpful.

Termination and Maintenance

I would not expect relapse to be a major problem for Bonita, unlike Bob. I would anticipate that she will to be able to make these changes relatively quickly. For Bonita, the key derailer will be complacency, prematurely thinking that she has mastered the requisite skills.

To guard against this possibility, I would suggest that she set up regular mentoring sessions with her CEO. She may also find it useful to actively mentor her team members, transferring her learning to them, and to consciously act as a role model for other African-American women.

Finally, I would encourage her to take the time to celebrate her successes, for her family, for her team, and most importantly, for herself. Long-term change will rest on her ability to integrate her leadership goals into her broader vision of herself. Her development as a leader in the workplace is as much about her own personal development as an individual as it is about team functionality.

CONCLUSION

Coaching is necessarily a goal-directed activity. The integrative goal-focused approach to executive coaching presented in this chapter is a multifaceted methodology for helping individuals and organizations create and sustain change.

By understanding the different types of goals and their relationship to the process of change, and through facilitating the goal alignment process, professional coaches can work more efficiently with their clients, helping them to achieve insight and behavioral change that enhances their workplace performance, their professional working lives, and, most importantly, their own personal well-being and sense of self.

REFERENCES

Argyris, C. (2002). Double-loop learning, teaching and research. *Academy of Management Learning and Education, 1*(2), 206–218.

Aspinwall, L. G., & Taylor, S. E. (1997). A stitch in time: Self-regulation and proactive coping. *Psychological Bulletin, 121*(3), 417–436.

Bandura, A. (1977). Self-efficacy: Toward a unifying theory of behavioral change. *Psychological Review, 84*(2), 191–215.

Bandura, A. (1982). Self-efficacy mechanism in human agency. *American Psychologist, 37*(2), 122–147.

Bar-On, R., & Handley, R. (1999). *Optimizing people.* New Braunfels, TX: Pro-Philes Press.

Bass, B. M. (2002). Cognitive, social, and emotional intelligence of transformational leaders. In Riggio, Ronald E. et al. (Eds.), *Multiple intelligences and leadership: LEA's organization and management series* (pp. 105–118). Mahwah, NJ: Lawrence Erlbaum Associates, Publishers.

Berglas, S. (2002). The very real dangers of executive coaching. *Harvard Business Review* (June), 87–92.

Bloor, R., & Pearson, D. (2004). Brief solution-focused organizational redesign: A model for international mental health consultancy. *International Journal of Mental Health, 33*(2), 44–53.

Bono, J. E., & Judge, T. A. (2003). Self-concordance at work: Toward understanding the motivational effects of transformational leaders. *Academy of Management Journal, 46*(5), 554–571.

Bridges, W. (1986). Managing organizational transitions. *Organizational Dynamics, 15*(1), 24-33.

Bridges, W. (1991). *Managing transitions: Making the most of change.* London: Nicholas.

Briere, N. M., & Vallerand, R. J. (1990). Effect of private self-consciousness and success outcome on causal dimensions. *Journal of Social Psychology, 130*(3), 325–332.

Carver, C. S., & Scheier, M. F. (1998). *On the self-regulation of behavior.* Cambridge: Cambridge University Press.

Cavanagh, M. (2005). Mental-health issues and challenging clients in executive coaching. In M. Cavanagh, A. M. Grant, & T. Kemp (Eds.), *Evidence-based coaching: Vol. 1. Contributions from the behavioural sciences* (pp. 21–36). Queensland: Australian Academic Press.

Cavanagh, M., & Franklin, J. (2001). *A controlled clinical trial of attention training as a treatment for hypochondriasis.* Conference paper presented at the World Congress of Behavioural and Cognitive Therapies, Vancouver, Canada, July 2001.

Chapman, T., Best, B., & Van Casteren, P. (2003). *Executive coaching: Exploding the myths.* New York: Palgrave Macmillan.

Chulef, A. S., Read, S. J., & Walsh, D. A. (2001). A hierarchical taxonomy of human goals. *Motivation & Emotion, 25*(3), 191–232.

Church, A. H. (1997). Managerial self-awareness in high-performing individuals in organizations. *Journal of Applied Psychology, 82*(2), 281–292.

Coats, E. J., Janoff-Bulman, R., & Alpert, N. (1996). Approach versus avoidance goals: Differences in self-evaluation and well-being. *Personality and Social Psychology Bulletin, 22*(10), 1057–1067.

Collier, R. M. (1957). Consciousness as a regulatory field: A theory of psychotherapy. *Journal of Abnormal & Social Psychology, 55,* 275–282.

Costa, P. T, & McCrae, R. R. (1992). *Revised NEO personality inventory and NEO five-factor inventory: Professional manual.* Florida: Psychological Assessment Resources.

de Shazer, S., & Lipchik, E. (1984). Frames and reframing. *Family Therapy Collections, 11*, 88–97.

Deci, E. L., & Ryan, R. M. (1980). Self-determination theory: When mind mediates behavior. *Journal of Mind & Behavior, 1*(1), 33–43.

Deci, E. L., & Ryan, R. M. (Eds.). (2002). *Handbook of self-determination research.* Rochester, NY: University of Rochester Press.

Dweck, C. S. (1986). Motivational processes affecting learning. *American Psychologist, 41*(10), 1040–1048.

Doherty, K., & Schlenker, B. R. (1991). Self-consciousness and strategic self-presentation. *Journal of Personality, 59*(1), 1–18.

Drewery, W., & Winslade, J. (1997). The theoretical story of narrative therapy. In G. Monk, J. Winsdale, K. Croket & D. Epston (Eds.), *Narrative therapy in practice: The archaeology of hope* (pp. 32–53). San Francisco, CA: Jossey-Bass.

Elliot, A. J., & Harackiewicz, J. M. (1996). Approach and avoidance achievement goals and intrinsic motivation: A mediational analysis. *Journal of Personality & Social Psychology, 70*(3), 461–475.

Elliot, A. J., & McGregor, H. A. (2001). A 2 X 2 achievement goal framework. *Journal of Personality and Social Psychology, 80*(3), 501–519.

Elliot, A. J., Sheldon, K. M., & Church, M. A. (1997). Avoidance personal goals and subjective well-being. *Personality & Social Psychology Bulletin, 23*(9), 915–927.

Ferrari, J. R. (2000). Procrastination and attention: Factor analysis of attention deficit, boredomness, intelligence, self-esteem, and task delay frequencies. *Journal of Social Behavior & Personality, 15*(5), 185–196.

Goleman, D. (1995). *Emotional intelligence.* London: Bloomsbury.

Goleman, D. (2000). Leadership that gets results. *Harvard Business Review* (March–April), 70–90.

Gollwitzer, P. M. (1996). The volitional benefits of planning. In P. M. Gollwitzer & J. A. Bargh (Eds.), *The psychology of action.* New York: Guilford.

Gollwitzer, P. M., & Kinney, R. F. (1989). Effects of deliberative and implmentational mindsets on illusion of control. *Journal of Personality and Social Psychology, 73*, 186–199.

Grant, A. M. (2001). Coaching for enhanced performance: Comparing cognitive and behavioural coaching approaches. Paper presented at the 3rd Spearman Conference, Sydney, Australia.

Grant, A. M. (2003). The impact of life coaching on goal attainment, metacognition and mental health. *Social Behavior & Personality, 31*(3), 253–264.

Gresham, F. M., Evans, S., & Elliot, S. N. (1988). Academic and social self-efficacy scale: Development and initial validation. *Journal of Psychoeducational Assessment, 6*(2), 125–138.

Grimley, D. M., & Lee, P. A. (1997). Condom and other contraceptive use among a random sample of female adolescents: A snapshot in time. *Adolescence, 32*(128), 771–779.

Heckhausen, H., & Gollwitzer, P. M. (1987). Thought content and cognitive functioning in motivational versus volitional states of mind. *Motivation and Emotion, 11*, 101–120.

Hogan, R., & Hogan, J. (2001). Assessing leadership: A view from the dark side. *International Journal of Selection and Assessment, 9*(1/2), 40–51.

Hollenbeck, J. R., & Brief, A. P. (1987). The effects of individual differences and goal origin on goal setting and performance. *Organizational Behavior & Human Decision Processes, 40*(3), 392–414.

Howard, A., & Bray, D. W. (1988). *Managerial lives in transition.* New York: Guilford Press.

Howell, J. M., & Hall-Merenda, K. E. (1999). The ties that bind: The impact of leader-member exchange, transformational and transactional leadership, and distance on predicting follower performance. *Journal of Applied Psychology, 84*(5), 680–694.

Hudson, F. M. (1999). *The handbook of coaching.* San Francisco: Jossey-Bass.

Janis, I. L., & Mann, L. (1977). *Decision making: A psychological analysis of conflict, choice and commitment.* New York: Free Press.

Jordan, P. J., & Troth, A. C. (2002). Emotional intelligence and conflict resolution: Implications for human resource development. *Advances in Developing Human Resources, 4*(1), 62–79.

Karniol, R., & Ross, M. (1996). The motivational impact of temporal focus: Thinking about the future and the past. *Annual Review of Psychology, 47*, 593–620.

Khan, M., & Quaddus, M. (2004). Group decision support using fuzzy cognitive maps for causal reasoning. *Group Decision & Negotiation, 13*(5), 463–480.

Kirschenbaum, D. S., Humphrey, L. L., & Malett, S. D. (1981). Specificity of planning in adult self-control: An applied investigation. *Journal of Personality & Social Psychology, 40*(5), 941–950.

Kristof-Brown, A. L., & Stevens, C. K. (2001). Goal congruence in project teams: Does the fit between members' personal mastery and performance goals matter? *Journal of Applied Psychology, 86*(6), 1083–1095.

Lee, F. K., Sheldon, K. M., & Turban, D. B. (2003). Personality and the goal-striving process: The influence of achievement goal patterns, goal level, and mental focus on performance and enjoyment. *Journal of Applied Psychology, 88*(2), 256–265.

Levesque, D. A., Prochaska, J. M., & Prochaska, J. O. (1999). Stages of change and integrated service delivery. *Consulting Psychology Journal: Practice & Research, 51*(4), 226–241.

Linnenbrink, E. A., Ryan, A. M., & Pintrich, P. R. (1999). The role of goals and affect in working memory functioning. *Learning & Individual Differences, 11*(2), 213–230.

Locke, E. A. (1996). Motivation through conscious goal setting. *Applied & Preventive Psychology, 5*(2), 117–124.

Locke, E. A., & Latham, G. P. (2002). Building a practically useful theory of goal setting and task motivation. *American Psychologist, 57*(9), 705–717.

Ludeman, K., & Erlandson, E. (2004). Coaching the Alpha male. *Harvard Business Review* (May), 58–67.

Manderlink, G., & Harackiewicz, J. M. (1984). Proximal versus distal goal setting and intrinsic motivation. *Journal of Personality & Social Psychology, 47*(4), 918–928.

Mansell, W. (2000). Conscious appraisal and the modification of automatic processes in anxiety. *Behavioural & Cognitive Psychotherapy, 28*(2), 99–120.

Marcus, B. H., Eaton, C. A., Rossi, J. S., & Harlow, L. L. (1994). Self-efficacy, decision-making, and stages of change: An integrative model of physical exercise. *Journal of Applied Social Psychology, 24*(6), 489–508.

Marlatt, G. A. (1996). Models of relapse and relapse prevention: A commentary. *Experimental & Clinical Psychopharmacology, 4*(1), 55–60.

Midgley, C., Kaplan, A., & Middleton, M. (2001). Performance-approach goals: Good for what, for whom, under what circumstances, and at what cost? *Journal of Educational Psychology, 93*(1), 77–86.

Norris, S. L., Lee, C., Cea, J., & Burshteyn, D. (1998). Performance enhancement training effects on attention: A case study. *Journal of Neurotherapy, 3*(1), 19–25.

Oishi, S., Schimmack, U., Diener, E., & Suh, E. M. (1998). The measurement of values and individualism-collectivism. *Personality & Social Psychology Bulletin, 24*(11), 1177–1189.

Pintrich, P. R. (2000). Multiple goals, multiple pathways: The role of goal orientation in learning and achievement. *Journal of Educational Psychology, 92*(3), 544–555.

Prochaska, J. M. (2000). A transtheoretical model for assessing organizational change: A study of family service agencies' movement to time-limited therapy. *Families in Society, 81*(1), 76–84.

Prochaska, J. O., & DiClemente, C. C. (1984). Toward a comprehensive model of change. In J. O. Prochaska & C. C. DiClemente (Eds.), *The transtheoretical approach: Crossing the traditional boundaries of therapy.* Homewood, IL: Dow-Jones.

Prochaska, J. O., DiClemente, C. C., & Norcross, J. C. (1998). Stages of change: Prescriptive guidelines for behavioral medicine. In G. P. Koocher, J. C. Norcross & S. S. Hill (Eds.), *Psychologists' desk reference* (pp. 203–236). Oxford: Oxford University Press.

Rapisarda, B. A. (2003). The impact of emotional intelligence on work team cohesiveness and performance. *Dissertation Abstracts International: Section B. The Physical Sciences & Engineering, 63*(9-B), 4357.

Rawsthorne, L. J., & Elliot, A. J. (1999). Achievement goals and intrinsic motivation: A meta-analytic review. *Personality & Social Psychology Review, 3*(4), 326–344.

Sarrazin, P., Vallerand, R., Guillet, E., Pelletier, L., & Cury, F. (2002). Motivation and dropout in female handballers: A 21-month prospective study. *European Journal of Social Psychology, 32*(3), 395–418.

Schlossberg, N. K. (1981). A model for analysing human adaptation to transition. *Counseling Psychologist, 9*(2), 2–18.

Seijts, G. H., & Latham, G. P. (2001). The effect of distal learning, outcome, and proximal goals on a moderately complex task. *Journal of Organizational Behavior, 22*(3), 291–307.

Sheldon, K. M. (2002). The self-concordance model of healthy goal striving: When personal goals correctly represent the person. In E. L. Deci & R. M. Ryan (Eds.), *Handbook of self-determination research* (pp. 65–86). Rochester, NY: University of Rochester Press.

Sheldon, K. M., & Elliot, A. J. (1998). Not all personal goals are personal: Comparing autonomous and controlled reasons for goals as predictors of effort and attainment. *Personality & Social Psychology Bulletin, 24*(5), 546–557.

Sheldon, K. M., & Elliot, A. J. (1999). Goal striving, need satisfaction and longitudinal well-being: The self-concordance model. *Journal of Personality and Social Psychology, 76*(3), 482–497.

Sheldon, K. M., Elliot, A. J., Ryan, R. M., Chirkov, V., Kim, Y., Wu, C., et al. (2004). Self-concordance and subjective well-being in four cultures. *Journal of Cross-Cultural Psychology, 35*(2), 209–223.

Sheldon, K. M., & Kasser, T. (1995). Coherence and congruence: Two aspects of personality integration. *Journal of Personality & Social Psychology, 68*(3), 531–543.

Sheldon, K. M., & Kasser, T. (1998). Pursuing personal goals: Skills enable progress, but not all progress is beneficial. *Personality & Social Psychology Bulletin, 24*(12), 1319–1331.

Taylor, S. E., & Gollwitzer, P. M. (1996). Effects of mindset on positive illusions. *Journal of Personality and Social Psychology, 69*, 213–226.

Thomas, K. W., & Klimann, R. H. (2003). *Thomas-Klimann Conflict Mode Instrument.* Mountain View, CA: Consulting Psychologist Press.

Trapnell, P. D., & Campbell, J. D. (1999). Private self-consciousness and the five-factor model of personality: Distinguishing rumination from reflection. *Journal of Personality & Social Psychology, 76*(2), 284–304.

VandeWalle, D., Brown, S. P., Cron, W. L., & Slocum, J. W., Jr. (1999). The influence of goal orientation and self-regulation tactics on sales performance: A longitudinal field test. *Journal of Applied Psychology, 84*(2), 249–259.

Velicer, W. F., Rossi, J. S., & Prochaska, J. O. (1996). A criterion measurement model for health behavior change. *Addictive Behaviours, 21*(5), 555–584.

Walter, J. L., & Peller, J. E. (1996). Rethinking our assumptions: Assuming anew in a postmodern world. In S. C. Miller, M. A. Hubble & B. L. Duncan (Eds.), *Handbook of solution-focused brief therapy* (pp. 9–27). San Francisco, CA: Jossey-Bass.

Weldon, E., & Yun, S. (2000). The effects of proximal and distal goals on goal level, strategy development, and group performance. *Journal of Applied Behavioral Science, 36*(3), 336–344.

Winters, D., & Latham, G. P. (1996). The effect of learning versus outcome goals on a simple versus a complex task. *Group & Organization Management, 21*(2), 236–250.

CHAPTER 7

An Adult Learning Approach to Coaching

Elaine Cox

In this chapter I will be considering how theories associated with adult learning also have critical relevance for coaching. Despite its rapid growth in popularity there has been very little academic writing that positions coaching in relation to adult learning theory. In this chapter, therefore, I aim to address this situation by outlining a number of concepts relevant to adult learning and exploring the links between these and coaching practice. Using two case studies, I also introduce a coaching process based on adult learning principles, theories, and approaches that illustrates the theories in practice.

In the first part of the chapter I identify eight learning theories that have a particular relevance to coaching. Each theory has a particular part to play in adult learning and has been identified because of its practical application to the coaching process. Briefly, these eight theories are:

1. *Andragogy,* which Knowles (1980, p. 43) defines as the "art and science of helping adults learn." Knowles developed his theory specifically to contrast the needs of adult learners with those of children.
2. *Transformative learning* theory, introduced by Mezirow (1990, p. 18), and described as involving a "particular function of reflection: reassessing the presuppositions on which our beliefs are based and acting on insights derived from the transformed meaning perspective that results from such reassessments."
3. *Reflective practice,* described by Boud et al. (1994, p. 9) as consisting of "those processes in which learners engage to recapture, notice, and re-evaluate their experience."

4. *Experiential learning* draws on the work of John Dewey, Kurt Lewin, and Jean Piaget, but has been extensively developed by Kolb (1984). It can be summarized as learning by doing. The experiential learning model is an inductive learning cycle comprising four stages: concrete experience, reflective observation, abstract conceptualization, and active experimentation.

5. *Learning styles* were introduced by Kolb (1984) as individual orientations toward learning based on the four different forms of knowledge production identified in the experiential learning cycle.

6. *Lifecourse development* is concerned with whether there are particular phases that human beings pass through during the course of their lives. Levinson (1978), for example, argues that the life cycle comprises a sequence of four eras, each lasting for approximately 25 years. He also identifies a number of developmental periods within these eras, concentrating on early and middle adulthood.

7. *Values and motivation.* Values are ideas about what is good and what is bad, and how things should be, and motivation is the internally generated state (feeling) that stimulates us to act. Motivation is linked to needs (Maslow, 1998), but also to values and as Locke (1996) argues, values have a central correlation with intrinsic motivation.

8. *Self-efficacy* (Bandura, 1994) has its roots in social learning theory and can be described as the general or specific belief that people have regarding their capacity to succeed at tasks.

Following a discussion of these theories in more detail, I then introduce an adult learning informed model of coaching that I apply to two case studies. In my conclusion I reinforce the claim that an understanding of adult learning principles is vital to effective coaching practice.

KEY CONCEPTS IN ADULT LEARNING

FROM ANDRAGOGY TO COACHING

Andragogy builds on the theory of constructivism, which suggests that learning is an active process where experience is used by learners to construct new learning based on their previous understandings. Constructivist learning theory maintains that learning is a process of constructing meaning from experience and connects directly to beliefs about the central role of experience in adult learning "as both a resource and a stimulus for learning" (Merriam & Caffarella, 1999, p. 263). Many of the aspects of constructivism, such as encouragement of ownership in learning and the emphasis on experiential learning, can be observed within the principles of andragogy (Knowles, 1978). For example, Knowles claims that adults accumulate a growing reservoir of experience that becomes an increasing resource for learning and that readiness to learn is oriented increasingly to the developmental tasks of the social role.

Rachal (2002, p. 212) argues that "the significance of andragogy and Knowles continues to engage us" and verifies this, reporting that Knowles has "garnered more journal citations over the last six years than any of the half-dozen of the field's most well-known and well-published authors." Thus, although there have been concerns about the empirical underpinning for the theory, it is evident the principles of andragogy have been assimilated into the learning culture. I would argue, in fact, that andragogy has reached its zenith with the advent of coaching as a learning approach: Knowles' definition of andragogy in 1980 confirms the birthright; the learner is perceived to be a mature, motivated, voluntary, and equal participant in a learning relationship with a facilitator whose role is to aid the learner in the achievement of his or her primarily self-determined learning objectives.

In Table 7.1 Knowles' six principles of andragogy are presented alongside some of the key elements of coaching in order to make the association explicit.

From this comparison the elements of coaching can be seen to reflect the principles of andragogy. It could be argued, therefore, that andragogy, as well as providing the core principles that underpin adult learning, also, since coaching is an adult learning situation, too, offers the philosophy for coaching. The goals and purpose may differ from individual to individual and from context to context, but the principles remain. As an example, in Flaherty's (1999) model, for coaching to succeed, there must be true enrollment into the coaching process; that is, there must be voluntary, intrinsic motivation—it must not be coerced or extrinsic. If coaching is mandated as part of, for example, a remedial program, the coach will need to work on achieving client enrollment or buy-in to the process. This aligns nicely with andragogical principles.

Another example of where adult learning practice parallels coaching is in relation to learning contracts. Learning contracts are similar to the contracts or action plans frequently used in coaching to help organize learning/performance more effectively. In the adult learning context learning contracts are used to negotiate learning programs. The learning contract is viewed as a means of giving learners control of the learning event by helping them with planning subsequent activities (Hiemstra & Sisco, 1990; Knowles, 1978). In coaching, the action plan indicates what clients will do to achieve their goal. Introducing written,

Table 7.1
Coaching: Andragogy's True Heir

Andragogy: Six Assumptions about Adult Learners (Knowles, Holton, & Swanson, 1998)	Some Corresponding Principles of Coaching
Adults are self-directed in their learning.	• The agenda comes from the client. The relationship is a designed alliance (Whitworth, Kimsey-House, & Sandahl, 1998, p. 3). • The client sets the agenda (Rogers, 2004, p. 8).
Adults are goal-oriented: they need to know why they are learning something before they learn it; that is, learning needs to be relevant.	• Coaching links inner purpose to outer work (Hudson, 1999, p. 15). • Each client has his or her own commitments and immediate concerns (Flaherty, 1999, p. 11).
Adults have a vast wealth of life experiences to bring to their learning.	• The client is resourceful and the coach's role is to spring loose the client's resourcefulness (Rogers, 2004, p. 7). • The client is naturally creative, resourceful, and whole (Whitworth et al., 1998, p. 3). • Clients are not empty vessels (Flaherty, 1999, p. 11).
Adults are interested in learning to solve real-life dilemmas. Learning needs to be relevant.	• Coaching means action and learning (Whitworth et al., 1998, p. 5). • Coaching is a collaborative solution-focused, result-oriented, and systematic process (Grant, 2003).
Adults have a practical orientation. Their learning needs to have application in their personal and professional lives.	• Coaching addresses the whole person—past, present, and future (Rogers, 2004, p. 8). • People will seek to engage in those activities that help them to meet their needs (Whitmore, 1996, p. 104).
Adults respond more to intrinsic motivators (increased self-esteem and quality of life) than to extrinsic motivators such as qualifications.	• The focus is on connecting a sense of purpose with a vision of a coaching result (Hudson, 1999, p. 30). • Coaching is unlocking people's potential to maximize their own performance (Whitmore, 1996, p. 8).

manageable goals is one way to bolster clients' confidence in managing their own progress and accomplishments.

Fahrenkamp (2001) reminds us that where change is necessary, in a leadership context for example, personal transformation creates the possibility for organizational transformation. Transformative learning theory has had an important influence on adult learning, beginning back in the early 1970s with Paulo Freire's emancipatory philosophy of transformation, developing through the work of Jack Mezirow, and culminating now, I would contend, with its essential application to coaching.

Transformative learning involves a deep, fundamental alteration in beliefs, principles, and feelings (Mezirow, 1990). It is a shift of perception that radically alters understanding of ourselves and others, and our sense of possibilities. Merriam (2004, p. 61) supports this view: "In transformational learning, one's values, beliefs, and assumptions compose the lens through which personal experience is mediated and made sense of." Personal transformation usually begins with a disorienting dilemma, and the process includes critical reflection, self-examination, and a reorientation that results in revised action and deep learning.

Mezirow (1991, p. 78) claims that engaging in such discourse leads us to "more developmentally advanced meaning perspectives." Tennant and Pogson (1995, p. 119) summarize this as representing a developmental shift, a new world view "rather than simply developmental progress" and suggest that researchers and practitioners need to recognize this distinction in order to avoid confusing perspective transformation with normal development. Crucial to the notion of transformative learning then, is the element of social and historical critique: taken-for-granted assumptions have to be challenged from all perspectives in order for transformation to occur (Mezirow, 1991; Tennant & Pogson, 1995).

Mezirow has proposed that there are three types of meaning perspectives: psychosocial, sociolinguistic, and epistemic. Epistemic meaning perspectives are those that connect with what we know and how we come to know it. They are embedded in our developmental phase (Kegan, 1994), cognitive or learning style (Kolb, 1984), and sensory preferences. These preferences can be well developed or distorted. For example, clients who insist they learn only from concrete experience, "activists" in Honey and Mumford's (1992) classification, may need to have their epistemic meaning perspective challenged in order to develop a more inclusive style. Sociolinguistic meaning perspectives relate to the social norms, language use, and cultural codes that underpin all our assumptions and often lead to prejudices, stereotypical judgments, and the like. Psychological meaning perspectives relate to our understanding of ourselves as individuals and how we are shaped by our self-concept, inhibitions, defense mechanisms, and psychological type preferences.

Thus a meaning perspective is a "habitual set of expectations that constitutes an orientating frame of reference that we use in projecting our symbolic models and that serves as a (usually tacit) belief system for interpreting and evaluating the meaning of experience" (Mezirow, 1991, p. 42, cited in Cranton, 1996). It is these meaning perspectives that need to be challenged if deep learning is to occur. Cranton (1996, p. 83) also reminds us that "to grow, one has to question," but suggests that it is not possible to articulate assumptions without the help of others. This suggests some work for the coach. A coach can help the client understand assumptions and beliefs and uncover their roots. Such beliefs may lie in childhood or in past experience, may be embedded in culture or language, or may be influenced by the media, as suggested by Mezirow, but once beliefs are understood in this way, then there is freedom to choose whether to maintain the beliefs.

Strategies for articulating and questioning meaning perspectives make use of different types of reflection. Mezirow suggests three types: content reflection, process reflection, and premise reflection. Only the third of these, where the reflection involves probing the relevance of the problem itself, can lead to perspective transformation. Through premise reflection assumptions, beliefs and values are questioned and this questioning process leads to transformative learning. Thus techniques for promoting transformative learning include critical incident analysis, role-play, journal, and biography. Later in this chapter, I describe a process whereby autobiography that takes account of social and historical standpoints is used as the basis for the coaching process, leading ultimately to perspective transformations.

It can be seen from this account that the questioning techniques of coaching have the potential to achieve perspective transformation. In addition, there are several popular strategies for challenging others in this way: Nancy Kline's "Time to Think" (2001) and Susan Scott's "Fierce Conversations" (2002) are examples of two strategies designed for challenging beliefs through dialogue.

REFLECTIVE PRACTICE

Brookfield (1986), like Mezirow, suggests that the most effective way of externalizing deep-seated assumptions that lead to transformation is through critical questioning and reflectivity. This is where learning occurs. Brookfield argues that significant personal learning "cannot be specified in advance in terms of objectives to be obtained or behaviours (of whatever kind) to be performed. Thus, significant personal learning might be defined as that learning in which adults come to reflect on their self-images, change their self-concepts, question their previously internalised norms (behavioural and moral), and reinterpret their current and past behaviours from a new perspective" (Brookfield, 1986, p. 213). West and Milan (2001, p. 8) describe how the coaching task is to create the right conditions for reflective learning. They suggest that the coach can do this by creating a "psychological space" that allows the client to stand back from the workplace. The coach then provides the support and challenge necessary to help the client "gain perspective on his or her experiences and self, and on his or her leadership task within the organisation."

Reflective practice involves examining actions in order to challenge beliefs and has its origins in the work of John Dewey (1963). Subsequently, the idea has been bolstered by the work of Donald Schön (1987), whose notions, such as "reflection in action," have become part of the language. Again, underpinning reflective practice is the theory of constructivism, where learning is viewed as an active process involving reflection on current and past knowledge and experiences to generate new ideas and concepts.

Elsewhere I have argued that the regular use of a reflective practice tool or model makes learning from experience a more reliable and faster method of gaining access to necessary knowledge and wisdom about our work processes and about ourselves (Cox, 2005). Thorpe (2004, p. 339) discusses how reflective learning journals, although demanding and time-consuming, are essential to professional development and professional practice. Thus both coaches and clients need to engage actively in the process.

Reflection, then, is where professionals come to terms with their feelings, learn from their mistakes, explore their successes, and develop empathy and understanding. It is an important practice for both the client and the coach. An individual identifies a critical event or incident, describes it in writing, and then thinks deeply about how the person's beliefs, attitudes, and knowledge influenced the outcome.

Bolton (2001, p. 11) reports that the practitioners she is working with consider that discussions with supervisors/mentors about their reflections are a process of "re-storying," which is just as much a part of the process as reflective writing. Later, in the analysis of the case studies, I describe the reflective process of identifying life chapters, which is also a form of re-storying. The choices made in the identification of the life chapters indicate how the client frames his/her life now, and illustrate how the self is an emergent and changing project, not a stable and fixed entity: "Over time our view of ourself changes and so, therefore, do the stories we tell about ourselves" (Goodson, 1998, p. 11).

In autobiography, therefore, life is transformed into a story. As Gusdorf (1980, p. 35) explains: "The author of an autobiography gives himself the job of narrating his own history; what he sets out to do is to reassemble the scattered elements of his individual life and to regroup them in a comprehensive sketch." Autobiography differs from a private journal that records the writer's experiences, impressions, and mental states. Rather, it requires one to take a distance with regard to oneself, to draw the meaning from one's life, to reconstruct "the unity of a life across time" (Gusdorf, 1980, p. 37), and to find the "larger story" that distinguishes one's life from that of another (Houston, 1987). Learning in these contexts results from finding patterns and meaning in our life, perhaps even building a theory of our life, or of life in general. Having stepped back and reflected, we know something now that we did not know before. Our knowledge has been extended (Olney, 1980).

Adult learners who reflect on their lives in this way embark on a process of recollection, distillation, and analysis that can yield both insight into life's meaning and purpose and understanding of self and others. Learning in the service of self-awareness and self-understanding involves processes of critical reflection, self-awareness, meaning making, and perspective change (Mezirow, 1991; Tennant & Pogson, 1995).

EXPERIENTIAL LEARNING

Experiential learning theory is a theory that operates on the premise that individuals learn best through experience. Boud et al. (1994, p. 8) claim that experience cannot be bypassed as "it is the central consideration of all learning" and that "learning builds on and flows from experience: no matter what external prompts to learning there might be." The insights and learning revealed during a coaching session by the examination of experience illustrate this theory in practice.

Kolb (1984), building on the work of Dewey (1933) and Lewin (1951), introduced an experiential learning model to explain how people learn from experience and process that experience in different ways in order to generate understanding. He suggested that the process is cyclical and comprises four elements: concrete experience, reflective observation, abstract conceptualization, and active experimentation.

Kolb and Fry (1975) suggest that the learning process often begins with a person experiencing and reporting on a particular action (concrete experience). Following this, the second step (reflective observation) is to reflect on the effects of the action and understand these effects so that if the same action is taken again in the same circumstances it would be possible to anticipate what would follow from the action. The third step (abstract conceptualization) would be to understand the general principles that affect the action. The last step is planning a new course of action. It was also suggested that the learning cycle can begin at any one of the four points—and that it should really be approached as a continuous spiral.

There is a significant role for the coach in ensuring that each of these four elements is addressed: Coaches can augment a discussion of the concrete experience by encouraging full descriptions of the experience, perhaps even sharing their own experience, if appropriate; the reflective observation element invites consideration of feelings and an exploration of different perspectives on the same experience; abstract conceptualization involves trying to make sense of the experience by drawing on prior knowledge and understanding in order to shed light on the experience; the planning phase, sometimes called active experimentation, requires a pragmatic approach to the whole. This is the opportunity to pull the learning from the experience and plan how to do things differently in the wake of the new understandings.

In models of coaching, the Kolb learning cycle can often be seen guiding the process. For instance, the GROW model (constructed by Graham Alexander in the mid-1980s and made popular by Whitmore, 1996) maps directly onto the cycle as depicted by Kolb (1984, p. 33). "Goal setting" equates to an actual or proposed concrete experience; the exploration of "Reality" is equivalent to reflective observation; "Options" involves abstract conceptualization, and "What will you do?" suggests active experimentation.

LEARNING STYLES

Kolb and Fry (1975, pp. 35–36) also argue that effective learning involves the development of four different abilities that echo the four poles of the learning cycle: concrete experience abilities, reflective observation abilities, abstract conceptualization abilities, and active experimentation abilities. They suggest that people develop strengths in, or orientation to, one of the poles of each dimension. As a result a learning style inventory was developed (Kolb, 1976) that placed people on a line between concrete experience and abstract conceptualization, and between active experimentation and reflective observation. Using this, Kolb and Fry proceeded to identify four basic learning styles.

Building on Kolb's work, Honey and Mumford (1992) built a typology of learning styles around this same sequence, identifying individual preferences (or styles) and naming them Activist, Reflector, Theorist, and Pragmatist. It is claimed that neglect of some styles can prove to be a major obstacle to learning.

In a coaching situation it is often useful to introduce some kind of learning styles questionnaire in order to gauge client preferences for working in one area of the learning cycle. This enables the discussion of strengths and weaknesses in relation to learning and is also useful in promoting an understanding of the strengths and weaknesses of others (Jackson, 2004). This knowledge can then be used to bolster weak areas and capitalize on existing strengths.

LIFE COURSE DEVELOPMENT

In addition to learning styles, it is also valuable to consider whether clients are affected by the phase in life that they have reached. Such an understanding can enable self-understanding and help significantly with goal setting.

The most influential study of life phases was undertaken by Levinson (1978), whose longitudinal research with 40 men, 10 from each of four different occupations, revealed that their lives fell into distinct phases, characterized by stable periods and periods of transition. Levinson (1978, p. 321), building on Erikson's work (1959), described how, within each phase, a man also does some work on the tasks of other periods; "tasks that will become primary in later periods may be activated early." The major transitions Levinson identifies are times of significant discomfort, questioning, reassessment, and redirection in a man's life. They are followed by a period of consolidation and stability.

Levinson (1996) also researched the lives of women, interviewing a diverse group of 45 women—both homemakers and career women. This study substantiates Levinson's thesis that all human beings go on developing throughout their lives. While the transitions are different for each person and the results are different for each person, each phase has to be worked through.

It is important for the coach to have an understanding of life phases and adult life course development since, as Levinson demonstrates, the phase is often linked to the realization of particular goals. The goals of the young man or woman will have a different emphasis than those of someone approaching, say, the midlife transition or someone in late adulthood.

VALUES AND MOTIVATION

Learning to understand their own motivations is an important step for coaching clients.

McKenna (2000, p. 89) has described motives as consisting of "inner states that energise, activate, and direct the behaviour of the individual as he or she strives to attain a goal." Smith and Spurling (2001, p. 2) contend that "in real life, motivation is not just a person's keenness for something; it always favours that action or goal against some perceived alternative(s)," which may or may not be clearly perceived. Smith and Spurling (2001, p. 7) also describe how motivation is not single-valued: "it is inherently multi-valued or fragmented, taking up different values even when directed towards the same action or decision." What this "multi-valuing" suggests is that no action or goal has an inherent ability to motivate.

Vroom's (1964) expectancy theory is pertinent here. He argues that people are motivated by the value of the outcome to them as well as the expected results of their actions. He claims that the force of motivation is a product of:

- *Valence*—the value of the outcome to the individual.
- *Expectancy*—the probability that effort will result in success.

The theory suggests that individual motivation has its genesis in what we value and what is imperative for us, as well as being governed by what we believe we can achieve. For coaching, this emphasis on values is extremely important. The coach therefore needs to help clients to recognize their multiple values and explore how these relate to life goals and project-level goals in an attempt to understand motivations.

Setting negotiated goals for learning using learning contracts is seen by Knowles (1978) as a means of empowering and motivating the learner. Thus the ownership of the goals by the client is central. Locke (1996, p. 119) confirms that high commitment to goals is attained when the individual is "convinced that the goal is important." He further suggests that "events and situations seen as threatening to one's values give rise to negative emotions (e.g., fear, anxiety, dissatisfaction), whereas events and situations seen as furthering one's values produce positive emotions (e.g., happiness, satisfaction, love)" (1996, p. 119).

SELF-EFFICACY

Closely related to motivation is the notion of self-efficacy. Self-efficacy is rooted in a view of human agency "in which individuals are agents proactively engaged in their own development and can make things happen by their actions" (Pajares, 2002). It is defined by Bandura (1994, p. 1) as "people's beliefs about their capabilities to produce designated levels of performance that exercise influence over events that affect their lives." Thus self-efficacy determines how people feel, think, behave, and motivate themselves. It can be seen, alongside valence, as the other vital element in Vroom's (1964) expectancy theory equation.

Self-efficacy is built from four main starting points that are each important for the coach to consider:

1. *Mastery experience.* Self-efficacy is built upon previous successful experience, which suggests that attention should be paid to goal setting. Locke (1996, p. 120) also explains that in addition to having a direct effect on performance, self-efficacy influences the difficulty of the goal chosen and the commitment to the goal. This theme has been picked up by Csikszentmihalyi (1997), who suggests that "flow" can be achieved only if goals are clear and at the right level.
2. *Vicarious experience.* Self-efficacy is encouraged through the sharing of experience or modeling behaviors. Thus mentors can be advantageous in promoting self-efficacy.
3. *Verbal persuasion.* Self-efficacy is heightened through the provision of positive, but honest, feedback on achievement to date.
4. *Physiological states.* Positive moods and well-being enhance self-efficacy.

Bandura claims that people with a strong belief in their capabilities approach difficult tasks as challenges to be mastered rather than as threats to be avoided. Such an efficacious outlook, he says, "fosters intrinsic interest and deep engrossment in activities." He also highlights how self-efficacy changes following failure: A strong sense of self-efficacy enables people to attribute failure to insufficient effort or deficient knowledge and skills that are acquirable. They approach threatening situations with the assurance that they can exercise control over them. Such an outlook produces personal accomplishments, reduces stress, and lowers vulnerability to depression (Bandura, 1994, p. 1).

IMPACT—A MODEL FOR COACHING

Readers who like mnemonics may want to follow what I have called the IMPACT model for coaching. This is an adult learning–informed process model of coaching that I now use here to describe the coaching process with Bonita and Bob. Throughout the discussion I draw on the theories highlighted earlier to point up the adult learning approach to coaching.

The process has six elements (Identify Life Chapters, Make Sense of Transitions, Plan, Act, Consider, Track), and is basically similar to other coaching models, such as GROW, that follow the Kolb learning cycle. However, this model differs in that the emphasis at the beginning of the coaching process is on identifying and making sense of life transitions through the introduction of the "Identifying Life Chapters" and "Making Sense of Transitions" exercises. Thus there is a strong initial element of structured reflective practice and the potential for transformative learning. The model then provides opportunities to explore life experience in depth and to identify transitions before following through on the learning cycle. I would argue that this method of getting to know clients and helping them to know themselves is fascinating and rewarding for both the coach and the client and produces excellent material that can be worked with throughout the coaching engagement.

CASE STUDIES

The Case of Bonita

Potential Issues

Our case study client, Bonita, is, I would suggest, in transition. For an event to be classed as transitional, Hopson suggests that there should be personal awareness of a discontinuity in the life space and "new behavioural responses required because either the situation is new, or the required behaviours are novel, or both" (1986, p. 136). Both of these are in evidence in Bonita's case, and on the Holmes and Rahe social readjustment rating scale changing to a different line of work is rated 18th out of the 43 transitional events identified (Hopson, 1986, p. 133).

It is likely that Bonita will be experiencing a mixture of excitement and fear in relation to her advancement at work.

The promotion to a new working situation requires extra responsibility and involvement with a different team of people. Bonita is unsure, from her own track record, whether she can deal with the situation.

Confidence is therefore an issue for her. She is concerned with her performance abilities and is particularly unsure of her leadership capabilities. She has already received patronizing and critical remarks from Ken, her supervisor. This antagonism appears to be related to Ken's sponsorship of Bill in the recent promotion round and the fact that he admires Bill's more forceful leadership style. From an early assessment of the situation it is likely that this will be one of the main areas that Bonita will want to work on, as the relationship with Ken is likely to affect her confidence and self-efficacy. Fortunately, she appears to be a self-directed learner and is eager to learn and develop.

Bonita's style is one of conflict avoidance: She prefers a logical, persuasive, and more collaborative style of communication. She likes to communicate by thinking out loud, and this may be an area that she will want to work on, since this degree of openness could be a risk in a more senior position. However, she likes to receive feedback from her colleagues and team, and this can be made to work to her advantage. There is an example in her previous role where Bonita's style has been effective, and this demonstrates that she may not have to change her style in order to work successfully with Ken.

Bonita, like many working mothers, anticipates difficulties in maintaining her work-life balance while managing a challenging work role. She has two school-age children, aged 12 and 8, and her husband also has a demanding job. However, she does have extended family living nearby and it is hoped that, at least in the short term, the help coming from this area will be an advantage. Bonita needs to ensure that her family life and the demands it could make on her time do not make her vulnerable to criticism and so undermine her leadership position. Any need to take time off from work during the workweek could be seen as a weakness by Ken, especially in the early days.

Adult Learning Approach

Identify Life Chapters
The use of autobiography as a tool for learning has been described in detail by Karpiak (2000) and advocated by Hudson and McLean (2001, p. 49) as a way of "finding meaning and opportunity in valleys as well as peaks, in transitions as well as the chapters of life." Thus it provides an opportunity for critical reflection, and ultimately may lead to considerable transformative learning.

In the first meeting with Bonita, therefore, I would want to ask her to review her life events by writing the outline of an autobiography (see Table 7.2). This would entail shaping her life events into a number of chapters, with the ending of each chapter reflecting a transition point. The potential for the exploration of historical and social elements, required by Mezirow as fundamental to perspective transformation, can be seen in the exercise, and can be elaborated if desired.

This alternative to the more conventional time line, or other forms of assessment, enables clients to identify significant transition points in their lives. The recent promotion can then be seen in the context of Bonita's whole life. The process will also highlight the phase in her life that she has reached. Levinson's work (1996) shows that career women begin the midlife transition at around age 40. Coaching may need to prepare Bonita for this. I would suggest that life transitions are easier to manage if there is an understanding of the processes involved, and so I would try to include some discussion about this with Bonita.

The life chapter process may also reveal other issues, such as any racial or gender reservations that Bonita may have, and there would be an opportunity to transform any firmly held beliefs that may be holding her back.

Make Sense of Transitions
The next step in the process, which I would probably begin in the second meeting, is to make sense of the current transition by drawing out the continuity and contributory factors in Bonita's life chapters. This has several benefits. First, it

Table 7.2
Identifying Life Chapters Exercise

Chapter 1:   *Title:*

Dates: *From _____ to _____*

Critical events:

Significant places:

Significant people:

Main challenges:

Themes of this chapter:

Features of the ending and transition to Chapter 2:

[Add as many chapters as needed.]

Adapted from Hudson and McLean (2001).

helps to emphasize coherence. Ibarra and Lineback (2005, p. 68) claim that coherence is crucial to a life story of transition because it is the characteristic that most generates trust. I would argue that belief in oneself through recognition of a coherent life story is important in the formation and maintenance of self-efficacy. Second, making sense of transitions allows the exploration of values, which, as suggested earlier, are intimately linked to motivation. The five phases in the "Making Sense of Transitions" process are outlined in Table 7.3.

The results from this initial work will provide a foundation for future coaching sessions. For example, we will be able to build self-efficacy by exploring how previous events had been handled successfully. We will also have more certainty

Table 7.3
Making Sense of Transitions

1. Emphasize coherence.

   Ask questions of the life chapters, such as:

   What have I always been interested in?

   What have I always been good at?

2. Keep the reasons for future change or transition grounded in enduring values and character traits.

   What have I always valued?

   What kind of person am I?

3. Provide multiple reasons for the change.

   Why is this happening now?

   What in my life story has prompted this change?

   How will accepting this change affect my values?

4. Review explanations that extend back in time.

   Why could I not pursue this goal earlier?

   Why is the time right now, and not, say, 10 years ago?

5. Reframe your past in light of the change you want.

   How is what I am involved with now linked to previous employment, interests, learning, and so on?

   What are the similarities to previous events or experiences?

   What skills can I bring from my past experiences to the new situation?

Adapted from Ibarra and Lineback (2005).

about why Bonita is pursing her career to this new level and how this fits with her values and life goals.

Additional work at this initial stage therefore will involve examining Bonita's values. It will be necessary to look at what success looks like for her and what is important to her and why. I would not presume, at this stage, to understand fully what the goals are, even though this may be evident from early conversations, but it is vital that performance, or project-level, goals relate directly back to life goals and ultimately to Bonita's value system. This will ensure that her approach to her work is congruent and will help particularly with the work-life balance issue. If Bonita's values are mainly related to her home and family, then work may need to be reframed to be shown to be contributing to family values. Then the conflict that Bonita, as a working woman, may feel can be ameliorated.

Development of the Relationship

Plan, Act, and Consider

The Plan, Act, Consider elements of the coaching process reflect Kolb's (1984) learning cycle.

Planning sessions would focus on exploring and planning for some specific project-level goals (Smith & Spurling, 2001). Initially we would check that all the goals were congruent with the reasons for change identified in the "Making Sense of Transitions" exercise, and then we would prioritize to ensure we address the most important first.

Only then would it be appropriate to build together a negotiated learning or action plan in relation to each goal. If the goals were identified, for example, as leadership skills, conflict management, and work-life balance, then, having explored the options for development available for each, the three action plans may begin to be developed in the following way.

Leadership Skills

1. Find leadership style that is congruent with own style (reading, Internet search, etc.).
2. Keep diary of leadership opportunities, how and whether taken, how responded to, and so on.
3. Review plan of action once this data has been gathered (after one month).

Conflict Management

1. In all dealings with Ken, maintain open and collaborative style that worked previously with Rita.
2. Keep diary of actual and potential conflict encounters. In particular, reflect on critical incidents with Ken.
3. Review plan of action after one-month trial.

Work-Life Balance

1. Ensure that contingency arrangements are in place for childcare, and ensure that family members realize this may be only a short-term commitment while credibility in the job is established.
2. Check out clubs and other after-school activities for children.
3. Discuss sharing of household chores with husband and children.
4. Set up systems for managing household (cleaner, gardener)—again these arrangements could be short-term.
5. Note in diary what is working and what isn't, and make swift, expedient adjustments.

Each action plan would incorporate a large chunk of reflective journal keeping, which is then reviewed in subsequent coaching sessions and plans are modified accordingly. This ensures that experiential learning is maximized.

Track and Terminate

At future meetings it is essential to review the actions detailed in the action plan and to provide feedback. Feedback is important to Bonita, and in the follow-up sessions the coach can use the appropriate point in the learning cycle, possibly augmenting the feedback with reflections on his/her own experience if appropriate in order to encourage different perspectives. The coach could also encourage Bonita to use evaluations and feedback from colleagues, including Ken. Bonita's learning style analysis (Honey & Mumford, 2000) may reveal a preference in one particular area. The feedback may confirm this, and she should then be encouraged to build strengths in other areas.

I would imagine working with Bonita for about a year, in order to ensure that she becomes established in her new role and is able to deal effectively with the issues she has identified. It is important to remember that opportunities for reinforcing self-efficacy and for significant transformative learning may occur at any stage of the coaching process; so follow-up sessions, which may be spaced further apart as time goes on, can also provide opportunities for learning.

Griffiths and Tann (1991) have suggested that reflection on practice has five eras:

1. Rapid reaction (immediate).
2. Repair (habitual/pause for thought).
3. Review (time out to reassess, hours/days).
4. Research (systematic, focused over weeks/months).
5. Retheorize and reformulate (abstract, rigorous, over months/years).

This hierarchy suggests that reflecting on past events over a longer time span, described in eras 4 and 5, would produce diverse and very useful results. The separate iterations of reflection each enable a different kind of understanding to be made explicit. Orange, Burke, and Cushman (n.d.) suggest that each iteration "progressively refines and enhances the individual's knowledge and expertise through reflection." This staged reflection can also identify recurrent issues and problems. Therefore, the value of using a variety of modes and levels of reflection cannot be stressed too strongly.

Challenges for Bonita

The main challenges for the adult learning coach supporting Bonita will be in relation to those times of uncertainty that are inevitable as she establishes herself in her new, senior role. Particular attention will need to be paid to the development of her relationship with Ken. This is pivotal to her success and to her sense of self-efficacy. The coach may need to encourage Bonita to revisit her values many times in order to build authenticity and confidence that what she is doing is right.

It should be fairly easy to convince Bonita of the value of reflection, especially since she will already begin to see the results from the "Identifying Life Chapters" exercise. Encouraging her to keep a journal to reflect on her leadership style and opportunities plus any conflict situations will be crucial to her success. Ken appears to be the main obstacle here: Initially Bonita will need to work on proving herself to him, but definitely not by conceding her values and integrity, nor by compromising her collaborative style.

Bonita will also need to put very clear work-life balance plans in action and include contingency arrangements for children's illness and so on. Having a specific action plan to set this course of actions in place should help in this respect, not least by relaying to the family the importance of these practical arrangements in the overall plan.

The Case of Bob

Potential Issues

Like Bonita, Bob is in transition. The company of which he is CEO is undergoing a merger, plus, at 58 years old, Bob may be approaching the late adult transition described by Levinson (1978). Bob will need to learn how to lead a successful merger. He may not be able to rely on his existing style of leadership. For example, previously Bob has relied very much on personal charisma to lead his organization. This may not be his best ally now. It will be necessary, through coaching, to explore what strengths he has and how these can be marshaled in order to ensure success. This exploration may reveal some weaknesses that will need to be addressed. He tends to have very clear and definite views in relation to the organization. He does not share Bonita's collaborative style, for instance, and fails to take on board the perspectives of others. This "persuade or purge" style of leadership may not work during the merger. However, Bob is good at using people to get things done and there may well be an opportunity to capitalize on this strength and to delegate to someone with a different, more collaborative style.

Bob's interest in the results that coaching has achieved for others is an area to explore with him in order to pinpoint what has impressed him. This suggests that Bob is results oriented, and the danger is that he may only be looking for bottom-line results.

The main goal for Bob is to negotiate a productive merger, and it will be necessary to explore with him what he means by "productive" and to consider what success looks like for him. His longer-term goal is to leave the business running perfectly. Any coach would also want to investigate what "perfect" means to Bob and why this is so important.

Adult Learning Approach

Identify Life Chapters

The explanation of the "Identifying Life Chapters" process will need to be different for Bob. Whereas Bonita may have been interested in developing the chapters for her own learning, the emphasis for Bob will need to be more instrumental and focus on uncovering good practices that may be of benefit during the merger. He will need to see the practical importance of such an exercise.

The use of the life chapters exercise, however, is key for Bob, and preferable to other more psychometric assessment tools, because it will provide insight into how his priorities might have changed over time. Bob will be approaching the late adult transition, as described by Levinson (1978, p. 35), and it might be that the goal to leave a perfect business when he retires is linked to this phase in his life course. Levinson suggests that the task for a man entering this phase is to sustain his youthfulness in a new form appropriate to late adulthood. So, rather than needing to prove that he is as good as he has always been by seeking perfection, perhaps there are other options available. The use of the life story facilitates a discussion of life phases and the differences between the drivers of the younger man and the needs of the older man.

"Identifying Life Chapters" also enables the discussion of values and of life and project-level goals. Questions that could arise from these conversations might include: What is still valuable to Bob? What if he can't leave the business "perfect"? What would an acceptable compromise look like? What would be unacceptable?

Make Sense of Transitions
The "Making Sense of Transitions" exercise will again help Bob to explore continuity and congruence in his life and make it easier for him to see what he values and what is important to him. The exercise will help uncover his motivation. Is his desire for perfection, for instance, linked to a need for respect? Does uncertainty or insecurity about the future underpin his uncompromising approach? The coach would need to tease out the answers to these questions, as well as examine the skills and attributes that Bob used previously that would be useful in the current situation, and also explore what might not work now.

It might be advantageous also, to use an appreciative inquiry (AI) approach (Cooperrider & Whitney, 2003). Appreciative inquiry is very much in tune with andragogical principles; it is based on valuing prior experience and best practice—looking at what has gone right, rather than what has gone wrong. The AI process begins by asking people to tell stories about their successful experiences and to relate these stories to their dreams for the future. With Bob's level of experience this would be a valuable method of exploring development needs.

Plan, Act, and Consider
Once motivation and values have been clarified, the speedy development of an action plan for Bob will be important. He will want to see or feel some results fairly quickly.

If Bob's goal is to negotiate a productive merger, it will be necessary to help him to map out how he could achieve this. Having first explored what "productive" means for him, and bearing in mind the need for quick, practical results, the plan for negotiating a productive merger might involve these initial three steps:

1. *Information gathering.* Bob would need to think about what information he needs to gather in order to ensure merger success. Are there pieces of information missing that would help the process?

2. *Identifying helpful people.* Part of the plan might be to include identifying the people he needs to help him make the merger a success. He has a history of using people to help him achieve his aims. In this case perhaps he could delegate some of the merger detail to someone with a more collaborative communication style, and thus achieve his aims. This would have two purposes: first to help him achieve his aim, and second to help him begin to see that other people have strengths that he can capitalize on, and therefore points of view that may be useful to augment his own vision.

3. *Keeping a logbook.* Instead of a reflective journal, which suits Bonita well, I would probably ask Bob to keep a log of merger processes and outcomes to consider at our meetings. This will begin the reflective process for Bob, but calling it a log will make it appear more systematic and businesslike to him.

In future coaching sessions, because Bob is not being expected to spend time reflecting in depth in his logbook, it will be necessary to provide time and space for this to happen in the session. Bob is probably an Activist or a Pragmatist (Honey & Mumford, 2000) and so will need encouragement to recognize the value of reflecting, theorizing, and planning. Using the logbook we would undertake a structured debrief, formulating checklists for further action, where necessary. This should meet Bob's learning style while at the same time strengthening his reflective and theorizing capability.

Bob has demonstrated his ability to create a vision for the organization, and so I would also use scenario planning with him. Scenario planning provides descriptive narratives of plausible alternative futures (van der Heijden, 1998). It does not predict the future, but does provide a safe platform for formulating policies and contingency plans that are flexible and pragmatic. They are a valuable mode of learning that will help Bob to think critically and creatively about the merger. I would ask him to envisage, for example, three scenarios: one where the merger, or a crucial meeting or other significant event related to the merger, had gone supremely well, beyond expectations; one where it had gone hopelessly wrong; and one where the outcome was acceptable. We would then explore these three scenarios in some depth, looking at cause and effect, strengths and weaknesses of parties involved, and so on.

Scenario planning and appreciative inquiry are complementary approaches that are constructivist, nonthreatening, and results oriented.

Track and Terminate

At future meetings with Bob it will be vital to monitor the actions detailed in the action plan.

Maintaining Bob's commitment to goals should not be a problem once these have been seen to be based on his values. The logbook that Bob will keep will provide a way for him to track his own progress.

I would anticipate working with Bob until he is confident that the merger is going to be successful. As he becomes more skilled at structured reflection and begins to enjoy the coaching process, I would like to think that he would begin to coach himself. There is also the possibility that he might like to mentor others in the organization, so that his knowledge is not lost in his retirement.

I would hope to have follow-up sessions with Bob in order to support his arrangements for leaving the business at retirement, but suspect that he would consider the work finished at the completion of the merger. I anticipate that he would want to see a real bottom-line benefit were coaching to continue.

Challenges for Bob

The main challenges for the adult learning coach supporting Bob will be in encouraging Bob to reflect critically on his own experience. Where people have closed their minds to other possibilities from an early age, as Bob appears to have done, it is particularly difficult to help them reflect and see things from different perspectives. Getting Bob to consider whether the leadership style that has stood him in good stead in his earlier career will do so again in this situation may be difficult. I would therefore want to use some of the tools that Mezirow (1990) advocates in order to help Bob to look at this experience in different ways. It may be ambitious to expect the fundamental changes that come via perspective transformation, but I feel that Bob's goals may be realized if only some progress can be made toward this.

Another challenge will be in maintaining Bob's motivation for coaching. It is hoped that this will be achieved by focusing on immediate goals and bringing a sense of instrumentality and urgency to the encounter. The success in this relationship will also depend on ensuring that Bob's goals are really relevant to him and making visible progress toward them.

CONCLUSION

Adult learning has emerged from psychology, not as a distinct discipline, but as a field of application. Similarly, coaching relies on approaches from a number of other disciplines and these approaches would need to be incorporated into the coaching program in order for it to be a fully effective, rounded coaching program. However, an attempt has been made in this chapter to distinguish a particular approach to coaching informed by theories of adult learning.

Consequently, the chapter has explored Bonita's and Bob's coaching experiences largely from the perspective of adult learning. The influential theory of andragogy popularized by Knowles was taken as a starting point for the elaboration of an adult learning (informed) framework for coaching. The chapter highlights that there is already considerable synergy between andragogy and coaching, and the influences of adult learning theories can be seen clearly in current coaching practice.

The IMPACT framework for coaching includes two initial exercises that provide clients with the opportunity to explore their previous life experiences through life chapters and to reflect on continuity and congruence in order to inform their values and project goals. The Kolb learning cycle provides a framework to develop a coaching process that closely follows adult learning principles and practices.

REFERENCES

Bandura, A. (1994). Self-efficacy. In V. S. Ramachaudran (Ed.), *Encyclopedia of human behavior* (Vol. 4, pp. 71–81). New York: Academic Press. Reprinted in H. Friedman (Ed.), *Encyclopedia of mental health*. San Diego: Academic Press, 1998. Accessed February 27, 2005, at www.emory.edu/EDUCATION/mfp/BanEncy.html.

Bolton, G. (2001). *Reflective practice: Writing and professional development*. London: Paul Chapman Publishing.

Boud, D., Cohen, R., & Walker, D. (1994) *Using experience for learning*. Buckingham, England: SRHE and Open University Press.

Brookfield, S. (1986). *Understanding and facilitating adult learning.* Buckingham, England: Open University Press.

Cooperrider, D., & Whitney, D. (2003). *Appreciative inquiry.* Bedford Heights, OH: Lakeshore Communications.

Cox, E. (2005). Adult learners learning from experience: Using a reflective practice model to support work-based learning. *Reflective Practice, 6*(3), 459–472.

Cranton, P. (1994). *Understanding and promoting transformative learning: A guide for educators of adults.* San Francisco: Jossey-Bass.

Cranton, P. (1996). *Professional development as transformative learning.* San Francisco: Jossey-Bass.

Csikszentmihalyi, M. (1997). *Living well.* London: Orion Publishing.

Dewey, J. (1933). *How we think.* New York: Heath.

Dewey, J. (1963). *Experience and education.* New York: Collier.

Erikson, E. (1959). *Identity and the life cycle.* New York: International Universities Press; reprinted, New York: W. W. Norton, 1980.

Fahrenkamp, P. (2001). Developing coaching in a consulting context. In L. West & M. Milan (Eds.), *The reflecting glass.* London: Palgrave.

Flaherty, J. (1999). *Coaching: Evoking excellence in others.* Oxford: Butterworth Heinemann.

Freire, P. (1974). *Education for critical consciousness* (M. B. Ramos, L. Bigwood, & M. Marshall, Trans.). London: Sheed-Ward.

Goodson, I. (1998) Storying the self. In W. Pinar (Ed.), *Curriculum: towards new identities.* London: Taylor & Francis.

Grant, A. (2003). The impact of life coaching on goal attainment, metacognition and mental health. *Social Behaviour and Personality, 31*(3), 253–264.

Griffiths, M., & Tann, S. (1991). Ripples in the reflection. In P. Lomax (Ed.), *Managing better schools and colleges: The action research way*, Clevedon, England: Multilingual Matters.

Gusdorf, G. (1980). Conditions and limits of autobiography (J. Olney, Trans.). In J. Olney (Ed.), *Autobiography: Essays theoretical and critical* (pp. 28–48). Princeton, NJ: Princeton University Press.

Hiemstra, R., & Sisco, B. (1990). *Individualizing instruction: Making learning personal, empowering, and successful.* San Francisco: Jossey-Bass.

Honey, P., & Mumford, A. (1992). *The manual of learning styles.* Maidenhead, UK: Peter Honey.

Honey, P., & Mumford, A. (2000). *The learning styles questionnaire: 80 item version.* Peter Honey Publications. Accessed February 13, 2005, at http://www.peterhoney.com/product/23.

Hopson, B. (1986). Transition: Understanding and managing personal change. In Herbert, M. (Ed.), *Psychology for social workers.* London: British Psychological Society and Macmillan.

Houston, J. (1987) *The search for the beloved: Journey in sacred psychology.* Los Angeles: J. P. Tarcher.

Hudson, F. (1999). *The handbook of coaching.* San Francisco: Jossey-Bass.

Hudson, F., & McLean, P. (2001). *LifeLaunch.* Santa Barbara, CA: Hudson Institute Press.

Ibarra, H., & Lineback, K. (2005) What's your story. *Harvard Business Review*, January 2005, 65–71.

Jackson, P. (2004). Understanding the experience of experience: A practical model of reflective practice for coaching. *International Journal of Evidence Based Coaching and Mentoring*, 2(1), 57–67.

Karpiak, I. (2000). Writing our life: Adult learning and teaching through autobiography. *Canadian Journal of University Continuing Education*, 26(1), 31–50.

Kegan, R. (1994). *In over our heads: The mental demands of modern life.* Cambridge, MA: Harvard University Press.

Kline, N. (1999). *Time to think.* London: Ward Lock.

Knowles, M. (1978). *The adult learner: A neglected species.* Houston, TX: Gulf Publishing Company.

Knowles, M. (1980). *The modern practice of adult education: From pedagogy to andragogy.* Englewood Cliffs, NJ: Prentice Hall/Cambridge.

Knowles, M., Holton, E. F., & Swanson, R. A. (1998). *The adult learner* (5th ed.). Houston, TX: Gulf Publishing Company.

Kolb, D. A. (1976). *The learning style inventory: Technical manual.* Boston: McBer.

Kolb, D. A. (1984). *Experiential learning: Experience as the source of learning and development.* Englewood Cliffs, NJ: Prentice Hall.

Kolb, D. A., & Fry, R. (1975). Toward an applied theory of experiential learning. In C. Cooper (Ed.), *Theories of group process.* London: Wiley.

Levinson, D. (1978). *The seasons of a man's life.* New York: Ballantine Books.

Levinson, D. (1996). *The seasons of a woman's life.* New York: Alfred A. Knopf.

Lewin, K. (1951). *Field theory in social science: Selected theoretical papers.* D. Cartwright (Ed.). New York: Harper & Row.

Locke, E. (1996). Motivation through conscious goal setting. *Applied & Preventive Psychology*, 5, 117–124.

Maslow, A. (1998). *Toward a psychology of being* (3rd ed.). R. J. Lowry (Ed.). New York: Wiley.

McKenna, E. (2000). *Business psychology and organisational behaviour.* Hove, England: Psychology Press.

Merriam, S. (2004). The role of cognitive development in Mezirow's transformational learning theory. *Adult Education Quarterly*, 55(1), 60–68.

Merriam, S., & Caffarella, R. (1999). *Learning in adulthood.* San Francisco: Jossey-Bass.

Mezirow, J. (1990). *Fostering critical reflection in adulthood: A guide to transformative and emancipatory learning.* San Francisco: Jossey-Bass.

Mezirow, J. (1991). *Transformative dimensions of adult learning.* San Francisco: Jossey-Bass.

Olney, J. (1980). Autobiography and the cultural moment: A thematic, historical and bibliographical introduction. In J. Olney (Ed.), *Autobiography: Essays theoretical and critical* (pp. 3–27). Princeton, NJ: Princeton University Press.

Orange, G., Burke, A., & Cushman, M. (n.d.). *An approach to support reflection and organisation learning within the UK construction industry.* Accessed February 25, 2005, at http://is.lse.ac.uk/b-hive/pdf/bitworld.pdf.

Pajares, F. (2002). *Overview of social cognitive theory and of self-efficacy.* Accessed February 25, 2005, at www.emory.edu/EDUCATION/mfp/eff.html.

Rachal, J. (2002). Andragogy's detectives: A critique of the present and a proposal for the future. *Adult Education Quarterly, 52*(3), 210–227.

Rogers, J. (2004). *Coaching skills.* Maidenhead, UK: Open University Press.

Schön, D. (1987). *Educating the reflective practitioner.* San Francisco: Jossey-Bass.

Scott, S. (2002). *Fierce Conversations.* London: Judy Piatkus (Publishers) Ltd.

Smith, J. & Spurling, A. (2001). *Understanding motivation for lifelong learning.* Leicester, UK: National Institute of Adult and Continuing Education (NIACE).

Tennant, M. & Pogson, P. (1995). *Learning and change in the adult years.* San Francisco: Wiley.

Thorpe, K. (2004). Reflective learning journals: From concept to practice, *Reflective Practice, 5*(3), 327–343.

van der Heijden, K. (1998). *Scenarios—The art of strategic conversation.* London: Wiley.

Vroom, V. (1964). *Work and motivation.* New York: Wiley.

West, L., & Milan, M. (Eds.) (2001). *The reflecting glass.* London: Palgrave.

Whitmore, J. (1996). *Coaching for performance.* London: Nicholas Brealey.

Whitworth, L., Kimsey-House, H., & Sandahl, P. (1998). *Co-active coaching.* Palo Alto, CA: Davies-Black Publishing.

CHAPTER 8

Positive Psychology: The Science at the Heart of Coaching

CAROL KAUFFMAN

WHAT YOU WILL understand by the end of this chapter is how the new field of positive psychology provides a robust theoretical and empirical base for the artful practice of life and executive coaching. But first, what exactly is positive psychology, and how is it different from business as usual? Through the years, traditional psychology has focused on ways to help make ill people better by finding clinically valid and empirically supported methods to help fix things that are wrong with them. The mission of positive psychology is to develop sound theories of optimal functioning and to find empirically supported ways to improve the lives of ordinary and extraordinary people.

In this chapter the author will present a number of emerging trends in positive psychology theory and research and explore their applications to coaching. I'll walk you through studies of positive emotion, flow (accessing the zone), hope therapy, and classification of strengths. Each set of studies offers a rich resource of knowledge that can be mined for potential coaching interventions. The chapter is not an overarching perspective on the coaching process, as this is described in other chapters

Author note: The author wants to express her gratitude to James Pawelski and Martin Seligman for their profound contribution to this paper. Particular thanks to Dr. Pawelski for many lively discussions and active participation in an early outline of this paper. Dr. Seligman's mentoring was a crucial inspiration for this chapter. His course in Authentic Happiness Coaching was the springboard for my thinking about positive psychology coaching and provided the context for my learning and practicing the AHC exercises described here. The author would like to dedicate this chapter to the memory of our beloved C. R. Snyder.

in this volume. Instead the focus is more narrow as we examine primary and secondary source material in positive psychology and invite coach practitioners to integrate what they learn into their ongoing professional practices. One model of applied positive psychology, Authentic Happiness Coaching (AHC), developed by the former president of the American Psychological Association and the father of positive psychology, Dr. Martin Seligman, will be described in detail. A process-coaching application of AHC with two clients follows.

The heart of positive psychology, like coaching, lies in the practitioner's choice to shift attention away from pathology and pain and direct it toward a clear-eyed concentration on strength, vision, and dreams. Despite this intent, many coaches are still steeped in the culture of therapy and can find it difficult to transcend the medical model (Williams & Davis, 2002). A review of the executive coaching literature by Kauffman and Scouler (2004) suggests that practitioners still carry a deficit-conflict perspective of clients even when working with high-level executives. One aspect of this challenge is that most psychological language and nearly all assessment tools are firmly grounded in the mission of identifying pathology and problems. As a result we are steeped in a medical model culture and often aren't aware of how it forms the background of our thinking. The ramifications of this are enormous in terms of what issues are framed, how clients are assessed and what interventions are selected.

An explicitly positive psychology framework suggests that a language of strength and vision rather than weakness and pain be the firm foundation upon which the coaching work rests. Coaches with a positive psychology orientation also develop a different internal decision tree when selecting what material to follow, what to let pass by, and what cause-effect sequences to focus on. In essence, the clinician is trained to follow the trail of tears. If someone is dissatisfied with life, for example, a coach needs to resist the inclination to immediately hone in on client skill deficits or automatically search for signs of depression, anxiety, or emotional conflict as the true cause of the client's challenge. Instead coaches need to get their bearings by attending to how clients can use their existing strengths to identify their vision of what they want and turn it into reality. To follow this new train of thought, one follows different signposts and landmarks. In essence, coaches shift attention from what causes and drives pain to what energizes and pulls people forward. They follow the trail of dreams.

From the outset, I must emphasize that positive psychology is not interested in pretending all people are paragons of virtue, maturity, and mental health. As you will see, for example, too much "positivity" isn't good for you or your work team's level of performance (Fredrickson & Losada, 2005). We are interested in disseminating information that offers theoretical and empirical support to the coaching orientation of attending to client wholeness and strength. Of course pathology exists, but we tend to focus upon it exclusively. To illustrate this kind of shift, you may recall the famous gestalt picture of a black vase on a white background. When you reverse focus and concentrate on the background (instead of the vase), you see two profiles facing one another. One perception isn't real and the other false, or a defense; both are equally true and each informs the other. Without the vase all you have is pale blankness, but if you zoom in and see only the vase, you lose perspective and imagine all is darkness. Coaches and clinicians need to learn how to shift attention back and forth as necessary (Lopez, Snyder, and Rasmussen, 2003). New research is even suggesting there is an optimal ratio of balance of how much you zoom in on the positive or negative (described below; Frederickson and Losada, 2005).

An additional challenge coaches face is describing how and why coaching is effective. Often testimonials and anecdotal evidence are used to support their assertions. Practitioners are often hard-pressed to have access or find theoretical, scientific, or empirical explanations to support their assertions of coaching effectiveness. The body of positive psychology research, however, indicates that a coaching orientation is an effective and valid perspective. *It is our belief that positive psychology theory and research will provide the scientific legs upon which the field of coaching can firmly stand.*

Throughout the twentieth century psychology developed an extensive technology to measure and address human pathology. There is now in the twenty-first century a movement toward developing equally robust assessment tools, interventions, and research methods to study human strengths and virtues. Lopez and Snyder (2003), for example, have compiled a handbook of psychometrically robust assessments of such "soft" phenomena as hope, optimism, and spirituality. Ed Diener, Chris Peterson, Martin Seligman, and others have also developed standardized, reliable, and valid measures of levels of well-being, strengths, approaches to happiness, life satisfaction, and more (see http://authentic happiness.org). As a result we can now "diagnose" strengths, hope, optimism, and love in as precise and reliable ways as we measure anxiety or depression. Effectiveness studies of positive therapy (Irving et al. 2004) and positive psychology-based coaching are showing them to be very effective with sustainable impact (Seligman, Steen, Park, & Peterson, 2005).

RESEARCH EVIDENCE FROM POSITIVE PSYCHOLOGY FOR COACHING

We now explore positive psychology research in four areas. For each one I'll describe some of the main concepts, offer a sample of research studies, and suggest possible coaching applications. The first area of theory/research is positive emotion and the surprisingly powerful role it plays in personal and professional effectiveness. Second I present the concept of "flow," the conditions that foster it and how coaches might use this information. Third I give a short overview of the components of hope and the effectiveness of hope therapy. Last is a description of the classification of strengths, the Values in Action survey (or as some have dubbed it, the "unDSM").

WHAT ARE POSITIVE EMOTIONS GOOD FOR?: PASSING THE "SO WHAT" TEST

Positive psychology focuses on understanding how positive emotions work. It is quite reasonable to wonder, why bother? After all, many clients, particularly corporations, are going to want something that will impact the bottom line—why would they pay for coaching to increase happiness? The answer to this question is found in several streams of research in positive psychology. Fredrickson (2001, 2002) has developed an empirically supported theory that shows how positive emotions help us thrive. Her work examines the powerful day-to-day benefits of positive emotion.

Until now, most psychological research has focused on negative emotion, how we cope or overcome fear, stress, anger, sadness, disgust, and so on. Exploration of the positive emotions such as: joy, love, awe, gratitude, hope, or desire is now in progress. To begin, it seems clear that positive and negative emotions have very different purposes in our lives. Negative ones tend to ensure survival by galvanizing people into action when faced with life-and-death challenges. At those moments success requires an individual to have a narrow and sharp focus on the problem that must be solved quickly. In contrast, Fredrickson's research shows that positive emotions boost other psychological functions. For example, they empower individuals to open up their focus of attention, to "widen the lens" and see the big picture.

A series of studies supports Fredrickson's theory that positive emotions serve to "broaden and build" access to personal competencies (Fredrickson, 2001; Fredrickson & Branigan, 2005). The research shows it is possible to precisely measure how positive emotions "broaden people's momentary thought-action repertoires and build their enduring personal resources, ranging from physical and intellectual resources to social and psychological resources" (Fredrickson, 2001; Fredrickson & Branigan, 2005). In the physical realm, positive emotions have been shown to: increase immune function, improve resilience to adversity, reduce inflammatory responses to stress, increase resistance to rhinoviruses, lower cortisol, and impact brain symmetry, and a number of studies show they predict longevity (see Fredrickson and Losada, 2005).

Positive emotions are central to psychological flourishing and have been found to have a significant impact on increasing intuition and creativity, and widening scope of attention.

They increase our capacity to use multiple social, cognitive, and affective resources and to take in an integrated long-term perspective—crucial skills in today's complex world. With a moment's reflection it becomes clear; positive emotions foster the very kinds of skills corporations want in their leadership teams and that our coaching clients would like to build in themselves. For example, positive priming of one's emotions directly translates into increasing cognitive flexibility, speed, and accuracy. This pattern has been shown throughout the developmental spectrum, starting with preschool. One study (Isen, Rosenzweig, & Young, 1991) compared how quickly and accurately groups of internists made diagnoses of a patient with complex liver disease. Those primed to feel good (with a small gift of candy!) showed more flexible thinking and made accurate diagnoses more quickly than those primed to think humanistic thoughts or those not primed at all. Positive priming of one's emotions directly translates into increasing cognitive flexibility, speed, and accuracy.

Another series of studies has shown that positive emotions have a powerful impact on how well work teams function and how this in turn has a direct impact on profitability. Losada (1999) studied 60 business teams and found that positive emotion played a primary role in how well the teams functioned. During strategy meetings, every statement was coded, and the ratio of positive (approving/supportive) to negative (disapproving/critical) was calculated. At the same time the positivity ratio of the 60 teams divided them into high, medium, or low performance in terms of profitability, customer satisfaction, and performance evaluations. The results are remarkably strong and show that the positivity/negativity ratio was the key variable that differentiated team performance. High-performance teams had a ratio of about 3 to 1 (three positive emotion or support statements for every negative emotion or disapproving/critical statement). The lower the positivity ratio the lower the level of function and effectiveness of the team.

When the researchers assessed the moment-to-moment group interactions, they found the high-performance teams had a much wider range of behavior. Their discussions were more fluid and flexible. While there were more positive comments, there were strong criticisms and challenges as well. When negativity occurs in the context of high amounts of support and approval (e.g., ratio of 2.9:1) workers bounced back quickly after being criticized (Losada & Heaphy, 2004). In fact, pointing out problems or challenges served to ignite performance and inspire the executives to think with greater clarity and effectiveness. In essence, these strategy teams had the "wider behavioral repertoire" that Fredrickson's theory would predict. In the groups where the positive/negative ratio was under 3:1 there was less resiliency and a narrower range of behavior. In particular, after negative comments, people seemed to lose creativity and authenticity.

The Losada research also refutes the notion that one should be positive all the time. When people get *really* positive team performance levels fall. It seems that if everyone is supportive and approving without a healthy balance of criticism (e.g., real reactions) the behavior range is constricted, just as was found in the highly negative groups. According to Fredrickson and Losada (2005) there is an upper limit of positivity. If the ratio of positive to negative comments goes above about 12:1 (11.6:1) behavior seems rigid and unresponsive. This is true with groups as well as with individuals. If one reflects on this information the implications for coaches are enormous. First, it suggests an ideal of being positive, and second a clear limit on how positive to be; in other words, you need enough sugar, but not so much as to make the relationship unpalatable.

Fredrickson examined positivity ratios with individuals and found very similar results. When she examined students' month-long diaries, the positive/negative ratio seemed to differentiate those who were languishing from those who were flourishing. Subjects whose diaries showed an average ratio of 3.2:1 (a bit above the 3:1 ratio) or higher were doing much better than those at 2.3:1 or below. What bears notice is that the difference between those who are flourishing and those who are languishing was very stable, but quite small; sometimes just a couple of positive experiences a day swings the balance. This has important ramifications for life coaching, as it suggests that just a bit more positive experience leads to a very different quality of life. Research on couples found similar results. Studies used the positive/negative affect quality to predict (on the basis of three minutes of observation) which newlyweds would divorce (Gottman, 1994).

This confluence of data supports the idea that positive emotion plays a crucial role in life. While negative emotions serve to quickly negotiate life/death challenges, positive emotions are interconnected with the kinds of competence needed a majority of the time. This work also has enormous ramifications for executive coaches, as it shows the importance of positive emotion and also the importance of grounded, critical thinking, and the most ideal ratio between the two. As such it provides an empirical, theoretically grounded model for optimal performance that can guide executive coaches on how to assist companies in management consultation, communication, and training.

In addition, it provides compelling, scientifically informed rationale with empirical support for why coaching, which clients often describe as a joyful experience, might have a very positive impact.

ROYAL ROADS TO HAPPINESS

The key question examined here is: what makes people happy, and is there a happiness "set point"? This is a basic research question that has important implications for coaching. Csikszentmihalyi (1990) described happiness as very much in one's personal control, "a condition that must be prepared for, cultivated, and defended privately by each person," while others suggest it's inborn.

A series of national and international studies collected data on hundreds of thousands of subjects in order to examine what makes people happy. Ed Diener (2000) has pioneered the study of "subjective well-being" and examined national norms, comparisons among countries, different professions, and so on. Mihalyi Csikszentmihalyi has also been exploring this issue for more than 30 years with thousands of subjects from all over the world. Together these two research traditions give us a fairly good idea of the contours and correlates of happiness. They've explored how happiness is (or is not) associated with macrosocial factors, genetics, chance, personality, behavior, and many other variables.

Implicit in the research are possible avenues, or even "royal roads," to increased well-being. Research shows that our automatic assumptions of what brings happiness are often incorrect. For example, in contrast to the popular belief that attaining the American dream of financial success will make you feel good, this belief is not strongly associated with happiness. In fact, the reverse is often found, as in the case of lottery winners (Brickman, Coates, & Janoff-Bulman, 1978). Diener (2000) and Csikszentmihalyi and Hunter (2003) found clear correlations between a sense of well-being and having one's survival and safety needs met, but beyond that there is a surprisingly low correlation. The usual pattern shows us that jumps in success have a short-lived impact that wears off as individuals acclimate to their new possessions or positions. This phenomenon leads to what has been called the "hedonic treadmill." Some studies indicate there is a negative relationship between materialism and happiness. For example, when you control for preexisting cheerfulness and parental income, having monetary reward as a primary goal has a negative effect on satisfaction with family life, friendships, and one's job (Nickerson, Schwartz, Diener, & Kahneman, 2003).

People also assume that happiness is a response to what happens in life, such as getting a great job or finding or losing a spouse. While obviously big events do have an impact, if you study people over time, they usually return to their preexisting level of happiness (or unhappiness) leveling off after joy and rising up after sorrow. This leads us to a core issue: can one's long-term sense of well-being be significantly increased or are we limited by how far we can rise? Diener (2000) suggests that people have a happiness set point, similar to the phenomenon of a weight set point. Events may shift one's level of emotional well-being, but other homeostatic forces pull one back over time. Fujita & Diener (2005) examined this with life satisfaction, and about one-fourth of the study participants made significant shifts over 17 years; 10 percent shifted very significantly. Some suggest that happiness might be hardwired in, but further exploration challenges this notion. Studies of subjective well-being of identical twins show, however, that only about half of the variation of happiness seems to be based on genes (Lykken & Tellegen, 1996). Longitudinal studies show that over a two-year period, happiness seems to have a stable set point. However, if you widen the timeline and study people over four years, there is far greater variation (Csikszentmihalyi & Hunter, 2003). These research programs on normal populations suggest that over the short run people do have a tendency toward a set point of happiness, but if you study them over time there can be significant shifts. Other authors suggest that since external factors (events, success, etc.) are not the key to understanding variation in a person's happiness, we should focus instead on internal ones. In other words, it isn't what happens to people; it's how they construct and interpret those events (Schwarz & Strack, 1999). In light of the hedonic treadmill, for example, it might not be what you have that matters, but how mindfully you experience it.

IMPLICATIONS FOR COACHING

The research on what does and does not lead to happiness has significant implications for coaching. First, it suggests that there is a role coaching can play to help people make upward shifts in their happiness set points. Second, remembering Frederickson's diary studies, very small increases in positive emotion can tilt the overall balance and lead to significant differences in the extent to which people flourish or languish. Third, the studies have implications for understanding the ephemeral impact of success and the so-called American dream. This last point bears a moment's reflection. What often surprises newcomers to coaching is that goal setting in coaching is often less tangible and concrete-goal driven than outsiders presume. Whitworth, Kimsey-House, and Sandahl's (1998) coaching text suggests that one always balance the client's agenda with a larger view of fulfillment that keeps an awareness of the alignment of the client's vision and values. A sweep through the research in positive psychology suggests that the coaching goals of "furthering the action and deepening the learning" are congruent with empirical findings on the nature of happiness.

WHEN TIME FLIES: FINDING FLOW AND A STATE OF GRACE

Emotional well-being is one road to what we think of as happiness. However, an equally powerful route is being "vitally engaged" in one's life and grounded in a sense of meaning and purpose (Nakamura and Csikszentmihalyi, 2003; Seligman, 2002). For the past 40 years Csikszentmihalyi has studied the capacity to be a full participant in life. He describes optimal living as "being fully involved with every detail of our lives, whether good or bad" (1990, p. 2). Thus, he sees the capacity to fully take in and metabolize one's experience as core to psychological health. Using the "experience sampling method" (buzzing people at random times to assess their state of mind) on thousands of subjects, he has carefully assessed what people actually feel at numerous points in a day. As a result, he has been able to establish the conditions that generate positive experience. His primary focus has become the "flow" state, or as the French translate it, *état de grâce* (Demontrond-Behr, Fournier, & Vaivre-Douret, 2004). The experience of flow is when you are able to be completely caught up in what you are doing and time flies.

Flow, or "being in the zone," is often described as an elusive, spiritual state that is available to only a chosen few. In contrast, Csikszentmihalyi has examined the conditions that make flow possible for ordinary, as well as extraordinary, individuals. His research shows that a number of conditions increase the likelihood of entering a flow state. Coaches can learn and then tailor this information to help clients find their own ways to access this high-performance state. What follows is a description of some of Csikszentmihalyi's "conditions of flow" accompanied by examples of how to apply the information to coaching or peak performance training.

Imagine you are coaching a client—an executive, or an athlete—who is doing well, but wants to move toward higher performance. What can help?

- *Clear and immediate feedback.* Feedback keeps the performer centered in reality. To keep at peak performance one needs to know how one is doing in order to meet the demands being faced (e.g. racers knowing their split times). However, feedback isn't necessarily external; *inner clarity* seems crucial. For example, you hear athletes describe their capacity to self-reflect and incorporate performance feedback as they are in the midst of a game. *I could feel if it was right. . . . It's hard to explain. . . . I knew I had made the right move* (Demontrond-Behr et al., 2004).
- *Absence of self-consciousness.* In a state of flow the individual is so fully engaged in the performance that he or she can let go of "over thinking and over trying" (Jackson, 2003). Exercises to increase mindful focus on the present and detaching from the outcome may help athletes or performers transcend themselves. Clients report things like: *I don't know how I did it, I just did it.* Or: *I let go of winning and just went for it.*
- *Merging action and awareness.* A coach can help the client manage the dialectical tension between transcending the moment and also being completely aware of and flexibly responding to new information coming in at the periphery (Kauffman, 2005b). *It's like blinders that come and go when I need them. My focus opens up to absorb what's happening, then narrows back down.*
- *Sense of control.* In any challenge there are elements one can control and elements one cannot. Help clients to focus clearly on the first and defocus from the last. A motto the author asks clients to repeat regularly, particularly when facing overwhelming challenge, is: *I'm not in control of my destiny but I AM in control of my probabilities* (Kauffman, in press).
- *Intrinsic motivation/autotelic experience.* Flow comes when doing what you want. If it isn't automatically present in a task, help clients find aspects of the challenge that are intrinsically rewarding. A key intervention (the Authentic Happiness Coaching model, described later) is helping the client identify signature strengths and find new ways to use them in the service of the task (Seligman, Steen, et al., 2005).
- *Balance skills and challenge.* The optimal match between having a high level of skill and a high task demand is one of the crucial aspects that makes flow possible. When the balance is off you see the following: High challenge with low skill = anxiety; low challenge with high skill = relaxation/boredom; low challenge with low skill = apathy (Nakamura & Csikszentmihalyi, 2002). To coach for flow, help clients find the right balance by either increasing skill level or decreasing challenge. The coach can help clients decrease

challenge by breaking the task into smaller pieces and building skills until they feel equipped to handle the task at hand. Alternatively, if the client is feeling untapped or bored, the coach can help the client find ways to make the task harder and expand the client's vision of the size and scope of the project at hand (Kauffman, 2004b).

- *Time transformation.* When in a flow state time transforms. For example, during a fencing match, a flow state heightens perception and the foils seem to move more slowly. Alternatively, a flow experience can feel like a wrinkle in time—hours go by in what feels like minutes. This one is hard to coach in a direct way, although laser-like visualization techniques can help build the perception skills. You can also have clients intensely recall past experiences of their own peak flow states to see if it becomes easier for them to replicate and access this state-dependent experience.

Those who apply Csikszentmihalyi's work to coaching executives, athletes, and performers also describe how important it is to adjust the external environment to support and enhance flow (Jackson, 2003). Jackson also emphasizes how the interpersonal environment is an important, if not crucial, factor in fostering flow during athletic or performance situation. The Frederickson and Losada work described above would support the idea that there probably is an ideal combination of encouragement and criticism/challenge that facilitates optimal performance. Sports psychologists also describe the importance of group support (Demontrond-Behr et al., 2004). Kauffman (2004a) emphasizes that multimodal resource training helps clients keep their foundation skills strong and increases their chances to have sustained flow states and "tap into turbo" for peak performance bursts. Clearly, the concept of flow and engagement has many potential applications that coaches can harness in their work.

Triumph of Hope Based in Reality

A key area that has received significant attention from positive psychology is the experience of having hope. Many dozens of studies have provided empirical support for the crucial role that hope plays in a person's life. High-hope (vs. low-hope) individuals enjoy better physical health and have higher academic functioning, interpersonal effectiveness, athletic performance, psychosocial adjustment, capacity for emotional self-regulation, and superior abilities to face and overcome obstacles (Snyder, 2000). When the highly hopeful person's progress toward a goal is blocked he or she is able to search for and find other pathways to the goal and maintain a sense of agency (sense of being able to act). In contrast, those low in hope tend to become confused, avoidant or ineffective when they find themselves thwarted; see Snyder (2002) and Snyder & Lopez (2002) for reviews.

Snyder (2002) has developed one of the first empirically supported programs for an application of positive psychology, called hope therapy. Over the past 20 years he has developed a complex theory of hope; a reliable and valid test to measure it (Snyder et al., 1991); and empirically supported interventions that have been shown to improve hope in children, adolescents, adults, and elders (Wrobleski and Snyder, 2005). This semistructured or narrative approach is described in detail in Snyder (2002). While hope therapy works well on its own, it also can be joined to other interventions. A five-week hope training orientation program with clients on a wait list was shown to boost the effectiveness of subsequent psychotherapy regardless of whether it was behavioral or dynamic (Irving et al., 2004). When other psychological factors were held constant, it appears that increasing hopefulness, not the client's subjective well-being or level of coping skills, was a key reason for improvement.

Hope has two elements according to Snyder's theory, and both components can be strengthened by hope training. These are: pathways thinking and having a sense of agency. Pathways thinking means that when the first route you try is blocked, you can produce alternative routes to get to your destination. High-hope individuals can think flexibly and change or correct course as needed. Low-hope people are less flexible and a second or third pathway does not feel viable to them. Thus, coaching to increase a client's capacity to find alternate routes is a core component of having hope, which in turn sustains one's effort.

The second aspect of hope is to have agency, a sense one can reach desired goals. There are numerous ways to coach clients to greater efficacy, either by developing more precise and attainable goals or by helping them vividly recall past successes and solidify the cognitive/ affective state associated with their individualized sense of "I can-ness." High hope individuals have both multiple pathways thinking and a sense of agency. One without the other does not foster maximum success. High pathways with low agency can surface as the client feeling: I know what to do, but I don't think I can. Low pathways with high agency appear as: I feel strong and ready but don't know what to do. Hope training can teach and coach people to develop both components of hope.

The power hope has on performance can be startling. For example, one study with female track athletes found that hope was the number one predictor of race performance (Snyder, 2002). When the authors statistically held raw athletic ability constant, hope still accounted for 56 percent of the variation in how well the athletes raced. The implications of these studies are that coaches will be well served by learning techniques to help clients become more hopeful. In turn this can have significant impact on the clients' capacities to regroup when faced with difficulty and to feel more empowered.

Coaches may find Snyder's work sheds light on explanations for the perceived effectiveness of well-known coaching interventions that, while not based on psychological theory, are in fact supported by it. For example, one familiar coaching intervention is brainstorming. From the perspective of Snyder's work, brainstorming is a type of pathways training—for example, "Let's think of five ways to get there!" An additional common practice in coaching is the use of positive affirmation and visualization exercises. These may help clients build a clear self-perception of "I can," or a sense of agency.

The famous wheel of life or pillars exercise is another case in point (Whitworth, Kimsey-House, & Sandahl, 1998; Dean, 2004). For this the coach asks the client to identify a series of life domains (career development, relationships, leisure time, etc.). Then the client rates on a scale of one to ten how satisfied he is in that domain. For example, a client rates herself as a 4.0 in her satisfaction with use of leisure time. The coach asks the client to describe in detail what that aspect of life would look like if it were a 10 and if neither time nor money were an issue (10 might be going to the Cannes film festival, yachting, skiing the Alps). Then the coach asks (and brainstorms as necessary) what the client could do in the next six weeks to become a 4.5 (e.g., go to three movies or attend the local film festival, check out community boating, and/or, in season, sign up for ski lessons). One can see how this type of exercise, aided by brainstorming and clear visualization, could possibly foster both pathways and agency thinking, particularly when paired with accountability and occurring in the context of a warm coaching relationship.

"DIAGNOSING" STRENGTHS

Positive psychologists Christopher Peterson and Martin Seligman (2004) have developed a classification system of strengths called the Values in Action (VIA) strengths survey. The questionnaire measures human strengths in a consistent, reliable, and valid manner; to date it has been tested on hundreds of thousands of individuals. It has proven useful for researchers and coaches. It begins to create a clear way to identify strengths and serves as a foundation for psychology practitioners to reliably measure them, find ways to help individuals cultivate strengths, and have a way to assess changes over time. The Mayerson

Foundation has donated the VIA to the public domain, and it is available for free at http://authentichappiness.org.

The VIA classification of character strengths identifies six primary categories of strength (described as core virtues). Each of these has a number of subcategories, resulting in 24 potential signature strengths. After taking the test, individuals' strengths are ranked from the top five (signature strengths) to the least developed. Usually, coaches focus on clients' top strengths and help them harness these qualities. It is also possible to identify important less-developed strengths and bolster them.

The 24 strengths are organized by categories and subcategories:

1. *Wisdom and knowledge:* cognitive strengths related to accruing and using knowledge.
   - *Creativity:* thinking in novel, productive ways, with originality or ingenuity.
   - *Curiosity:* interest in experience for its own sake, openness to experience, finding things fascinating.
   - *Open-mindedness:* thinking things through, not jumping to conclusions, having good critical thinking and judgment.
   - *Love of learning:* enjoying learning and systematically organizing experience; also surfaces as love of teaching others.
   - *Perspective:* being able to make sense of the world to oneself and others, having wisdom.
2. *Courage:* emotional strengths that involve the will to accomplish goals in the face of external or internal opposition.
   - *Bravery:* not shrinking from challenge or pain; speaking up, standing up for convictions.
   - *Persistence:* finishing what you start and getting it out the door.
   - *Integrity:* presenting oneself in a genuine, honest way, taking responsibility for one's feelings and actions.
   - *Vitality:* feeling alive and activated, with zest, vigor, and energy.
3. *Humanity:* interpersonal strengths, tending and befriending others.
   - *Love:* valuing close relations.
   - *Kindness:* doing good deeds for others, nurturance, compassion, and altruism.
   - *Social intelligence:* being aware of motives and feelings of others and oneself.
4. *Justice:* civic strengths that would foster healthy community life.
   - *Citizenship:* working well with a team, loyalty, social responsibility.
   - *Fairness:* treating people equally, not swayed by personal feelings.
   - *Leadership:* encouraging your group to get things done while maintaining good relations.

5. *Temperance:* strengths that protect against excess.
   - *Forgiveness and mercy:* not being vengeful; giving others a second chance.
   - *Humility:* not seeking the spotlight; modesty.
   - *Prudence:* farsightedness; being careful about choices.
   - *Self-regulation:* controlling appetites and emotions.
6. *Transcendence:* strengths that provide meaning and connect with a larger universe.
   - *Appreciation of beauty and excellence:* notice and appreciation of nature, performance; able to experience awe and wonder.
   - *Gratitude:* being aware and thankful for the good things that happen and for life itself, accompanied by warm goodwill.
   - *Hope and optimism:* expecting the best and believing a good future is something you can help bring about.
   - *Humor:* playfulness, enjoying laughter, making people smile.
   - *Spirituality:* coherent beliefs about the higher purpose in life and connection to the purpose and meaning.

At first glance the list of strengths may seem overwhelming, but after coach and client become familiar with the test and its results, the information can be very useful for coaching. Identification of top strengths provides a unique profile of who the client is at his or her best. In turn this information highlights what motivates and inspires each client. One can make choices of how to select interventions that might most powerfully help clients in the light of knowing their strengths. For example: a client trying to work through a challenging situation whose top strengths are love of learning and open mindedness might benefit from a different set of interventions from a client who has the top strengths of capacity to love and appreciation of beauty. Coaches can also use their knowledge of client strengths to design more optimal relationships as well as individually tailor homework assignments. When clients learn to bring their strength to a challenge it helps them tap into their intrinsic motivations and can help them improve performance and find more satisfaction in the task accomplishment.

There is strong empirical evidence that supports the effectiveness of working with clients' signature strengths. For example, in one exercise (described later) people were asked to use their top strengths in new ways for one week (vs. a placebo exercise). The results showed that those who worked with their strengths in new ways were happier, less depressed, and more engaged in their lives that those in the control group. The effect of this one-week self-administered exercise was still strongly evident at follow-up assessments six months later. Extensive research data comparing strengths across culture, gender, and age suggest few differences across categories. Of all the 24 strengths, the five most strongly correlated to happiness are gratitude, curiosity, vitality, hope, and the capacity to love and be loved. These last results suggest that strength-building exercises in these subcategories might be useful.

As a coach, the author has found the strengths survey to be quietly radical. Many clients have never had their strengths assessed and find that just reading the survey results helps them label or understand themselves in new ways. Our society has many words for nuances of pathology, but a much less developed language to depict subtle but profound differences in profiles of strength. In addition, my experience is that the survey offers information that is not readily apparent from simple observation and interaction, and it deepens our understanding and connection with clients.

TRIAGE FOR HAPPINESS: THE AUTHENTIC HAPPINESS COACHING MODEL

I will now present one model of positive psychology coaching that has been developed from the outset with an empirically based orientation. The Authentic Happiness Coaching model evolved directly from the research described above; many studies are continually in progress (Seligman et al., 2005). The goal of Seligman and others in creating the AHC model is to provide a theoretically grounded and empirically supported set of techniques to foster happiness. While the interventions and exercises are useful to help people move from feeling unhappy or neutral to being happier, these psychologists were particularly interested in developing ways to help people move from a "+2" to a "+5" (Seligman, 2004; Seligman, Steen, et al., 2005).

The exercises described in the following paragraphs are for the CEOs, entrepreneurs, performers, and soccer moms and dads who are psychologically healthy but also want to lead more joyful, engaged, and meaningful lives. These are the individuals who can be well served by our being able to expand the repertoire of services available to include tested methods to achieve these ends, not just to reduce depression and anxiety. As we've seen, increasing happiness is not only an end unto itself; it also correlates with and may even help create greater competence, resilience, access to personal as well as social resources, improved physical health, and deeper connection to society and sense of personal mission.

I will describe a number of exercises and techniques from AHC in the hope that coaches will adapt them to fit into their own style of working.

One can pick and choose among exercises or use them as a whole, in a more stepwise, manual-like manner. Process-oriented coaches can incorporate the exercises as issues unfold in coaching. They can be offered to clients as between-session homework assignments or as in-session experiential exercises. The material can also be presented in a didactic-process format to individuals or groups. For the latter, sessions can begin with 15 minutes of personalized teaching, then segue into process discussion. The members can then pair up with one another during a group/workshop session or between sessions, to practice the exercise and debrief. Pairs (or triads) can then share what they learned when they return to the larger group with subsequent process discussion. While not describing specific session format at this time, my hope is coaches can integrate the material to their own training or coaching programs.

In order to coach to increase happiness, we must first arrive at a working definition. Seligman has identified three pathways to happiness: (1) through the emotions, (2) through connection with internal or external activity, and (3) through personal meaning. He calls these the Pleasant Life, the Engaged Life, and the Meaningful Life. Most often people think only of emotion and Hollywood impressions of life when they think of being happy. However, the second two pathways are equally, and probably more, compelling and lead to greater life satisfaction. The Engaged Life refers to being fully involved in life activity in work, relationships, and avocational pursuits. Coaching to increase engagement focuses on helping clients find what is intrinsically rewarding to them. Positive emotion and engagement together, however, don't automatically lead to deep satisfaction, as one can happily be engaged in "fidgeting one's life away." This leads us to develop access to the third pathway, finding meaning and purpose and connection to a greater cause. Together the three lives, Pleasant, Engaged, and Meaningful, help us to create the Full Life.

IDEALIZED SESSION PLANNING FOR AUTHENTIC HAPPINESS COACHING

The first step is to establish initial contact and then have clients take tests described in the appendix at the end of this chapter, which are all available at http://authentichappiness.org. I request that clients take baseline measures of depression and current happiness, as well as taking tests for approaches to happiness, life satisfaction, and strengths testing. Clients can retest themselves to assess their progress.

POSITIVE INTRODUCTION EXERCISE A good way to begin is to ask clients to describe themselves at their very best and to base this information on concrete events from the previous week. This exercise builds rapport and begins training clients to identify and focus on their strengths. In further discussion we help them anchor their strengths, explore for details, and so on.

Variations: Ask some clients to write an introduction, as this draws on the natural strengths of those who are less verbally spontaneous. In workshops, having participants break into pairs for positive introductions is often very energizing. Peterson, Park, and Seligman (2005) use this when interviewing prospective graduate students and find it shifts the tone of the process substantially.

POSITIVE TRIAGE: PICKING A PATH TO HAPPINESS

The "approaches to happiness" questionnaire (Peterson, et al., 2005) assesses how high a person scores on three types of happiness: pleasure, engagement, and meaning. Clients can then pick what pathway to well-being they would like to work on first, either burnishing strongest areas or developing less-used pathways. Depending on their choice, the AHC coach picks from among numerous exercises available that have been developed to increase well-being in each of these three dimensions. Each exercise can be tweaked to fit with the client's particular interest and style.

For simplicity's sake the exercises are presented here in the following sequence: first the focus is on those that increase positive emotion; second, those aimed toward increasing engagement; and finally, those to increase one's sense of purpose and meaning. In actual sessions there is great flexibility in what exercises a coach chooses and whether they are presented in a structured or process oriented way (see coaching scenarios below).

COACHING TO INCREASE POSITIVE EMOTION: THE PLEASANT LIFE

For those who work too hard or don't open up to pleasurable emotions easily, these exercises help strengthen the capacity to enjoy life more fully. The exercises can help increase positive emotion about the present, the past, or the future.

Exercises to Increase/Enhance Positive Emotion in the Present

SAVORING A BEAUTIFUL DAY Ask the client to set aside a period of time—a half hour or even an entire day—and devote it to one's favorite pleasurable activities. Savoring skill is increased by experimenting with such techniques as mindfully experiencing the moment, sensory memory building (taking mental pictures or finding physical souvenirs), focusing on sharpening one's perceptions, attaining complete absorption in the activity, and later sharing the moment with others. The client notes any kind of "killjoy thinking" that arises and tries to find the best method for disarming it (Bryant & Veroff, in press).

Purpose: This exercise is a pleasure/mindfulness experience that can help clients who are on the hedonic treadmill. In other words, they have acclimated to success and good fortune and no longer feel as happy as their life circumstances would seem to merit. It is also a useful balance for the work-driven client who moves quickly from success to success without stopping to notice or absorb their lives. Over time clients learn to weave this skill into every day life.

THREE BLESSINGS EXERCISE Each night before going to bed, clients write down (or at least think about) three good things that happened that day. Then (this part is crucial) they ask themselves what they did to make each good thing happen. Often people are unaware of their own role in good fortune. For example, someone cannot make a beautiful sunset, but they can choose to take it in (or not).

This exercise is so simple it may feel simpleminded to many. However, it is receiving strong empirical support. Subjects participating in the three blessings (vs. placebo exercise of writing about childhood) were happier and less depressed six months after one week of three blessings homework.

Variation 1: In a work setting the coach can switch the question: What three things went right with the project today? What did the client do to make those good things happen?

Variation 2: When lying in bed at night and unfinished business pulls at the clients' thoughts, suggest they mull over: "When was I at my best today?" Often clients remember events that otherwise would have been overlooked.

Increasing/Enhancing Positive Emotion about the Past

GRATITUDE VISIT The client identifies someone in his or her life who has been especially kind but whom the client has never properly thanked. The client writes a letter indicating specifically the reasons for his or her gratitude. The letter states concretely what that person had done and what results this has had in the client's life. Then the client calls the person and makes an appointment to meet, without indicating the reason for the meeting beyond that there is something important he or she would like to talk about. The client then meets the person and reads the letter aloud. People find this to be an enormously powerful experience. Early data suggest it has strong short-term (one-month) impact.

Purpose: Research suggests gratitude is one of the key strengths most associated with overall well-being. Beyond the specifics of the visit, learning the skill of having gratitude for people in your past has potential positive ramifications. Can the client transfer this to people in the present?

When clients would like to feel more positive about someone who has had a negative impact on them, another exercise might be useful.

LETTING GO OF GRUDGES The issue of forgiveness is complex and controversial, and may need to be balanced with issues of accountability and justice. However, when bitterness interferes with capacity to have more joy about one's life and the past, this exercise may help put things in a different perspective.

The client chooses a person he knows well who has done something hurtful. On a piece of paper he writes that person's name down in the middle of the paper, captures in a few words what he did (the grudge) and circles it. Then the client makes 15 circles on the page and fills each one in with a phrase describing what that same person did that was helpful and generous and for which the client is grateful. The client then holds the page at arm's length and tries to find the balance between how the person helped and hurt. Does the hurt get lost in what else this person did? Encourage the client to allow the situation to be complex and not black/white.

Variation for a work setting: If an executive is having a challenge with a boss/subordinate, have him write the problematic behavior/situation in the middle of the page and then balance it with 15 other things. This exercise can be used with both individuals as a precursor to conflict management sessions.

Increasing/Enhancing Positive Emotion about the Future

ONE DOOR CLOSES, ONE DOOR OPENS This is an optimism-building exercise. In this exercise, the client is instructed to think back over his or her life and make a list of times when he or she met with failure or loss or when plans were thwarted. Then the client searches for what good thing happened as a result of the first door closing.

Variation: The client practices this in a small way during a week as events unfold. For example, one event is canceled—what takes its place?

OPTIMISM BUILDING This exercise teaches clients the explanatory style of optimists, who tend to see what goes wrong as temporary and a result of circumstance or choices rather than seeing failure as related to one's core. Then when things go right optimists tend to see this as more permanent and related to their core self, not simple luck. Clients are asked to go over a past failure and a past success. When something went wrong, they are to analyze it from the following perspective: to search for circumstances (not personal reasons) for the setback/failure, or to focus on specific actions (I'm a good planner, but didn't plan that day well). When they did something right they are to search for what character strengths accounted for the success.

RAPID-FIRE DISPUTATION When pessimistic thoughts interfere with a sense of hope, clients are taught the ABCDE method of disputing the pessimistic assessment. A = adversity (the problem/pessimistic thought); B = your automatic beliefs about it; C = the usual consequences; D = your disputing your routine belief; and E = the energizing you can get when you dispute effectively. To help clients dispute negative beliefs, urge them to get outside the box of their thinking and search for evidence that concretely challenges the thought; have them find just one thing that disputes their conclusion (e.g., I'm a bad boss or bad parent). Then search for alternate explanations for challenges and look for aspects the client can control (see Seligman, 2002).

Variation: Clients can do this as homework, or they can pick someone to help them "argue" with the pessimistic thought. The partner may also play devil's advocate to help the client increase the capacity to dispute it.

COACHING TO INCREASE FLOW AND INVOLVEMENT: THE ENGAGED LIFE

The Engaged Life is the pathway that involves the identification of one's strengths and learning how to use them at work, in relationships, and in leisure. As a result one can be more vitally involved with what one is doing, and therefore with one's own life (Nakamura & Csikszentmihalyi, 2003). By pulling more strongly on natural strengths, the client can find that certain tasks become more intrinsically rewarding and motivating. For example, if love of learning is a top strength, one can learn to harness it to make activities more enjoyable (see below).

Engagement with Activity

USING STRENGTH IN A NEW WAY Clients choose one of their top strengths and during the week find a designated time to exercise the strength in a new way at work, home, or leisure. The exercise is to first go through a day (in real time or through recall) to identify situations where one's signature strengths are already in action. Then the clients brainstorm new ways to use the strength (see case example of Bonita, described later).

Variation 1: Finding ways clients can use their strengths under adversity. When a situation is challenging coach and client brainstorm and practice how the client's signature strength can be applied to improve or make the most of the situation. For example: For public speaking anxiety, how might clients pull on gratitude, love of learning, or capacity to love in order to center themselves in their core strength/value and find the energy or resolve to continue?

Variation 2: When engaged in an action that increases anxiety, read over the conditions of flow and slightly alter the parameters of the task to be in line with natural strengths.

Increasing Engagement with Others

STRENGTHS DATE   A client chooses someone with whom to share some time. Both participants identify their signature strengths through the VIA Signature Strengths Survey. Then they plan an activity that puts into play one or more of the signature strengths of each. For example, if one client has appreciation of beauty and excellence as a signature strength, and the other has love of learning, then they might plan a trip to the local art museum so that they can learn about beautiful art objects together.

Variations: In a work or team setting, take members' natural skills into account when delegating (or volunteering) for particular tasks. Have work teams all take the VIA if they are interested. If a colleague or friend is unable or uninterested in taking the VIA, have the client guess what the other's signature strengths might be and use that when planning an activity or choosing a gift for the friend.

RELATIONAL ENGAGEMENT   Practice active, constructive responding based on findings that being active and constructive in responding to another fosters interpersonal flow. Being passive and constructive or active/passive and destructive does not predict interpersonal engagement (Gable, Ries, Impett, & Asher, 2004).

Variations: Practice active/constructive responding in the work setting, saving criticisms until afterward. Notice whether conflicts are reduced and if behavioral repertoire of the team shifts.

COACHING TO INCREASE SENSE OF PURPOSE: THE MEANINGFUL LIFE

The third pathway involves the use of one's strengths in the service of something larger than oneself. The focus shifts to the positive effects one can have on one's family, on one's community, and even on the world at large. Pilot research shows that tapping strengths in the service of others or a larger cause increases life satisfaction and experience of feeling fulfilled.

FUN VERSUS PHILANTHROPY Clients are asked to plan one act for personal enjoyment and then follow through. On another day they plan one altruistic act to bring joy to another. Each of these days they fill out the happiness rating scale (see Appendix on page 249) to see what actually makes them feel better at the end of the day.

STRENGTHS FAMILY TREE A client asks members of his family to take the VIA Signature Strengths Survey and report the results. The client creates a family tree, and notes each person's strengths on the tree. For grandparents, great-grandparents, or others who are no longer alive, family members can discuss together what they think those persons' strengths might have been. Once the strengths have been listed on the tree, family members can take turns telling anecdotes that illustrate the various strengths of the other family members and then note and discuss any insights that arise as a result of knowing each other's signature strengths.

Variation: In the Work Strengths Tree exercise, clients repeat the Strengths Family Tree exercise with people they work with on a daily basis. They think through the key strengths of colleagues, bosses, or subordinates and plan to relate to them differently in light of this information.

GIFT OF TIME, OR POSITIVE SERVICE Interventions for cultivating the Meaningful Life are intended to help clients put their signature strengths to work in the service of something larger than themselves. Here a client is asked to think about the various domains of life beyond herself that would benefit from the gift of her time and the application of her signature strengths. These domains could be institutions the client cares about, groups of underprivileged people, or ideals the client believes are worth fighting for. The client is then asked to develop a plan for intentionally using one or more of her signature strengths in the service of this institution, population, or idea. While it might be powerful for a client to analyze service she is already engaged in to see which of her strengths it makes use of, the point of this exercise is to go beyond that to the intentional creation and execution of a new plan of strengths-based service.

THE LIFE SUMMARY This is an exercise where a client writes out an account of his life as he might want a great-grandchild to perceive it. What are the things that the client finds most meaningful in life and for which he would most want to be remembered? Some of these things may already be present in a client's life, and some may be things he will want to move toward. The Life Summary exercise is intended to help a client focus both on maintaining important things that are already present in his life and on cultivating those new things he wants to include in his life. By writing out the Life Summary and then reading it periodically, a client can help maintain a meaningful perspective on his life. Meaningful Life is intended to help clients gain perspective on what is most important in their lives.

EXERCISES FOR ALL THREE PATHWAYS TO HAPPINESS:
FINDING THE FULL LIFE

This exercise can help your clients develop the capacity to observe their own levels of happiness.

DIARY EXERCISE   The client is instructed to go through a regular day and answer the following questions on an hourly basis. What did I do? To what extent was it enjoyable? To what extent was I in flow? To what extent did the activity have meaning? Review the day. Develop hypotheses about what fosters happiness in the way that feels most satisfying and/or important.

PLAN FOR HAPPINESS   Apply the information learned in the Diary Exercise. Then take a day, even if it's busy, and think through how the client can plan three activities: one that is pleasurable, one that is engaging, and one that is meaningful. Notice which ones come easily and which ones do not. Make sure to do all three! At times this can mean just stopping to notice what one is already doing that's been pleasurable, engaging or meaningful, but could enjoy more if one was mindful of the experience. Anecdotal evidence suggests that engaging in small positive behaviors can shift the balance of how one experiences the day and overcome the hedonic treadmill.

The preceding exercises are currently being tested for effectiveness for increasing happiness, reducing depression, and increasing engagement and meaning. While on the surface these interventions are most obviously related to individual and personal coaching, it is fairly clear how one might apply these in work settings. The Gallup Organization, for example, first assesses signature strengths of all the primary leaders of an organization, then continues down through the organizational hierarchy until every person in the entire institution has been tested on Gallup's Strength Survey (Buckingham & Clifton, 2001; Stone, 2004). Then, once everyone is familiar with the language and comfortable with the philosophy, programs to make companywide shifts in optimal task assignment and management communication are implemented. In this way the strengths culture can permeate the system prior to explicit changes in management.

USING AUTHENTIC HAPPINESS COACHING IN A SESSION

Given how clear it is to see how you could use these exercises in a structured manner, the case examples here illustrate how a coach might use positive psychology and authentic happiness coaching in process oriented coaching. These vignettes are not intended to give an overarching sense of coaching sessions, but are glimpses into the process. In both cases we'll hone in on just one area: how to help clients orient to their challenge in a way that pulls on their strengths. For Bonita, the experience is supportive in nature; for Bob, it requires positive confrontation.

Case Example of Bonita

Bonita was recently promoted to vice-president of HR at her firm. Her goals are to improve her conflict management and leadership and work toward better work-life balance. We focus on her strengths and conflict management in the following snippet.

After making contact I'd ask Bonita for a positive introduction. As Bonita tells her story I'd listen for her natural strengths and notice her preferred relational style. Afterward I'd ask questions about her introduction in order to augment her appreciation of her strengths and help anchor this information more firmly into her consciousness and self-image. If she slips into describing weaknesses, first listen, provide support, but also redirect attention back to her best self.

The next few sessions would explore Bonita's signature strengths. I'd expect her VIA top strength profile to be:

- Bonita has a strong capacity to love and be loved; she cares deeply about others and often puts their needs first.
- She also has a very strong love of learning and building her knowledge. (This strength exists in tandem with the love of teaching, which surfaces in her ways of interacting with colleagues.)
- Similar to many who have survived hardship and thrived, she would also be very high in gratitude. We see this surface in her relationship to her father.
- Persistence is also a top strength. She works hard and follows through on her promises.
- In the domain of civic strengths she'd show a very high strength in citizenship, as the needs of many are of key importance, as is fairness to others.

The positive psychology orientation suggests that teaching Bonita to harness her natural strengths would be an optimal pathway to increase effectiveness in both these areas. Bonita has many avenues to increase her ability to engage in constructive conflict. The first work I'd do with signature strengths includes the assignment to identify top strengths and find new ways to use them in the current week. Then I would focus in on her goals regarding conflict and leadership.

Our work might evolve as follows:

Coach: So you feel your leadership skills would be more complete if you were less afraid of conflict?

Bonita: Yes, it's the one area where I feel over my head, especially with Rick.

Coach: What's the challenge?

Bonita: Every time he makes a criticism or remark I just try harder to appease him.

Coach: Does that work?

Bonita: Not really. Last time my team, instead of me, wound up confronting him. I need to be more in the lead now.

Coach: What would that look like?

Bonita: I'd have to confront him myself. I don't know, maybe get a little angry? *(With the last phrase Bonita's voice tone suddenly rises, becoming high-pitched and questioning, like a little girl.)*

Coach: I hear your voice getting littler as you speak. What's that about?

Bonita: I'm not good with getting angry. I don't think well on my feet.

Coach: You know, there are many pathways to engaging in conflict. It sounds like getting angry doesn't play to your strengths.

Bonita: That's for sure! *(She laughs, suddenly sounding more energetic and grown-up again.)*

Coach: Well, let's play to your strengths. How would the perfect you, functioning at your very best, manage a conflict with Rick? *(Coach is pulling for images of agency from the client.)*

Bonita: I'd head it off at the pass by connecting with him early on and engaging in a dialogue. *(Client is smiling but lowers her eyes; coach senses shame.)*

Coach: That makes sense. It pulls on your primary strength of the capacity to love and be loved. I bet you already do that very well. *(Coach works to reframe the self-deprecating subtext.)*

Bonita: Yes, that's true, but sometimes it isn't enough.

Coach: That's why we have other strengths. How might you pull on your second strength to help you manage conflict? *(Coach is helping client deepen awareness of strengths and begin to consider using them in a new way.)*

Bonita: Love of learning? I've read quite a lot about conflict management.

Coach: Love of learning also surfaces as a love of teaching. *(Coach is not interested in asking about her intellectual understanding, but flies another aspect of this strength past to see if it catches her attention.)*

Bonita: Oh, teaching . . . *(Looking out the window, thinking.)* I could teach him to share his ideas in a less disruptive way? *(Voice tone rises in pitch—she sounds tentative, not as much as before.)*

Coach: How could you do that?

Bonita: Well, I could talk to him when he isn't being disruptive—I know, I could set up a conflict management seminar for the entire team, and have us all learn more about it together.

Coach: That might be useful. *(This is a noncommittal response; coach senses client is sidling up to more core material and is quiet to help create more space for self-inquiry.)*

Bonita: Yes, but you know if I'm honest, that avoids the real issue.

Coach: Which is?

Bonita: Confronting Rick and being comfortable with being angry with him directly.

Coach: Can I put on my consultant hat for a minute? *(Coach points out role shift by asking permission. Client is clearly stuck in an aggression model of conflict that makes her feel badly and is therefore not able to think flexibly. Goal here is to provide alternative and help her access positive sense of self and expand behavioral repertoire.)*

Bonita: Please do!

Coach: When there's conflict and you have to decide whether to address it, most of us think along the lines of: Is this so bad I simply must say something or I'll burst? That particular decision tree does not pull on your strengths. You're not a natural fighter. I wonder if you're putting yourself in a too small a box by thinking you have to be angry to engage in conflict. What would it be like if you thought more along the lines of: What could I say to Rick that would teach him how to work with me and the team more effectively?

Bonita: You mean I could put on my teacher hat? *(Client is sounding intrigued and energetic again.)*

Coach: Exactly. Now, if we go back to my question—how might the perfect you, you at your best, manage conflict with Rick?

Bonita: That's easy—the perfect me would say, "Rick, I appreciate your suggestions. For me, it would work best if you shared them before the main meeting so we could use your input more effectively." It would help him, you know. He winds up alienating people when he shoots me down, and he does it to co-workers as well.

Coach: Have you noticed your voice tone?

Bonita: What about it?

Coach: You don't sound little anymore.

By helping Bonita back to her central strengths, the coach empowers her to more easily access her already well-formed teaching and communication skills and use them in the service of conflict management. If her signature strengths were in the area of justice, the coach could tailor the conversation quite differently. In that situation, the coach might harness the client's core values of fairness and justice. For each person, whatever the nature of the challenge, the coach tries to find the bridge connecting that challenge to the client's primary strengths.

Case Example of Bob

Bob is a CEO having difficulty managing a major upward transition. As occasionally happens, his board has gathered to "fix" him. We'll imagine that coaching was initiated after a previous consultant did a traditional 360-degree feedback session. This consists of lengthy interviews from all the people surrounding Bob and reflecting back what they think of him as a CEO and leader as well as a person. The information from board members, top management, middle management, and a few employees is a combination of superlative performance ratings and strong criticisms. After the previous executive coach tried to get Bob to become a kinder and gentler corporate magnate, Bob initiated a series of moves that resulted in the coach being placed elsewhere. The data from the 360-degree feedback session has been forwarded to a positive psychologist who is implicitly requested to "fix" Bob so things will go well.

The primary challenge Bob is facing is that his multinational company is merging with its main competitor, a South Korea–based company, and his board worries that his high-powered American cowboy style will not be nuanced enough to allow the merger to go through. Bob's goals are for the merger to go well and to leave his company in "perfect order" when he retires a few years down the road. He has been clear that he is not interested in the "soft side" of coaching.

As a positive psychology coach I would begin the first session in the usual manner by asking Bob to tell a story about himself at his best during a specific experience the previous week. As he gives the introduction, I'd build rapport, assess his strengths and values, and afterward explore these more fully.

Bob would also take the Values in Action questionnaire to assess his signature strengths. The second session would engage him in dialogue about these strengths and how he uses them in everyday life. People often have the invigorating "aha" experience of finding words for experiences they could never name until learning their strengths. Those not initially interested in psychological interventions often find it energizing to develop self-reflection skills in the context of exploring a new language for real and specific strengths (vs. flattery) and by focusing on health rather than pathology.

Bob's top signature strengths would probably include:

- Persistence—industriousness and overcoming obstacles.
- Bravery—not shrinking from threat or difficulty.
- Vitality—zest, enthusiasm.
- Leadership—encouraging a group to get things done.
- Humor/hope (these might be tied for fifth place).

I'd discuss and explore with Bob how these strengths have formed the powerful building blocks for his success. In Bob's case he shows extraordinary strengths in two areas, courage and transcendence. In major leadership positions one hopes for a greater breadth of strengths, ideally one highly developed strength for at least four areas.

For Bob, it might be best to tailor a different signature strength exercise, for example, ask him to pick five people of importance to the merger and have them take the VIA. I'd then ask Bob to guess their strengths and assess his accuracy. The purpose here would be to make it interesting for him to begin thinking in a strengths language about others, and have the implicit support or confrontation of his social intelligence by how well he did.

Bob is a CEO with major strengths; to reach his goals, however, he is going to need to acknowledge the importance of areas in which he is not as strong. At home, he has his wife to cover him in these areas of weakness. At work, he apparently doesn't have people he respects to fill this role. There is no way around this issue, and like the previous coach, we need to address his liabilities. As good coaches, we remain as unattached as possible to whether our interventions will get us fired. Circling the truth is a good way to lose a consultation job.

Coach: So, Bob, what was it like to see all that feedback? *(I don't shrink from bringing up touchy topics just because I'm "positive.")*

Bob: Most of it was great, but of course there were the requisite amount of kicks in the head.

Coach: Like what?

Bob: That I'm seen as a superficial glad-hander who doesn't listen or follow through with being nice to people. That's true enough—I just move forward when things get tough.

Coach: What do you make of that?

Bob: You have to break eggs to make an omelet.

Coach: That's true, but what else might be going on?

Bob: People like to take potshots at the leader. What else is new?

Coach: Leaders are targets; that's the truth. But they're also the ones who inspire their communities to greatness. If you kick that part of yourself in gear, what would you like to do with the negative feedback? *(Notice the coach refocusing Bob's attention to himself at his best and using what he shared in his positive introduction to do that. The coach also is using Bob's "kick" image, which reflects strong affect, and channeling it in a growth-promoting direction.)*

Bob: Learn from it—or get them to change their minds about me. What did you learn from it? You're the expert.

Coach: I imagine I learned what's probably obvious—you are incredibly successful, you're courageous, and you get things done that other people find utterly overwhelming.

Bob: (Interrupting) That's for damn sure, but what about the bad stuff?

Coach: You know, Bob, spectacular people have spectacular flaws. It goes with the territory. What makes leaders great is how they manage those flaws. Your challenge, if you choose to accept it, is to look this problem in the eye and figure out how to fix it. *(Notice the implicit use of the 3:1 ratio, being clear about the positive and the negative, then calling on Bob's strengths of bravery and persistence to galvanize his effort.)*

Bob: I never run from a fight.

Coach: Where do you want to start?

Bob: I'm not sure. That touchy-feely stuff isn't my cup of tea.

Coach: That's true. According to the VIA your top three strengths are all in the category of courage: persistence, bravery, and zest. And these contribute to your other top strength of leadership. This is an incredible combination, but the humanity strengths lag pretty far behind—and I wonder if that gets in your way at times.

Bob: I'm a big picture guy. Relationships aren't high on my radar.

Coach: Is that true in all aspects of your life?

Bob: Personally, no—things at home work perfectly. Professionally, my priority is making sure all systems interface optimally. People aren't my focus.

Coach: They don't have to be. But from your big picture perspective, what costs might you pay if you don't bump up your awareness of human interfaces? *(Coach is pulling on Bob's strengths to help create a context where he can think more flexibly.)*

Bob: (Pauses, looks combative for a second, then sighs.) Damn, I don't want to think about this. . . . *(Another long pause; coach nods, smiles slightly, but remains silent.)* Okay, it's obvious, isn't it? The cost could just be my legacy. If people resent me, all hell could break loose when I leave.

Coach: Empires don't always outlast their founders. *(Coach resists reassurances, but also doesn't leap in to blare out the obvious problem.)* Any thoughts on what could lessen the chance of that happening?

Bob: Most of what I do works, but you know, I'm in up the stratosphere now, with the highest fliers. Things can get tricky and smaller problems can surface in big ways.

Coach: Like not being interested in people?

Bob: Right. But I am who I am; that isn't going to change.

Coach: Most people can't change their core selves very much. But if people skills aren't your natural strength, what do you think makes sense?

Bob: Having someone around who does this stuff more naturally than I do. That would leave me free to do the strategic work.

Coach: You know, Bob, didn't you say your personal life works perfectly? From what I've heard others think you've done this balancing act brilliantly in your personal life. *(Coach is trying to help Bob generalize from one domain to another, something he tends not to do as he's very compartmentalized.)*

Bob: You mean-with my wife? *(Bob hesitates, making the connection.)*

Coach: Exactly. Didn't you say that you do what you do best, she does what she does and you're great complements to each other?

Bob: Right, but lightning doesn't strike twice. I don't think I could find such a great match at work.

Coach: Bob, is there anything in this life that you've ever really wanted that you haven't gotten? *(Coach throws down the gauntlet safely in Bob's greatest strength—persistence. If Bob values solving this problem, he clearly will.)*

Bob: No, and I see where you're heading. I could get it if I really wanted to *(he grins)*—I could sink my teeth into that.

Bob now feels ready to connect to the challenge. If Bob's primary strengths were in a different area, the coach would shift, framing the core issue in a way that would pull on what is intrinsically rewarding to the client, for instance, curiosity, justice, and so on. It is very important for the coach to set up assignments, inquiries, or confrontations based on the client's signature strengths, not the coach's strengths or agenda.

CONCLUSION

Positive psychology has the potential to provide a theoretical and empirical underpinning, an internal scaffolding if you will, to the emerging profession of coaching. There is evidence-based support for the utility of attending to a client's wholeness, fostering hope and helping that client hone his vision of the future. There is a firm base of data that the increases in joy and positive emotion that we often see in coaching are not a woo-woo phenomenon. It can be reliably and validly measured, and its positive impact on fostering cognitive and social skills is very amenable to the light of scientific scrutiny.

Advances in the field also explicitly and implicitly offer a wide range of possible applications. There are psychometrically robust measures to assess strengths, and empirically testable positive interventions that have been found to increase happiness, productivity, and life satisfaction. For those who have seen the power of coaching on a personal level, it behooves you to be aware of the larger science base that can support this perspective. Obviously all coaching doesn't work; we are a new field and must make mistakes to move the process of discovery forward. While coaching is an art, it is one that can be built on science. At each phase of growth as individuals and as a profession, there is an optimal dialectical tension of art and science as the art informs the science which in turn can inform the art. It is time to transcend the notion that it is one or the other, and for coach-practitioners to become adept at both.

APPENDIX: TESTS USED IN AUTHENTIC HAPPINESS COACHING

POSITIVE AND NEGATIVE AFFECT SCHEDULE (PANAS)

This scale (Watson, Clark, & Tellegen, 1988) provides a snapshot of the clients' current, momentary affective state. Interestingly, positive affect and negative affect are almost independent of each other. So it is possible, for example, for a client to feel both high positive affect and high negative affect at the same time.

FORDYCE EMOTIONS QUESTIONNAIRE

This questionnaire (Fordyce, 1988) is a very quick, one-item assessment used to measure clients' typical level of happiness. This measure is not domain specific.

SATISFACTION WITH LIFE SCALE

This scale (Diener, Emmons, Larsen, & Griffen, 1985) measures clients' general satisfaction with life as a whole. This measure is not domain specific.

APPROACHES TO HAPPINESS QUESTIONNAIRE

This questionnaire (Peterson, Park, & Seligman, 2005) is designed to measure the extent to which clients are using each of the three pathways to happiness. This questionnaire measures the use of each of the three pathways and gives a score for each.

AUTHENTIC HAPPINESS INVENTORY QUESTIONNAIRE

This questionnaire (Peterson, 2005) is intended to measure changes in overall happiness levels across time.

CENTER FOR EPIDEMIOLOGICAL STUDIES DEPRESSION SCALE (CES-D)

This Scale (Radloff, 1977) measures changes in overall depressive symptoms across time. Using this scale in tandem with the others can help to indicate whether clients are becoming less depressed as well as more happy.

REFERENCES

Brickman, P., Coates, D., & Janoff-Bulman, R. (1978). Lottery winners and accident victims: Is happiness relative? *Journal of Personality and Social Psychology, 36*, 917–927.

Bryant, F. B. (2003). A scale for measuring beliefs about savoring: The Savoring Beliefs Inventory. *Journal of Mental Health, 12*, 175–196.

Bryant, F. B., & Veroff, J. (in press). *The process of savoring: A new model of positive experience.* Mahwah, NJ: Lawrence Erlbaum Associates.

Buck, D. (2004) *Extreme productivity.* Paper presented at the Annual Meeting of the International Coaching Federation, Quebec, Canada.

Buckingham, M., & Clifton, D. (2001). *Now, discover your strengths.* New York: Free Press.

Carrere, S., & Gottman, J. (1999). Predicting divorce among newlyweds from the first three minutes of a marital conflict discussion. *Family Process, 28*(3), 293–301.

Csikszentmihalyi, M. (1991). *Flow.* New York: Harper.

Csikszentmihalyi, M. (1997). *Finding flow: The psychology of engagement with everyday life.* New York: Basic Books.

Csikszentmihalyi, M., & Hunter, J. (2003). Happiness in everyday life: The uses of experience sampling. *Journal of Happiness Studies, 4*, 185–199.

Dean, B. (2004). *MentorCoach Foundation skills training manual.* Baltimore: MentorCoach.

Demontrond-Behr, P., Fournier, J., & Vaivre-Douret, L. (2004). *Investigation of flow in French sport setting.* Communication affichée: Second European Conference on Positive Psychology, Verbania, Italy.

Diener, E. (2000b). Subjective well-being: The science of happiness and a proposal for a national index. *American Psychologist, 55*(1), 34–43.

Diener, E., Emmons, R. A., Larsen, R. J., & Griffen, S. (1985). The satisfaction with life scale. *Journal of Personality Assessment, 49*, 71–75.

Diener, E., & Kahneman, D. (2003). Zeroing in on the dark side of the American dream. *Psychological Science, 14*(6), 531–164.

Fordyce, M. (1988). A review of research on the happiness measures: A sixty-second index of happiness and mental health. *Social Indicators Research, 20*, 355–381.

Fredrickson, B. (2001). The role of positive emotions in positive psychology: The Broaden-and-Build theory of positive emotions. *American Psychologist, 56*(3), 218–226.

Fredrickson, B. L., & Branigan, C. A. (2005). Positive emotions broaden the scope of attention and thought-action repertoires. *Cognition and Emotion, 19*, 313–332.

Fredrickson, B. L., & Joiner, T. (2002). Positive emotions trigger upward spirals toward emotional well-being. *Psychological Science, 13*, 172–175.

Fredrickson, B. L., & Losada, M. (2005). Positive affect and the complex dynamics of human flourishing. *American Psychologist, 60*(7), 678–686.

Fujita, F., & Diener, E. (2005). Life satisfaction set point: Stability and change. *Journal of Personality and Social Psychology, 88*(1), 158–164.

Gable, S., Reis, H., Impett, E., & Asher, E. (2004). What do you do when things go right? The intrapersonal and interpersonal benefits of sharing positive events. *Journal of Personality and Social Psychology, 87*(2), 228–245.

Gottman, J. M. (1994). *What predicts divorce? The relationship between marital processes and marital outcomes.* Hillsdale, NJ: Erlbaum.

Irving, L. M., Snyder, C. R., Cheavens, J., Gravel, L., Hanke, J., Hilberg, P., & Nelson, N. (2004). The relationships between hope and outcomes at the pre-treatment, beginning, and later phases of psychotherapy. *Journal of Psychotherapy Integration, 14*(4), 419–443.

Isen, A. M., Rosenzweig, A. S., & Young, M. J. (1991). The influence of positive affect on clinical problem solving. *Medical Decision Making, 11*, 221–227.

Jackson, B. H. (2003). *In search of peak experiences through life: Understanding the strategies for replicating the flow experience; A developmental perspective.* Unpublished doctoral dissertation, The Fielding Graduate Institute, Santa Barbara, CA.

Kauffman, C. (2004a). *Multi modal coaching.* Third Annual International Summit of Positive Psychology, Washington, DC.

Kauffman, C. (2004b). *Pivot point coaching.* Annual Meeting of the International Coaching Federation. Quebec, Canada.

Kauffman, C. (2005a). *Pulling it all together: Developing and organizing positive psychology interventions.* Fourth Annual International Summit of Positive Psychology, Washington, DC.

Kauffman, C. (2005b). *The dialectics of peak performance.* Psychology Lecture Series at McLean Hospital, Belmont, MA.

Kauffman, C. (in press). *Pivot points: Small choices with the power to change your life.* New York: Evans Press.

Kauffman, C., & Scouler, A. (2004) Toward a positive psychology of executive coaching. In A. Linley & S. Josephs (Eds.), *Positive psychology in practice.* Hoboken, NJ: Wiley.

Lopez, S., & Snyder, C. R. (Eds.). (2003). *Positive psychological assessment: A handbook of models and measures.* Washington, DC: American Psychological Association.

Lopez, S. J., Snyder, C. R., & Rasmussen, H. N. (2003). Striking a vital balance: Developing a complementary focus on human weakness and strength through positive psychological assessment. In S. Lopez & C. R. Snyder (Eds.), *Positive psychological assessment: A handbook of models and measures.* Washington, DC: American Psychological Association.

Losada, M. (1999). The complex dynamics of high performance teams. *Mathematical and Computer Modelling, 30*(9-10), 179–192.

Losada, M., & Heaphy, E. (2004). The role of positivity and connectivity in the performance of business teams: A nonlinear dynamics model. *American Behavioral Scientist, 47*(6), 740–765.

Lykken, D., & Tellegen, A. (1996). Happiness is a stochastic phenomenon. *Psychological Science, 7*, 186–189.

Nakamura, J., & Csikszentmihalyi, M. (2002). The concept of flow. In C. R. Snyder & S. J. Lopez (Eds.), *Handbook of positive psychology*, 89–105. New York: Oxford University Press.

Nakamura, J., & Csikszentmihalyi, M. (2003). The construction of meaning through vital engagement. In C. Keyes & J. Haidt (Eds.), *Flourishing: Positive psychology and the life well-lived.* American Psychological Association, Washington DC.

Nickerson, C., Schwartz, N., Diener, E., & Kahneman (2003) Zeroing in on the dark side of the American dream: A closer look at the negative consequences of the goal for financial success. *Psychological Science 14*(6), 531–536.

Peterson, C. (2005). Introduction Remarks at the Fourth Annual International Summit of Positive Psychology, Washington, DC.

Peterson, C., Park, N., & Seligman, M. E. P. (2005). Orientations to happiness and life satisfaction: The full life versus the empty life. *Journal of Happiness Studies, 6*, 25–41.

Peterson, C., & Seligman, M. (2004). *Character strengths and virtues: A handbook and classification.* New York: Oxford University Press.

Radloff, L. S. (1977). The CES-D scale: A self-report depression scale for research in the general population. *Applied Psychological Measurement, 1*, 385–401.

Schwarz, N., & Strack, F. (1999). Reports of subjective well-being: Judgmental processes and their methodological implications. In D. Kahneman, E. Diener,

& N. Schwarz (Eds.), *Well-being: The foundations of hedonic psychology*. New York: Russell Sage Foundation.

Seligman, M. (2002). *Authentic happiness*. New York: Basic Books.

Seligman, M. (2004). Introductory Comments, Third International Summit in Positive Psychology, Washington, DC.

Seligman, M. E. P., Parks, A. C., & Steen, T. (2004). *A balanced psychology and a full life*. University of Pennsylvania, unpublished manuscript.

Seligman, M., Steen, T., Park, N., & Peterson, C. (2005). Positive psychology process: Empirical validation of interventions. *American Psychologist, 60*(5), 410–421.

Snyder, C. R. (2000). *Handbook of hope: Theory measures and applications*. New York: Guilford Press.

Snyder, C. R. (2002). Hope theory: Rainbows in the mind. *Psychological Inquiry, 13*(4), 249–275.

Snyder, C. R., Harris, C., Anderson, J. R., Holleran, S., Irving, L. M., Gibb, J., Sigmon, S. T., Yoshinobu, L., Langelle, C., & Harney, P. (1991). The will and the ways: Development and validation of an individual differences measure of hope. *Journal of Personality and Social Psychology, 60*, 570–585.

Snyder, C. R., & Lopez, S. (Eds.). (2002). *Handbook of positive psychology*. New York: Oxford University Press.

Watson, D., Clark, L. A., & Tellegen, A. (1988). Development and validation of brief measures of positive and negative affect: The PANAS Scales. *Journal of Personality and Social Psychology, 54*, 1063–1070.

Whitworth, L., Kimsey-House, H., & Sandahl, P. (1998). *Co-active coaching: New skills for coaching people toward success in work and life*. Palo Alto, CA: Davies-Black Publishing.

Williams, P., & Davis, D. (2002). Therapist as life coach: Transforming your practice. New York: W.W. Norton.

Wrobleski, K., & Snyder, C. (2005). Hopeful thinking in older adults: Back to the future. *Experimental Aging Research, 31*, 217–233.

CHAPTER 9

Coaching from
a Cultural Perspective

Philippe Rosinski and
Geoffrey N. Abbott

Coaching from a cultural perspective requires a willingness by the coach to explore and make use of the influence of culture as it operates within client contexts. We do not see the consideration of culture as an extra or different way of coaching. Taking a cultural perspective will enhance the impact of any coaching intervention. Consistent with the general philosophy of coaching, it will bring to the surface relevant issues and assumptions related to culture and to harness them toward unleashing client potential and facilitating positive change. This chapter highlights the benefits leveraging differences that may be culturally based, rather than treating them as obstacles, threats, or irrelevancies. The evidence for the work—in addition to the research base for coaching generally—is from a very large body of research literature including material from cross-cultural psychology, intercultural communication, cultural values and dimensions, international business, and anthropology. Much of the material here is drawn from Philippe Rosinski´s book *Coaching across Cultures: New Tools for Leveraging National, Corporate and Professional Differences* (Rosinski, 2003a), including the concept of a Global Coaching Process. Global coaching invites coaches and clients to connect their personal voyages with the journeys of their families, friends, work colleagues, organizations, communities, and society in general. The process is one of creativity and possibilities that is anchored in a belief in the human potential.

KEY CONCEPTS AND ASSUMPTIONS
OF CULTURAL COACHING

In describing the cultural perspective in coaching, we are working from some assumptions: Culture results in differences between people, culture is everywhere, and valuing those differences allows for potential growth.

DIFFERENCES DUE TO CULTURE

One assumption is that there are differences between people due to culture. These differences result in people seeing the world from different perspectives. Edward T. Hall (1989) observes that culture in its many forms determines what we pay attention to and what we ignore (p. 85). As a result, there are, in effect, multiple realities. The American pragmatist William James preferred the term *multi-verse* to *universe* (James, 1907a). Coaching is a pragmatic humanism and it does require a genuine acceptance of different views of the world. Such a stance is not an automatic abandonment to an "anything goes" relativism. Realism is consistent with coaching from a cultural perspective. James commented, "Reality may exist distributively just as it sensibly seems to, after all" (James, 1907a, p. 135). As humanists, we emphasize care of self and of others, quality of life, and human growth. We will therefore work with clients toward approaches that are ethical and consistent with the humanist stance. Coaching from a cultural perspective is inconsistent, for example, with racial discrimination or exploitative practices by businesses operating in developing countries. Another assumption is that moving outside one's own perspective to look at how others see the world will provide rich material for leveraging differences for personal, professional, and societal growth. The overarching assumption is that culture matters.

DIFFERENT FORMS OF CULTURE

This chapter may have particularly attracted readers interested in the theory and practice of coaching in situations where national culture is a defining feature of the coaching assignment (e.g., multinational corporations, cross-border joint venture companies, and multicultural work teams). There is a large body of recent literature that gives emphasis to the effects of national culture on business (e.g., Adler, 2002; Hofstede, 1997, 2001; Trompenaars, 1993). However, groups of all kinds have cultures. Groups originate from various categories, including geography, religion, profession, organization, social life, gender, and sexual orientation. Our individual identities can be viewed as a personal and dynamic synthesis of the cultures of the multiple groups to which we belong. Often, people are surprisingly unaware of the characteristics of various group cultures to which they are connected. They can therefore be oblivious of the influence culture is having on their thoughts, behaviors, and emotions. Coaching from a cultural perspective can raise awareness of identity and mobilize culture as a positive force in change processes.

CULTURE AS A SOURCE OF STRENGTH

The philosophy of valuing differences rather than imposing your norms, values, and beliefs applies to all forms of culture. Here we define coaching as the art of unleashing people's potential to reach meaningful, important objectives. Coaching from a cultural perspective allows the unleashing of additional human potential by systematically tapping into the richness of cultural diversity, into the wisdom that lies in alternative cultural perspectives (Rosinski, 2003a). Considering alternative belief systems, as they are represented in different cultures, helps clients to broaden their perspectives.

DEFINITIONS OF CULTURE

There are various definitions of culture, probably more than there are people who have written about culture. Tayeb (2001) observes that "Culture is a woolly concept, almost impossible to observe and 'measure' in all its visible and hidden corners; like the air that we breathe, we cannot see it or weigh it, we cannot put our arms around it and feel its strength and power, but we know it is there" (p. 92). Each perspective on culture helps to capture its essence. The working definition we use in this chapter is: "A group's culture is the set of unique characteristics that distinguishes its members from another group" (Rosinski, 2003a, p. 20). Looking at culture in this way enables the coach and client to look at various affective, behavioral, and cognitive characteristics of groups that may provide relevant information about the impact of culture.

Edgar Schein (1999) defines culture as "the sum total of all the shared, taken-for-granted assumptions that a group has learned throughout its history. It is the residue of success" (p. 29). Francis Fukuyama (1996) sees culture essentially as inherited social habit. Coaching can foster opportunities to question and possibly change embedded habits and assumptions using proven approaches from various disciplines, including psychological, medical, and management research. Coaching provides a mechanism for engaging clients with culture and with change.

Geert Hofstede proposes that culture is the collective programming or software of the mind (Hofstede, 1997). Fons Trompenaars offers the perspective that culture is "the way in which a group of people solves problems and reconciles dilemmas" (Trompenaars, 1993, p. 6). These approaches point toward the active and dynamic nature of culture. Coaching is similarly active and dynamic in aiming to unleash potential. As coaches, we facilitate the creation of solutions and new meanings for our clients. When culture is conceptualized as ways of solving problems and reconciling dilemmas, its centrality to coaching is clear.

Coaching from a cultural perspective requires that we look beneath the surface. Hofstede (1997) conceptualizes various layers of culture with the analogy of an onion ring. The outer layers contain the practices of culture through symbols, heroes, and rituals, while at the center lie the values of the culture. Coaching can move back and forth from the external symbols and routine practices of culture to work with the internal values and associated desires of clients that are keys to unleashing potential.

CULTURAL ORIENTATIONS FRAMEWORK

A common and useful way of examining how values differ (or are similar) across cultures is to conceptualize them as to how people face universal challenges that confront them. Rosinski (2003) has adapted the work of anthropologists, cross cultural consultants and communications experts such as Geert Hofstede (2001), Shalom Schwartz (Schwartz & Bardi, 2001), Edward T. Hall (1989), and Fons Trompenaars (1993) to identify challenges that are common across coaching situations. Different cultures choose different approaches in response to the challenges. These can be termed cultural orientations. Table 9.1 sets out the Cultural Orientations Framework (Rosinski, 2003a).

There are many ways of identifying and leveraging from cultural orientations in coaching. Our experience is that the Cultural Orientations Framework is an effective tool. Clients are asked to identify their existing orientations and to examine other alternatives. Through experimentation and reflection, they then explore alternative orientations and work toward an approach that best suits their identities and contexts. This is an ongoing process of personal and professional growth and does not require a letting go of original orientations or a surrendering of self. The approach is pragmatic in seeking to build on existing characteristics and strengths (James, 1907b). Clients are encouraged to be authentic in exploring and developing their preferred orientations.

In considering cultural orientations, we seek to leverage differences.

Table 9.1

Cultural Orientations Framework

Categories	Dimensions	Description
Sense of Power and Responsibility	Control/Harmony/Humility	*Control:* People have a determinant power and responsibility to forge the life they want. *Harmony:* Strive for balance and harmony with nature. *Humility:* Accept inevitable natural limitations.
Time Management Approaches	Scarce/Plentiful	*Scarce:* Time is a scarce resource. Manage time carefully! *Plentiful:* Time is abundant. Relax!
	Monochronic/Polychronic	*Monochronic:* Concentrate on one activity and/or relationship at a time. *Polychronic:* Concentrate simultaneously on multiple tasks and/or people.
	Past/Present/Future	*Past:* Learn from the past. The present is essentially a continuation or a repetition of past occurrences. *Present:* Focus on the here and now and on short-term benefits. *Future:* Have a bias toward long-term benefits. Promote a far-reaching vision.
Definitions of Identity and Purpose	Being/Doing	*Being:* Stress living itself and the development of talents and relationships. *Doing:* Focus on accomplishments and visible achievements.
	Individualistic/Collectivistic	*Individualistic:* Emphasize individual attributes and projects. *Collectivistic:* Emphasize affiliation with a group.
Organizational Arrangements	Hierarchy/Equality	*Hierarchy:* Society and organizations must be socially stratified to function properly. *Equality:* People are equals who often happen to play different roles.
	Universalist/Particularist	*Universalist:* All cases should be treated in the same universal manner. Adopt common processes for consistency and economies of scale. *Particularist:* Emphasize particular circumstances. Favor decentralization and tailored solutions.
	Stability/Change	*Stability:* Value a static and orderly environment. Encourage efficiency through systematic and disciplined work. Minimize change and ambiguity, perceived as disruptive. *Change:* Value a dynamic and flexible environment. Promote effectiveness through adaptability and innovation. Avoid routine, perceived as boring.

(Continued)

259

Table 9.1 *(Continued)*

Categories	Dimensions	Description
	Competitive/Collaborative	*Competitive:* Promote success and progress through competitive stimulation. *Collaborative:* Promote success and progress through mutual support, sharing of best practices, and solidarity.
Notions of Territory and Boundaries	Protective/Sharing	*Protective:* Protect oneself by keeping personal life and feelings private (mental boundaries), and by minimizing intrusions in one's physical space (physical boundaries). *Sharing:* Build closer relationships by sharing one's psychological and physical domains.
Communication Patterns	High-Context/ Low-Context	*High-Context:* Rely on implicit communication. Appreciate the meaning of gestures, postures, voice, and context. *Low-Context:* Rely on explicit communication. Favor clear and detailed instructions.
	Direct/Indirect	*Direct:* In a conflict or with a tough message to deliver, get your point across clearly at the risk of offending or hurting. *Indirect:* In a conflict or with a tough message to deliver, favor maintaining a cordial relationship at the risk of misunderstanding.
	Affective/Neutral	*Affective:* Display emotions and warmth when communicating. Establishing and maintaining personal and social connections is key. *Neutral:* Stress conciseness, precision, and detachment when communicating.
	Formal/Informal	*Formal:* Observe strict protocols and rituals. *Informal:* Favor familiarity and spontaneity.
Modes of Thinking	Deductive/Inductive	*Deductive:* Emphasize concepts, theories, and general principles. Then, through logical reasoning, derive practical applications and solutions. *Inductive:* Start with experiences, concrete situations, and cases. Then, using intuition, formulate general models and theories.
	Analytical/Systemic	*Analytical:* Separate a whole into its constituent elements. Dissect a problem into smaller chunks. *Systemic:* Assemble the parts into a cohesive whole. Explore connections between elements, and focus on the whole system.

© Philippe Rosinski. Reproduced with permission from "Coaching Across Cultures" by Philippe Rosinski, published by Nicholas Brealey Publishing, London 2003.

The idea is not to select one approach or another, but to synthesize for maximum advantage. Put in algebraic terms, we do not seek to choose either *a* or *b*, nor to average them, but to add them—that is, to accept both *a* and *b*. The approach suggested here is dialectical where we seek to maximize through contrast. We are therefore open to the possibility that the net result is greater than *a* + *b*. The practice of deliberately accepting and building from apparently opposite approaches requires a certain comfort with paradoxes and complexity. One central paradox is that while major differences between people can provide a barrier to effective communication, differences can also be levers for positive change. Differences generally are seen as challenges and opportunities rather than problems or threats to be navigated.

AVOIDING OVERGENERALIZING

When seeking to identify the distinctive characteristics and orientations that define group culture, there is a risk of stereotyping, particularly when an attempt is made to quantify culture along dimensions or orientations. In fact, some writers have gone so far as to argue that the whole notion of measuring along cultural dimensions promotes a form of sophisticated stereotyping, particularly when applied to national culture (Osland, Bird, Delano, & Jacob, 2000; Tayeb, 2001). Here is another paradox: Knowledge of cultural dimensions—including measurements on dimensions—can provide invaluable insights about group and even individual behavior; yet knowledge of cultural dimensions can be misleading and destructive. For example, to coach a Malaysian businessman from an assumption that he strongly favors a hierarchical and directive leadership style could restrict the effectiveness of the coaching relationship. (Malaysia is ranked highest on Hofstede's power distance scale, which aims to measure the distance between managers and employees.) However, to be aware that such a style is common in Malaysia and to have it as valuable knowledge of context for the coaching relationship provides the potential for enhancing the effectiveness of the coaching. Cultural diversity within national culture means that there is often considerable variation in style. Australia, for example, is a multicultural society with many people exhibiting cultural characteristics more typical of their homelands than of the statistical norm in Australia. At the same time, it is useful to know that there are certain ways that many Australian companies tend to do business. The same need for informed caution holds when considering work group and organizational cultures. There is variation within as well as across groups—that is, cultures within cultures. Also, there are individual personality differences that are based on genetic factors. Put in statistical terms, quantifying where cultures sit on particular dimensions requires averaging and normal curve distributions. In coaching we often come across outliers! We look to leverage differences rather than to statistically wash them out.

CULTURAL INTELLIGENCE (CQ)

Conventional notions of intelligence have been questioned as a strong or valid predictor of success in business, or functionality generally—particularly across different cultural contexts. Various other forms of intelligence have been proposed as important variables, and culture has begun to inform discussions on the influence of intelligence in predicting success in different contexts. Sternberg (2003) comments that the strength of cultural approaches to intelligence is their recognition that intelligence cannot be fully understood outside its cultural context. Coaching literature and practice have often drawn on the work of Daniel Goleman (1995, 1998) and others in the area of emotional intelligence (referred to as EQ) (e.g., see Greene & Grant, 2003, pp. 125–126). Goleman includes coaching as one of six leadership styles, noting that it is the least used but delivers bottom-line results (Goleman, 2000). Goleman argues that EQ is a better predictor of success than IQ and focuses on factors such as self-awareness, self-regulation, motivation, empathy, and social skills. These, of course, are the areas where coaching focuses. There has been some debate about the validity of EQ (Sternberg, 2003). Nevertheless, the concept has definitely struck a chord with managers and practitioners in business. More recently, several academics and practitioners (Earley & Ang, 2003; Peterson, 2004; Thomas & Inkson, 2004) have given emotional intelligence a cultural perspective and suggested that cultural intelligence (called CQ) goes beyond EQ in predicting success in working across cultures. Their work has been on national culture. However, the principles appear consistent when applied to culture across groups of different kinds.

Earley and Ang (2003) define CQ as "a person's capability for successful adaptation to new cultural settings, that is, for unfamiliar settings attributable to cultural context" (p. 9). They suggest that a person with high EQ can in fact be quite ineffective in cross-cultural adaptation. High CQ requires effectiveness across the cognitive, affective, and behavioral domains. What is required for cultural adaptation is knowledge of cultural context (cognitive), a willingness to change ways of behaving (affective), and the ability to change behavior (behavioral). The affective element is often overlooked. Neither training nor coaching can assist a manager in cross-cultural effectiveness if the manager is, for example, passionately committed to the superiority of his or her own culture and has no interest in shifting focus. There is a compelling case for a special consideration of culture in contexts where people are confronted with cross-cultural situations. The construct of CQ provides some ideas as to how coaches might work with clients to maximize their effectiveness in cross-cultural situations. Coaching can, for example, increase what Thomas and Inkson (2004) term "mindfulness," an element of CQ defined as the ability to pay attention in a reflective and creative way to cues in the cross-cultural situations (p. 15).

Importantly, all of the writers about CQ agree that it can be increased through learning, though the exact processes have not been made explicit. Coaching would seem to provide an excellent vehicle for increasing CQ because it provides a process for experimentation and reflection. An element of CQ that provides a coaching challenge is the need for clients to be knowledgeable about cultural issues and the specifics of the cultures from which and within which they are operating. The means by which people effectively process information vary across cultures. For example, a direct message about cultural awareness and sensitivity delivered to someone whose cultural orientation for communication is indirect may be viewed as disrespectful. Similarly, in some cultures it might be of marginal effectiveness—or even counterproductive—to send unsolicited written material to clients. The delivery of information about culture may be better delivered or introduced in the coaching conversations. Coaches need to be aware of the culture of their clients, as well as their own styles, to maximize opportunities for effective communication of relevant information. CQ is a useful concept for coaches who are working across cultures. Beyond CQ, we encourage our clients to reach in their learning journeys a point of intercultural excellence. At this point, not only can they work effectively across cultures through an appreciation of cultural differences, but can also synthesize and leverage these differences (Rosinski, 2003b).

ACCEPTANCE OF SELF AND OTHER IDENTITIES

Taking a cultural perspective encourages clients (and coaches) to be authentic, which in effect means acting from a sense of who they really are, rather than from a perspective of what others expect or desire. Being authentic requires an exploration and understanding of individual identity, which is shaped by a synthesis of the multiple cultures by which we are influenced. A model that is useful in coaching and flows naturally from this process of clarifying and establishing authenticity is transactional analysis (TA) (Berne, 1973; for a summary of TA theory, see Rosinski,

2003a, pp. 260–265). One insight from TA that works well across cultures is the choice of an "okay (self)–okay (others)" mind-set. "Okay" refers to our image of someone worthy of respect, with positive intentions, and able to make a difference. Taking an okay–okay mind-set is a subjective choice. It does not matter that you could rationally also make a case for the other combinations (okay–not okay, not okay–okay, not okay–not okay). The okay–okay perspective encourages the creation of virtuous circles of respect, productive behaviors, and creativity (Rosinski, 2003a, pp. 6–7). Nevertheless, to sustain an okay–okay mind-set clients must genuinely believe that they are okay. Coaching from a cultural perspective can assist them in reaching this point and in doing so provide a basis for more authentic relationships in their work and social lives.

Coaching—particularly executive coaching—is often associated with psychology, and in particular psychotherapy (e.g., *The Economist*, 2003). The popular vision is of a faceless coach, often with a background in psychology, working secretly and off-site with the CEO. The rest of the company may only be aware of some mysterious process that seems to be making the CEO behave in unusual ways. This model is sometimes the reality, though a broader view of coaching such as the Global Coaching Process offers expanded possibilities. Certainly, the principles and techniques of counseling and psychotherapy are very useful for coaching, though the two are not the same (see Peltier, 2001; Rotenberg, 2000). One major contrast is that the emphasis in coaching is on increasing joy rather than decreasing pain and suffering. Clients are usually highly productive. We tend to work with issues of the present and future, in contrast to unraveling problems stemming from past experiences (though we might do this). From a cultural perspective, psychodynamic approaches can be extremely effective in exploring beneath surface layers of culture. Issues of confidentiality are still crucial—though different—and it is often appropriate and effective for the coach to move out of the office and into clients' cultural environments. A consideration of culture is a consideration of context, and it can be very useful for the coach to observe firsthand the interactions of the client with colleagues. The coaching sessions can then be informed with new data in the form of the coach's observations. The aim is not for the coach to say, "This is what was really occurring," but to provide another perspective: "This is what I observed." Conversations can then occur that leverage differences between the two perspectives.

As with psychotherapy, a strong, trusting client-coach relationship is paramount. It requires an okay (self)–okay (others) mind-set from both parties. It requires that the coach adopt a benevolent approach to the client. The inherent bias is a belief in client potential. Solomon and Flores (2001) argue that true trust is what they term *authentic trust*. This form of trust is "an ongoing, delicate dance of trust and distrust, the tests and trials of commitment, the careful scrutiny and reassessment of the relationship" (p. 102). It is not simple trust such as that of child for a parent, or blind trust such that of follower for a charismatic religious leader. Authentic trust is a mature trust built up through routine, experiment, and experience. The routine of a successful coaching process over an extended time frame is perfectly positioned to promote and develop such a relationship. Key elements are authenticity, confidentiality, and commitment. Clients can use a trusting coaching relationship as a model to extend into their work and social domains.

GLOBAL COACHING PROCESS

Coaching from a cultural perspective in practice sees coach and client working through developmental stages toward the ultimate stage of leveraging cultural differences. The six developmental stages toward intercultural sensitivity proposed by interculturalist Milton Bennett provide a structure that is useful for the coaching process (Bennett, 1993). The early stages can be described as ethnocentric, where clients are locked into their own cultural perspectives. In the later ethnorelative stages clients are more open to different perspectives and realities. Rosinski (2003) proposes a seventh developmental stage of leveraging cultural differences. At this stage, clients not only accept in both their hearts and their guts that different truths or ideals are legitimate, but they engage in synthesis and leverage for growth (Rosinski, 2003a, pp. 29–41).

Step 1 of the Global Coaching Process involves stepping back and imagining what others expect, followed by exploration, gradual emergence of objectives, and preview of the use of the Global Scorecard (Rosinski, 2003a, pp. 209–240) in step 2. This means of facilitating an effective goal-setting process, aiding clients' self-assessment, and providing valuable information for coaches as they seek to work with the client through the developmental journey described earlier. In the assessment phase, the coach will encourage clients to assess approximately where they might be in relation to these developmental stages, and to discuss their associated levels of effectiveness in cross-cultural adjustment and functioning. This information is revealed through the early coaching conversations and appropriate use of tools such as 360-degree feedback. Fundamentally, the coaching will begin at the level of the client. Sessions can then move to increasingly higher levels of complexity in maximizing the client's impact and sense of personal fulfillment.

Setting targets is step 2 of the Global Coaching Process. The Global

Scorecard (Figure 9.1) invites the client to devise measures of internal and external success across a broad variety of stakeholders, including self, family and friends, organization, and community and world. This process emphasizes the centrality of human relationships in personal and professional growth and extends the coaching outside of individual experiences and perceptions. Solomon and Flores (2001) argue, "Any conception of the good life (except to the rare hermit or lone mountaineer) that leaves out the importance of human relationships is pathetic and unrealistic" (pp. 10–11). Step 3 focuses on monitoring and making progress toward the targets, and on revising them as new experiences and new learning are integrated.

The categories help to incorporate the various cultural perspectives that influence the client's reality. There are various other indicators that are effectively used in coaching and in management development. What has been missing is a comprehensive framework for conceptualizing and tying together previous and disparate scorecards and extending the scope. The Global Scorecard seeks to fill this gap.

By including the stakeholder category of community and world, the

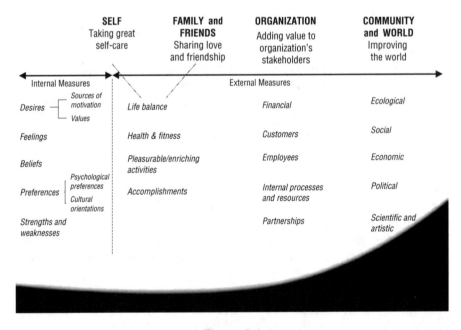

Figure 9.1

The Global Scorecard: Devising Appropriate Measures of Global Success (Drivers and Outcomes)

© Philippe Rosinski, www.CoachingAcrossCultures.com. Reproduced with permission from "Coaching Across Cultures," published by Nicholas Brealey Publishing, London 2003.

Global Scorecard focuses attention on an area that individual coaching sometimes neglects. Coaching from a cultural perspective means looking beyond the individual's immediate reality and into the broader impact that executives in particular can have on society. Coaching relationships then enter the challenging and critical areas of business ethics, sustainable development, corporate citizenship, human rights, poverty, and human creativity. These are areas that have not sat comfortably within the traditional consideration of business bottom lines and economic rationalism.

In addition to focusing on the client, coaching from a cultural perspective encourages the coaches to look deeply at themselves. The Global Scorecard can help with this. Our own desires, strengths, weaknesses, contexts, and cultural and psychological preferences are directly relevant to how we interact with clients. We need to be authentic in our coaching if we are to be effective in encouraging authenticity in our clients. We need to open ourselves to the possibility that our own cultural values, assumptions, or backgrounds may potentially inhibit our effectiveness with a client. By being aware of ourselves and sensitive to our clients, we can be ready to develop authentic strategies to leverage differences and contrasts we encounter.

CULTURAL APPROACH TO CASE STUDIES

In approaching the case studies of Bob and Bonita, we can only offer some ideas on what might happen in the coaching relationship. Our approach is holistic and can draw on multiple perspectives, of which culture is one. Our intention always is to work with the possibilities and potentials of the clients. We assume and look for positive intentions from which to build creative coaching experiences. As we do this, culture often emerges as a critical issue in ways that could never be anticipated based on information presented by the client or client organization. For Bob and Bonita, we have picked up on some likely areas where there is opportunity for creative development.

Case Study: Bob

The presenting information suggests to us that Bob has a high degree of positive intention in approaching the coaching situation. The very fact that Bob has decided to engage a coach—in the face of his own skepticism about the softer side of the profession—is a pointer toward a successful coaching outcome. There are other elements that suggest to us that Bob is open to a creative and exciting coaching experience that will be valuable to him as he establishes his legacy and prepares for retirement. Very obviously, Bob has a deep reservoir of successful experiences from which to draw, including a strong company, a long-term marriage, and his interest in community service. He is charismatic and energetic, and has demonstrated a capacity to follow through on his ideas and projects. As he approaches a new international merger with a South Korean company, he recognizes the need to be flexible in the face of different environments, nations, and cultures.

Right now, it is apparent that Bob may not be at a point where he can take full advantage of the possibilities that surround him. Even without Bob working through the Cultural Orientations Framework, it is clear that Bob places emphasis on doing rather than being. His focus is on accomplishments and visible achievements such as leaving a perfect company as a legacy. From a transactional analysis perspective, Bob seems to be commonly adopting an okay (self)–not okay (other) mind-set. In the coaching we would encourage Bob to acknowledge the perspectives of those whom he manages and with whom he interacts socially and professionally. We would encourage Bob to take a long-term view of the coaching process—to step back and consider carefully where he wants to go with his company and his life beyond short-term objectives of achieving bottom-line results.

Initially, we would familiarize Bob with the Global Coaching Process and the Cultural Orientations Framework. The Global Scorecard tool will assist Bob in clarifying his aims through the coaching. Equally importantly, it is likely that the 360-degree feedback process would give him some new perspectives on those around him—his subordinates, his South Korean colleagues, his friends, and even his wife. Our coaching conversations are likely to move into the nature of the relationships that Bob has with the key people in his life. For example, we might reflect with Bob that his partnership with his wife, like each of his relationships, seems heavily colored by his "doing" approach. Across all of his relationships, we would encourage Bob to look for the possibilities for greater depth through his also adopting a "being" approach. Our aim would be to help Bob connect the patterns in his life and to be open to new approaches.

One immediate issue that we would be dealing with in the coaching session is the merger of Bob's company with the South Korean partner. By reference to the Cultural Orientations Framework, we might contrast Bob's style with those of his South Korean partners and also of some of his key managers. We would then encourage him to consider ways of using the differences constructively. We know Bob is results driven and is likely to be open to new approaches to the merger that contain hard data. Information from Hofstede's studies of cultural dimensions might be a very powerful way of introducing ideas about cultural difference in the language of hard data. For example, South Korea scored very low on the individualism index (18) while the United States is at the high end (91). We could provide Bob with a graphical or tabular representation of the scores of the United States and South Korea on each of Hofstede's dimensions (Hofstede, 2001). The resulting conversations might be very powerful in assisting Bob in seeing possibilities for making the most of differences.

As preparation, we might inform ourselves about aspects of South Korean business culture. For example, Francis Fukuyama's book on the nature of trust in different societies (Fukuyama, 1996) includes chapters on South Korea and America that deal with the complexity of trust as it operates in those business cultures. We would check whether Bob is a keen reader of management literature. If so, we would encourage a conversation about the best ideas he has drawn from literature or his education. We would also refer him to Hofstede, Fukuyama, and other relevant material on cross-cultural business. We might introduce the idea of cultural intelligence as a way of conceptualizing cross-cultural adjustment, and also offer some insights from examples of high-profile companies that worked successfully to leverage culture during mergers and acquisitions. If Bob's resistance is strong we might take the angle that it is his staff that could benefit from understanding more about culture, and suggest, for example, that each of his senior managers be given a copy of a text such as *Cultural Intelligence* by Brooks Peterson (Peterson, 2004), or even *Coaching across Cultures* (Rosinski, 2003a).

Bob is aware that in the past his capacity to customize environments to different cultures and environments has been restricted by the human interactions. We would explore with Bob what did and did not work in his past experiences. We would then use the South Korean merger as a platform for trying new approaches, informed by the research, by previous experience, and from the outcomes of the exercise with the Cultural Orientations Framework. In a learning journal, Bob could track the impact of different approaches and the way that his various relationships are developing.

As a further lever for change, we would encourage Bob to look at his vision for his future and the future of the company in very broad terms, discussing for example the way global corporations are developing. A task for Bob could be to work up a model global corporation with the idea of his leaving a model corporation as part of his legacy. These discussions would flow from the community and world category of the Global Scorecard. Bob could use his learning journal to reflect on how well his company is progressing toward the model, and also to revise his model to accommodate new insights. Our discussions might move across the Cultural Orientations Framework to look at how his human interactions in his company are functioning in relation to his evolving idea of a model global company. One measure of success for Bob would be that the company model is starting to look like his ideal for a global corporation.

Bob might find it difficult to change from an okay (self)–not okay (others) mindset. Similarly, incorporating a "being" approach to relationships is likely to take time. However, if Bob commits himself early in the coaching process to achieving better relationships through adopting additional approaches, then we would be confident of his being successful. If progress is slow, the learning journal entries may reveal, for example, that Bob is inhibiting a successful company merger by stepping in (doing) to persuade and cajole at sensitive points where his managers are developing their own relationships across the corporate and national boundaries. Our role as coaches would be to encourage Bob to take responsibility for the impact his actions might be having in the process and to set in place some new strategies for achieving his objectives. We may canvass the benefits of adopting an alternative approach of providing support by his very presence, authority, and accessibility (being). Such a situation could be an opportunity to demonstrate that it is possible to achieve more doing by being.

It is conceivable that Bob would set narrow target objectives from the coaching that would automatically restrict his capacity for growth. However, this is unlikely to happen because we would challenge him from the beginning to expand his horizons. Not to do so would contribute to the restriction of possibilities from the coaching experience. If we continued coaching Bob while he retained a preference for a pushy, bottom-line focus, we could well end up making him more efficient in this style—but less likely to create a rich legacy. Bob's model company would remain a reflection of his existing style. The possibility remains that Bob could reject our efforts to engage him in reflective conversations about possibilities of more productive and creative models for global success. Then it would become a judgment based on retaining our integrity as coaches about whether to continue the assignment.

More likely, we would anticipate continuing to work with Bob, and he would continue to encourage his key people, including those in South Korea, to work with coaches. In summary, Bob enters the coaching with a high level of goodwill. Provided we harness that goodwill to assist Bob in opening himself up to new possibilities, the coaching should progress positively and creatively.

Case Study: Bonita

Bonita enters the coaching relationship in a frame of mind that invites success. She is excited about the future, open to new ideas, and armed with a record of achievement within her company. We would anticipate dynamic and creative coaching sessions from day one. At 38, she is in midcareer and full of energy and potential. The Global Coaching Process should be a springboard for a period of considerable personal and professional growth.

Like all new executives, Bonita is facing a challenge in her new role. She appears to have a leadership style that may not fit easily with the culture of the company's senior management. The main contrast seems to be between Bonita's collaborative leadership style and a competitive management culture. The fact she is presenting to the coaching program with the issues of leadership skills, dealing with conflict, and work-life balance suggests she may be anticipating a difficult transition. Encouragingly, there is a strong interest in coaching among senior ranks. At least at first glance, this looks like an organizational culture that is open for change. The time ahead for Bonita is one of challenge and opportunity rather than threat.

We would start by a conversation around Bonita's feelings, hopes, and expectations as she takes up her new role. Specifically, we would explore presenting issues: what leadership skills she wishes to acquire and change, her experiences with conflict in the workplace, and what she envisages to be an appropriate work-life balance. Bonita would complete the Cultural Orientations Framework. This is likely to confirm that in facing organizational challenges, Bonita's preferred approach is collaborative, in contrast to competitive. We might suggest that Bonita choose some of her colleagues and make some assessments of them through the Cultural Orientations Framework.

Through the Global Coaching Process we would encourage Bonita to assess her desires, strengths, weaknesses, present situation, and preferences. In this process,

Bonita would be invited to assess the expectations of her stakeholders, and in particular of her executive colleagues, including Ken. The differences between her and their expectations would be the subject of coaching conversations. We might talk with her about contrasting leadership styles and what type of leader she would like to be. She may find that while the culture of the executive team may be more competitive than her own, there may be some on the team who are more in tune with her approach and would make valuable allies through the transition stage. This process might also reveal some new perspectives for Bonita about how her family might view Bonita's promotion.

The coaching process would explore issues around Bonita's transition and look for opportunities for making the most of differences. There will be some stark contrasts between Bonita's way of operating as a manager and colleague in comparison with those of the majority of the executive team she has joined. For example, the relationship with Ken presents a major challenge for Bonita and for the coaching program. Nevertheless, the fact that Ken has not actively opposed her appointment provides a positive entry point to explore strategies for approaching this relationship. Through a learning journal, Bonita could monitor her relationships with her executive colleagues, including Ken. The coaching sessions would provide her with ideas for strategies to build those relationships.

Bonita's tendency to avoid conflict and the difficulties she has in asserting herself are two indications that she is taking a "not okay (self)–okay (other)" mind-set. We would discuss with Bonita the things that are preventing her from being more assertive in the workplace. In encouraging Bonita to be okay about herself and to be assertive, we open up a conversation about what an acceptable style of assertiveness entails for her. Calmness in the face of aggressive behavior might be one element. A quiet persistence in presenting her own point of view might be another. At the same time, we would explore and highlight the effectiveness of Bonita's approach in enabling her to reach a senior position. We would work with Bonita in assisting her in remaining true to herself (i.e., in being authentic) as she goes through this period of transition. There may be a temptation for Bonita to give up some of her essential characteristics in attempting to fit in.

Much of the coaching is likely to be about leveraging difference between the style of operating that Bonita brings to the executive team and the existing management culture. Through synthesis with different styles, we might work on modifying aspects of Bonita's management style to add new dimensions. The coaching emphasis would be on encouraging Bonita to be assertive in a positive way through an okay (self)–okay (other) approach. We would introduce to Bonita the model of the dramatic triangle from transactional analysis (TA) which describes the roles that people tend to adopt when they "play games." Negative energy is created as people take on and move between roles of Persecutor, Rescuer, and Victim. Bonita's tendency to adopt the not okay (self) mind-set makes it likely that she would enter dramatic triangles in a Victim role. Her colleagues would be the Persecutors in the negative games that tend to flow from the dramatic triangles (Rosinski, 2003a). We might also explore if in different situations—such as with her family—Bonita is assuming different roles. Assertiveness would provide a means for Bonita to stay out of destructive games in the workplace and to better manage her work-life balance.

Our sense is that Bonita is very open to learning. The coaching would include a considerable amount of action and experimentation by Bonita as she establishes herself in the new management role. We would encourage Bonita to experiment with risking conflict by being deliberately assertive in situations with some of her colleagues. Conversely, it may be that one weakness Bonita identifies in the management culture is a lack of willingness or capacity to be collaborative. She might set a goal of using her apparently considerable people skills to establish collaborative relationships with her competitive colleagues that could over time assist the management culture to become more creative and effective.

The potential for Bonita to leverage the difference between collaborative and competitive styles is a good example of how the dialectic can operate and synthesis can be achieved. We would discuss with Bonita the opportunities for her to continue to gain benefits in her new role by continuing her collaborative approach. Benefits include mutual support, sharing of best practices, and team solidarity. We would then explore how a competitive approach might also be introduced by Bonita to achieve greater success. This might include the perspective that competition does not have to mean destruction—and it can even be fun, provided one's ego is not too tied up in winning! We might refer to the example of coaching. Coaches often collaborate with each other in ad hoc project teams, while at the same time they gain motivation through a sense of competition in striving to be at the top of their field.

We would encourage Bonita to look for allies. During the sessions, Bonita might develop some strong relationships with people within the organization or outside who share some of her perspectives on life and work. For example, we might discuss with Bonita the idea of identifying a mentor in another company who has faced and overcome similar challenges in his or her career. Bonita's coach might be able to play this role, depending on experiences and the nature of the relationship formed during the sessions. Bonita might also act as a mentor to someone within the company with whom she has established a rapport. Such an arrangement would assist Bonita by strengthening her appreciation of her own effectiveness and strengths, while at the same time contributing to a gradual shift in organizational culture. Consistent with our approach, we might suggest she look for allies who have perspectives very different from her own.

We would assist Bonita in monitoring her work-family balance and discussing strategies for her to manage that situation if balance is not achieved. We would refer back to a discussion of her family's desires from the Global Scorecard and check with Bonita on how they are managing with Bonita's enhanced responsibilities. The objective here is not to look at their desires as having a greater priority than those of Bonita, but to create strategies that would meet both the family's needs and Bonita's. Strategies could include assisting Bonita in preparing for conversations with her husband Martin about the likely pressures on the family during the transition period.

We would be confident that through coaching Bonita would achieve her aim of more highly developed leadership skills. Some of the targets she might set and achieve would be to become more self-aware and more assertive in working from an okay (self) position. Ideally, Bonita would be operating authentically, still with leadership style of collaboration but with the capacity to confront when necessary. This adjusted mind-set would reduce the chances of Bonita being caught in destructive dramatic triangles, not just at work but also with her family.

How Bonita's family and work colleagues react to Bonita's personal and professional growth is not something that Bonita can control. However, her more assertive approach may have an influence on those around her. Family members may develop a better understanding of Bonita's issues in fulfilling her work duties and a respect for her achievements and desires in the new role. This may assist her in achieving her objective of better work-life balance. Bonita's colleagues may be influenced by Bonita to adopt a more collaborative style and to be more open to Bonita's requests for flexible working hours to meet her family responsibilities—or they may not. Idealistically, Ken could grow to respect Bonita and begin to model some of his workplace behavior on her style.

The corporate culture seems to be receptive to change. Nevertheless, her colleagues may be inflexible and reject Bonita's collaborative management style as inappropriate. They might also refuse to allow Bonita sufficient flexibility to meet her desires regarding her family. At worst, Ken could lead a move to remove Bonita from the management team and push for Bill to replace her. Such a scenario is unlikely given the management support of executive coaching and Bonita's track record of success in the company. Also, such a development would not be a failure on Bonita's part.

Changing organizational or management culture is a difficult process. If Bonita rates that her chances of achieving success in meeting her goals seem slim, we might discuss with Bonita the possibility of looking for other options. This possibility would be best raised early on in the process so that Bonita does not confuse a failure to change on the part of others to be a failure in her goals for personal and professional development. Bonita could then explore opportunities in other organizations that might have cultures more receptive to Bonita's style that allow her to be fully authentic in her work.

CONCLUSION

This chapter may have assisted the reader in testing the assumption that culture matters in coaching. We emphasize that culture is not all that matters, but it is an element in executive, team, organizational, and personal coaching that requires consideration and offers great possibilities. In explaining the cultural perspective we draw from developmental, cognitive, behavioral, psychodynamic, and other perspectives. In the case studies, we aim to demonstrate the value of the cultural perspective. We would begin with Bob's and Bonita's possibilities and potentials and encourage them toward visions of global success. The result of a global perspective is that clients' worlds are expanded and they are better able to harness their potentials across relationships in work, family, and social lives—as well as in the community generally.

The practice of leveraging differences provides scope for broader societal success in reconciling and synthesizing differences, rather than just tolerating or even dismissing them. Through a ripple effect, individual coaches who work with leaders can play a part in creating more harmonious organizations and even societies. The metaphor of the human brain is relevant in explaining this effect. In the human brain, synapses provide flexible and organic bridges between neurons that allow the regrouping and succession of neurons into a gigantic number of possible combinations or circuits. This process unlocks our individual neural potential. On a broader scope, human potential can be unleashed when coaches act as synapses, drawing an influx from various disciplines and cultures and connecting people. Coaches operating in this way can cross-fertilize ideas, enhance the depth and quality of communication, and foster the circulation of positive energy.

While we do this, we are also on our own journeys. A privileged side product of coaching from a cultural perspective is growth for the coach. By opening ourselves up to the alternative cultural perspectives we encounter through our clients, we can achieve constant personal and professional growth.

REFERENCES

Adler, N. J. (2002). *International dimensions of organizational behavior* (4th ed.). Cincinnati, OH: South-Western.

Bennett, M. J. (1993). Towards ethnorelativism: A developmental model of intercultural sensitivity, In R. M. Paige (Ed.), *Education for the intercultural experience* (pp. 21–71). Yarmouth, Maine: Intercultural Press.

Berne, E. J. (1973). *The games people play: The basic handbook of transactional analysis.* New York: Ballantine Books.

Earley, P. C., & Ang, S. (2003). *Cultural intelligence: Individual interactions across cultures.* Stanford, CA: Stanford University Press.

The Economist. (2003). Executive coaching: Corporate therapy. *The Economist, 15* (November), 61.

Fukuyama, F. (1996). *Trust: The social virtues and the creation of prosperity.* New York: Simon & Schuster.

Goleman, D. (1995). *Emotional intelligence.* New York: Bantam Books.

Goleman, D. (1998). *Working with emotional intelligence.* New York: Bantam Books.

Goleman, D. (2000). Leadership that gets results. *Harvard Business Review* (March–April), 78–90.

Greene, J., & Grant, A. M. (2003). *Solution-focused coaching: A manager's guide to getting the best from people.* London: Pearson Education Limited.

Hall, E. T. (1989). *Beyond culture.* New York: Anchor Books.

Hofstede, G. (1997). *Cultures and organizations: Software of the mind.* New York: McGraw-Hill.

Hofstede, G. (2001). *Culture's consequences: Comparing values, behaviors, institutions and organizations across nations* (2nd ed.). Thousand Oaks, CA: Sage.

James, W. (1907a). A pluralistic universe. In L. Menand (Ed.), *Pragmatism: A reader* (pp. 132–138). New York: Random House, 1997.

James, W. (1907b). *What pragmatism means.* New York: Longmans, Green & Co.

Osland, J. S., Bird, A., Delano, J., & Jacob, M. (2000). Beyond sophisticated stereotyping: Cultural sensemaking in context. *Academy of Management Executive, 14*(1), 65–79.

Peltier, B. (2001). *The psychology of executive coaching.* New York: Brunner Routledge.

Peterson, B. (2004). *Cultural intelligence: A guide to working with people from other cultures.* Yarmouth, Maine: Intercultural Press.

Rosinski, P. (2003a). *Coaching across cultures: New tools for leveraging national, corporate and professional differences.* London: Nicholas Brealey.

Rosinski, P. (2003b). The applications of coaching across cultures. *International Journal of Coaching in Organizations, 1*(4), 4–16.

Rotenberg, C. T. (2000). Psychodynamic psychotherapy and executive coaching: Overlapping paradigms. *Journal of the American Academy of Psychoanalysis, 28*(4), 653–663.

Schein, E. H. (1999). *The corporate culture survival guide: Sense and nonsense about culture change.* San Francisco: Wiley.

Schwartz, S. H., & Bardi, A. (2001). Value hierarchies across cultures: Taking a similarities perspective. *Journal of Cross-Cultural Psychology, 32*(3), 268–290.

Solomon, R. C., & Flores, F. (2001). *Building trust in business, politics, relationships, and life.* New York: Oxford University Press.

Sternberg, R. J. (2003). *Wisdom, creativity and intelligence synthesized.* Cambridge, UK: Cambridge University Press

Tayeb, M. (2001). Conducting research across cultures: Overcoming drawbacks and obstacles. *International Journal of Cross Cultural Management, 1*(1), 91–108.

Thomas, D. C., & Inkson, K. (2004). *Cultural intelligence: People skills for global business.* San Francisco: Berrett-Koehler Publishers Inc.

Trompenaars, F. (1993). *Riding the waves of culture: Understanding cultural diversity in business.* London: Nicholas Brealey.

CHAPTER 10

An Adventure-Based Framework for Coaching

TRAVIS KEMP

ADVENTURE PROGRAMMING IS a specialist field of practice within experiential education that shares close affiliations and informing bodies of knowledge with pedagogy, andragogy, counseling, psychotherapy, and psychology. A still embryonic subdiscipline within the broader field of adventure programming known as *adventure therapy* is increasingly being utilized within a range of clinical and developmental settings and with a diverse range of client groups. Like coaching, adventure programming continues to accumulate an empirical, efficacy-based body of knowledge while practitioners continue the process of defining it as a distinctly unique developmental intervention method. To date, the theoretical and case-based evidence exploring the outcomes of adventure programming appear promising, and the potential applications to a coaching context continue to emerge, driven by the many similarities, potentials, and opportunities for methodological cross-fertilization that exist between these two practice frameworks.

In this chapter, I explore the historical and contextual development of adventure programming and therapy, provide an overview of the informing bodies of knowledge central to their practice, and detail its subsequent application to a coaching context. Through the exploration of potential individual and group-based applications of the adventure method to the two selected coaching case studies, I explore how this methodology provides not only an innovative, accessible, and functional framework for a coaching intervention, but a valuable philosophical foundation for coaching more broadly through its human values focus, positive-developmental approaches, and proactive assumptions in relation to human potential.

FOUNDATIONS OF ADVENTURE

As Blattner (2005) subtly eludes, the process of executive coaching can be readily conceptualized as an "adventure" when one examines the phenomenology of the coaching relationship. In his case study, Blattner's client articulates an internal struggle with fear, anxiety, self-doubt, and uncertainty as he pursues his goals of increased courage and self-esteem, and through this sharing provides an intimate insight into his unique "adventure" within the coaching experience. However, while on this occasion the author stops short of articulating his rationale for applying this popular term to the coaching relationship, the current chapter outlines the full extent of this synergistic marriage of approaches and details the key elements of adventure programming and therapy that both define this field of practice and can be applied directly to coaching practice.

Adventure programming has been defined most broadly as "the deliberate use of adventurous experiences to create learning in individuals or groups, that results in change for society and communities" (Priest, 1999a, p. xiii).

However, as with all adventures, we begin by observing, questioning, and gaining an understanding of where we are currently and how we find ourselves to be here. Hence, any review of adventure programming must acknowledge, as do many other experientially based methodologies, two of its most influential contributors, John Dewey and Kurt Hahn.

According to Crosby (1995), John Dewey grappled throughout his career with the dualist notions of separating the human from the natural, with this struggle ultimately resulting in him developing a unique philosophical framework for education. Dewey argued strongly for the encouragement of freedom within education and a movement away from the central function of authority and secondary experience as its basic doctrine. Instead, Dewey professed a philosophy of reflective experience and balance between knowledge created through the learning process itself and the teaching of the established bodies of knowledge within academe (Hunt, 1995). It was this philosophical framework that spawned the emergence of an experiential philosophy of education, which, during the late nineteenth century, digressed markedly from the largely didactically driven pedagogical framework of that period and set in motion a radical new framework for learning.

Following in the philosophical footsteps of John Dewey was Kurt Hahn. Hahn is widely acknowledged as having had a profound influence on the development of experiential education (James, 1995; Priest, 1990; Schafermeyer, 1978). Hahn founded the internationally recognized Outward

Bound schools in Wales in 1941, and these schools have since multiplied across the globe, often seen as being synonymous with outdoor adventure education. The Outward Bound schools at that time focused on providing extended residential outdoor experiences that utilized a series of adventure programming and outdoor activities to facilitate personal growth and learning within their participants. The rationale for Outward Bound's methodology is built upon the belief that by taking groups of individuals and placing them in new, unfamiliar, and subjectively risky situations, a group dynamic process will emerge that will facilitate their achievement of a given objective or task (Schafermeyer, 1978). Schafermeyer further suggested that the primary outcome of participation in these experiences was personal growth and development, rather than achievement of the task itself. Hahn clearly stipulated that all courses conducted by Outward Bound were to be facilitated using the medium of outdoor activity, as participants needed to be placed in environments that were essentially wilderness in nature to achieve the desired developmental outcomes. In some respects this, together with Outward Bound's focus on utilizing outdoor pursuit–based activities such as rock climbing and mountaineering, both nurtured and constrained development within the field during these early years due to the exclusive and restrictive nature of this method for many potential clients.

As adventure education grew in sophistication, finer distinctions began to be made among a myriad of activities and pursuits that fell within this broad term. Indeed, today the term *adventure education* has come to include a myriad of activities and programs ranging from wilderness-based backpacking expeditions to the group games and initiative tasks such as those outlined by Rohnke (1984) and Kemp (1995), among numerous others. It was Miles and Priest (1990) who commented that the term had been used synonymously with experiential education, outdoor education, physical education, or outdoor pursuits. Similarly, Hirsch (1999) commented that the term *outdoor education* encompassed virtually any activity that was conducted outdoors and hence any activity that was apparently adventurous in nature.

DEFINING THE ADVENTURE

Most attempts by researchers and practitioners alike during the early growth of adventure programming focused on the identification of *activities* that defined the field, rather than the process and methods central to the field. Authors including Mortlock (1978), Iso-Ahola (1988), and Webster (1978) were among the first to contribute this activity-based approach to the definition. However, Raiola (1984) adopted a different approach. Instead of focusing on defining the activities themselves, he chose to explore the key elements of adventure. The fundamental element, he argued, was the presence of *perceptual risk* in the activity, and this risk was physical in nature.

Priest and Baillie (1987) broadened this perspective with their proposal of a second key element of adventure. Consistent with the thoughts of Raiola (1984), before any activity could be defined as adventurous, an element of perceptual risk needed to be present. In addition, though, this risk could be seen as being not only physical in nature, but also psychological. The second key element identified was an inherent *uncertainty* surrounding both the process of participating in the activity and its final outcome. As a result, instead of simply being a group of selected activities that defined adventure, a construct of adventure had now been conceptualized in the form of a client-centered perception and a unique paradigm for participation.

Carpenter and Priest's (1989) later explorations highlighted the highly subjective nature of risk. Essentially, they argued, risk was an individual's unique perception of a situation or event as opposed to being any externally definable and stable construct in and of itself. Moreover, participants' cognitive, behavioral, and emotional competence in responding to that experience played a critical role in their subjective judgment of the size and magnitude of the risk itself. Simply, this meant that:

> Adventures differ for individual participants. What is an adventure for one person may not be for another, and an adventure at a certain time or in a given place may not be the same at another time or place. (Carpenter & Priest, 1989, p. 67)

It is as a result of this insight that an adventure can be seen as a function not of the outdoors or outdoor activities per se, but of the participant's unique schemas and subjective interpretations of a situation or event. To clarify this proposition, Carpenter and Priest (1989) provided the example of an adventure as experienced by a newly divorced person. The adventure in this case can be seen as the event of participating alone in his/her first social gathering. First, the uncertainty and perceived risk inherent in this situation relates to the threat to the individual's self-concept and self-esteem. The commitment to recover from the divorce and establish a new social network provides the stimulus for this first social encounter, or, as we have conceptualized, the adventure. There is an element of doubt surrounding the person's rusty skills in social conversation and there is some fear of rejection or embarrassment among strangers. Regardless of the number of similar encounters the person has experienced previously, at this time and in this place, the person is embarking upon an adventure:

> Uncertainties determine whether an adventure takes place. In other words, adventures are merely a subset of leisure where uncertainty of outcome is present due to the interplay of perceived competence and risk. (p. 73)

There is a perceptual gap between the person's current level of perceived competence and the skill level required to be successful in the social activity. If this self-perception is accurate, then the potential outcomes of this gap may be embarrassment or psychological "injury." This is the key element that defines this experience as an adventure.

It is the behavioral *change* that emerges from the person's successful participation in an adventure that Priest (1996b) believed was the central objective of adventure programming. The adventure, he suggested, provides the opportunity for the participant to change by formulating new behavioral responses to the uncertainties faced in the adventure process.

In short, while a focus within the traditional constructs of adventure has been physical safety (Wade, 1990), Dickson, Chapman, and Hurrell (2000) more accurately capture the breadth of risk that defines an adventure by stating that "risk may be physical, social, psychological, financial, or spiritual" (p. 16).

However, it was Nadler (1993) who earlier outlined several key elements and critical factors of an adventure experience. Simply, he proposed that an adventure is any experience whereby the client experiences a state of disequilibrium by being placed in a novel setting and a *cooperative* environment. She is presented with opportunities for solving unique and new problems and these solutions lead to feelings of accomplishment, which are augmented by *processing* the experience. These learnings and successes are then transferred and generalized to the client's current reality.

As Priest (1999b) concluded, adventure could be seen as a *process* rather than an activity, and while outdoor activities may provide the vehicle for the adventure in some cases, it is the *process* of adventure that is central to the growth and developmental outcomes experienced by participants.

RISK AND UNCERTAINTY: THE ESSENCE OF THE ADVENTURE

With the emergence of risk being a central defining element of adventure programming, Vincent (1995) raises several pertinent questions regarding the management of the emotional component of adventure programs in developmental settings. Creating an environment of emotional safety is widely regarded as a fundamental requirement to the successful implementation of any adventure experience (Johnson, 1992; Schoel, Prouty, & Radcliffe, 1988). Vincent describes emotional safety as a continuum anchored at each end by feelings of safety and feelings of threat. The participant's position on the continuum is contingent upon his level of inter- and intrapersonal trust being experienced at a given moment. In her phenomenological study, Vincent targeted professionals practicing in the field of adventure programming to validate this definition of emotional safety, with positive interrater reliability being reported in relation to this model.

In extending the development of thinking associated with risk, Nadler (1995) introduced the notion of personal "comfort zones" in adventure programming. It is through the adventure experience that individuals are encouraged to move to the edge of their psychological or psychophysiological boundary or to a point that their inherent level of internal comfort begins to give way to overarousal and discomfort. Thus "edgework" is "a process that illuminates what is happening for the individual when they are at or close to their edge" (p. 53).

The aim of this process is to reflect, with the guidance of the facilitator, on one's unique experience while in the moment. This enables a "cognitive anchoring" of the experience for the client and an ability to return to this anchor at any point in the future when a similar "real-life" situation arises. Nadler proposes four key levels of processing of the adventure experience in order to facilitate edgework. Initially *awareness* of one's feelings and emotional responses in a given situation is the first step in the developmental process. This may include awareness at both an emotional and a physiological level. *Responsibility* sees participants begin to accept ownership of their behavior. They discover and acknowledge the similarities between their behavior in the activity and their responses to other situations in the external setting outside of the adventure experience. *Experimentation* by the participants with new responses or behaviors can then be attempted and a subsequent reevaluation and assessment of these attempts is made. Following feedback, appropriate adjustments are made, and these new responses and behaviors are *transferred* to the clients' external environment. This process is underpinned by the core exploratory areas of *edgework*, which include emotion, physiology, beliefs, conversation, support, defense, and participants' autonomous behavioral patterns.

It is apparent that the adventure paradigm as conceptualized by adventure core components of risk and anxiety coupled with an uncertain outcome closely aligns with the client's subjective experience of the coaching relationship. As change is central to achieving successful outcomes in coaching, the greater the coach's skill in normalizing the psychoemotional dynamics within the change process of coaching, the greater the likelihood of client success; and therein lies the potential of the metaphoric framing of the coaching relationship within an adventure-based paradigm.

PROCESSING THE ADVENTURE: FRAMEWORKS FOR COACHING CONVERSATIONS

The science of processing adventure experiences has developed significantly during the past 20 years. While numerous approaches to processing have been explored and utilized, it is the framework devised and presented initially by Bacon (1987) and progressively developed by Doughty (1991), Priest and Gass (1993, 1999), and later Priest, Gass, and Gillis (2000) that represents the contemporary benchmark for effective facilitation of adventure programming. These works represent a progressive generational development (Priest, 1999c, Priest & Gass, 1993) of understanding surrounding the processing of adventure experiences.

Priest and Gass (1993) first presented a model for processing adventure experiences that was directly tied to the purpose for which the adventure program was being implemented. They identified four key settings in which adventure programming could be utilized. Recreational adventure programming is primarily concerned with providing a fun and enjoyable experience for the participant. This style of programming would also encompass learning new motor skills, especially outdoor pursuit skills such as canoeing or rock climbing. Educational programming aims to provide participants with an understanding of key social concepts such as teamwork and communication. This program allows participants to gain a new insight into alternative aspects of behavior and facilitates a broadening of understanding and perception about the life experiences of themselves and others.

The final two types of adventure programming have perhaps the greatest direct transfer value to the coaching context. Developmental and therapeutic adventure both focus specifically on participants learning new behaviors. In the case of developmental experiences, these new behaviors represent different ways to respond to situations, allowing for behavioral adaptability. Therapeutic programming is differentiated from developmental programming by one key variable. Unlike the developmental program, which facilitates a broadening of already adequate behavioral competency, therapeutic programs seek to correct misbehaviors by teaching more functional behaviors. This may take the form of helping participants to replace their existing destructive behavioral responses to situations with more functional and effective behaviors. These categories were later reiterated by Ringer and Gillis (1995).

Each of these categories lends itself to the six progressive generations of facilitation technique that Priest and Gass (1993) outline. The first and second generations, "letting the experience speak for itself" and "speaking on behalf of the experience" appear best applied to the recreational program. The first of these methods allows participants to draw their own conclusions and learning from the experience. The facilitator simply provides an opportunity for participants to experience an adventure-based program and ensures their safety and well-being while they are participating. There is no facilitator-centered reflection about the experience, and participants are left to draw their own conclusions as to their learning, if any, from the experience.

In the second generation, the facilitator interprets the participants' experiences on their behalf and presents his/her interpretation of the benefits, learnings, and outcomes of their experience to the participants directly in the form of teaching. This method remains "facilitator-centric" with little input from participants with regard to their own perceptions of the value of the experience or the key learning outcomes. Instead, specific educational objectives are targeted and achieved through the process. Given the client-driven focus within the coaching context, however, these methods appear of limited direct value.

The third generation, called "debriefing," has been by far the most widely utilized form of adventure processing to date and the most relevant to direct application to the coaching relationship, as are the subsequent fourth, fifth, and sixth generations outlined next. Priest and Naismith (1993) developed the now-preferred model for best-practice debriefing of adventure experiences, *funneling*. Immediately after the program has ended, participants are asked to reflect on their adventure experience, behavior, and general participation while completing it. Participants learn through a facilitator-guided discussion at the conclusion of the experience during which participants are encouraged to accept responsibility for their actions within the activity. Several key questions are posed to the group to guide their reflection and progressively distill their learning through five key phases. These phases include reviewing, recalling, and remembering events within the experience; exploring the affect and effect these events had; a summation of the learning as a result of these insights; a plan for applying these insights outside the program; and finally a commitment to applying this learning.

The fourth generation of facilitation technique involves directly front-loading (Priest, 1996b) the experience by "prebriefing" (Gass, 1995, p. 3) the participants prior to their participation in the program. According to Priest and Gass (1994):

> Frontloading means punctuating the key learning points in advance of the adventure experience, rather than reviewing or debriefing any learning after the fact. (p. 8)

This prebriefing includes the key objectives of the activity, such as goals around behavior, participation, and interaction with other group members. This encourages participants to focus on these objectives throughout the experience, thus allowing the debrief to take the form of a guided reflection and analysis in line with the framework initially established.

The fifth generation of facilitation, *isomorphic framing*, utilizes metaphor to facilitate the transfer of learning from the adventure experience to the participant's wider life. This approach is still relatively uncommon in adventure programming (Priest & Gass, 1999) and is most appropriate for specific interventions with intact groups or for therapeutic settings.

Even rarer, however, is the sixth generation, indirectly frontloading the experience. This approach is used in conjunction with the techniques of *double binding* and *paradox*, presented initially by Priest and Gass (1994). Paradox takes the form of symptom prescription and displacement, illusion of alternatives, and proactive reframing. This technique is best understood through the example of a "win-win" frontloading double bind, which outlines one dysfunctional way that clients have completed the activity in the past. By doing this, if clients complete the task in this dysfunctional way, they win because this behavior will be obvious and highlighted by the activity. Alternatively, if they don't, they will be able to witness and subsequently reinforce their ability to behave functionally. When these last two methods of processing are utilized, transfer of learning from the adventure program to the external world is most likely to occur.

Itin (1998b) added a seventh generation to Gass and Priest's original model. The seventh generation, known as *flagging* the experience, describes the unconscious reinforcement of desired behavioral changes while participating in the activity following a specific type of frontload. The central tool for this type of processing is hypnosis, and this technique enables the unconscious establishment of metaphoric connections throughout the adventure experience to be achieved. To date, this last generation, as well as the potential use of hypnotic suggestion within the coaching relationship, has yet to be fully explored.

Regardless of the method utilized to process the adventure experience, however, successful processing is ultimately measured by how effectively the learning is transferred from the coaching adventure to the client's real-world experience. Gass (1985) outlines three distinct levels of transfer of learning that occur within the adventure experience. *Specific* transfer occurs when the direct application of skills learned within the activity is applied to other situations outside the activity. These are most often concrete skills such as those encountered in the traditional outdoor pursuit activities. *Nonspecific* transfer occurs when essentially generalizable principles learned through the activity are applied to diverse situations in the future. These principles may be teamwork or communication insight that is gained through adventure experiences. Finally, *metaphoric transfer* of learning occurs when the activities and experiences in the adventure program closely mimic the situation experienced by the participant outside of the adventure program. Although this progressive generational model of processing provides a sound framework for facilitating adventure processes, a myriad of innovative adjunct techniques have also been used successfully by adventure programmers.

Building on the theoretical perspective of providing innovative feedback mechanisms to facilitate behavioral learning, Kemp and McCarron (1998) presented a conceptual framework for teaching new behaviors through adventure programming that translated motor skill acquisition theory to a cognitive-behavioral learning context. Borrowing from Magill's (1995) multistage model, this sequential framework outlines the cognitive, autonomous, and mastery phases of behavioral skill development and identifies the key learning and feedback requirements necessary to enable learners to make a successful transition at each stage of behavioral development.

Greenaway (1992) developed a complementary four-stage model for exploring the adventure program. The "experience, express, examine, and explore" sequence provides a simple framework for reviewing adventure experiences. In addition, he presents a series of techniques for active reviewing that incorporate activities that include action replay, replay with puppets, and sketch mapping. *Action replay* centers around the replaying of a specific scene or interaction between people in the group by having them act out or repeat the interaction again during the debrief phase. *Replay with puppets* utilizes a similar framework; however, rather than the individuals themselves repeating the interaction, puppets or actors are used. *Sketch mapping* relates to members of the group drawing their experience visually and talking through the construction of their drawing with the group. In addition, Greenaway introduces the use of visual metaphor in the debriefing process. He uses the example of creating the picture of a swimming pool. The facilitator describes and outlines the pool to the group, including the edges, deep and shallow ends, and so on. Participants are then asked to use the metaphor to describe how they were feeling at various points throughout the activity. The pool in this case becomes the metaphor for the activity, and participants are encouraged to be creative in their use of this metaphor.

Narrative is a technique often used within a number of therapeutic settings to restructure clients' own stories of themselves and their experiences. Nadler and Luckner (1992) argue that this, too, is a powerful and beneficial processing technique available to the adventure practitioner. If facilitators can help the client create positive and valuable stories to describe his or her experiences in adventure programming, learning is generalized more effectively to the diversity of situations one faces outside the program.

Quinsland and Van Ginkel (1988) identified early on the value of journal writing for the processing of adventure experience. McKenna and Kiewa (1996) conducted an empirical study to investigate the impact of journal writing as a processing tool during a residential outdoor education program over a five-day period on self-concept. A control group who did not complete journal writing was utilized to isolate journal writing as the independent variable. Results indicated a higher level of stability in self-concept change in the journal-writing group than in the control group. The authors concluded that the reflection associated with the process of minimally structured journal writing is a valuable tool for processing adventure experiences. These sentiments were later echoed by Driver (1997).

Empirical studies have now been completed that investigate the specific effects of different styles of processing, including that completed by Priest (1996a) investigating two different debriefing methods used for processing a high ropes course experience. Results suggested a general enhancement of subjects' self-confidence across both treatment groups, but more sustained changes were reported at a four-month posttreatment follow-up within subjects in the specific debrief group.

In summary, it would appear that the sophistication of the processing and coaching that occurs prior to, during, and following any adventure experience is critical in achieving a successful change outcome. In particular, the use of metaphor is identified as central to adventure programming's developmental effectiveness and hence warrants a deeper investigation.

METAPHORS AND ISOMORPHS:
KEYS TO LEARNING TRANSFER THROUGH COACHING

Metaphoric transfer of learning occurs when the activities and experiences in the adventure program closely mimic the situation experienced by the participant outside of the adventure program. The activity becomes a reflection and a facsimile of an individual's wider life, and this parallel experience provides participants with an opportunity to identify key patterns and processes embedded in their behavior, then practice new behavior within a supportive gamelike and controlled situation.

Metaphor has been defined most broadly by Bryant, Katz, Becvar, and Becvar (1988) as "any verbal or concrete illustration, description, or reference designed to bring about perceptual and/or behavioral change" (p. 113), and more specifically by Priest and Gass (1993) as "the analogous connections made by a learner between the adventure and real life" (p. 24), whereas isomorphs, often used as an adjunct to metaphor, have been defined as "parallel structures added to the adventure experience by the facilitator so clients are encouraged to make certain metaphoric linkages" (Gladding, 1986, p. 25).

Gass and Priest (1993) articulated clearly how these methods are applied within an adventure programming context:

> In structured metaphoric transference, the facilitator purposefully frames the adventure experience in advance, often through a briefing that strengthens the metaphoric message, making discovery on one's own during the activity, and analogous recognition during the debrief session, much more likely. This latter approach of presenting activities as metaphoric frameworks rather than as fantasy games is becoming the leading creative edge of innovative work in adventure programmes with a counselling and therapy or training and development focus. (p. 19)

While metaphors and isomorphs are relatively recent additions to the adventure processing tool kit (Gass, 1995; Nadler & Luckner, 1992), these methods have been used widely to facilitate behavioral change within a variety of educational and developmental settings for some time. Metaphor has been utilized by behavioral, Gestalt, and family therapists previously (Bryant, Katz, Becvar, & Becvar, 1988), and both metaphors and isomorphs have been utilized within general and developmental counseling settings (Atwood & Levine, 1991; Hendrix, 1992; Roberts, 1987). They have been acknowledged as a highly valuable and functional tool for the facilitation of therapeutic outcomes (Gladding, 1986), and metaphor has been used with such diverse client groups as prison inmate populations (Romig & Gruenke, 1991) and those adjusting to blindness (Bowman, 1992). Metaphor has also been utilized within group-based growth and developmental settings to create an opportunity for safe dialogue and communication within the group (McClure, 1989).

Strong (1989) offers a finer distinction by suggesting that the adventure programmer needs to develop an understanding of the individual client's own existing metaphoric language for the metaphor to be successful. Only by doing this is the programmer able to fully utilize the client's unique experiences in the developmental process. The creation of metaphor is often a nonintentional act on the part of the client, which gives the therapist a valuable insight into the client's unique experiences. The challenge, Strong suggests, is to pick up on the client's unique subjective, metaphoric context and continue to construct new learning through the client's own metaphor where possible. Strong suggests that there are three main strategies that can be employed when using metaphors in client counseling, including explicating what is implicit, therapeutically extending or modifying the metaphor, and creating and delivering therapeutic metaphors. This final method has become a focus for many adventure therapists, although the importance of a deeper exploration and progressive development of each client's own metaphoric structures is of critical importance to the successful application of this method. Without an acute awareness of clients' own metaphors, adventure therapists may risk discounting frames of reference that are already meaningfully established in an effort to create their own metaphoric framing of the adventure program. Strong suggests that the delivery of the metaphor is far more complex than one might immediately think, requiring techniques such as "analogue marking" that represent significant but subtle changes in micro-cues such as vocal inflection or body language.

Ideally, Gass (1993b) argues, an *isomorphic* metaphor should be created for individuals operating within a therapeutic environment. The isomorphic framing of an activity centers on a specific issue, problem, or challenge presented by the participant and subsequently allows the adventure activity to become an isomorphic framework and context for this issue, problem, or challenge. The behavioral choices made by the participant within the adventure activity are hence analogous to the client's responses to their presenting problem outside of the activity. Facilitating a specific client-centric metaphoric transfer such as that described by Dolan (1986) and Gass (1995) relies heavily on the precise and accurate construction of a unique metaphor that is customized for the individual.

Hovelynck (1998a) later reflected similar perspectives when suggesting that adventure facilitators may become too focused on creating a specific metaphor for the task so that they may risk missing their participants' own metaphors and hence lose the opportunity to develop these metaphors further with their clients. Hovelynck (1998b) later succinctly articulated the process by which participants immerse themselves in the activity and generate new metaphors via the unarticulated sense of similarity that emerges through participation in the experience. Subsequent naming and framing of the metaphor follows with an explicit account of similarities and further behavioral mapping leads to new solutions being created. Hence, the metaphor becomes a "captured interruption" of a failing course of action. Once the initial metaphoric shift away from this action has been made, the creation of the body of a new metaphor is then pursued.

CRITICAL COACH COMPETENCIES
FOR ADVENTURE PROGRAMMING

While some authors have presented facilitation frameworks for adventure programming (Gass, 1993b) and others have presented philosophical frameworks (Pickard, 1998), little mention has been made of the personal skills and qualities required by the facilitator him/herself in order to be effective.

Knapp (1986) articulated the importance of the role the facilitator plays in adventure programming. This role is not the role of the traditional educator or teacher but rather one of presenter and monitor who outlines the task or challenge to the group, enforces the rules of the activity, identifies and manages unsafe situations, offers general encouragement, and promotes personal insight and growth. Unlike the traditional role of instructor, Knapp saw it to be inappropriate for the facilitator to become involved in the activity beyond this charter or to provide answers relating to the solution of the activity.

Vincent's (1995) study revealed several facilitator skills and attributes that were identified by adventure programming participants as being critical to success. These include an understanding and ownership of self-limitations, an awareness and evidence of having worked through one's own personal issues, and a willingness to be present in the moment with the group throughout their adventure experience. Additional educationally based skills valued by participants included an understanding of the group's issues, appropriately timed contributions of interpretations during the processing phase of the activity, and the ability to choose appropriate activities for the particular level of group development and type.

However, to gain a deeper level of insight around the more intangible skills of the adventure programmer, we need to explore more broadly. Corey (1991) identified 18 personal characteristics of counselors that were identified as being critical to becoming an effective change facilitator and therapeutic person (as distinct from a therapist). Effective counselors, he suggests, have a clear personal identity, respecting and appreciating themselves and their skills. They identify, acknowledge, and accept their own personal power, negating the need to draw on their clients to feed their sense of self-worth. They are open to change and are committed to expanding their awareness of self and others while being willing and able to tolerate ambiguity. They demonstrate their own unique counseling style while demonstrating a deeply sensitive and respectful empathy for their clients. Effective counselors embrace life proactively, exercising their own choices in an empowered manner, and demonstrate their honesty and integrity in all their communications and interpersonal interactions. While often dealing with challenging and confronting issues, effective counselors maintain a sense of humor and are willing to accept and own their mistakes. Therapeutic counselors live in the present, minimizing any fixation with the past or future. They are appreciative of the complexities and diversity of culture and its effect on the client and demonstrate a nonjudgmental and sincere interest in the welfare of others. Effective counselors become deeply involved in their work and derive great purpose and meaning from it, enabling them to continually grow, change, and develop themselves through the life-changing choices that they make about themselves. These skills serve to provide a solid foundation on which to build a coaching relationship, and indeed it was Corey himself who hinted at the skills crossover between facilitators operating within a development setting versus a counseling setting:

> My philosophy of counseling does not include the assumption that therapy is exclusively for the "sick" and is aimed at "curing" psychological "ailments." . . . Counseling, then, is viewed as a vehicle for helping "normal" people get more from life. (p. 4)

The clients (as opposed to patients) are therefore seen as predominantly "healthy people who see counseling as a self-exploratory and personal-growth experience" (p. 4).

While a vigorous debate continues surrounding the methods and processes used in therapy versus coaching and facilitation, it would appear that a shift toward client-centered factors defining the intervention and not the intervention methods themselves serves to offer a more considered and appropriate way forward in the future.

ADVENTURE INITIATIVES AS A GROUP-BASED COACHING LABORATORY

Group initiatives have had a long history within adventure programming and specifically within corporate training environments. These games have been utilized in a number of outdoor and indoor settings, broadening their accessibility and utility, an advantage that informed Priest and Gass's (1997) observation that these programs had all but replaced the traditional outdoor pursuits activities within the corporate environment.

Group initiatives have been known historically as "initiatives" (Luckner, 1986); "initiative games" (Darst & Armstrong, 1980); "initiative tasks" (Priest, 1986); "initiative problems" (Rohnke, 1989); "initiative tests" (Stich & Senior, 1984); "games" (Moore, 1984); "low risk adventure activities" or "minimal equipment activities" (Hyde, 1985); "Task Oriented Group Problem Solving Games" (Newman, 1985); "artificial activities" (Mortlock, 1978); and "group adventure initiative tasks" (Kemp & Piltz, 1995). Stich and Senior (1984) provided a comprehensive definition of group initiatives, describing them as:

> group games designed to provide concrete experiences in problem solving, cooperation, and personal involvement. Communication and interaction are essential. [They] offer opportunities for challenge, adventure, and creativity that can be used as a metaphor for daily living situations and to raise issues for peer discussion. These experiences are usually held within the span of one day, but they can be extended over a period of three consecutive days. (p. 104)

Later, Kemp and Piltz (1995) refined this definition, outlining them as:

> any task or game which requires a group to work together to achieve a goal. The goal cannot be achieved by an individual alone. The task is "artificial" in nature; that is, a fictitious scenario is created at the outset and the group may use any resources it has available to it within the rules of the task so as to arrive at a successful outcome. On the completion or achievement of the task the group is debriefed by a facilitator focussing on interactions and behaviours which were identified from the group process.

Hence, group initiatives, conceptualized most simply, are games. These games have a specific goal and rules within which a group of people must operate to achieve this goal. The outcome is normally not achievable by one person alone and hence group interaction is required. They are adventurous in their nature due to the inherent subjective perception of any one of a number of forms of risk, including physical, behavioral, psychological, or emotional risk.

Gillis and Bonney (1989) have applied psychotherapeutic group-based interventions, such as sociodrama, utilizing group initiatives. Both adventure programming and sociodrama are experiential methods that are active and group based and place participants in unfamiliar social and experiential contexts in which participants have few, if any, autonomous, learned, or rehearsed behavioral solutions. Both methods seek to transfer learning from the game-based situation to real issues in participants' personal life experience and context.

While group coaching has not enjoyed the same degree of market support as one-on-one coaching, the adventure initiative task offers a number of highly valuable learning laboratory opportunities to explore and experiment with new behaviors in a safe, supportive, and unique environment. In addition, these tasks may be used very successfully to highlight the need for clients to consider changing current behaviors prior to commencing a targeted and personalized coaching program.

THE EMERGENCE OF ADVENTURE THERAPY

The utilization of adventure programming within the context of therapy is by no means new. Thompson (1972) coined the term *recreational counseling* to describe the process of utilizing outdoor activities and initiative games within counseling settings. Further definitions of the content and processes used in adventure therapy were provided by Gillis and Thomsen (1996), but perhaps the broadest and simplest was offered by Gillis and Ringer (1999), describing it as "the deliberate, strategic combination of adventure activities with therapeutic change processes with the goal of making lasting changes in the lives of participants" (p. 29).

Recently, professionals in the field of adventure therapy have sought to "explore its boundaries" (Itin, 1998a) and as a result a growth in adventure therapy research has emerged. This has been stimulated by the positive impacts on personal growth and development that have been observed following participation in adventure programming (Kemp, 2001).

Adventure therapy has been widely and successfully utilized with a number of specific client groups including bulimia nervosa patients (Maguire & Priest, 1994); juvenile sex offenders (Simpson & Gillis, 1998); couples and families (Gillis & Bonney, 1989); and chronic psychiatric patients (Banaka & Young, 1985; Stich & Senior, 1984).

A wide range of therapeutic modalities has also been integrated into an adventure-based paradigm including psychosynthesis (Moore, 1991); Gestalt therapy (Gilsdorf, 1998); family therapy (Clift, 1972; Mulholland & Williams, 1998); psychodynamic therapy (Stouffer, 1999); hypnotherapy (Itin, 1995); group integrated reality therapy (Clagett, 1992); and Eriksonian hypnosis (Itin, 1994, 1995). It has also been utilized in conjunction with person-centered therapy, reality therapy, and behavioral therapy (Chase & Chase, 1992).

Adventure therapy is closely linked with the traditional clinical therapeutic paradigm. Clients are involved in both individual and group tasks and exercises for a short duration and complete repeated sessions, often in a clinical setting. Early activities from within adventure counseling included group initiatives, ropes courses, and low ropes elements, and these activities and programs have been widely documented (Schoel, Prouty, & Radcliffe, 1988).

Although the first focused attempt to construct a specific adventure-based counseling model was presented by Schoel, Prouty, & Radcliffe (1988), it was Gass's (1993a) efforts that successfully drew together a diverse range of therapeutic adventure experiences and facilitation methods into a cohesive and summative volume.

Gass's (1993b) rationale for using adventure programming in therapeutic environments appears sound. As an adventure places the client in an unfamiliar, novel, new, or unique environment, clients' expectations and preconceived generalizations about their competence and capability can be challenged. This process disrupts the clients' prevailing reality state and provides the opportunity to gain a new perspective on the old and develop new solutions to persistent challenges and issues. The process also focuses on clients' successful rather than dysfunctional behaviors. In an adventure setting, clients are presented with opportunities to focus on their skills and abilities rather than their shortcomings and hence the spontaneous formation of defensive responses normally demonstrated by the client are minimized.

Gass (1993b) acknowledged the diversity of knowledge informing the field:

> While the area of adventure therapy has developed as a discrete addition to the mental health field, many of the origins, principles, and philosophies of adventure therapy are founded in the field of experiential education. (pp. 3–4)

As the exploration of the field of adventure therapy has unfolded, progressively more refined perspectives have been articulated. Crisp (1996) offered a redefinition of the term, describing it as "a therapeutic intervention which uses contrived activities of an experiential, risk taking, and challenging nature in the treatment of an individual or group" (p. 5). Crisp, however, resigns himself to the perpetually problematic nature of resolving a consensual definition of the term.

At present, the definition of adventure therapy has come to include the use of wilderness expeditions and outdoor pursuits, ropes courses, extended residential experiences in standing camps or tenting environments, and clinically based and group centered initiative task programs. The foundations of a unique intervention method known as wilderness therapy have also begun to emerge (Davis-Berman & Berman, 1994).

Yet another method utilized within adventure therapy, long-term residential camping therapy, focuses on the placement of clients into long-term (up to one-year) standing camps or mobile programs. Examples of these programs include sail training on ocean-going sailing vessels or guided client/therapist expeditions led by therapists similar to those described by McNutt (1994). In these programs, the clients are responsible for meeting their own basic needs on a daily basis. Through self-sufficiency training and the acquisition of life skills including cooking, cleaning, and washing, clients learn self-sufficiency and the behaviors necessary for effective functioning. It is through this process of behavioral skill acquisition, combined with the need to develop coping strategies to address the inevitable interpersonal conflicts and day-to-day problems that arise, that therapeutic outcomes are achieved. Cason & Gillis (1994) acknowledged that these programs, historically known as adventure education programs rather than adventure therapy programs, have been widely used in the past and continue to gain increasing attention in the current literature (Crane, Hattie, & Houghton, 1997).

Although several empirical studies to date appear to support the benefits of using adventure activities in therapeutic programs, some contradictory evidence has also emerged, and hence calls for a deeper examination of the effects and outcomes of adventure-based interventions have been made (Parker & Stoltenberg, 1995).

With the emergence of clinical models for adventure therapy interventions such as the CHANGES model presented by Gass and Gillis (1995a), new ground has been gained in adventure therapy's search for acceptance. Of particular value is the unique opportunity that adventure experiences provide therapists to observe clients' autonomous behavior in real time. The application of this model is demonstrated in the case studies later in the chapter.

TOWARD A MODEL OF ADVENTURE-BASED COACHING

Strong support still exists for the application of broadly experiential learning cycle within the coaching process, albeit within a more broadly inclusive and integrated approach (Peel, 2005). In essence, the application of an adventure paradigm to the coaching process makes overtly explicit and normalizes the anxiety, fear, and uncertainty inherent in the change processes. Further, by framing the coaching relationship at its outset within an adventure paradigm, these affective consequences of the change process can be isomorphically transferred to similar situations and contexts of the clients' current reality. This subsequently provides an opportunity to create a circumvention mechanism for the resistance that is prone to surface in the initial stages of the change process. By framing adventure experiences in this way, clients' self-concept can be successfully modified while maintaining an appropriate level of self-esteem and self-efficacy. As Priest (1993) articulates, successful outcomes from adventure programming hinge on participants' willingness to embrace the perceptual risks induced by the experience, and hence a safe, supportive, and nurturing relationship is critical to achieving a successful outcome.

Founded on the work of Kolb (1984), the adventure-based coaching process integrates an experiential learning cycle with an adventure-based paradigm to create a coaching cycle that is framed within the broader metaphoric context of an adventure (see Figure 10.1).

The adventure cycle commences with the coach introducing the adventure paradigm and its application to the coaching process. It is critical at this point that the process be outlined in detail and the metaphoric structure of adventure as it applies to the coaching context is fully ex-

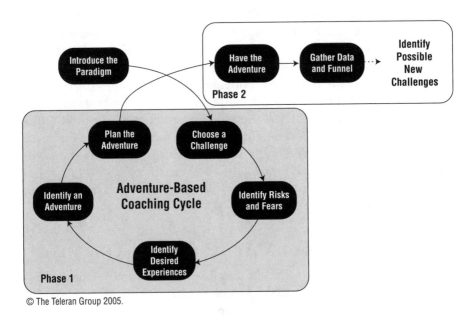

© The Teleran Group 2005.

Figure 10.1
The Adventure Based Coaching Cycle

plored with the client. This initial introduction also serves as a screening exercise to establish the appropriateness of fit of this framework for the current client. It is important to note that this approach may not be effective with all clients and clients' willingness to frame their experience in the context of an adventure is critical to the success of this method.

The challenge that is presented by the client is then explored. The presenting issue or broad developmental objective that the client presents to coaching is the basis for this conversation. Successful completion of this phase provides the client with a clearly defined and conceptualization developmental goal that is sufficiently attractive and compelling as to provide the appropriate level of motivation toward action.

Identifying perceptual risks and fears is central to the adventure experience, and this phase seeks to surface underlying fears associated with the change and new behavioral state. Challenging the client's autonomous behavior and thinking is central to completing this phase successfully, and various techniques to disrupt these autonomous patterns may be utilized at this point.

Identifying desirable experiences helps the client establish her desired state of performance and competence for the future. The client seeks to create a vision of a situation in which she can practice and demonstrate her goal behaviors and performance and begins to develop a catalog of multiple situations and interactions that call on her to demonstrate the desired behavior. At this point, the client begins the process of mental rehearsal whereby she imagines herself in these situations, demonstrating the desired behavior and experiencing successful outcomes as a result of this behavior.

Identifying the adventure that will be commenced is an important phase within the cycle. The adventure should be carefully chosen to facilitate edgework but not so challenging as to result in overarousal and performance decay. Client success in the first adventure is critical to future events and learning, so coach and client spend time collaboratively creating possible adventure activities and then choosing the most appropriate one for the client at her stage of development.

Planning the adventure then becomes an exercise in both logistics and cognitive-behavioral preparation. For example, the executive struggling to develop empathy may choose an adventure to volunteer at a homeless men's shelter for a period of two weeks. This adventure may be structured in a number of ways ranging from day visits to a full residential experience, depending on the client's level of current competence.

The client then participates in the adventure, gathering data and meta-data in the process on his unique experiences. When the adventure has been completed, this data is processed using a funneling technique outlined next and new behaviors are transferred to the client's real-life setting. This cycle is then repeated as the client progressively refines her behavioral capability.

This model provides a simple and flexible framework through which the coach can apply a number of specific and innovative techniques and processes with an adventure-based paradigm.

ADVENTURE COACHING FUNNEL

Adapted from Priest and Naismith's (1993) original funneling model, the coaching process funnel provides a framework for reflection on the adventure experience within the coaching relationship. (See Figure 10.2.) Simply, the coachee embarks upon and completes her chosen adventure and convenes with her coach. The process that must occur is a review of the adventure itself and the actual events that occurred. From the telling of this story by the client comes insights into what was most memorable and hence most impactful for the client. By using a narrative approach to questioning within this phase, the client is free to surface her most important memories at her own discretion and pace, and hence the free flow of recall

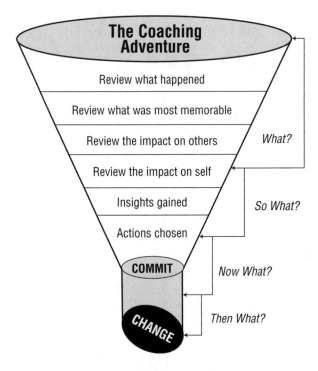

Figure 10.2
The Adventure Coaching Funnel

remains free of any potential coach biases in interpretation. This is also the phase in which the client's specific behaviors are examined and the outcomes of those behaviors are analyzed. Did you get the result that you wanted? If so, how so? If not, why not? Don't know? Who would know?

The next phase seeks to explore the impact of the client's behavior on others. Did you influence the person in a way that ensured your needs were met? Did you achieve this while respecting their needs? What was the outcome on the relationship between you? These questions begin to explore more deeply the impact of the behavioral dynamic among those people engaged in the process. It is critical at this point to explore both the *affect* and the *effect* within the adventure from the perspective of both the agonist (the client) and the antagonist (the recipient of the client's behavior) to ensure that the behavior that has been designed to achieve a specific outcome is in reality having that outcome.

From this phase flows a similar reflection on the client's unique affective experience of the adventure and through this reflection an understanding of the key elements of the experience. What worked? Why? What didn't work? Why? Following on from this, the coach works with the client to surface insights that these observations have stimulated in relation to the client's deeper understanding of their fears and anxieties along with their strengths and competencies. In addition, the underlying drivers for this behavior and the historical underpinnings to behavior are explored in this phase. In the final analysis phase, a suitable new action is chosen and committed to based on the insights gained through the funneling process.

The emerging trend toward the application of psychotherapeutic methods to coaching practice is clearly evident (Ducharme, 2004; Kemp, 2005; McAuley, 2003; Sherin & Caiger, 2004), and the inclusion of established, action based developmental interventions such as adventure programming into the coaching environment provides a new opportunity for providing diversity and impact within the coaching relationship. The progressive shift toward client-factor-based distinctions between coaching and therapy are proving less problematic than the intervention-methodology-driven approach that has dominated the theoretical and professional discourse to date, and as a result the broader application of nontraditional clinical intervention methods is gaining acceptance within the coaching dialogue.

CASE STUDIES

The Case of Bonita: Creating a Personal Adventure for Growth

Our client, Bonita, appears to be at a turning point in not only her career, but also in her broader life adventure. She has been promoted to a senior role within the organization, likely as a result of her "technical HR" competence that she has ex-hibited and her proven track record of producing tangible deliverables to her manager. Now the world has changed for Bonita. Reporting directly to a senior vice president, who subsequently most likely reports to the CEO of the organiza-tion, means that her exposure to the executive team and the organization has sud-denly become much greater.

Conflict is inherent in much of the communication that occurs at the table for Bonita now, and that conflict is essential to the organization making the best deci-sions for stakeholders. When conducted well, this conflict nurtures creative and innovative divergent thinking and solutions. When conducted poorly, however, this quickly takes its toll on the organization and its people.

While she expresses a desire to develop and maintain a degree of balance be-tween the time that she spends at work and the time that she has with Martin and her children, with a somewhat paternalistic and patriarchal boss, Ken, this may prove to be somewhat difficult.

Until now, her openness and inclusive and collaborative style have worked well for her, but from here on, work life may become tougher. Asserting herself among her peers at this new level will require a significant shift in her approach to this task.

By utilizing an adventure-based structure for the coaching relationship, Bonita will gain the opportunity to frame her development activity in a way that sees her taking progressively larger and more frequent personal risks within a relationship that supports her success and nurtures her courage to continue to stretch the boundaries of her comfort zone. These risk-taking opportunities will be progres-sively more challenging and her sequential successes will be isomorphically trans-ferred to her work environment, allowing her to draw on her increasing feelings of assertiveness and leadership self-efficacy. By using this method, her autonomous self-talk and self-perception will be disrupted and challenged by this unique ap-proach to learning. Increasing the level of novelty in Bonita's learning tasks while simultaneously reinforcing the metaphoric connections with her work environment will see a more integrated and proactive sense of self-concept emerge.

Metaphoric Framing of the Coaching Relationship

Stage 1—Collaboratively Building the Metaphor and Framing the Isomorphs for the Coaching Relationship
After an initial relationship-building conversation with Bonita, allowing the shar-ing of experiences and building of rapport, the coach frames the developmental journey in coaching as a unique *adventure*. The coach outlines the key elements of the coaching relationship that define it as an adventure and normalizes the emotional and psychological risks that are inherent in the adventure process, hence strengthening the metaphoric transfer. The client is invited to share parallel adventures that she has experienced in her life previously and capture her suc-cesses to date. The metaphor is progressively built with sequentially finer detail (for a detailed examination of using metaphor in adventure programming, see Gass, 1995a).

Stage 2—Framing the Coaching Process

By using a processing framework such as the CHANGES model (Gass & Gillis, 1995a), we establish the goals and desired outcomes of the coaching engagement.

Context

In Bonita's case, we may explore her presenting goals and related underlying drivers for these—for example, the need for assertiveness, elevated self-esteem, and sense of self-efficacy in her new role. Core questions relating to why she is here, what she wants to achieve in coaching, and what commitment and effort she is prepared to make are critical.

Hypotheses

A deeper examination and exploration of Bonita's current situation, analysis of the data that support these perceptions, engaging in a process of collaborative hypothesizing on her current strengths, and the identification of potential opportunities for development and possible directions for these development opportunities may be presented. The more skilled the coach, the more deeply this exploration may proceed. Coaching psychologists may also explore the underlying psychodynamic drivers of recognition and perfectionism that appear to be surfacing in Bonita's behavior (Freud, 1923).

Action

Bonita would be encouraged to try something that directly attempts to address her development need. In Bonita's case, it may be to assert her specific needs around finishing work at an appropriate time to ensure that she spends the evening with her husband and children. The important part of this phase is to try something different in relation to her behavioral responses to her current life situations.

Novelty

Unfamiliar experiences cause people to struggle with spontaneity. They don't have an autonomous or spontaneous behavioral act in these unfamiliar situations, and therefore a more authentic and less contrived behavioral pattern is likely to emerge. In Bonita's case, it may be that she chooses an adventure that requires her to assert her own needs in the face of conflict. Together with her coach, she may choose to visualize a series of experiences that create fear or anxiety for her and describe in detail these situations. These may range from sending an unsatisfactory meal back to the chef in a restaurant, returning unwanted goods to a department store and requesting a refund, or challenging her mother-in-law when she next critiques the washing powder she uses. The key in this phase is to choose a situation that is dissimilar to her work environment and that requires her to draw upon authentic behaviors of assertion within a potentially difficult environment.

Generating

Generate information about what happened. Determine how and why Bonita's chosen behaviors make sense to her. Use the funneling process (see Figure 10.2).

Evaluation

Ask the questions required to fully evaluate the impact of Bonita's behavior on herself and others. Did you get what you expected? Was it what you wanted? What needs to change for next time? Are you happy with the way you see your performance now? Continue to utilize the funneling process.

Solutions

Explore possible solutions to the current adventure. Where do we go from here? What now needs to change? What now is holding you back or driving you forward in relation to this change? How can we collaboratively design a solution to this challenge?

This process can be used in collaboration with the adventure coaching model to achieve a multiple-adventure learning cycle with each subsequent adventure building on the learning and insights gained from the previous one. By utilizing this progressive model, Bonita will ensure that her self-concept shift occurs simultaneously with her behavioral competence growth and a progressive movement to a more balanced and effective operating approach to her new role can be achieved. Most importantly, each subsequent successfully negotiated adventure becomes a metaphoric anchor for the next, and as a result Bonita will develop a stronger sense of generalized self-efficacy given the multitude of diverse and novel environments in which she has now demonstrated her capability.

The Case of Bob: Creating an Adventure from Without

Bob is successful. Regardless of his methods, values, and views of the world, he is CEO of a multinational company that has achieved significant growth and expansion, and from a commercial and financial perspective it is difficult to dispute this success. While one may argue that only one of the "triple bottom line" metrics (people, financial, and cultural organizational performance measures) is being met here, the prevailing focus on short-term stockholder returns means that financial performance remains of disproportionate importance in this trio of performance indicators. The challenge for this coaching intervention is to surface Bob's cognitive and behavioral shortcomings by utilizing a sufficiently impactful method while at the same time creating a strong enough value proposition for personal change. Simultaneously, we must ensure Bob maintains a sufficient level of self-esteem and perceptual authority among his team to allow him the personal safety to readjust his self-concept and a move toward demonstrating new behavior.

His tendency toward autocratic and top-down approaches lends itself perfectly to an adventure-based intervention as a mechanism to stimulate an impetus for change. It is unlikely that Bob will respond favourably to any direct business-issue-based intervention beyond the core challenge of completing the current acquisition process successfully. Likewise, his ability to treat human capital clinically and with limited emotionality places him in a robust position to deflect any isolated or adverse performance feedback.

His resolve and commitment to his current course of action has already proved to be a success. Even his view that human capital can, like any other piece of capital, be amortized over a suitable time frame and later written off as a cost of delivery has remained quantitatively and pragmatically unchallenged.

Intervention

Within a highly controlled and carefully facilitated environment, the coaching relationship may be instigated by bringing the new executive team from the merged organization together under the guise of reviewing acquisition issues and to facilitate further strategic planning. As a part of this process, a review of the executive team's dynamics and communication patterns could be seen as a valuable adjunct to understanding the quantitative aspects of the merger.

As a part of the education process for the executive team, they would participate in a series of sessions identifying key leadership behaviors that will be critical to the successful integration of the newly acquired organization. This outcome is particularly attractive to Bob given his need to have the new business running smoothly prior to his retirement. After all, every additional month that he feels he needs to be in the business is another month taken away from time that he spends with his new grandchild.

As a way of surfacing the team's spontaneous and automatic behavior they would participate in a series of group initiative games outlined earlier. These games would be designed and metaphorically framed within the context of the new organization. Participation in these games will highlight the learned patterns of behavior demonstrated in the workplace within a safe and "frivolous" environment, and through appropriate frontloading followed by progressively deepening funneling within the debrief, the functional and less functional behaviors will be highlighted and explored. The team will then have an opportunity to modify these patterns in subsequent activities as they progress through the adventure coaching cycle.

To ensure that the metaphoric framing of the initial activity provides a solid foundation for later learning, the following double-bind brief could be used. To elaborate, according to Priest, Gass, and Gillis (2000) "bind means to restrict movement and double means to provide two choices" (p. 125).

> Most executives approach this task by asking one or two questions initially then cutting to the chase, solving the problem in front of them and directing the others to implement their solution. If there is a positive outcome, most executives usually take credit for the idea and use this success as a validation of their own problem solving and leadership capability. If there is a negative outcome, they usually blame the others for not executing the solution in the way that it was communicated. When executives come to reflect on these events with their coaches, they typically identify their impatience, autocratic behavior, and poor listening as problems and want to discuss ways of addressing these.

The executive team then completes the activity while the coach makes observations of the processes, dynamics, and results. Each activity, inclusive of the initial framing and processing of the event, may take between 30 minutes and three hours depending on the complexity of the activity. (For excellent sources of adventure-based activities for corporate settings see Priest & Rohnke, 2000; Rohnke, 1996a, 1996b, 1998; Rohnke & Butler, 1995).

Once completed, this initial session provides a rich source of cultural and experiential capital on which to gain future developmental returns for the executive team. The unique events of the program anchor desirable and undesirable behaviors, and the establishment of an adventure-based context for the continuing coaching relationship allows Bob to venture into unknown and uncertain territory by taking risks with new behaviors and new ways of communicating. By this time a solid foundation of trust has been created in the coaching relationship and subsequent feedback may be gathered and processed within the work environment as the isomorphic transfer between the adventure tasks and real-world challenges takes effect.

By utilizing the adventure-based coaching cycle and funneling, Bob will successfully complete a succession of behavioral adventures. As Bob's behavioral risk taking increases, his need for control should begin to decline and the subsequent increase in engagement, dialogue, and collaboration between members of the executive team should serve to increase the likelihood of a successful organizational integration for Bob.

By continuing with a funneling methodology and questioning cycle similar to the one used in Bonita's case, Bob will progressively gain a deeper insight into the impact that his perceptions and beliefs have on those around him. He will deepen his understanding of his behavioral drivers and create progressively more complex and stretching adventures as his ability to take risks increases and his fear subsides.

Over successive adventure cycles, Bob's ego-defense mechanisms, including repression, sublimation, projection, reaction formation, denial, rationalization, regression, and intellectualization, which have been used to defend his self-image, will recede (Freud, 1923).

CONCLUSION

By utilizing an adventure-based approach to coaching, many of the core barriers to successful behavior change, such as personal schemas and resistance, can be circumvented. The use of personal risk taking, normalizing fear and anxiety, and participation in novel activities with uncertain outcomes all serve to actively disrupt conditioned cognitive-behavioral patterns and hence create a dissonance for clients through which growth can occur. The parallel metaphoric and isomorphic framing of these experiences facilitates the effective transfer of learning from the adventure experience to the real world as the adventure coaching cycle is completed. By utilizing this method, coaches can provide a safe, nurturing, and progressively developmental coaching experience for clients while at the same time maximizing their potential success in stimulating and maintaining core cognitive and behavioral change.

REFERENCES

Atwood, J. D., & Levine, L.B. (1991). Ax murderers, dragons, spiders and webs: Therapeutic metaphors in couple therapy. *Contemporary Family Therapy, 13*(3), 201–217.

Bacon, S. (1987). *The evolution of the Outward Bound process.* Greenwich, CT: Outward Bound Press. (ERIC Reproduction Service No. 295 780).

Banaka, W. H., & Young, D. W. (1985). Community coping skills enhanced by an adventure camp for adult chronic psychiatric patients. *Hospital and Community Psychiatry, 36*(7), 746–748.

Blattner, J. (2005). Coaching: The successful adventure of a downwardly mobile executive. *Consulting Psychology Journal: Practice and Research, 57*(1), 3–13.

Bowman, G. (1992). Using therapeutic metaphor in adjustment counselling. *Journal of Visual Impairment & Blindness, 86*(10), 440–442.

Bryant, L., Katz, B., Becvar, R. J., & Becvar, D. S. (1988). The use of therapeutic metaphor among members of the AAMFT. *American Journal of Family Therapy, 16*(2), 112–120.

Carpenter, G., & Priest, S. (1989). The adventure experience paradigm and non-outdoor leisure pursuits. *Leisure Studies, 8,* 65–75.

Cason, D., & Gillis, H. L. (1994). A meta-analysis of outdoor adventure programming with adolescents. *Journal of Experiential Education, 17*(1), 40–47.

Chase, M., & Chase, R. (1992). Counselling techniques for outdoor leaders. *Journal of Adventure Education and Outdoor Leadership, 9*(4), 5–7.

Clagett, A. F. (1992). Group-integrated reality therapy in a wilderness camp. *Journal of Offender Rehabilitation, 17*(3/4), 1–18.

Clift, J. E. (1972). Family recreational therapy: A new treatment technique. *Therapeutic Recreation Journal, 6*(1), 25–27, 36–38.

Corey, G. (1991). *The theory and practice of counselling and psychotherapy* (4th ed.). Pacific Grove, CA: Brooks Cole Publishing.

Crane, D., Hattie, J., & Houghton, S. (1997). Goal setting and the adventure experience. *Australian Journal of Psychology, 49*(1), 6–13.

Crisp, S. (1996). *International models of best practice in wilderness and adventure therapy: Implications for Australia.* 1996 Winston Churchill Final Report. Department of Child, Adolescent & Family Psychiatry, Austin & Repatriation Medical Centre, Melbourne.

Crosby, A. (1995). A critical look: The philosophical foundations of experiential education. In K. Warren, M. Sakofs, J. S. Hunt Jr. (Eds.), *The theory of experiential education* (3rd ed.). Dubuque, IA: Kendall/Hunt.

Darst, P. W., & Armstrong, G. P. (1980). *Outdoor adventure activities for school and recreation programs.* Minneapolis, MN: Burgess.

Davis-Berman, J., & Berman, D. S. (1994). *Wilderness therapy: Foundations, theory and research.* Dubuque, IA: Kendall/Hunt.

Dickson, T. J., Chapman, J., & Hurrell, M. (2000). Risk in outdoor activities: The perception, the appeal, the reality. *Australian Journal of Outdoor Education, 4*(2), 10–17.

Dolan, Y. M. (1986). Metaphors for motivation and intervention. *The Family Therapy Collections, 19*, 1–10.

Doughty, S. (1991). Three generations of development training. *Journal of Adventure Education and Outdoor Leadership, 7*(4), 7–9.

Driver, J. (1997). The place of journal writing on an outdoor experience. *Journeys, 2*(4), 24–27.

Ducharme, M. J. (2004). The cognitive-behavioral approach to executive coaching. *Consulting Psychology Journal: Practice and Research, 56*(4), 214–224.

Freud, S. (1923). The ego and the id. In J. Strachey (Ed. & Trans.), *The standard edition of the complete works of Sigmund Freud* (Vol. 19, pp. 3–66). London: Hogarth Press and Institute of Psychoanalysis, 1961.

Gass, M. (1985). Programming the transfer of learning in adventure education. *Journal of Experiential Education, 8*(3), 24–32.

Gass, M. (Ed.). (1993a). *Adventure therapy: Therapeutic applications of adventure programming.* Dubuque, IA: Kendall/Hunt.

Gass, M. (1993b). Foundations of adventure therapy. In M. Gass (Ed.), *Adventure therapy: Therapeutic applications of adventure programming.* Dubuque, IA: Kendall/Hunt.

Gass, M. (1995). *Book of metaphors: Vol. 2.* Dubuque, IA: Kendall/Hunt.

Gass, M. A., & Gillis, H. L. (1995a) CHANGES: An assessment model using adventure experiences. *Journal of Experiential Education 18*(1), 34–40.

Gass, M. A., & Gillis, H. L. (1995b). Focusing on the "solution" rather than the "problem": Empowering client change in adventure experiences. *Journal of Experiential Education 18*(2).

Gass, M. & Priest, S. (1993). Using metaphors and isomorphs to transfer learning in adventure education. *The Journal of Adventure Education and Outdoor Leadership, 10*(4), 18–23.

Gillis, H. L., & Bonney, W. C. (1989). Utilizing adventure activities with intact groups: A sociodramatic systems approach to consultation. *Journal of Mental Health Counselling, 11*(4), 345–358.

Gillis, H. L., & Gass, M. A. (1993). Bringing adventure into marriage and family therapy: An innovative experiential approach. *Journal of Marital and Family Therapy, 19*(3), 273–286.

Gillis, H. L., & Gass, M. (2003). Adventure therapy with groups. In J. L. DeLucia-Waack, D. A. Gerrity, C. R. Kalodner, & M. Riva (Eds.), *Handbook of group counseling and psychotherapy.* Thousand Oaks, CA: Sage Publications.

Gillis, H. L., & Ringer, T. M. (1999). Adventure as therapy. In J. C. Miles and S. Priest (Eds.), *Adventure programming.* State College, PA: Venture Publishing.

Gillis, H. L., & Thomsen, D. (1996). A research update (1992–1995) of adventure therapy: Challenge activities and ropes courses, wilderness expeditions & residential camping programs. Invited presentation for the Coalition for Education in the Outdoors Symposium, Bradford Woods, Indiana University, Martinsville, IN.

Gilsdorf, R. (1998). Gestalt and adventure therapy: Parallels and perspectives. In C. M. Itin (Ed.), *Exploring the boundaries of adventure therapy: International perspectives.* Leederville, Western Australia: Camping and Outdoor Education Association of Western Australia.

Gladding, S. T. (1986). Imagery and metaphor in counselling: A humanistic course. *Journal of Humanistic Education and Development, 25*(1), 38–47.

Grant, A. (2003). The impact of life coaching on goal attainment, metacognition and mental health. *Social Behaviour and Personality, 31*(3), 253–264.

Greenaway, R. (1992). Reviewing by doing. *Journal of Adventure Education and Outdoor Leadership, 9*(1), 21–25.

Hendrix, D. H. (1992). Metaphors as nudges toward understanding in mental health counselling. *Journal of Mental Health Counselling, 14*(2), 234–242.

Hirsch, J. (1999). Developmental adventure programs. In J. C. Miles and S. Priest (Eds.), *Adventure programming.* State College, PA: Venture Publishing.

Hovelynck, J. (1998a). Facilitating processes of metaphor change: Envisioning behavioural alternatives. In C. M. Itin (Ed.), *Exploring the boundaries of adventure therapy: International perspectives.* Leederville, Western Australia: Camping and Outdoor Education Association of Western Australia.

Hovelynck, J. (1998b). Facilitating experiential learning as a process of metaphor development. *The Journal of Experiential Education, 21*(1), 6–13.

Hunt, J. S., Jr. (1995). Dewey's philosophical method and its influence on his philosophy of education. In K. Warren, M. Sakofs, & J. S. Hunt Jr. (Eds.), *The theory of experiential education* (3rd ed.). Dubuque, IA: Kendall/Hunt.

Hyde, R. (1985). Minimal-equipment activities. *Adventure Education, 3*(2), 16–17.

Iso-Ahola, S. E. (1988). Research in therapeutic recreation. *Therapeutic Recreation Journal, 22*(2), 7–13.

Itin, C. M. (1994, November). Ericksonian approach to experiential education: Part 3. Applying specific Ericksonian techniques. *Experiential Education: A Critical Resource for the 21st Century.* Proceedings Manual of the Annual International Conference of the Association for Experiential Education, Austin, Texas. ERIC Document Reproduction Service No. ED 377 009.

Itin, C. M. (1995). Utilizing hypnotic language in adventure therapy. *Journal of Experiential Education, 18*(2), 70–75.

Itin, C. M. (Ed.). (1998a). *Exploring the boundaries of adventure therapy: International perspectives.* Proceedings of the 1st International Adventure Therapy Conference, Perth, Australia. Leederville, Western Australia: Camping and Outdoor Education Association of Western Australia.

Itin, C. M. (1998b). The seventh generation in adventure therapy. In C. M. Itin (Ed.), *Exploring the boundaries of adventure therapy: International perspectives.* Proceedings of the 1st International Adventure Therapy Conference, Perth, Australia. Leederville, Western Australia: Camping and Outdoor Education Association of Western Australia.

James, T. (1995). Kurt Hahn and the aims of education. In K. Warren, M. Sakofs, & J. S. Hunt Jr. (Eds.), *The theory of experiential education* (3rd Ed.). Dubuque, IA: Kendall/Hunt.

Johnson, J. A. (1992). Adventure therapy: The ropes-wilderness connection. *Therapeutic Recreation Journal, 26*(3), 17–26.

Kemp, T. J. (1995). *The influence of an adventure learning program, using group adventure initiative tasks, on participant self-esteem.* Unpublished master's thesis, Deakin University, Melbourne. Australia.

Kemp, T. J. (2001). *Playing to learn: Exploring personal awareness and growth through facilitated adventure programming.* Unpublished doctoral dissertation, University of South Australia, Adelaide.

Kemp, T. J. (2005). Psychology's unique contribution to solution-focused coaching: Exploring clients' past to inform their present and design their future. In M. Cavanagh, A. M. Grant, & T. Kemp (Eds.), *Evidence based coaching: Volume 1. Theory, research and practice from the behavioural sciences.* Queensland: Australian Academic Press.

Kemp, T. J., & McCarron, L. (1998). Learning new behaviours through group adventure initiative tasks: A theoretical perspective. In C. M. Itin (Ed.), *Exploring the boundaries of adventure therapy: International perspectives.* Leederville, Western Australia: Camping and Outdoor Education Association of Western Australia.

Kemp, T. J., & Piltz, W. (1995). Teaching personal responsibility through group adventure initiative tasks: An introduction to the model of responsible action. *Journal of Adventure Education and Outdoor Leadership, 12*(2), 22–26.

Knapp, C. E. (1986). Group initiative educational games: Teaching students how to think, not what to think. *The International Association for the Study of Cooperation in Education Newsletter, 7*(3 & 4), 3–4, 7–8.

Knowles, M. S. (1980). *The modern practice of adult education: From pedagogy to andragogy* (2nd ed.). Wilton, CT: Association Press.

Kolb, D. (1984). *Experiential learning: Experience as the source of learning and development.* Englewood Cliffs, NJ: Prentice Hall.

Luckner, J. L. (1986). *Outdoor adventure education as an ancillary component in rehabilitation programs for the hearing impaired: A pilot study.* ERIC reproduction EC 201 226.

Magill, R. A. (1995). *Motor learning: Concepts and applications* (2nd ed.). Dubuque, IA: W. C. Brown.

Maguire, R., & Priest, S. (1994). The treatment of bulimia nervosa through adventure therapy. *Journal of Experiential Education, 17*(2), 44–48.

McAuley, M. J. (2003). Transference, counter-transference and mentoring: The ghost in the process. *British Journal of Guidance and Counselling, 31*(1), 11–23.

McClure, B. A. (1989). What's a group meta-phor? *The Journal for Specialists in Group Work, 14*(4), 239–242.

McKenna, P., & Kiewa, J. (1996). The efficacy of journal writing as a reflective tool. *Australian Journal of Outdoor Education, 2*(2), 17–23.

McNutt, B. (1994, April). *Adventure as therapy: Using adventure as part of therapeutic programs with young people in trouble and at risk.* Proceedings of a National One-Day Conference "Adventure-Based Interventions" and a Study Weekend "Enabling Troubled Youth," Ambleside, England, 932–934.

Miles, J. C., & Priest, S. (Eds.). (1990). *Adventure programming.* State College, PA: Venture Publishing.

Moore, I. (1984). The games we play. *Adventure Education, 1*(6), 18–19.

Moore, J. (1991). *Psychosynthesis and adventure counselling.* Proceedings of the International Conference and Workshop Summaries Book of the International Association for Experiential Education, October 24–27.

Mortlock, C. (1978). *Adventure education.* Keswick, UK: Ferguson Publishers.

Mulholland, R., & Williams, A. (1998). Exploring the outdoors: A family therapy approach based in the outdoors. In C. M. Itin (Ed.), *Exploring the boundaries of adventure therapy: International perspectives.* Leederville, Western Australia: Camping and Outdoor Education Association of Western Australia.

Nadler, R. S. (1993). Therapeutic process of change. In M. Gass (Ed.), *Adventure therapy: Therapeutic applications of adventure programming.* Dubuque, IA: Kendall/Hunt.

Nadler, R. S. (1995). Edgework: Stretching boundaries and generalizing experiences. *The Journal of Experiential Education, 18*(1), 52–55.

Nadler, R. S., & Luckner, J. L. (1992). *Processing the adventure experience: Theory and practice.* Dubuque, IA: Kendall/Hunt.

Newman, V. (1985). Forum: Playing games. *Adventure Education, 3*(2), 15–16.

Parker, M., & Stoltenberg, C.D. (1995). Use of adventure experiences in traditional counseling interventions. *Psychological Reports, 77*, 1370–1372.

Peel, D. (2005). The significance of behavioural learning theory to the development of effective coaching practice. *International Journal of Evidence Based Coaching and Mentoring, 3*(1), 18–28.

Pickard, J. (1998). Choosing your style: Approaches to leading adventure therapy programmes. In C.M. Itin (Ed.), *Exploring the boundaries of adventure therapy: International perspectives.* Leederville, Western Australia: Camping and Outdoor Education Association of Western Australia.

Priest, S. (1986). Training the facilitators of group initiatives. *Adventure Education, 3*(3), 28–29.

Priest, S. (1990). Foundations of adventure education: An overview. In J. C. Miles & S. Priest (Eds.), *Adventure education.* State College, PA: Venture Publishing.

Priest, S. (1993). A new model for risk taking. *Journal of Experiential Education, 16*(1), 50–53.

Priest, S. (1996a). The effect of two different debriefing approaches on developing self-confidence. *Journal of Experiential Education, 19*(1), 40–42.

Priest, S. (1996b). The relationships among change, programme type and facilitation technique in adventure programming. *Journal of Adventure Education and Outdoor Leadership, 13*(2), 22–26.

Priest, S. (1999a). Introduction. In J. C. Miles & S. Priest (Eds.), *Adventure programming.* State College, PA: Venture Publishing.

Priest, S. (1999b). The semantics of adventure programming. In J. C. Miles & S. Priest (Eds.), *Adventure programming.* State College, PA: Venture Publishing.

Priest, S. (1999c). Introduction. In J. C. Miles and S. Priest (Eds.), *Adventure programming.* State College, PA: Venture Publishing.

Priest, S., & Baillie, R. (1987). Justifying the risk to others: The real razor's edge. *Journal of Experiential Education, 10*, 6–22.

Priest, S., & Gass, M. (1993). Five generations of facilitated learning from adventure experiences. *Journal of Adventure Education and Outdoor Leadership, 10*(3), 23–25.

Priest, S., & Gass, M. (1994). Frontloading with paradox & double binds in adventure education facilitation. *Journal of Adventure Education and Outdoor Leadership, 11*(1), 8–10.

Priest, S., & Gass, M. (1997). Trends and issues. *Journeys, 2*(4), 13–21.

Priest, S., & Gass, M. (1999). Six generations of facilitation skills. In J. C. Miles & S. Priest (Eds.), *Adventure programming.* State College, PA: Venture Publishing.

Priest, S., Gass, M., & Gillis, L. (2000). *The essential elements of facilitation.* Dubuque, IA: Kendall/Hunt.

Priest, S., & Naismith, M. (1993). The debriefing funnel. *Journal of Adventure Education and Outdoor Leadership, 10*(3), 20–22.

Priest, S., & Rohnke, K. (2000). *101 of the best corporate team-building activities we know!* Dubuque, IA: Kendall/Hunt.

Quinsland, L. K., & Van Ginkel, A. (1988). How to process experience. *Adventure Education and Outdoor Leadership, 5*(3), 27–30.

Raiola, E. O. (1984). *Outdoor adventure activities for new student orientation programs.* ERIC Document Reproduction No. RC 014 144.

Ringer, T. M. (2002). *Group action: The dynamics of groups in therapeutic educational and corporate settings.* London: Jessica Kingley Publishers.

Ringer, T. M., & Gillis, H. L. (1995). Managing psychological depth in adventure programming. *Journal of Experiential Education, 18*(1), 41–51.

Roberts, S. D. (1987). Therapeutic metaphors: A counselling technique. *Journal of the Academy of Rehabilitative Audiology, 20*, 61–72.

Rohnke, K. (1984). *Silver bullets: A guide to initiative problems, adventure games and trust activities.* Dubuque, IA: Kendall/Hunt.

Rohnke, K. (1989). *Cowstails and Cobras 2: A Guide to Games, Initiatives, Ropes Courses, and Adventure Curriculum.* Dubuque, IA: Kendall/Hunt.

Rohnke, K. (1996a). *Funn Stuff: Vol. 1.* Dubuque, IA: Kendall/Hunt.

Rohnke, K. (1996b). *Funn Stuff: Vol. 2.* Dubuque, IA: Kendall/Hunt.

Rohnke, K. (1998). *Funn Stuff: Vol. 3.* Dubuque, IA: Kendall/Hunt.

Rohnke, K., & Butler, S. (1995). *Quicksilver: Adventure games, initiative problems, trust activities and a guide to effective leadership.* Dubuque, IA: Kendall/Hunt.

Romig, C. A., & Gruenke, C. (1991). The use of metaphor to overcome inmate resistance to mental health counseling. *Journal of Counselling and Development, 69*(5), 414–418.

Schafermeyer, H. (1978). Adventure programming—Wilderness and urban. *Journal of Physical Education and Recreation, 49*(1), 30–32.

Schoel, J., Prouty, D., & Radcliffe, P. (1988). *Islands of healing: A guide to adventure based counseling.* Hamilton, CA: Project Adventure.

Sherin, J., & Caiger, L. (2004). Rational-emotive behavior therapy: A behavioral change model for executive coaching? *Consulting Psychology Journal: Practice and Research, 56*(4), 225–233.

Simpson, C., & Gillis, H. L. (1998). Working with those who hurt others: Adventure therapy with juvenile sexual perpetrators. In C. M. Itin (Ed.), *Exploring the boundaries of adventure therapy: International perspectives.* Leederville, Western Australia: Camping and Outdoor Education Association of Western Australia.

Stich, T. F., & Senior, N. (1984). Adventure therapy: An innovative treatment for psychiatric patients. *New Directions for Mental Health Services, 21,* 103–113.

Stouffer, R. (1999). Personal insight: Reframing the unconscious through metaphor-based adventure therapy. *Journal of Experiential Education, 29*(1), 28–34.

Strong, T. (1989). Metaphors and client change in counselling. *International Journal for the Advancement of Counselling, 12*(3), 203–213.

Thompson, G. (1972). Outline for development of a recreational counselling program. *Therapeutic Recreation Journal, 6*(2), 83.

Vincent, S. M. (1995). Emotional safety in adventure therapy programs: Can it be defined? *Journal of Experiential Education, 18*(2), 76–81.

Wade, I. R. (1990). Safety management. In J. C. Miles & S. Priest (Eds.), *Adventure education.* State College, PA: Venture Publishing.

Webster, S. E. (1978). Project Adventure: A trip into the unknown. *Journal of Physical Education and Recreation, 49*(4), 15–17.

CHAPTER 11

Coaching from a Systemic Perspective: A Complex Adaptive Conversation

Michael Cavanagh

As coaches, we are pattern recognition experts.
—Paul Mitchell, coach and founder of "The Human Enterprise"

COACHING IS A JOURNEY in search of patterns. Our clients come to us, sometimes with fuzzy problems, sometimes with clear goals, but always with a desire to understand their experience in a way that enables them to move forward. We, as coaches, undertake to work with them to develop this new understanding, and to support them in taking the actions that flow from it. The value we add to our clients resides in our ability to help them see their experience in a new way. We do this by helping them to discover or notice previously unnoticed (or ignored) patterns in the complex mix of experience, thoughts, actions, and reactions that is their story. Coaching, then, is a journey in search of patterns.

The difficulty is that, in the complex world of human experience, there are many possible patterns to be found and many ways of helping the client make meaning of their experience. Precisely which patterns we detect as coaches will depend on the theories, models, and assumptions that we bring to bear on the client's story. Our theories (like our clients' theories) are the lenses we use to filter out what is important

313

and what is not. They allow us to understand our world, and they guide both prediction and action. The best coaches are able to take multiple perspectives and select those that are most helpful for the client.

This chapter explores one way of finding patterns in coaching, one set of lenses through which to view the coaching engagement—complex systems theory. In order to do this, I first describe the main features of complex adaptive systems, exploring some of the implications for coaching as we go along. Given that the cases we are discussing are situated in an organizational leadership context, I also consider some ways in which complexity theory informs our approach to leadership. I then explore Stacey's (2000) metaphor of systems as conversations, and present a model of the coaching engagement that I have found useful in helping me understand what it is I am doing in coaching. Finally, we look at the cases of Bob and Bonita from this systemic perspective.

SYSTEMS THEORY BACKGROUND

Systems theories are a wide range of theoretical approaches, stretching from cybernetics (Wiener, 1948), family systems theory (Bowen, 1978), and complexity theory (Lewin, 1993; Stacey, 2000) to chaos theory (Gleick, 1998; Lorenz, 1963). One of the founders of the systems approach was the biologist Ludwig von Bertalanffy. Von Bertalanffy developed General Systems Theory from the 1920s to the 1960s in an attempt to provide a unifying approach to science that overcame many of the limitations of the dominant reductionistic approach to knowledge about the world. He suggested that the world was made up of interdependent and hierarchical systems that interact with their environments (von Bertalanffy, 1968). In other words, he held that the world could be usefully viewed as a series of systems within systems, which all display some common characteristics. Figure 11.1 gives a simplified graphical representation of this in terms of the human person within the corporate environment.

General Systems Theory was said to be a unifying theory in that the systemic nature of the world can be seen in both the natural sciences, such as biology, physics, and chemistry, and the social sciences such as psychology and sociology. It is not surprising then that a host of systems theories have been developed via parallel streams of research. It is not possible here to outline the differences and similarities between the multitudes of particular theories. Rather we will focus on the branch of systems theories that deals with complex adaptive systems, or complexity theory.

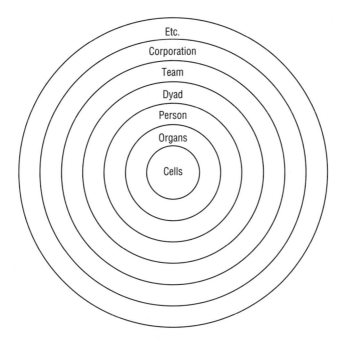

Figure 11.1
The Hierarchical Nature of Systems

WHAT IS A COMPLEX ADAPTIVE SYSTEM (CAS)?

A system, as opposed to a collection, is a group of interacting or interdependent elements that form a complex whole that unfolds over time. A defining feature of all true systems is that they form entities that are greater than the sum of their parts. Complex adaptive systems are so named because the parts that make them up are whole systems in their own right (Dimitrov, 2003). These whole systems interact according to their own rules and goals, adapting to each other, and it is this interaction that brings about order of the larger system. The human body is a good example. It is made up of organ systems that in turn are made up of cells, which are made up of smaller systems. Each goes about its business, being influenced by and influencing the systems around it. If the environment changes or some challenge occurs, or if any of the subsystems sustain damage, others adapt so as to continue to achieve their goals and maintain the overall functioning of the system.

Relatively simple systems, such as a clock or a car, fit the general description of a system, but are not complex adaptive systems in that they are unable to adapt their functioning. They are made up of parts, rather than systems. For example, if we took even a minor cog out of a clock it would cease to function. The principal differentiating feature of complexity theory is that it focuses on systems in which systems members act locally and in so doing produce order at a global level.

There are a number of important features of complex adaptive systems. Many of these are common to all systemic approaches and are important to take into account in coaching.

HOLISM AND INTERDEPENDENCE

A fundamental understanding common to all systemic approaches is that the systems are holistic. To understand the system one must attempt to step back from the level of the particular, and examine the systems in terms of what is created when the parts interact. One cannot view, for example, the human person as a mere collection of functioning organ systems without losing the essence of what it means to be a unique person. We are more than the sum of our parts.

In scientific terms this is a relatively new approach. The scientific worldview under Newton utilized a predominantly mechanistic and reductionistic approach. It explored and understood the world by breaking it down into its constituent parts and looking for linear chains of cause and effect governing the behavior of those parts (Haines, 1998). The assumption underlying this approach is that the parts of a system have a fundamental nature that is independent of the system in which it is embedded, and which governs their interactions. Logic and the scientific method are the means by which we attempt to access this reality.

We see this linear approach in organizations when we see the traditional "name, blame, and shame" approach to team failures. In this approach, the locus of dysfunction is seen to be the individual's choices or even the individual's personality. Blaming the collapse of Barings Bank on the so-called rogue trader Nick Leeson is an example of the reductionist approach.

Reason's (1990) "Swiss Cheese" model of human error shows clearly that when things go awry (as clearly they did at Barings) typically a host of factors have been at work in an interdependent way to create the outcome. These factors include organizational culture, supervisory practices, time and task pressure, and individual choices. Rawnsley's (1995) analysis of the Barings collapse clearly shows that there was much more at work than the deviant actions of one individual. That is not to say that Leeson bears no responsibility for the collapse. On the contrary, his actions show a significant failure of adult responsibility for which Leeson was and is responsible. Taking a systems approach, however, means dealing with the system in all its complexity and tailoring one's coaching to address issues at every level of the system—including the personal. Leeson's behavior shows that he clearly had some significant issues to work on—as did the rest of the system!

Systems theories see reductionist approaches as incomplete. Rather than focus on the parts of the system in isolation, systems theories focus much more on the relationships between parts. This approach is based on the belief that the parts of the system are essentially *interdependent*. In other words, their functioning within the system depends on the nature of the relationships between them and the other parts of the system.

This interdependence can be seen in the way we often operate differently when in different groups. Many of us may have had experiences of being in relationships or groups that draw the best (or the worst) out of us. In such a situation, how we respond is not so much about who we are in isolation as it is about the nature of the complex interactions and relationships that exist between us and the system in which we are operating.

KEY IMPLICATION FOR COACHING

Holism and interdependence show us that in order to understanding our clients, we must understand how they are related to the situations, events, and systems in which they are involved—there is always more to the story than the blame game. Here the notions of openness, transformation, and entropy are important.

OPENNESS, TRANSFORMATION, AND ENTROPY

All systems have boundaries. Typically, in human systems these boundaries are more or less fuzzy. Who makes up a team? Where do the boundaries of an organization start and end? Are customers part of the organizational system? Are subcontractors part of the company? Who is in your family? The best answer to these questions typically depends on what level of analysis we are working with.

The notion of openness refers to the permeability of systems boundaries, or the ability of the system to effectively communicate with, and be affected by, the wider environment. Openness is a dimensional property that is able to change over time; that is, systems can be more or less open or closed. In human systems feedback and communication processes enable the system to remain open to its wider environment. For example, an organization that is unable to hear its customers may be said to have dangerously closed boundaries. A sales team that is unable to effectively communicate with marketing or supply is in trouble.

A manager who is unable to seek or hear feedback without defensiveness is facing potential derailment.

The degree of openness of a system is important because of the process of entropy. Technically, this is the tendency for all things to move to lower levels of energy—the tendency for things to disintegrate or fragment. Openness enables new energy to be brought into the system. For a system to maintain itself through time it must embody an input-transformation-output process (Haines, 1998). This can be seen in the human body. We must continually bring in resources (food, ideas, etc.) that we transform into energy and action. At a physical level, if we don't eat, we die. At a psychological level, if we are not stimulated by our world or cannot put back into the world our thoughts, ideas, and other expressions of our individuality (for example, if we are not loved or able to love others), then we begin to disintegrate psychologically. All systems embody some form of transformational process. It is what keeps the system alive. If a system's boundaries become closed, and they are no longer able to input energy and resources or output production, then the system suffers—it begins to lose energy and fragment. All closed systems eventually run down and die.

Openness enables systems to grow and develop beyond simple maintenance. Growth is a process of the internal elaboration of the system in response to the challenges meted out by the environment (Haines, 1998). The old saying "Necessity is the mother of invention" is apropos here. Feedback and challenge from outside the system are sources of perturbation for the system that stimulate change. Growth is the ability of a system to develop more effective structures and processes in response to the inevitable challenges of life.

KEY IMPLICATIONS FOR COACHING

Coaching's focus on feedback and the development of new structures of meaning and new patterns of action requires us to attend to how new information enters the system, what is done with it, and how feedback occurs. We need to have an understanding of how to nurture effective levels of openness. Too little openness and there is not enough new information to nourish change—everything is repetitive sameness. Too much openness and the system cannot cope with the amount and diversity of information—it becomes chaotic. Coaching seeks to help the person and organization maintain themselves at the border between chaos and sameness—a place complexity theory calls the "edge of chaos" (Lewin, 1993).

DYNAMIC EQUILIBRIUM AND THE EDGE OF CHAOS

The inevitable disturbance that comes with openness in systems can lead to instability in system functioning. Early theorists (such as von Bertalanffy, 1968, and Bowen, 1978) suggested that systems incorporate homeostatic mechanisms—responses that help the system return to stable functioning, or equilibrium, when disturbed. Problem solving, defensiveness, and resistance are familiar examples of homeostatic mechanisms in human systems. They serve to protect the normal functioning of the system when it is challenged. In early theories, it was assumed that stable predictable functioning was the desired state of any system. This assumption is still regularly made about individuals, teams, and organizations.

More recently, complexity theorists have identified that, rather than seeking steady-state functioning, complex adaptive systems are *necessarily* marked by a sort of sustainable instability or dynamic equilibrium (Haines, 1998; Stacey, 2000). By this is meant a sort of paradoxical bounded instability that is able to produce new forms of behavior and creative action. Both stability and instability are important. Too much instability and the system becomes chaotic and breaks down. Too much stability and the system becomes closed—it is unable to do anything new or to adapt to its environment—and entropy sets in. This place between chaos and stability is called the "edge of chaos." It is *not* a place of balance between stability and instability, but a paradoxical state of unresolvable contradictory forces (Stacey, 2000). The tension between these forces elicits creativity and innovation. According to Stacey, the edge of chaos is created where there is sufficient energy and information flow, diversity, and connectivity between system elements (Stacey, 2000). Most human systems typically function best at the edge of chaos.

We can see the edge of chaos operating in most innovative human behavior. We need a certain paradoxical instability of thinking to create something new. The tension created by the juxtaposition of diverse ideas enables us to make connections where they don't usually exist, and out of this tension new forms emerge. We see this juxtaposition of diverse ideas in Jørn Utzon's design for the Sydney Opera House. Utzon connected the idea of sailing with a building for performance of the arts. While instability is necessary for creativity, thinking cannot be completely random or chaotic. There must be sufficient discipline or orderedness to enable the selection of meaningful connections. (It is perhaps this paradoxical bounded instability that explains why so many creative geniuses lead such messy lives!)

The development of internal tension is important in coaching. One of the differentiation points between therapy and coaching is that in therapy, the level of instability, anxiety, or tension is so high as to be destructive of the person's ability to function effectively in his systems. They have slipped from the edge of chaos into chaos itself. Hence often one of the proximal goals of therapy is to help the person reduce distress so as to enable the emergence of new order. In other words, therapy seeks to comfort the afflicted.

In coaching, however, the coach is often called upon to afflict the comfortable! We often seek to increase information flow, energy, and diversity to a level that helps the person move out of stable mind-sets and behaviors so as to create new insights, understandings, and actions.

Creativity and the generation of novel behaviors, ideas, and structures illustrate another important feature of all complex adaptive systems—emergence (Lewin, 1993).

AGENCY, EMERGENCE, AND FEEDBACK

According to systems theories, it is the pattern of relationship between system elements that gives rise to the observable properties of the system. Let us take a simple example—water. Water is made up of molecules of H_2O. These are the system's elements. However, whether I am looking at a glass of water, a pile of snow, a block of ice, or a cloud of steam will depend on the specific pattern of relationship between the H_2O molecules. The properties of the system (wetness, hardness, whiteness, crystalline structure, etc.) are not to be found in the H_2O molecules themselves. Rather, they emerge in the context of relationships the H_2O molecules have with each other and the wider environment.

In human complex adaptive systems, human behavior can be seen as an emergent property. We do not go through the world emitting robotic behavior in isolation from the pattern of events and relationships in which we are involved. Rather, we have agency. We respond to events, strive for goals, and introduce novel behaviors in attempts to work within our systems. Human systems are able to adapt in novel ways (as are many other complex systems, like a flock of birds, fisheries, forests, and other environmental systems), because they incorporate complex positive and negative (amplifying and balancing) feedback loops and feed-forward loops that impact on the emergence of behavior (Lewin, 1993; Stacey, 2000).

Feedback and feed-forward loops are critical to the operation of complex adaptive systems in that they provide the nonlinear causality that marks such systems (Senge, 1990; Stacey, 2000; Wheatley, 1999). A systemic approach to coaching requires a familiarity with the workings of feedback and feed-forward loops.

Amplifying or positive feedback describes a system dynamic where elements of the system reinforce the behavior of the system such that the behavior grows. Vicious and virtuous cycles are examples of amplifying feedback. For example, the compounding of interest in a bank account is a form of amplifying feedback (and a virtuous cycle for the owner of the bank account!). Anxiety may also create amplifying loops with respect to defensive behavior. The more anxious a management team feels, the more defensive they become (a vicious cycle).

The action of amplifying loops is moderated by negative (balancing or regulatory) loops. These function to reduce system growth, or focus it at a specific level. For example, commercial fishing creates a balancing loop that reduces the growth of fish stocks. Other common examples of balancing loops include price regulating demand and aggressive criticism curtailing open exchange of information.

Human systems also incorporate feed-forward loops. These are the ability to anticipate the future in a way that causes the emergence of behavior in the present. For example, investors may anticipate an interest rate rise and decide to shift their investments from property to the stock market. Like feedback loops, feed-forward loops can be amplifying or regulatory (Stacey, 2000). For example, in team settings, patterns of past responding can lead team members to anticipate either positive or negative reactions when they put forward novel ideas. Anticipating positive reactions to new ideas is likely to increase creativity and innovative behavior. Creativity and innovation will be reduced if the anticipated response is negative.

Much has been written on the process of identifying and mapping different patterns of feedback loops. In the interests of brevity, the reader is referred to several sources for a fuller description (see Argyris, 2004; O'Connor & McDermott 1997; Senge, 1990; Senge, Ross, Smith, Roberts, & Kleiner, 1994).

Feedback is important in coaching at a number of levels. The nature, quality, and timeliness of feedback are critical for good coaching, regardless of whether the coach is operating from a systemic perspective. Here feedback is used in its broadest sense, as information flow that links action and outcome. Feedback functions to help the coachee identify goals and changes, track progress, and adjust behavior. From a systemic perspective, the coach's role is to help the client become sensitive and responsive to the many forms of feedback produced by the system. For example, at an individual level this might involve building sensitivity to others' reactions or using 360-degree feedback. At a team level, this might involve helping the client identify where amplifying and regulatory loops are operating in a way that subverts the achievement of the client's or organization's goals.

Systemic coaching also uses feed-forward loops when it seeks to explore the potential impacts that may be created by any changes the client makes. Take the case of a manager seeking to increase productivity in her team. There are multiple avenues open to the manager to influence the team—for example, she may institute bonus incentives, or she may introduce a policy of sacking the lowest-performing team members each year (as has been tried in some multinationals). Both of these strategies are likely to have unintended side effects. One side effect of a bonus system might be to focus people's efforts on achieving metrics at the expensive of genuine improvements in productivity (a pattern not dissimilar to governments reclassifying underemployed workers as employed so as to improve employment figures). Sacking the poorest performers regardless of actual performance is likely to create an atmosphere of hostile competition in which team members seek to secure their own jobs by withholding information and assistance from other team members for fear the others will be too successful.

Both of these are examples of unintended system patterns that function as negative or regulatory loops with respect to productivity. The coach may assist the manager in examining the potential effects of implementing such strategies. It may be that the manager can redesign the strategy so as to minimize negative outcomes. It may be that, once the potential feedforward or feedback loops are discovered, an entirely new strategy is called for. Whatever the outcome, by discussing feedback and feed-forward, the coaching conversation has moved the discussion to a place of tension. That tension is evidence of the edge of chaos, and is the place where creativity can emerge.

KEY IMPLICATION FOR COACHING

Rarely are the unhelpful behaviors, properties, and outcomes elicited by feedback loops deliberately malicious. Rather they can be seen as the unintended consequences that emerge as a result of the system's dynamics. We can sometimes understand the system's dynamics by looking for emergent properties, and then seeking to identify the feedback and feedback loops that give rise to them. To do this we need to see the system from the client's perspective. In order to understand this important feature of complex systems, the concepts of attractors and sensitivity to initial conditions are important (Lewin, 1993).

ATTRACTORS AND SENSITIVITY TO INITIAL CONDITIONS

An attractor can be thought of as the complex pattern of influences that cause system properties to gravitate to particular values (Harris & Scherblom, 1999). The way a group of people talk together, competitiveness, defensiveness, cooperativeness, and energy levels can all be thought of as emergent properties of the system. The intricate pattern of stories, goals, concerns, power relations, and positive and negative feedback loops that exist in an organization may tend, for example, to elicit different levels of competitiveness or defensiveness. These patterns of forces are attractors.

Perhaps the easiest way to think of attractors is to imagine a three-dimensional model of a landscape—say a large relief map such as you might find in the visitors' center of a national park. Now imagine throwing a marble into the model. It will tend to travel downhill, into the valleys until it reaches the lowest local point. That valley or the area bounded by that set of hills is an attractor—when the marble comes into the field of its influence, it attracts particular types of behavior from the marble. Attractors are more or less stable places in the landscape. If you somehow disturb the marble as it is sitting in the valley, it may move around the valley floor a bit, but it will tend to stay somewhere in the valley. Moving the marble to a new valley takes a lot more energy. You need to either change the shape of the mountains or push the marble up and over and into another valley. But remember that attractors can be powerful. You may end up like Sisyphus, putting in enormous effort for little result.

Attractors are like the valleys. They exert forces that shape behavior in systems. In organizations, remuneration and bonus systems act as attractors. People, mental models, rules, assumptions, events, and even objects can elicit more or less stable patterns of behavior over time. Things as simple as the lunchroom, photocopier, or watercooler can act as attractors in the system—they can become places where people meet, talk, and make decisions.

Of course, like our model landscape, attractor valleys differ enormously in shape. Some have steep walls and small floors, and it is easy to identify where the marble will come to rest. Others have shallow walls or wide flat areas that make it very hard to identify exactly where the marble will end up. You know it is likely to be somewhere in the valley, but just where is unpredictable. Still others, called strange attractors, cause behavior to move in one direction at some times and in other directions at other times. Small differences may be all it takes to cause a discontinuous shift in the attractor!

So, from a coaching perspective, being alive to the shape of the system landscape is important. Unfortunately, unlike marbles and model landscapes, real-life attractor landscapes are not always easily identifiable, particularly in advance. However, we often can begin to see the shape of attractors in patterns of behavior they elicit. For example, budget meetings in one organization may be a mad scramble to secure as many resources as possible from the collective pot. In another organization, budget meetings may revolve almost exclusively around cost cutting. In such situations, systemic coaching does not seek to ask who is to blame for undesired behaviors. Rather, it asks, "How useful are each of these behavioral patterns in terms of the client's goals? What are the assumptions, rules, and feedback loops that elicit these behaviors? What changes could be made to elicit different, more useful behaviors?"

Noticing patterns is made even harder by another feature of complex adaptive systems, namely, sensitivity to initial conditions. Human systems often show huge sensitivity to very fine differences in the initial state of the system—so much so that it is often impossible to even identify precisely what is causing the final emergent behavior of the system.

This sensitivity was first shown by the meteorologist Lorenz (1963) in his work on weather systems. He found that even the most minute changes in the initial condition of a weather system tend to amplify over time to produce major changes in the outcome of the system. This is what is meant by the famous "butterfly flapping its wings in Brazil" analogy.

Some authors suggest that the complexity created by nonlinear feedback, amplification, and sensitivity to initial conditions makes all complex adaptive systems radically unpredictable (Stacey, 2000). To a large degree this is true. One can never predict with precision or certainty how systems will react to the things we do, particularly in the long term. They are too complex. Yet experience shows us that many systems respond in a broadly predictable way.

For example, if I forget a close friend's birthday, I can predict the friend will be hurt and that tension may arise between us. It is likely that something will need to be done to repair the relationship before it returns to a relatively even keel. What I cannot predict is exactly what this process will look like. It may also be that my forgetting will prove to be the undoing of the friendship because it has come on the heels of several other slights (by me or others). Equally, it is possible that my friend might see that I was under unusual pressure at work, be understanding of my neglect, and let the incident pass without mention.

While precise prediction may be impossible, human behavior in systems is often predictable in a fuzzy way a good deal of the time. The further we move away from the present, the less predictable or more fuzzy the potential outcomes. At the same time, human behavior is typically not utterly random. When it appears so, it is seen as either an indicator of mental illness or a sign that we have missed some important feature of the event landscape. For example, I would normally have a high degree of confidence that my friend will not respond to my failure to remember his birthday by becoming vegetarian, joining the French Foreign Legion, or attacking me with a cauliflower.

IMPLICATIONS FOR COACHING—THE AUTONOMOUS CLIENT?

The dynamics of attractors, emergence, and sensitivity to initial conditions in complex adaptive systems have many significant implications for coaching. First, the dynamics of system attractors suggest that attempts to locate blame for system failures in individuals, while perhaps emotionally satisfying, will be largely unhelpful. Behavior is often best thought of as an emergent property of the system. In other words, the behavior of one part of the system (i.e., a person or team) is called forth by the complex web of relations in which that person or team finds themselves.

Yet, as coaches we are often asked to treat system members as if they are isolated units. This is particularly true in situations involving remedial coaching. It is not unusual for individuals to be referred for coaching in the hope that they will be "fixed" and that their negative impact on team or group performance might be alleviated. This is analogous to something that often happens in family therapy. Parents will bring a child to therapy for behavioral problems, when in fact the child's behavior is actually a symptom of the distress evident in the wider family system. In recognition of this, family therapists typically say that the child is the "identified patient," and then proceed to work with the whole family system (Parry, 1996).

One might argue that in executive coaching we are not dealing with helpless and hapless children. We deal with adults, and adults are accountable for their behavior. Furthermore, this accountability is important because an individual's actions within a system can have a significant impact, for good or ill, on the system as a whole. One has only to think of Sir Bob Geldof and Band Aid, or Nick Leeson and the failure of Barings Bank to see the impact an individual can have. However, as unique as these individuals might appear, treating them as entities isolated from the wider systems in which their actions occurred is problematic. Band Aid's achievements would have been impossible but for the cooperation of a host of people. Leeson's activities were enabled by a system that lacked appropriate feedback mechanisms or the will to implement them. Leeson's fraud was enacted within a culture that placed a premium on success, regardless of how it is achieved. According to a colleague at Barings Bank, "The management trusted him too much. . . . Nick was the star trader at Barings because his trades contributed a huge amount of money. Because of this, a lot of the checks and balances that should have been noted were ignored" (Borthwick, 2003).

The idea that the individual is the only agent contributing to an organizational outcome can be reassuring for the organization. It enables the members to have heroes and scapegoats, and to explain outcomes in ways that do not call for significant personal change. While locating causality in the individual may protect system members from having to face their complicity in the outcome, in the long run it fails to address problematic systemic patterns. Colluding with this avoidance serves to undermine the coaching engagement and weaken both the client and the organization.

An example of unhelpful collusion occurs when coaches act as go-betweens, delivering management feedback to the coachee or advocating on behalf of the coachee. Such behavior has the potential to subvert more mature channels of communication in the organization, weaken relationships, foster dependence, and maintain the very patterns of poor communication the coaching was meant to address.

The failure to acknowledge the wider system can be just as damaging in times of success. A common example of this is the impact on team members when a narcissistic leader fails to properly acknowledge the contributions of the team in times of success. Such behavior weakens team morale and commitment, and reduces the leader's influence at the very time when success should be enhancing both! If done often enough, the legacy can be a cancerous resentment that team members feel unable to openly express, but which undermines every project undertaken.

That is not to say that coaching individuals to more effectively participate in their organizations is pointless. Just as the team is a complex adaptive system, so, too, is the individual. The individuals' *potential* to effectively participate in positive interaction, along with their ability to resist the pull of destructive attractors, is an emergent property of their complex interaction of the parts that make them up. These parts include their mental models, personalities, habitual behaviors, emotions, physiologies, and genetics. We will explore this area more fully later in the chapter.

Coaching from a complex adaptive systems perspective does not draw a dichotomy between the individual and the team. Rather, working with an individual *is* working with the team/wider organization. Similarly, one cannot work with a team without having an impact at the level of the individual. Nevertheless, it is important for the coach to be aware of, and intentional about, which level of the system is being engaged (individual, team, or organization) at any given time in the coaching process, and to consider, as best one can, the foreseeable impacts on the other levels of the system.

Almost all interventions in coaching are multilayered in that they have impacts on many levels. For example, one might be coaching an executive with a goal of developing a more family friendly work-life balance. A typical behavioral change might be to leave the office at a reasonable hour in the evening (say, 6:00 P.M.). It is important to consider how that change might be perceived. This will be very context dependent. For example, when other staff feel they must stay late because the company is struggling, seeing the boss leaving on time may lead to increased stress and tension in the workplace. In other contexts (such as in some law firms) this behavior may be interpreted as a lack of suitability for advancement or even a thinly veiled criticism of the dominant culture. That does not mean the goal of leaving by 6:00 P.M. must be abandoned. Rather, it indicates that the resultant stress and tension or misinterpretation may need to be addressed so as to keep it within reasonable bounds.

ENGAGING WITH THE UNPREDICTABLE AND UNCONTROLLABLE NATURE OF COMPLEX SYSTEMS

System sensitivity to initial conditions means that often small changes can result in large shifts in outcomes. For example, spending time with an executive practicing reflective listening or even something as simple as smiling when he greets his direct reports can have a major impact on employee engagement and morale and overall team performance.

Unfortunately, sensitivity to initial conditions also carries with it a difficulty that is often downplayed or ignored by coaches and consultants working from a linear approach—the problem of long-term unpredictability. We can often present our solutions or develop plans with clients that have an aura of authority about them. We are easily seduced by the apparent certainty of linear thinking. The old image of the corporate leader standing at the helm of the organization, guiding it through the stormy waters of life, is a powerful one. It leads to the expectation, at all levels of management, that a skilled leader should know the right levers to pull in order to enact change, and what will happen when they are used. The most skilled leader is the one who can turn the ship around quickly and with the greatest grace! This is the fundamental assumption of command and control leadership.

The traditional or classical command and control leader, according to Crawford and Brungardt (2000), was well suited to the industrialized world, where work flow depended on stable, predictable structures. While the methods of industry resulted in relatively stable output, they paid scant attention to the human resources they used in the process. However, in today's world where knowledge and information drive an increasingly service-oriented economy, success requires the adaptive and diverse contribution of all employees. Command and control models of leadership are not well suited to eliciting free-flowing contributions to innovation and knowledge creation (Crawford & Brungardt, 2000).

If we are to take the process of emergence in complex systems seriously, then we must acknowledge that the leader can never stand outside the system and operate on it in such a clinical way. Leaders are fundamentally part of the system. The very notion of leadership can be understood as an emergent property of the co-created relationship between leader and follower (Dimitrov & Lederer, 2003). Even the simple act of observation affects system behavior. We have all experienced how behavior changes in a meeting when the boss enters the room. We take these changes for granted, but they show powerfully the interdependence of systems agents, and demonstrate the principle that systems agents tend to act locally—that is, according to local goals.

This radical unpredictability and interdependence has far-reaching implications for leadership and for coaching (Stacey, 2000). If leaders cannot stand outside the organization in order to direct it in predictable ways, what is their role? If coaches cannot assist leaders to find predictable solutions, what value are they to the organization?

One of the reasons why complexity theory has been so slow to infiltrate leadership theory is that it raises these highly anxiety-provoking questions. It weakens our ability to see the world as predictable and controllable. This is an existentially terrifying position to take. It undermines the very reason for being so many of us have taken for granted in our roles as leaders and change agents.

At another level, though, complexity theory is enormously liberating. If control and predictability are illusions, and stable order is a sign of decay, then no longer do leaders have to struggle under so heavy a burden of responsibility for forces they cannot, *as a matter of principle*, predict or control. But this does not mean that leaders at all levels of the system have no role. Their role remains crucial to the organization—it is simply no longer one characterized by disengaged diagnosis, command, and control (Crawford & Brungardt, 2000). Rather, as we shall see, complexity theory shows us that the leader's role is perhaps more usefully conceived in terms of engaging with the system in a way that is characterized by ongoing responsive dialogue.

Attempts have been made to maintain a traditional command and control approach to organizational leadership by suggesting that the role of the leader is to push the organizational systems toward the edge of chaos so as to capitalize on the creativity found there (for example, Brown and Eisenhardt, 1998). Some of the techniques associated with this include setting stretch goals, establishing cross-functional teams, flattening hierarchical management structures, downsizing, and so on. However, such an approach neglects that inherent unpredictability of complexity and also assumes the leader is able to stand outside the system and see where, and in what way to push the system into creativity. There is no guarantee that new order created at the edge of chaos will be a beneficial one for the organization (Stacey, 2000). It also neglects the fact that most human systems typically gravitate toward the edge of chaos, because this is where self-organization occurs.

> It is the very essence of self-organisation that none of those individual agents is able to step outside the system and obtain an overview of how the whole is evolving, let alone how it will evolve. It is the very essence of self-organisation that none of the agents, as individuals, or any small group of them on their own, can design, or even shape the evolution of the system other than through their local interaction. (Stacey, 2000, p. 303)

Leaders (and coaches) cannot stand outside the system in order to manipulate it in predicted ways, because they are part of the system, and their actions are immediately swept up into the web of nonlinear feedback and information flow. Rather than intervening in the functioning of the organization from time to time, the leader needs to be engaged in an ongoing dialogical relationship with the system.

An ongoing responsive engagement within the system as it unfolds over time would seem to be the model of leadership most in keeping with the dynamics of complex adaptive systems. In this way the leader can participate in, rather than seek to control, the self-organization of the system. Four broad areas of activity have been held to be important in sustaining organizations in the creative tension on the edge of chaos. These are: setting vision, creating boundaries, ensuring adequate communication flow, and empowerment (Crawford & Brungardt, 2000; Fraser & Greenhalgh, 2001; Plsek & Wilson, 2001; Stacey, 2000; Wheately, 1999; Youngblood, 1997).

This ongoing responsive engagement is highlighted in the work of Ralph Stacey. Stacey (2000), building on the work of ethnologists such as Goffman and Boden, has developed a metaphor that I believe captures well the dynamic nature of complex systems and sheds light on the roles of both leaders and coaches in complex systems. Stacey (2000) suggests that human systems (and the human person) are constructed by the complex responsive process of conversation.

> How do new organisations come into being? The intention to form a new organisation emerges as a theme in the conversations those forming it have with each other and with other people with whom they are in relationship.
>
> Why do they cease to exist? The pattern of relationship, the pattern of conversation which shapes the actions of members does not survive in competition with other conversations. (Stacey, 2000, p. 402).

How does a marriage come about? It starts with a conversation between two people. How does it end? They stop talking (or talk about the wrong things!). The same is true for companies, clubs, and nations.

INDIVIDUALS AND ORGANIZATIONS AS CONVERSATIONS

Stacey points to several ways in which conversation is an apt metaphor for the dynamic processes from which organizational character, culture, and behavior emerge. Firstly, conversation is the construction of narratives of meaning, from which emerge themes and mental models. These themes and mental models both enable behavior and communication and constrain it. The conversation enables some types of action, and constrains other types of action.

Communication is creative of organization at both the individual and the wider systems level. We become who we are via the complex process of communication with other human beings. Case studies of people who are raised in isolation show that normal human development is arrested when people are deprived of the opportunity to interact with other people (Pines, 1997). Interacting with our external conversations is the stream of internal dialogue that is an essential part of the creation of meaning. It is a conversation we have with ourselves in which we seek to form intentions and to elaborate ideas, models, explanations, and other narratives so as to resolve the tensions that arise when we are faced with challenges, or to discharge or avoid emotional states that arise within us, or to elicit other desired emotional states. It is out of this ongoing dialogue that our sense of self develops and is maintained (Stacey, 2000).

So what are the system elements in conversation within the person? Figure 11.2 shows that this internal dialogue involves the whole person. All aspects of the self both inform and are informed by each other in an ongoing inner dialogue. Our genetics determine the broad boundaries

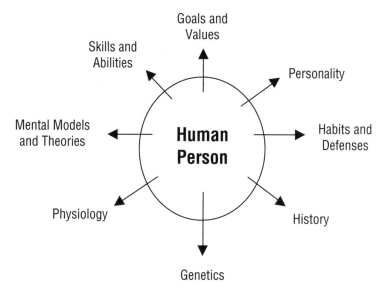

Figure 11.2
The Dynamic Components of the Human Person,
or the Personal Reflective Space

of the system. Our personalities, habits, and defenses act as attractors for particular types of conversations, behaviors, and conclusions. Our physiology is a powerful player in our internal dialogue. Physiology includes our emotions, our health, and our ever-changing physical states. Our changing goals and values inform our intentions, as do our mental models and the theories and metaphors that guide us. All of these factors interact together, and in that interaction emerges our experience of self, our intentions, and our knowledge.

That knowledge is an emergent property is an important point. We often think of knowledge as something we acquire (or lose in forgetfulness). Yet careful examination of our experience shows us otherwise. The story of Avril illustrates this.

I met Avril on a train going from London to Stanstead Airport on my way to run a communication skills workshop for a group of general practitioners. Avril, a bright, engaging, and intelligent woman in her 40s, was the conductor on the train. As she took my ticket, she asked where I was going, and I told her I was going to teach doctors how to communicate with patients.

"Well!" she said, planting her hands on her hips. "They can certainly use some of that! You know, whenever I go to the doctors, I know exactly what I want to say, but when I get in there he asks me all these questions, and in no time flat I am hopelessly confused and I don't even know why I am there."

We can all relate to Avril's experience of being undone by the conversation. We have probably all been dumbstruck or discombobulated by others at one time or another. This occurs whenever the conversations we are engaged in (both inner and outer) do not allow our knowledge to emerge in consciousness.

Just as our sense of self and our knowledge emerges in a complex mix of inner and outer conversations, so, too, the organizations of which we are a part are defined in the complex conversations that emerge among systems members. Organizational conversations seek to make meaning, form intentions, discharge, elicit, and avoid emotional states via ongoing narrative. In our workplace conversations we seek to make sense of what we see happening. We discuss and form plans of action. We hold conversations that are designed, consciously and unconsciously, to reduce anxiety, discharge frustration, and respond to and exercise power. We do all of this while attempting to maintain a sense of belonging or connectedness to the system. These competing demands hold us on the edge of chaos—the place of emergence and creativity.

Our mental models are key elements in these conversations. They are constructed by and emerge from within the complex responsive dialogue that goes on between people and within the person. They both enable meaningful conversations to be held and constrain the limits of meaning. They help us to select certain information out of the miasma of stimuli that surrounds us, and reject other stimuli as mere noise (Parry, 1996).

When the conversation strays from the meaning enabled by our current mental models, we experience ourselves as moving further toward chaos, and the resultant tension is creative of innovation. If the conversation strays too far from our mental models, then it becomes meaningless and we are thrown into disarray until a radical new understanding can be discovered (or the system disintegrates). This is a paradigm shift. Interestingly, if our conversations become repetitive and add nothing new to our mental models, we experience boredom and restlessness (Parry, 1996). Notice that the problematic movement here is toward stability. The system becomes closed and vulnerable to entropy. Our boredom and restlessness serve to motivate us to seek new and stimulating conversations. It seems we are constantly drawn to that place between sameness and radical newness—the edge of chaos again.

At the simplest level of mental model making, we learn what behaviors are acceptable and not acceptable in both the subtle and covert conversations that go on in response to those behaviors. The system tells us, often in no uncertain terms, that different types of action, gestures, themes, and narratives are acceptable or not. Coming late for a meeting, telling the wrong joke for the situation, making a speech that captures the feeling of the audience, all elicit responses (feedback) from the system members with whom we are in relationship. The latecomer observes others as they glance at their watches; the inappropriate comic receives polite smiles, confused concern, or looks of disapproval. The speaker observes the audience's attentive gaze, affirmative gestures, and heartfelt applause.

At more complex levels of model making, we elaborate theories and metaphors to explain the world of our experience. This is done, once again, both in conversations with others and in our internal dialogue. In this dialogue we test the theories and metaphors against our experience, seek for congruencies and areas of disjunction. Our mental models and the patterns of our conversations are attractors through which we reproduce themes and narratives (Stacey, 2000). We are often able to see the attractors at play in the recurrent patterns and themes that our conversations reproduce.

> Nonscientists tend to think that science works by deduction. But actually science works mainly by metaphor. And what's happening [when change happens] is that the kinds of metaphor people have in mind are changing. (Waldrop, 1992, p. 327)

THE IMPORTANCE OF EMOTION
FOR THE FREE FLOW OF INFORMATION

All conversations are embodied. All human communication is initiated in bodies, and is interpreted through bodies. Our emotional states are the physical reactions we have to the communication in which we are involved. Emotion provides us both with the energy that drives (or depletes) ongoing dialogue and action, and provides us with a visceral level of feedback about the nature and quality of the conversations in which we are involved. For the client and the coach, emotions can be a rich source of data to inform the coaching conversation.

According to Stacey (2000), the free flow of conversation enables the emergence of new forms, understandings, and action. When the conversation becomes repetitive, the behavior of the organization becomes stuck—the boundaries of the system become closed and the organization is unable to adapt to changes in the environment. Bureaucracies are typical examples of stereotyped repetitive conversation patterns. They are stultifying for both the bureaucracy members and its customers.

Stacey (2000) identifies three factors associated with the free flow of conversation: connectivity, diversity, and anxiety. By connectivity is meant the richness of the themes and associations within the conversation. If system members are connected by a few loose themes, their communication is apt to be stereotyped. We can often see this in the pattern of communication of old school friends who do not meet regularly. Their communication tends to revolve around reminiscing over their schoolday experiences. Repeated contact tends to allow more connected and richer themes to emerge in the conversation.

Diversity enables the free flow of conversation by supplying novelty, difference, and tension. People from diverse backgrounds and experience hold different perspectives on events. These differences provide the critical levels of misunderstanding and cross-fertilization needed to stimulate novel connections (Stacey, 2000). Too much diversity and the communication falls into chaos. This is consistent with communication theorists such as Shannon, who found that messages had to have the correct mix of redundancy (or repetition) and surprise (or novelty) in order to be effective. Too much of what is already known and the listener will switch off. Too much novelty and the message becomes chaotic (Parry, 1996).

Anxiety is the third critical factor in the free flow of communication. Too little anxiety and the conversation lacks energy. Too much and the free flow of conversation is destroyed. People who are overly anxious will tend to close down communication (destructive stability again), or open a flood of information that leads to chaos. The facilitatory and inhibitory effects of anxiety have been long known in the psychological literature (Druskat & Wolff, 2001; Harris & Scherblom, 1999; Yerkes & Dodson, 1908). Hence, for the free flow of communication there must be what Stacey calls the "good enough holding of anxiety" (Stacey, 2000, p. 391).

Allied to anxiety is the notion of the use of power. Power is an attractor that constrains (and enables) behavior. Used in a coercive fashion, power is likely to elicit passivity and compliance (the closing down of free conversational flow) or rebellion and disintegration of the conversation (Stacey, 2000). At the same time, when power is absent from the conversation, connectedness and cohesion suffer.

The more senior the leadership role, the more connectivity and power the leader is able to wield, and the more diversity the leader is able to introduce. This means that leaders are able to influence the pattern and quality of organizational conversations in a way many others cannot. An old saying, "The leader casts a long shadow, and small movements by the leader are translated into large movements at the end of the shadow," speaks to the power leaders wield. The follow-up question, "What is the single most common activity in organizations? Shadow watching!" speaks to the connectivity of leaders!

The conversational metaphor, as discussed so far, is consistent with the work of Dimitrov (1997) on fuzzy logic in teams. Dimitrov suggests a remarkably similar set of preconditions for effective group dynamics. Using fuzzy logic rules, he sees "preparedness to act together" as a function of willingness to engage in dialogue, trustworthiness, and creativity. Both the correspondence with connectivity, anxiety, and diversity, as well as the conversational dynamic of the system are clear.

> The paradoxical and chaotic nature of social reality causes a great deal of uncertainty and vagueness in human decision-making. Under conditions of uncertainty and vagueness, when no ultimate answers or best solutions exist, the search for understanding and consensus between people becomes crucial for the management of social complexity. (Dimitrov, 1997, section 3.2, para. 4)

If organizations are emergent properties organised by the models, themes, and dynamics of the conversations engaged in by system members, then we can say, along with Parry, Dimitrov, and Stacey, that the quality of the conversation determines the quality of the organization.

What gets said, how it is said, by whom and where, whose voice is heard, what can and can't be talked about openly, what values and emotions energize our conversations, what patterns our conversations take—they all point to the attractors that shape the behavior of system members, and indicate the health of the organization. The quality of the conversation determines the quality of the organization. One has only to look at the way our current discourse around the war on terror is shaping our societies in order to see this.

Figure 11.3 summarizes the implications of the preceding discussion for coaching leaders at every level in an organization.

Complexity theory not only shows us what may be profitably focused on in the coaching conversation, it also helps us to understand how we might approach the coaching conversation so as to foster change and the open flow of communication.

Ten Points of Focus in Coaching

1. The quality of the organizational conversations that create the intentions that managers convey to the organization—and focus on the responses to those intentions by organization members.

2. The types of conversation had within the organization—what themes emerge, what rhetorical ploys are used to block the free flow of conversation, and what is not said.

3. The quality and richness of connection between system members. How are system members connected to each other, customers, suppliers, competition, etc.? (Feedback loops become important here.)

4. Power relations embodied in those organizational conversations: who is ruled in, and who is left out—what is their perspective?

5. How is anxiety being dealt with? Is anxiety held in a good enough way—so as to allow continued change and innovation?

6. Trust: How is the client generating good enough trust to allow the difficult conversations to be had?

7. Diversity: Is there enough deviance and difference in the system to allow for the emergence of new ideas, themes, and ways of doing things? Is there some degree of subversive activity going on that is able to challenge the dominant ways of thinking and doing in the organization?

8. Taking unpredictability and paradox seriously—the name, blame, and shame game is pointless and counterproductive.

9. Action: Action must be taken in the absence of clear knowledge and predictable outcomes. Nonaction is likely to lead to less adaptive fit as the environment changes and as competitors discover more adaptive spaces.

10. Fit and Value: Unpredictability means that the quality of action should not be judged by outcome. A quality action is good because:
    - It fits with the demands of the environment at the time.
    - It creates a platform from which other options can be taken (it does not lead to a dead end).
    - It is one that enables errors to be detected quickly.
    - It is fundamentally moral and ethical in nature.

Figure 11.3

The Ten Focal Points of Coaching in Complex Adaptive Systems

Source: Adapted from Stacey (2000).

A DYNAMIC MODEL OF THE COACHING ENGAGEMENT

If the preceding discussion is correct, then the coaching relationship is itself a complex adaptive system. The coaching engagement is an organization that emerges from the complex interaction of the coach and client—it is a co-created conversation. This contrasts with an expert-centric view of coaching that suggests that coaches "add value" either by providing expert knowledge or by their ability to view the client's system from a more objective perspective. If the coach is a co-creator of the coaching conversation, then such an objective stance is impossible.

Similarly, the preceding discussion also calls into question overly simplistic client-centric approaches such as the common or received version of the solutions-focused approach often seen in coaching. In this version, the solution is claimed to lie within the client. The coach's role is to merely facilitate the client's discoveriy of what the client already has within himself or herself. "Ask, don't tell" is the catch cry. Yet sometimes no matter how long we ask the solution does not emerge, because it is not "in" the client, nor are the raw materials available for it to emerge via a process of questioning.

(It should be noted that the more sophisticated solutions-focused approach, such as that articulated by Jackson and McKergow (2002) is consistent with a complex adaptive systems approach. It sees the solution to a client's problem in interactional terms, and as an emergent property of the interaction between the client and the coach.)

My experience as a coach, and as an educator and a supervisor of coaches, suggests that both the simplistic client-centric approach and the expert-centric approach are often more about managing the coach's anxiety than they are reflective of what actually happens in effective coaching sessions. Effective coaches often do tell. They educate their clients. They share their mental models, and tell them things when the answer eludes the client. They also spend a lot of time asking. But the questions they ask are not atheoretical, as stated in the solution-focused texts (Jackson & McKergow, 2002). Rather, they are informed by their hypotheses about what is going on for the client. These hypotheses are built on the foundation of the coach's understandings about what it means to be human, or in relationship, or in business, or healthy, or whatever else the coaching is about. Their domain-specific knowledge is constantly in play, but never overpowering the client. The coach's telling is timely, the questions genuinely curious.

A very wise clinical supervisor I had years ago used to say to me, "The art of good therapy is to wait for the learning moment, and notice it when it arrives."

So how then does the coaching conversation proceed in a way that opens the client's situation for change, while remaining respectful of the skills, experience, and knowledge of both the client and coach? How do we notice the learning moments, and what do we do with them? The process illustrated in Figure 11.4 is untested except in the laboratory of the mind. It comes out of my experience as a coach and supervisor, and as a client of coaching and supervision. While I have shared this model with many coaches and it seems to resonate with their experience, it does not yet qualify as an evidence-based model. I present it here because I find it a useful metaphor that helps me understand what I am doing when I coach.

It is named "The Three Reflective Spaces" because it is a system made up primarily of three spaces that contain three conversations that interact together to create the coaching conversation.

The first reflective space is the internal conversation within the client.

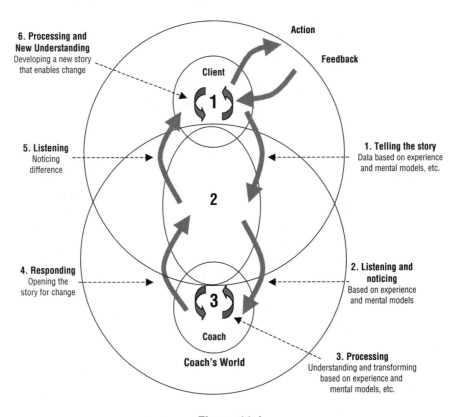

Figure 11.4
The Three Reflective Spaces—A Dynamic Model of the Coaching Conversation

It is here that the coaching conversation starts. For the sake of simplicity, the client is here defined as the person we are coaching. The second reflective space is the shared space created between the coach and client. It is the space in which the external coaching conversation is conducted. The third reflective space is the space within the coach. As with the client, this is the space where the coach's internal dialogue happens. It is the space where meaning and understanding emerge for the individual.

The external coaching conversation begins as clients tell their story. In other words, they put data into the shared space between the coach and client. This data is the product of their internal conversation and the myriad of conversations they have outside the coaching relationship. It is informed by and expressive of their experience, mental models, personality, physiology, goals and values, emotions, and habits and defenses. Everything that the client puts into this shared coaching space is a potentially rich source of information about the client in his/her world.

The coach listens to this rich data as it enters the shared space—noticing and selecting through the filter of his/her own experience, mental models, and emotional responses. We try to notice what is said, both verbally and non-verbally. We notice the story and the way it constrains possibilities and enables them. We notice what is not said, and what is avoided. We notice the feeling tone in the client, and the feeling tone it elicits in us. In this way the client's communication enters into the coach's personal reflective space. Here it continues to interact with the coach's experience, mental models, emotions, personality, history, and so on, and we begin to see patterns as the client's data elicits ideas, images, metaphors, and theories. Meaning or knowledge begins to emerge for us in this process. This processing often continues postsession and during the coach's supervision.

The knowledge that is elicited is *new* knowledge—we coaches see it in the connections between what the client is experiencing and our own experience and understandings. When we are truly engaged in the conversation, this emergent knowledge has the character of insight, rather than of the mechanical overlay of our preexisting models on the client's situation. It is an "aha" experience (Lewin & Regine, 2001). Yet the insight is tentative until shared and agreed—"Aha, *perhaps* this is what it means for them."

Our experience, mental models, values, and intentions help us as coaches to see the data in a way that raises the possibility of change. The coach's experience, theories, values, and intentions inform the dialogue, rather than predetermine its outcome. It is through this internal dialogue that data first disclosed by the client is transformed in an attempt to make it understandable in a way that facilitates change and goal attainment.

The fourth step is to put this transformed data back into the shared space for ongoing consideration in the conversation. The coachee then picks it up and, all going well, takes it into the crucible of his own internal dialogue. The conversation continues in an iterative way until both coach and client have developed a shared understanding, or shared mental model, that opens the way forward to action. In effect, new knowledge has been created in the coaching encounter. For that knowledge to be useful, it must result in action in the client's world, and feedback on that action needs to be returned to the client and the coaching system.

For the coaching process to remain an effective conversation, the coaching system must be open. The input-transformation-output process is required at every level of the system. Information can (and often should) flow in from many points in the wider environment. This introduces both connectivity and diversity into the conversation—two of the three critical variables for fostering the conversation. Figure 11.5 illustrates some of the many sources of new information that may nourish the coaching conversation. The cycle of information flow, conversation, action, and feedback continues in an iterative way throughout the coaching engagement.

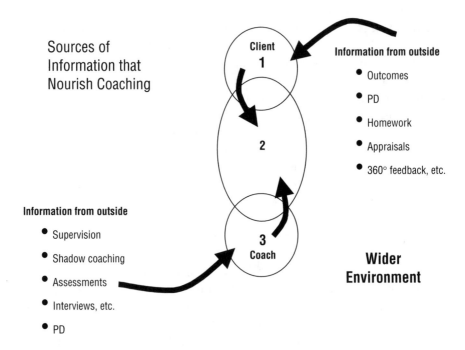

Figure 11.5
Maintaining Adequate Diversity and Connectivity with the Wider System

Anxiety and trust must also be held at good enough levels in the conversations. Deep respect for the client, an empathic and curious attitude, rapport building and listening skills, sensitivity to the emotional impact of the conversation, clear confidentiality boundaries, and an understanding of personality are all critical coaching competencies here. Holding anxiety in a good enough way is an ongoing process in the conversation. As we have discussed, too much or too little anxiety is destructive of the type of open disclosure needed for effective coaching.

The exercise of expert power is also an important issue in the coaching space. The three reflective spaces model helps us to understand the noncoercive use of domain-specific knowledge and expertise in coaching. Our traditional understanding of an expert is someone who holds a high level of domain-specific knowledge and skills. Expertise is the effective application of that knowledge and skill. However, if complexity theory is correct, then true knowledge is an emergent property of the intrapersonal and interpersonal conversation process.

In the same way, expertise, or the effective application of expert knowledge, is an emergent property of the conversation. It emerges in the creation of a shared mental model that opens the way for change. This understanding of expertise seems to tally with experience. We have all had coaching sessions that went poorly—where we felt inexpert and acted inexpertly, even though we had the raw materials for expertise. Sometimes this is because the conversation is such that it does not allow knowledge to emerge in the individual (as in the case of Avril), or because conversation did not enable the production of a useful shared mental model. A multitude of factors can derail the emergence of expertise. These include: inattention, anxiety, lack of trust, avoidance, defensiveness, lack of expert information, failure to empathize, or other internal or external conversations overwhelming the coaching conversation.

There appear to be at least six common internal conversations that derail coaching. These all involve failure to engage with the conversation in the creative space at the edge of chaos. They can occur within either the client or the coach, and frequently both coach and client collude in them together. They are:

1. Intolerance of ambiguity.
2. Rushing to closure on the goal.
3. Being the expert (imposing one's knowledge rather than using it to inform).
4. Thinking it's about me!
5. Objectifying the client or overidentifying with the client.
6. Avoidance of difficult issues.

All of these involve conversations that block the free flow of information. They seek to resolve the tension of being on the edge of chaos by either prematurely imposing order on the conversation, constraining what can be talked about, or introducing a level of anxiety that closes down communication. They stop us from really seeing our clients and meeting them where they are.

Expert knowledge is critically important to the coaching conversation. Without it, we are simply well-meaning amateurs. Expert knowledge helps us, and our clients, understand experience in new ways. It helps open the system boundaries. While expert knowledge must be held, it must be held lightly! The danger with expert knowledge is that we can make it a priori to the lived experience of the client. In other words, we can give our "expert mental models" a privileged status and then try to fit the data to the theory. When our theories and models move from being perspectives that nourish the conversation to the necessary conclusion of that conversation, they have moved from being information to ideology. When this happens, we, as coaches, have moved from a stance of curiosity and service to one of coercive arrogance!

> *We cannot make spontaneous coherence emerge according to our desire—*
> *but we can seed it and nourish it.*
> —Dimitrov and Lederer (2003)

DEVELOPING CONVERSATIONAL FITNESS— THE TASK OF COACHING AND A TASK FOR COACHES

The three reflective spaces model shows that both the individual and the system are important. Ultimately, the task of coaching is to help the individual develop his fitness to be involved in the conversational process, both internally and externally. In other words, coaching seeks to help clients improve their ability to participate in the process of meaning making via open and reflective engagement with all the data their world provides.

Carl Rogers' often quoted exhortation "all facts are friendly" reflects this open, or nondefensive, reflective engagement. Learning to take this stance is the work of a lifetime. It is no less than the process of growth and maturation. It requires the individual to engage constantly with the tension found at the edge of chaos, so as to seek new understandings that enable ever more effective, value-based action in the world.

This process is inherently challenging. It calls us to examine our assumptions, mental models, habitual ways of responding, goals, and values. It calls us to engage in honest dialogue both within ourselves and with others When done well, this reflective engagement not only issues in double loop learning (Argyris, 2004) and effective action, it also nourishes the spirit; and by calling us into ever more authentic engagement with others, it nourishes the world in which we live.

This is no less true for the coach than it is for the client. As coaches, we have an ethical imperative to develop our fitness to engage in the complex responsive system that is the coaching conversation. This involves ensuring that we as coaches dance within the tension at the edge of chaos. At a practical level this means entering into supervision, ongoing professional development, a commitment to informing our skills through rigorous learning and evidence-based practice, and the hard work of dealing with one's own personality issues and personal growth. These are the behaviors that keep us in the dance, and develop richness and depth to our inner and outer dialogue.

While it may sound a daunting task, as they say, "We aim for progress, not perfection." It is an ongoing iterative process. But in learning to engage more fully and effectively with an ever more diverse range of clients, we ourselves are nourished. All the facts are indeed friendly!

Let us now look at how complexity theory may inform the coaching conversations with Bonita and Bob.

COACHING CASE STUDIES

The fundamental assumption of the three reflective spaces model is that the coaching conversation is a complex adaptive system. Both an understanding of the precise nature of the issue and the solution unfold in the complex interaction of the coaching conversation. This means that a detailed discussion of how I would coach Bonita and Bob would be somewhat nonsensical. About the only thing I know that I would do would be to welcome Bob or Bonita, ask why he/she was there, and inquire about what he/she hoped to get out of the coaching. Beyond that point, the coaching conversation would unfold in a unique and unrepeatable way.

So, rather than invent a coaching dialogue, I have chosen to discuss some of the potential issues I found myself wondering about (my internal dialogue) as I read Bonita's and Bob's case studies, and point to some of the questions and techniques that might be useful to explore.

As is often the situation, both Bonita's and Bob's cases show that there is work needed at the level of the personal and the wider organizational conversations. In the interest of brevity I will focus more on the personal conversations in Bonita's case, and more on the organizational conversation in Bob's case.

The Case of Bonita

At the levels of the individual and the dyad, one of the first things that jumped out of Bonita's case study was that there appears to be something going on in the system created by the conversation between Bonita and Ken that silences her and causes her to avoid confrontation. Note that I did not say Ken silences Bonita. It is not Ken that silences Bonita. Silence, or avoidance, is the emergent property of the complex interaction between the external conversation they have and their internal conversations.

There are a number of feedback loops potentially operating here. One (and only one of many) potential feedback diagrams is illustrated in Figure 11.6. We are told that Ken reluctantly agreed to Bonita's promotion, and there are clear signs of tension in his internal dialogue around Bonita. It is possible that resentment, or a degree of dismissive contempt, is leaking into the external conversation with Bonita. This leakage can be conscious or unconscious, overt or extremely subtle. Nevertheless we are often very adept at feeling it, even when we find it hard to rationally identify what is wrong.

Something in the external conversation triggers an internal conversation for Bonita, which seems to create for her a sense of anxiety and powerlessness. This leads her to not speak her mind and/or to avoid difficult issues. We can see signs of this internal dynamic in a number of places in the case study. It is seen with Rick and with Rita, and in Bonita's difficulty managing boundaries between work and home. It may also be seen in her need to syndicate ideas with her colleagues. There thus appears to be some sort of attractor at work here. Precisely what the boundaries of that attractor are, and the internal and external pattern of behavior that attractor elicits, we are yet to discover. At a theoretical level, we might guess that it is likely to involve Bonita's personality and history.

One of the tasks of coaching, then, would be to inquire into the meaning of these events and relationships—to ask Bonita to talk about the stories she tells herself in these situations, and how this impacts on the unfolding conversation in the external world. Often one can discern a common pattern to these stories and the processes they set in motion. My initial hunch (informed by my mental models, experience, and emotional responses or empathy) is that it may have something to do with overvaluing others' expectations, which generate feelings of responsibility, while at the same time leaving Bonita feeling like she can never really live up to those expectations. This set of assumptions, beliefs, rules, and expectations forms a mental model that causes Bonita to seek and notice particular types of feedback, and that functions to create an anticipatory or feed-forward loop in which Bonita does not speak her mind, and she avoids potential confrontations. This then serves to reinforce Ken's perception of her as not up to the task. Three self-reinforcing vicious cycles are created. The quality of the conversations determines the quality of the system!

In coaching, we are not so much interested in unpacking the history of Bonita's beliefs and feedback and feed-forward loops as we are interested in understanding how the story unfolds in the here and now, and what other stories might be told.

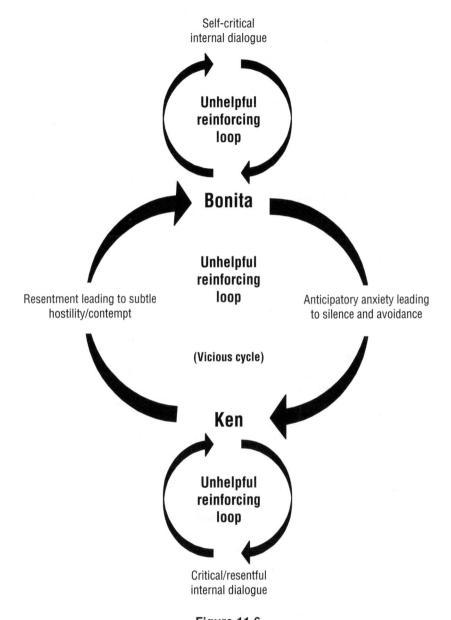

Self-critical
internal dialogue

**Unhelpful
reinforcing
loop**

Bonita

**Unhelpful
reinforcing
loop**

Resentment leading to subtle
hostility/contempt

Anticipatory anxiety leading
to silence and avoidance

(Vicious cycle)

Ken

**Unhelpful
reinforcing
loop**

Critical/resentful
internal dialogue

Figure 11.6
One Possible Representation of the Destructive Dynamic Feedback System
Created between and within Bonita and Ken

In the coaching conversation I would want to explore the features of the situation that tend to elicit that story. I would ask questions about when Bonita is able to tell herself different stories with different outcomes; for example, what is different about the story she tells herself with Ken and the somewhat more empowering story she tells herself with Rita? What other stories could she tell? Elements of cognitive behavioral, narrative, and psychodynamic models are likely to be useful in assisting Bonita in developing a new story or mental model that is more helpful. Figure 11.7 illustrates what this might initially look like.

Rather than engage in a self-focused critical inner dialogue, Bonita has engaged in the hard work of challenging her mental model, and is now more able to dispassionately notice what is going on in her, and in the conversation. The conversation is no longer "about her." Anxiety is held in check, and her emotional reactions can now be seen as information that helps her to understand the interaction and as signals to change the conversation. The boundaries of her system begin to open.

Understanding her own emotions, and the responses they elicit, is also a potent source of information in understanding others. What is most personal is often most common. By connecting with herself—her goals and her values—while at the same time holding a respectful and curious stance toward what is going on for Ken in this encounter, Bonita is now dancing with the tension on the edge of chaos. She is in the place where tension is most likely to stimulate the emergence of new more creative and adaptive responses.

Notice in Figure 11.7 that Ken's part of the conversation has not yet changed. There is most often a time lag between introducing change and the adaptive responses of others in the system. We cannot predict what Ken's response will be. We might hope that Bonita's respectful and courageous responding will elicit more respectful and positive responses from Ken—but this might not be the case! Ken's responses are radically unpredictable. The attractors at work for Ken may mean that he becomes more entrenched in his negative view of Bonita, interpreting her new behavior as contemptuous and manipulative. Whatever Ken's new response, Bonita is now in a better position to incorporate it as new data about which to be curious. As she slowly learns how to converse more effectively with Ken, she will become more and more adept at dancing in the tension, and more adept at holding good enough levels of anxiety and growing the degree of trust in the relationship.

Some of the coaching techniques that might be of use in developing more effective internal and external conversations are conversational mapping and role-play. Conversational mapping involves planning out a potential conversation and then examining it from as many perspectives as possible. What goals and values might others have in the situation? How might others feel, act, or respond to the conversation, and what does this mean for holding anxiety and trust at good enough levels? Role play is often a very useful way of both exploring these issues, practicing different conversations, and becoming adept at noticing what is going on in the inner dialogue.

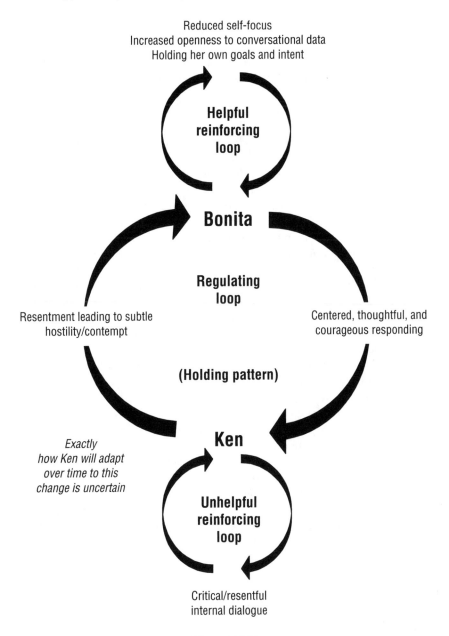

Reduced self-focus
Increased openness to conversational data
Holding her own goals and intent

**Helpful
reinforcing
loop**

Bonita

**Regulating
loop**

Resentment leading to subtle
hostility/contempt

Centered, thoughtful, and
courageous responding

(Holding pattern)

*Exactly
how Ken will adapt
over time to this
change is uncertain*

Ken

**Unhelpful
reinforcing
loop**

Critical/resentful
internal dialogue

Figure 11.7
Starting to Shift the Dynamic Feedback System

Conversational mapping, role-play, and introspection are useful techniques because they acknowledge that different system members have different goals and adapt in complex ways as the conversation unfolds. This adaptation is informed by their goals, values, mental models, and emotional responses. This is what is meant by the phrase "System members act locally." The process of conversational mapping and role-play is useful, but not because it allows the client to control or predict the way the conversation will unfold—interdependence and sensitivity to initial conditions means that the real conversation is often quite different to the one that was practiced. Rather, these techniques provide a forum in which to uncover the mental maps that are operating and develop new ones, and at the same time they give the client practice in engaging in the conversation in a more responsive and less reactive way. The exploration of which values, goals, and tone the client would like to have characterize the conversation also forms an attractor that helps the client maintain purposeful styles of communication behavior.

Bonita is likely to want to develop her ability to act assertively. This may have ramifications at a wider team or systems level. Behaving more assertively represents a change in the conversation between members in the system. Interdependence means that such changes typically raise anxiety in the system, and may elicit pushback. For example, as Bonita begins to be more open and forthright in her communication, some her direct reports may worry that she is unhappy with them. Still other system members may interpret Bonita's new behavior as in some way subversive of the established "way we do things here." Both interpretations may elicit defensive behaviors.

Exploration and role-play may be useful in developing strategies designed to introduce this new style of conversation into the workplace. Depending on the nature of the existing organizational conversation, there may be a need to gain buy-in from key team members, or even support for the change from senior leadership. The principle here is to assist Bonita in identifying some ways in which she and her team can develop a shared mental model of how they want to communicate together. Some potential strategies may include: just modeling the desired behavior, explicitly flagging the new communication style with individuals or the whole team, personal sharing of her experience, developing a new shared language through training, or facilitated examination of the team communication process.

Bonita's goals are also likely to include improving her leadership and increasing team productivity. At this level it is useful for Bonita to have an overview of attractors in the system, including how power is distributed through the system. Points to focus on here might include: What sort of things are spoken about at a team level? What is the tone and nature of the conversations that take place? Are they solution focused or problem focused, optimistic or pessimistic? What is spoken about, where, and with whom? What is not spoken about? How is communication curtailed in the organization? Who gets to speak? What values are actually enacted, and which values are merely espoused? What processes, rules, norms, and assumptions enable and constrain the organizational conversation? How do people feel about themselves and their work?

The selection and timing of questions, and the selection, timing, and type of sharing/education done by the coach are important. The coach processes the data Bonita brings to the coaching conversation by allowing his/her experience, training, models, theories, and humanity to grapple with data. The questions emerge out of this process, and are not a priori to it. They are asked and considered in the light of Bonita's intentions and aspirations for the organization and her role as a leader.

The task of coaching here is to help Bonita identify her goals as a leader and then to assist her in shaping ongoing, iterative, value-based conversations with the wider system and its members. In these ongoing conversations Bonita will be called on to manage boundaries, make decisions, implement actions, and have hard conversations while maintaining connectivity and diversity while keeping anxiety with reasonable bounds.

The coaching conversation is a developmental task whereby Bonita seeks to improve her ability to enter into these iterative, complex responsive exchanges. Coaching will cease to be needed as Bonita gains skill and confidence and fitness for sustaining this dance on the edge of chaos.

The Case of Bob

Bob's challenge, like Bonita's, is around creating high-value conversations that enable the organization to adaptively face some significant developmental and cultural challenges. However, as I read the case study, it seemed to me that Bob and his people appear to be quite good at co-creating low-value, superficial conversations characterized by emotional acting out, passivity, denial, and fear. In these conversations people are seen as subordinate to results, and vision is used as a substitute for integrity. Bob, as the bringer of vision, is protected from the superficiality of these conversations by the work of others who maintain the system's effective functioning by supplying the human connection that Bob lacks. There are signs that this pattern is present in a number of areas of Bob's life, including his relationship with his wife and his children. From a personality perspective one might suggest Bob falls in the narcissistic spectrum.

Bob appears to be an attractor for these types of conversations. One might expect that there will be a significant pull toward recreating this conversation in the coaching relationship. Hence the first question the coach must ask is whether he or she is able to enter into an effective coaching dialogue with Bob, or whether referral to someone better equipped to deal with challenging personalities is required (Berglas, 2002). Whether coaching or therapy is called for will depend on whether Bob is able to be open to the possibility that he will need to make significant changes in his own behavior (see Cavanagh, 2005, for a fuller discussion of working with challenging clients).

Let us assume the coach is appropriately qualified and Bob shows an ability to approach change. Given the long-term nature of Bob's behavior, the coaching engagement may need to be relatively long-term (one to two years) if effective and sustained change is to be achieved. The first significant challenge faced by the coach will be to establish empathic attunement with Bob while also establishing effective alignment for creating the type of conversations needed to leave the organization in a healthier state.

Establishing alignment and rapport may be achieved by first exploring what the "just right" organization would look like, and what this would mean for Bob. I would also want to explore Bob's understanding of the sort of relationships among the members that would qualify as "just right" functioning. Specifically, it will include exploring what this means in terms of the types of conversations Bob will need to shape with his people. Bob may well find it difficult to articulate the more empathic and integrity-based elements of that new conversation. For example, because Bob seems to lack empathy and sees the world through a mental model of winners and losers, his understanding of courageous honesty may be little more than apportioning blame.

The coach can assist Bob in discovering the meaning of empathy and honesty and courage in communication both by modeling this in his/her interactions with Bob and by creating good enough holding of anxiety to allow Bob to approach the blind spots in what appears to be a long-standing pattern of behavior. In order to do this the coach must be able to see the world from Bob's perspective, and demonstrate an understanding of the value Bob sees in that perspective. At the same time he/she must find a way to help Bob engage with the inherent tensions and contradictions that inevitably lie at the heart of his experience.

As in the case of Bonita, the use of conversational mapping, role-play, introspection, and feedback will be important in developing greater empathy and attunement in Bob for his people.

At the wider systems level, it will be important to explore the key differences in approach to organizational conversations between the merging South Korean/European and U.S. elements of the system. As we know from complexity theory, diversity needs to be held within critical limits if it is to have a positive impact on opening the system to change. Bob may need to assess the level of connectivity and diversity operating in the merging between these parts of the business.

Dimitrov's (1997) work on the use of fuzzy logic when dealing with social complexity may be very useful in helping Bob shape conversations that encourage participatory action. Dimitrov has found that preparedness to act together is a function of willingness to engage in dialogue, confidence in trustworthiness, and ability to create options (creativity). Willingness to engage in dialogue is fostered by effective listening and validation of differing perspectives. As leader of the organization, Bob can demonstrate this in his communication with the business. This will require Bob to begin to remember what is spoken about, follow up on communication, and respond to people's concerns and feelings. In other words, Bob will need to genuinely engage with individuals and teams.

Trustworthiness is built via shared responsibility and accountability (Dimitrov 1997). Demonstrating unidirectional accountability is destructive of trust. Follow-through and accountability in Bob's action are important conditions for increased trust. Similarly, Bob will need to entrust responsibility to his people. Learning to delegate power while holding in check his anxiety about not being in control may be important components of Bob's change program. Bob will need to ensure there are appropriate resources, training, and communication avenues available to enable effective power sharing. Similarly, the establishment of timely and effective feedback mechanisms to support accountability will be important.

The final condition, creativity, needs to be fostered. Punitive action in the event of mistakes is inimical to creativity. Permission to make mistakes, as well as rewards for novel approaches and diversity, are essential in building an atmosphere conducive to creativity. In particular, reward for combined creative action would encourage a sense of moving forward together, increasing cohesion and maximizing the organization's ability to adapt to its new circumstances (Dimitrov, 1997; Harris & Scherblom, 1999). Once again, Bob's ability to demonstrate this type of connectivity in his own relationships with organization members will be an important part of embedding this behavior in the organization.

These changes will be difficult for Bob. The quality of engagement Bob has with the organization is a critical part of modeling and supporting the emergence of a new organizational conversation. Equally so, the quality of the engagement the coach has with Bob will be critical in supporting the emergence of that new inner dialogue in Bob.

If the coach overidentifies with Bob, he/she will have no new perspective or information to bring to the conversation—no place from which to challenge Bob to growth. However, if the coach approaches Bob from outside—objectifying him and his behavior—then in order to protect his sense of self, Bob will almost certainly close his boundaries and the conversation will end up in silence or a useless cycle of accusation and denial. The coach must be able to maintain a paradoxical position of "attuned objectivity." (Once again, we are at the edge of chaos.) It is in this place of creative tension that feedback can be most effective, provided that anxiety and trust are held within appropriate bounds.

Maintaining a position of attuned objectivity is a type of loving of our clients. It requires us to consider them as whole people, struggling like the rest of us to do their best in the world. But like the rest of us, struggling means struggling! It means grappling with the inner dragons that threaten to derail us. Attuned objectivity means taking the presence of the dragons seriously, while seeing the beauty inherent in the person and in his/her attempts to grow.

As mentioned earlier, coaching in the case of Bob is likely to be a longer-term engagement, with much less certain success, than in Bonita's case. Relapse into old communication patterns is always a danger when more personality-based forces are at work. The impact of relapse in destroying trust and system openness is significant. At the same time, Bob's impending life transition may provide the personal openness and motivation Bob needs to maintain himself at the edge of chaos.

A Mental Health Diversion

For the sake of argument, let us suppose that the coach's initial assessment of Bob's fitness for the coaching conversation was erroneous, and Bob's native charm and energy actually masked a very low level of ego resilience. People with narcissistic personalities are vulnerable to rage, major depression, suicide, or other impulsive reactions when overwhelmed by unavoidable internal and external feedback (Sperry, 1995). From the perspective of complexity, this might represent a high degree of sensitivity to some types of initial conditions—namely shame and criticism. In the right conditions, this could give rise to a shame-based amplifying feedback loop that compromises Bob's safety.

There is potential for this to happen if events converge in such a way that the wider organization is destabilized and pushed into a highly reactive or defended state. Significant teething troubles with the merger, a major drop in share price, or the threat of downsizing may fit these conditions. A poorly conducted coaching-related feedback process at that point could elicit a level of blame and criticism toward Bob against which he is unable to defend. The more fragile Bob's ego defenses, the less blame or criticism is needed to overwhelm him.

On the face of the case study supplied, Bob appears quite resilient, and such a worst-case scenario is unlikely to occur. Nevertheless, as the butterfly effect attests, a combination of sensitivity to initial conditions and amplifying feedback can lead to unpredictable outcomes. Hence it would be important for the coach to be particularly aware of Bob's ability to engage with challenging feedback in a mature and resilient fashion, before initiating highly confronting feedback processes (e.g., public sharing of 360-degree feedback).

CONCLUSION

This chapter's application of complexity theory has only just begun to scratch the surface. We have not considered, for example, the role that third parties, such as human resources, line managers, and other stakeholders have in co-creating the context in which the coaching conversation takes place. Similarly, the impact of systems outside of the organization—such as family, the market, regulators, or the impact of environmental and geopolitical systems or global trends in employment and the organization of work—have not been considered. These are often present in one form or another in coaching engagement.

I believe that the metaphor of conversation offers us a rich image through which to understand the complexity of the human person, human systems, and the complex adaptive system that is the coaching engagement. Our role as coaches is to engage with our clients in the dialogue that carries us to the edge of chaos—to have the courage to approach the tensions that disturb us, yet paradoxically help us grow into more fully present and responsive human beings.

It is a great honor and responsibility with which we are entrusted. We honor that trust whenever we do the work of developing our fitness to enter into ever more effective conversations with our clients, so that they can enter into ever more life-giving and effective conversations with their families, colleagues, and the world.

REFERENCES

Argyris, C. (2004). *Reasons and rationalizations: The limits to organizational knowledge.* Oxford: Oxford University Press.

Berglas, S. (2002). The very real dangers of executive coaching. *Harvard Business Review,* June, 87–92.

Borthwick, M. (2003). *Leeson's legacy lives on in Singapore.* Retrieved October 5, 2005 from http://news.bbc.co.uk/2/hi/business/4288271.stm.

Bowen, M. (1978). *Family therapy in clinical practice.* New York: J. Aronson.

Brown, S. L., & Eisenhardt, K. M. (1998). *Competing on the edge: Strategy as structured chaos.* Boston: Harvard Business School Press.

Cavanagh, M. (2005). Mental health issues and challenging clients in executive coaching. In M. Cavanagh, A. Grant, and T. Kemp (Eds.), *Evidence-based coaching: Vol. 1. Theory, research and practice from the behavioural sciences* (pp. 21–36). Brisbane: Australian Academic Press.

Crawford, C., & Brungardt, C. (2000). Building the corporate revolution: Real empowerment through risk leadership. *Selected Proceedings, 1999 Annual Meeting, International Leadership Association.* College Park, MD: Academy of Leadership Press.

Dimitrov, V. (1997). Use of fuzzy logic when dealing with social complexity. *Complexity International, 4.* Retrieved September 25, 2005, from http://journal-ci.csse.monash.edu.au/ci/vol04/dimitrov1/dimitrov.htm.

Dimitrov, V. (2003). Chaos, complexity and fuzzy logic. In V. Dimitrov (Ed.), *Working with chaos and complexity: A book of readings* (pp. 85–93). Sydney: University of Western Sydney, School of Social Ecology and Lifelong Learning.

Dimitrov, V., & Lederer, B. (2003). Forward: An outline of the ecology of leadership. In V. Dimitrov (Ed.), *Leadership and change. A reader* (pp. 4–5). Sydney: University of Western Sydney, School of Social Ecology and Lifelong Learning.

Druskat, V., & Wolff, S. (2001). Building the emotional intelligence of groups. In *Harvard Business Review on Teams that Succeed* (pp. 27–51). Boston: Harvard Business School Press.

Fraser, S., & Greenhalgh, T. (2001). Coping with complexity: Educating for capability. *British Medical Journal 323,* 799–803.

Gleick, J. (1998). *Chaos: The amazing science of the unpredictable.* London: Vintage.

Haines, S. (1998). *Systems thinking and learning.* Amherst, MA: HRD Press.

Harris, T., & Scherblom, J. (1999). *Small group and team communication.* Boston: Allyn & Bacon.

Jackson, P., & McKergow, M. (2002). *The solutions focus: The simple way to positive change.* London: Nicholas Brealey.

Lewin, R. (1993). *Complexity: Life at the edge of chaos.* London: Phoenix.

Lewin, R., & Regine, B. (2001). *Weaving complexity & business: Engaging the soul at work.* New York: Texere.

Lorenz, E. (1963). Deterministic non-periodic flow. *Journal of Atmospheric Sciences, 20,* 130–141.

O'Connor, J., & McDermott, I. (1997). *The art of systems thinking: Essential skills for the creativity and problem solving.* London: Thorsons.

Parry, A. (1996). Love is a strange attractor: Therapy at the edge of chaos. In W. Sulis & A. Combs (Eds.), *Nonlinear dynamics in human behaviour* (pp. 235–236). Singapore: World Scientific.

Pines, M. (1997). The civilizing of Genie. In L. F. Kasper (Ed.), *Teaching English through the disciplines: Psychology.* New York: Whittier Publications. Retrieved 25/10/05 from http://kccesl.tripod.com/genie.html.

Plsek, P., & Wilson, T. (2001). Complexity, leadership, and management in healthcare organisations. *British Medical Journal, 323,* 746–749.

Rawnsley, J. (1995). *Going for broke: Nick Leeson and the collapse of Barings Bank.* London: HarperCollins.

Reason, J. (1990). *Human error.* New York: Cambridge University Press.

Senge, P. (1990). *The fifth discipline: The art & practice of the learning organization.* New York: Currency Doubleday.

Senge, P., Ross, R., Smith, B., Roberts, C., & Kleiner, A. (1994). *The fifth discipline fieldbook: Strategies and tools for building a learning organization.* London: Nicholas Brealey.

Sperry, L. (1995). *Handbook of diagnosis and treatment of DSM-IV personality disorders.* New York: Brunner/Mazel.

Stacey, R. D. (2000). *Strategic management and organisational dynamics* (3rd ed.). Harlow U.K.: Pearson Education.

Von Bertalanffy, L. (1968). *General system theory.* New York: George Braziller.

Waldrop, M. (1992). *Complexity: The emerging science at the edge of order and chaos.* New York: Simon & Schuster.

Wheatley, M. (1999). *Leadership and new science: Discovering order in a chaotic world.* San Francisco: Berrett-Koehler.

Wiener, N. (1948). *Cybernetics, or control and communication in the animal and the machine.* New York: Wiley.

Yerkes, R. M., & Dodson, J. D. (1908). The relationship of strength of stimulus to rapidity of habit formation. *Journal of Comparative Neurology and Psychology, 18,* 459–482.

Youngblood, M. (1997). Leadership at the edge of chaos: From control to creativity. *Strategy & Leadership 25*(5), 8–14.

CHAPTER 12

Toward a Contextual Approach to Coaching Models

DIANNE R. STOBER AND ANTHONY M. GRANT

THE PRECEDING APPROACHES to coaching practice are diverse in theoretical formulation, and each has particular contributions and insights. All of these systems of thought provide articulate frameworks for approaching the coaching scenario and in understanding our clients and our role as coaches.

While this leaves the coach, and for that matter, the informed client, to choose as best they can what fits and which approach(es) are most applicable, at this point it would be helpful to have some framework within which to place these theories. We believe that a contextual model of coaching might provide useful themes and a framework for evidence-based practice. In addition, there are some core principles that guide applications across the various approaches that can integrate various techniques. We discuss both and how they may form a framework for cross-disciplinary, multitheoretical evidence-based coaching.

THE MEDICAL MODEL AND COACHING

Within psychotherapy, one of the disciplines most closely related to coaching, the problem of how to comparatively evaluate different therapeutic approaches is long-standing. The dominant means of resolving this dilemma has been the application of the medical model.

The medical model draws on the notion that physical illness has biological causes and that physical illness can be cured by an appropriate medical intervention. In extending this to psychological and psychotherapeutic domains, the psychological or psychotherapeutic medical model holds that behavioral and emotional problems are analogous to physical diseases and such emotional problems can be diagnosed and cured, with the patient returning to normal functioning. Thus, the medical model relies on a number of components: a distressed client, an explanatory theory for the distress, a diagnosis based on a diagnostic system, and an accompanying treatment derived from the theory, with the resulting outcome seen as due to the specific ingredients of that treatment. The use of the medical model in psychotherapeutic domains has been consistently critiqued for its emphasis on pathology (Barbour, 1995; Hafner, 1987) and deficit reduction (Ingram, 2005), and such critiques are perhaps even more salient in the coaching realm where clients are not being treated for mental illnesses.

One by-product of the widespread use of the medical model is that there has been considerable evaluation of psychotherapeutic treatment and comparisons of the effectiveness of different psychotherapeutic approaches. However, as has been argued by Wampold and associates, among others (Wampold, 2001; Wampold et al., 1997; Wampold, Ahn, & Coleman, 2001), the medical model's requirement of determining the specific, active ingredients does not fit the data from psychotherapy outcome literature.

The literature tends to show that psychotherapies are generally equivalent, and this has become known as the Dodo effect (from Rosenzweig's 1936 perceptive proposition that different psychotherapies' success was likely due to common factors akin to the words of the Dodo in Lewis Carroll's *Alice in Wonderland*: "Everybody has won, and all must have prizes").

In discussing this topic and its relevance to the need for research and evaluation in coaching, Kilburg (2004, 2005) edited a two-part series on coaching in *Consulting Psychology Journal: Practice and Research*. Kilburg (2004) describes the tension between the empirical, logico-scientific tradition and the constructivist-narrative approach to ways of knowing. He notes that executive coaching as a discipline can benefit from both:

> So it would seem that as we consultants wait for the results of the correlations, analyses of variance, analyses of covariance, path analyses, and multiple regressions designed to test the efficacy of various forms of coaching to come rolling in to challenge and educate us, we could also curl up in front of our fires with some good stories of how our colleagues are entering into the worlds of their clients and trying to help them make sense and meaning of what they encounter along the roads they travel together. (p. 210)

Lowman (2005) in his contribution to this special issue, argues that without a scientific foundation, executive coaching runs the risk of becoming as extinct as the dodo. While he does not see narrative or more qualitative approaches as without value (he in fact concludes that both qualitative and quantitative approaches are needed), Lowman argues that grounding coaching in empirical research is required for the continued development of coaching. Lowman also specifies some common themes identified through the case studies contained in the special issue that are analogous to psychotherapy outcome studies and are germane to this discussion: (1) a trusting relationship may be critical to success; (2) the environmental context is key; and (3) the coach's belief in the efficacy of his or her approach may be more important than the particular approach itself. As we will see, this fits with an overarching framework different from the specific ingredient requirements provided by a medical model metaphor for psychotherapy, and in turn, coaching.

THE CONTEXTUAL MODEL AS A META-MODEL FOR COACHING: THEMES AND PRINCIPLES

A meta-model is a conceptual framework that models other models. A meta-model does not offer exact testable theories and propositions. Rather, by delineating higher-order *themes* and *principles* it offers a means to guide thinking and understanding, make complex ideas accessible, highlight interrelationships, and assimilate and understand apparently diverse cross-disciplinary and multitheoretical knowledge bases (King, 2004).

A meta-model that offers a different approach from the medical model and can also leverage the complementary nature of both empirical and constructivist-narrative approaches to theory and evidence is that of the contextual model. We propose a contextual model for coaching expanded from the four components described by Wampold (2001) for a contextual model of psychotherapy (which in turn was adapted from Frank & Frank, 1991).

The seven thematic factors of the proposed model are:

1. An *explicit outcome or goal* that both parties, coach and client, are collaboratively working toward.
2. A sensible *rationale* or explanation for how coaching as a process fits the client's needs and situation.
3. A *procedure* or set of steps that is consistent with the rationale and requires both the client's and coach's active participation.
4. A meaningful *relationship* between a client and coach such that the client believes the coach is there to help and will work in the client's best interest.

5. A *collaborative working alliance* in which the coach's explicit role is to expand the client's development, performance, or skill set, appropriately pacing the intervention to maintain challenge and facilitate change.

6. The *client's ability and readiness to change*, and the extent to which the client is both able and willing to do the work of change.

7. The *coach's ability and readiness to help the client create change*, in that the coach's ability to facilitate the client's change process will significantly rest on the coach's own personal ability to recognize and deal with the often personally poignant issues arising from the coaching process.

Thus the contextual approach seeks to understand the process of coaching, the "how" of coaching, rather than trying to compare the effectiveness of one coaching model to another. It asks the question, "What are the common themes that are effective in coaching and within what context?"

These common themes include such concepts as the coach-client relationship, characteristics of the client and the coach, and how these interface in the successful application of techniques to each individual client's context. Each coaching intervention needs to have a rationale for the techniques used that fits the particular coaching context of a particular client with a particular coach in a particular relationship. The contextual model emphasizes the importance of the meaning attributed to the procedures by practitioner and client, above and beyond the efficacy of any particular procedure (i.e., it works partly because we act from the belief it will be helpful).

THE CONTEXTUAL MODEL
IN EVIDENCE-BASED PRACTICE

The contextual model, with its seven contextual components, can hold the various knowledge bases represented in this volume within its frame. Each theory or approach to coaching has its view of an identified desired outcome, a rationale, a number of procedures or techniques that follow from the rationale, a meaningful relationship, a collaborative working alliance, the client's readiness to change, and the coach's ability and readiness to facilitate the client's change. For example, evidence and theory regarding building a positive relationship are essential features of a number of approaches, including the humanistic, the integrative goal-focused, and the psychodynamic approaches. The other perspectives also note the importance of a good working relationship between coach and client.

Likewise, a contextual model states that any approach to coaching should provide a context of positive potential growth by the client that is supported by the coach. This part of the meta-model highlights the importance of the shared view of why coaching is being done, regardless of the particular theoretical perspective. This factor can be contrasted with the medical model in which the practitioner is frequently positioned as the "expert who diagnoses and then repairs," rather than a collaborative partner in positive growth (Maudsley & Strivens, 2000).

Indeed, many coaches have noted the pitfalls associated with a coaching context in which the client feels mandated or forced into coaching (Latham, Almost, Mann, & Moore, 2005). Even if the coach is able to communicate an empathic, nonjudgmental, and authentic stance, as in the humanistic approach, if the client is unable to trust that the context is set up for his or her success, the likelihood of success is threatened. The systems and complexity theory approach might conclude that the openness of the system is suspect.

Taking the contextual model as a meta-model for coaching approaches, the importance of the rationale is immediately clear. Each perspective represented in this book uses a particular lens by which the coach is making sense of the client and his or her situation. Often the coach goes on to educate the client about the coach's expert hypotheses or assessments of the situation (Chapman, Best, & Van Casteren, 2003). So a coach using the adult development approach will use the framework of a particular stage of development or complexity of mind to understand clients and where their strengths, limitations, opportunities, or challenges might lie (Laske, 1999). Similarly, a psychodynamic or cultural approach might be used by other coaches in building a rationale for why X is happening for client Y in situation Z.

As a coach employs a rationale for helping a client make meaning of their experience, a contextual model requires the coach to use procedures consistent with that rationale in order to be effective. As the previous chapters have demonstrated, each perspective/rationale represented in this book has procedures by which the coach can engage the client in positive growth. A cognitive or behavioral coach may utilize specific homework assignments to further the client's development, as might a coach using a goal-oriented approach, but the rationale behind the procedure might differ.

A contextual model of coaching would also encompass an explicit outcome of what is expected in coaching. Many coaches, regardless of theoretical perspective, use the identification of specific goals for the coaching scenario as a way to shape the conversation and agree upon the aims of the coaching engagement. But the perspectives represented in this book might lead the coach to frame these goals differently. For example, a psychoanalytically informed coach might work with a client toward the goal of developing insight into the client's defense mechanisms in order to act more effectively in a specific situation. A coach using a positive psychology approach might explicitly contract with a client to increase his experience of fulfillment at work, with the idea that this goal will encompass other goals such as enhanced performance and reduced stress. The behavioral and integrative goal-focused approaches discussed would likely start with clearly articulating goals for action with the client.

In summary, the contextual model can act as an overarching framework in which various theoretical approaches, models, and applicable evidence can be placed. In using an evidence-based approach, and emphasizing the use of knowledge and expertise in the service of a particular client, the contextual model offers coaches a "meta" view, and this may be useful in enhancing recognition of the similarities and differences between different approaches and in this way help forward the development of coaching theory and practice.

AN INTEGRATION OF CORE COACHING PRINCIPLES ACROSS PERSPECTIVES: SEVEN PRINCIPLES OF EFFECTIVE COACHING

While a contextual view of different coaching approaches can help us understand the themes through which all of these approaches work in a similar manner, there are also some principles for effective coaching that these approaches share. If the contextual model gives us seven organizing themes that comprise a meta-model for knowledge bases for an evidence-based practice, the following principles may encapsulate the core of the coaching process, what is been done, and represent the means by which the contextual themes are enacted.

Drawing on the seminal work of Rosenzweig (1936), Prochaska and DiClemente (1984), and Egan (1974), we can delineate seven key principles that underpin the human change process. These seven principles are: (1) collaboration, (2) accountability, (3) awareness, (4) responsibility, (5) commitment, (6) action, and (7) results (see Figure 12.1).

Regardless of preferred theoretical perspective, the foundation of effective coaching is the successful formation of a *collaborative* relationship, within which the coach can hold the client accountable. The term *accountability* relates to the fact that, as an integral part of coaching, clients will be enacting specific action steps that move them toward their goals. Such actions are designed in collaboration between the coach and the client.

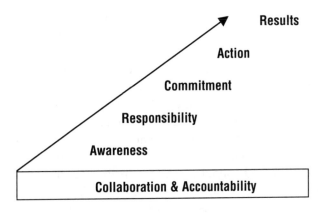

Figure 12.1
The Seven Principles of Effective Coaching

As we all know, change is not always easy, and we frequently procrastinate or avoid doing tasks that take us outside of our comfort zone. The coach needs to be able to hold the client accountable for the completion of such tasks. Many coaching engagements fail if the coach is not able, for one reason or another, to monitor and evaluate the client's progress toward goals and appropriately address any performance shortfalls directly and promptly.

To facilitate this process, it is important that the coach and client spend some time discussing the nature of their relationship, and that they jointly design the dynamics of their working alliance. Most problems in coaching can be circumvented by having a clearly articulated and shared understanding of the coach-client relationship. The perspectives in this volume all share recognition of the importance of a robust and positive working alliance.

It is from this platform that the coach can work with clients to raise their *awareness* of the issues, and help them find ways to take responsibility for change. The client's awareness levels can be raised in many different, ways including behavioral, cognitive, or emotional assessments, 360-degree feedback, direct real-life observations or shadow coaching, or feedback generated from within the coaching session itself, as in the use of immediacy (Egan, 1974), and such awareness-raising tools will again be chosen in line with the preferred theoretical perspective.

One useful understanding of the notion of *responsibility* is the ability to choose one's response (response-able) (Whitmore, 1992). To be response-able requires that the client have an awareness of the issues. Again, the various perspectives all note the importance of clients' understanding of their situation and their ultimate responsibility for any change, while coaches may differ in the methods they employ to help clients in this step.

Of course, awareness and response-ableness are insufficient in themselves. Clients also need *commitment* to action so that they can move forward toward the goals and results. Thus the coach needs to be able to enhance the client's motivation levels and build commitment to action, and to ensure that at any point in time, the action steps match the client's ability for change. Trying to change too much too soon can be a major derailer, and conversely, underchallenging action steps will fail to engage the client; so the coach needs to be mindful of the client's readiness for change.

The seventh principle is *results*, in that coaching should be directed toward a specific outcome or result, and such results orientation is the essence of good coaching.

Again, each theoretical perspective will have specific tools and techniques to operationalize these principles and use specific theoretically oriented language that describes these principles. Nevertheless, we hold that coaching is about the systematic enactment of these seven principles.

THE ROLE OF EXPERT KNOWLEDGE IN COACHING

In applying an evidence-based approach to coaching, there is a connection between a knowledge base (i.e., one's theoretical orientation or domain of expertise) and the coach's use of that knowledge and style of interaction. The contextual model with its themes and principles can help guide practice and the procedures required by a particular approach. While these themes and principles are shared by the various approaches, they may differ on some important dimensions. For example, using a contextual model, the appropriateness of direct provision of specific content knowledge, or expert knowledge, differs across approaches depending on the rationale and procedures of the approach.

What does expert knowledge in coaching look like? Expert knowledge in coaching can be understood as highly specialized or technical knowledge held by the coach in an area where the client has less expertise than the coach, and where such knowledge is related to the client's goals. For some coaches this will be about behavioral science or organizational change. For example, in leadership coaching the coach may have specialized knowledge of personality styles and how they relate to leadership styles and organizational effectiveness. Other coaches may have specific expertise in the application of economic science or business models, or in the assessment and enhancement of intrapersonal and interpersonal competencies. In a learning alliance such as coaching, wherever one individual holds more expert knowledge than the other, there is always a potential dynamic of the "coach as expert advice giver."

The notion of the "coach as expert advice giver" is somewhat controversial, and there is some difference of opinion as to the appropriate role of expert knowledge in coaching. A nondirectional ask-not-tell approach may be best characterized by the work of John Whitmore (1992), which emphasizes facilitation of client self-discovery, and the directional, tell-rather-than-ask approach may be characterized by the robust approach of Marshall Goldsmith (2000), which emphasizes direct feedback and advice giving.

However, these are not categorically different approaches to coaching. Rather these two approaches lie on a continuum. The issue is not which of these approaches is right and which is wrong, but rather which best helps clients reach their goals, and which is the most apt at particular points in any specific coaching conversation. In essence this issue is about striking the right balance between process facilitation and content or information delivery, and this balance varies at different points in the overall coaching engagement and within individual coaching sessions. The skillful and experienced coach knows when to move across the ask-tell dimension, and knows when and how to promote self-discovery and when and how to give expert-based authoritative or specialized information.

Clearly, in addition to the expert knowledge that a coach holds about the process of coaching, it is important for coaches to have a good understanding of the clients' issues and context. Furthermore, it would be unprofessional and unethical not to impart important expert information in a timely and appropriate fashion. However, a coach with highly developed applied coaching skills can deliver excellent outcomes purely through facilitating a process that operationalizes the principles of coaching, rather than through an instructor mode that emphasizes the delivery of expert knowledge.

It has been our observation in teaching coaching theory and skills to a wide range of individuals that some consultants making the transition to coaching tend to place greater value on the role of the expert advice giver. In contrast, many therapists and counselors transitioning to coaching often place greater emphasis on attending to the process and the asking aspect of the coaching process. These of course are generalizations. What is it that is happening here?

It is possible that coaches tend to rely more on the telling mode of expert advice giving than on facilitating the process of client self-discovery when their applied coaching skills are challenged by the situation, or where their coaching skills are not very well developed. In a sense, this is understandable as we all need something to fall back on when the coaching process may not be going as well as we would like, and slipping into the expert telling mode is one way to get the coaching conversation back on track. Not least, we may slip into the telling mode to unconsciously reassure ourselves that we are in fact bringing value to the conversation. These potentials require monitoring and reflection on the part of the coach.

In summary, different approaches may emphasize a particular range in the ask-tell dimension regarding expert knowledge. It is imperative for coaches to monitor their behavior on this dimension for potential overemphasis on either end. Domain-specific knowledge experts may find the contextual model useful in coaching practice. The seven thematic factors provide a means of analyzing *how* the coaching is conducted, whereas the seven principles provide a framework to analyze *what* is being done.

Evidence-based practice asks the coach to consider the questions of *why* they are acting in one way or another in the coaching session and whether their choice is *consistent* with the rationale and procedures from which they are operating. The evidence-based coach will incorporate regular reflection on their use of knowledge and its application, and we hope the proposed contextual model provides a useful framework for the development of an evidence-based, reflective coaching practice.

CONCLUSIONS

In this volume we have attempted to describe what an evidence-based approach to coaching might be. The contributors have linked existing knowledge bases to coaching theory and practice. While the collection of approaches contained here is not exhaustive, we hope our readers have found that the linkages made give them a richer picture of applicable knowledge.

We have particularly focused on applicable knowledge from a variety of perspectives and how that knowledge can be integrated with coach expertise. How these are utilized in specific client contexts remains for further explication and to individual coaches' discretion.

Evidence-based practice holds promise as a guide for critical evaluation and development in coaching. We have argued for a broad definition of applicable evidence and sources of knowledge. We think this is the most appropriate stance for an emerging area. We look forward to continuing development in terms of linking existing bodies of knowledge to coaching and in coaching-specific theory and evidence.

REFERENCES

Barbour, A. B. (1995). *Caring for patients: A critique of the medical model.* Stanford, CA: Stanford University Press.

Chapman, T., Best, B., & Van Casteren, P. (2003). *Executive coaching: Exploding the myths.* New York: Palgrave Macmillan.

Egan, G. (1974). *The skilled helper.* Pacific Grove, CA: Brooks/Cole Publishing Co.

Frank, J. D., & Frank, J. B. (1991). *Persuasion and healing: A comparative study of psychotherapy* (3rd ed.). Baltimore: Johns Hopkins University Press.

Goldsmith, M. (2000). Coaching change. *Executive Excellence, 17*(6), 4.

Hafner, H. (1987). The concept of disease in psychiatry. *Psychological Medicine, 17*(1), 11–14.

Ingram, R. E. (2005). Clinical training for the next millennium. *Journal of Clinical Psychology, 61*(9), 1155–1158.

Kilburg, R. R. (Ed.). (2004). Trudging toward Dodoville—Part I: Conceptual approaches in executive coaching [Special issue]. *Consulting Psychology Journal: Practice and Research, 56*(4).

Kilburg, R. R. (Ed.). (2005). Trudging toward Dodoville—Part II: Case studies in executive coaching [Special issue]. *Consulting Psychology Journal: Practice and Research, 57*(1&2).

King, G. A. (2004). The meaning of life experiences: Application of a meta-model to rehabilitation sciences and services. *American Journal of Orthopsychiatry, 74*(1), 72–88.

Laske, O. E. (1999). An integrated model of developmental coaching. *Consulting Psychology Journal: Practice & Research, 51*(3), 139–159.

Latham, G. P., Almost, J., Mann, S., & Moore, C. (2005). New developments in performance management. *Organizational Dynamics, 34*(1), 77–87.

Lowman, R. L. (2005). Executive coaching: The road to Dodoville needs paving with more than good assumptions. *Consulting Psychology Journal: Practice and Research, 57,* 90–96.

Maudsley, G., & Strivens, J. (2000). Promoting professional knowledge, experiential learning and critical thinking for medical students. *Medical Education, 34*(7), 535–544.

Prochaska, J. O., & DiClemente, C. C. (1984). Toward a comprehensive model of change. In J. O. Prochaska & C. C. DiClemente (Eds.), *The transtheoretical approach: Crossing the traditional boundaries of therapy.* Homewood, IL: Dow-Jones.

Rosenzweig, S. (1936). Some implicit common factors in diverse methods of psychotherapy. *American Journal of Orthopsychiatry, 6,* 412–415.

Wampold, B. E. (2001). *The great psychotherapy debate: Models, methods, and findings.* Mahwah, NJ: Lawrence Erlbaum.

Wampold, B. E., Ahn, H., & Coleman, H. L. K. (2001). Medical model as metaphor: Old habits die hard. *Journal of Counseling Psychology, 48,* 268–273.

Wampold, B. E., Mondin, G. W., Moody, M., Stich, F., Benson, K., & Ahn, H. (1997). Meta-analysis of outcome studies comparing bona fide psychotherapies: Empirically, "all must have prizes." *Psychological Bulletin, 122,* 203–215.

Whitmore, J. (1992). *Coaching for performance.* London: Nicholas Brealey.

Workplace and Executive Coaching: A Bibliography from the Scholarly Business Literature

ANTHONY M. GRANT

THIS CHAPTER PRESENTS a bibliography on workplace and executive coaching which is drawn from the scholarly business literature databases. Books, book reviews and non-scholarly articles, magazines, or publications were excluded. The inclusion of this bibliography is intended to be an aid for teachers, researchers, practitioners, and students of coaching. This bibliography does not include citations from the psychology, medical, or education databases. The business literature was selected for inclusion in this book as it is the domain most pertinent to executive coaching, which is the focus of this book's case studies.

This bibliography is not a definitive overview of the literature on coaching. Readers are referred to the following databases; *PsycINFO* for psychology-related literature on coaching and to find doctoral dissertations on coaching; *Medline* for health-related coaching; *ERIC* for coaching related to education. In addition, there are a number of coaching-focused journals that may not be indexed in the academic databases. These include the *International Coaching Psychology Review*, published jointly by the Australian and British Psychological Societies (APS and BPS), and the *International Journal of Evidence-based Coaching and Mentoring*, published by Oxford Brookes University, Oxford, UK.

In December 2005 a literature search was conducted using the broad search term "coaching." Citations that referred to educational tutoring or coaching were excluded, as were papers that referred to mental health issues. Citations were categorized as follows: **A** = Primarily a discussion article; **E** = Primarily an empirical study; **Ecase** = Primarily an empirical case study.

The use of coaching in workplace or organizations settings to enhance work performance and executive development is increasing in popularity. The number of published scholarly papers in the business literature has escalated since 1996. The first published scholarly paper on coaching in the business literature was published in 1955. Between 1955 and December 2005 there were a total of 393 published papers. (See Figure A.1.) Of these 78 were empirical studies and 314 were articles which discussed coaching, theories of coaching, or application of techniques. (See Figure A.2.) Of the 393 published papers, 318 were published since 1996. Of the 78 empirical studies, 67 were published since 2001. The majority of empirical investigations are uncontrolled group or case studies.

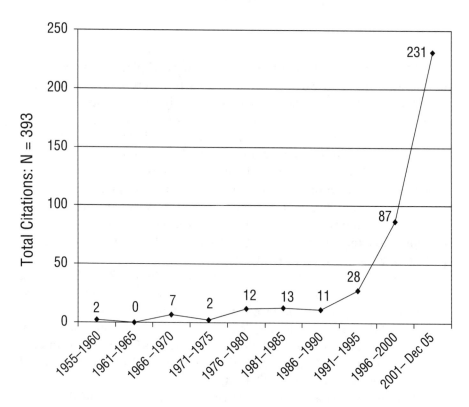

Figure A.1
Total Number of Citations in the Scholarly Business Literature 1955–2005

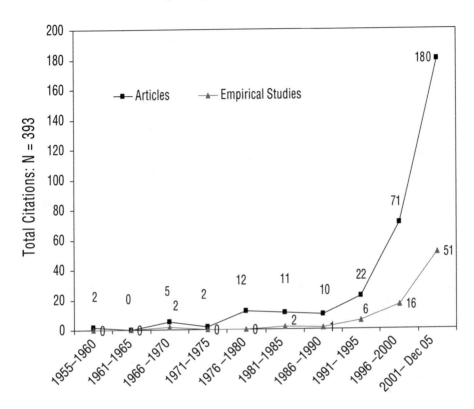

Figure A.2
Articles Compared With Empirical Studies in the
Scholarly Business Literature 1955–2005

Although coaching-related research is still in its infancy, there is an emerging body of empirical support for the effectiveness of workplace and executive coaching. Clearly, far more empirical research needs to be conducted. Such research should focus on the impact of coaching at both individual and organizational levels, as well as the establishment of validated, evidence-based coaching methodologies.

2001–2005 N = 231

2005

Ahern, G. (2005). Coaching professionalism and provider size. *Journal of Management Development*, 24(1), 94–99. **A**

Anon. (2005). Care and feeding of top performers. *Financial Executive*, 21(1), 12. **A**

APA Ethics Committee (2005). Report of the Ethics Committee, 2004. *American Psychologist, 60,* 523–528. **A**

Arnoudse, D. (2005). Commentary. *Reflections* (Society for Organizational Learning), *6,* 11. **A**

Beauchamp, M. R., S. R. Bray, et al. (2005). Leadership behaviors and multidimensional role ambiguity perceptions in team sports. *Small Group Research, 36*(1), 5–20. **E**

Blakey, J. (2005). Building a successful coaching environment at LogicaCMG. *Strategic HR Review, 4*(5), 8–9. **A**

Blattner, J. (2005). Coaching: The successful adventure of a downwardly mobile executive. *Consulting Psychology Journal: Practice & Research, 57*(1), 3–13. **Ecase**

Bluckert, P. (2005). The foundations of a psychological approach to executive coaching. *Industrial & Commercial Training, 37*(4), 171–178. **A**

Bluckert, P. (2005). The similarities and differences between coaching and therapy. *Industrial & Commercial Training, 37*(2), 91–96. **A**

Bolt, J. F. (2005). The Wild West of executive coaching. *Harvard Business Review, 83,* 145. **A**

Brown, J., R. Eagar, et al. (2005). BP refines leadership. *T+D, 59*(3), 33–41. **E**

Bryce, D. (2005). Senge sound bites. *T+D, 59*(4), 74–75. **A**

Byrne, C. (2005). Don't get stuck in a style rut. *New Zealand Management, 52*(6), 19. **Ecase**

Byrne, C. (2005). Getting to know me! *New Zealand Management, 52*(3), 21. **Ecase**

Cairo, P., D. L. Dotlich, et al. (2005). The unnatural leader. *T+D, 59*(3), 27–30. **A**

Chaundy, C. (2005). Creating a good practice center at the BBC. *KM Review, 8*(2), 24–27. **A**

Concelman, J. (2005). Referee bosses give leaders a bad rep. *Employment Relations Today, 32*(1), 47–53. **Ecase**

Dalton, C. M. (2005). Human resource management in a global environment: Keys for personal and organizational success: An interview with Eliza Hermann. *Business Horizons, 48,* 193–198. **A**

De Witte, H., J. Vandoorne, et al. (2005). Outplacement and re-employment measures during organizational restructuring in Belgium. *Journal of European Industrial Training, 29*(2), 148–164. **E**

Driscoll, J., & R. Cooper. (2005). Coaching for clinicians. *Nursing Management—UK, 12*(1), 18–23. **A**

Edelstein, B. C. (2005). The Wild West of executive coaching. *Harvard Business Review, 83,* 142. **A**

Frame, D. (2005). Tips for top challenges. *Nursing Management, 36*(1), 56. **A**

Frisch, M. H. (2005). Coaching caveats. *Human Resource Planning, 28*(2), 13–15. **A**

Frisch, M. H. (2005). Extending the reach of executive coaching: The internal coach. *Human Resource Planning, 28*(1), 23. **A**

Garvin, D. A., & M. A. Roberto. (2005). Change through persuasion. *Harvard Business Review, 83*(2), 104–112. **Ecase**

Goldberg, R. A. (2005). Resistance to coaching. *Organization Development Journal, 23*(1), 9–16. **A**

Grapentin, T. (2005). Segmenting the sales force. *Marketing Management, 14*(1), 29–34. **A**

Hackman, J. R., & R. Wageman. (2005). A theory of team coaching. *Academy of Management Review, 30*(2), 269–287. **A**

Hallowell, W. Z. (2005). The Wild West of executive coaching. *Harvard Business Review, 83*, 142–143. **A**

Hedin, G., L. Bendix, et al. (2005). Teaching extreme programming to large groups of students. *Journal of Systems & Software, 74*(2), 133–146. **Ecase**

Herman, R. E. (2005). HR managers as employee-retention specialists. *Employment Relations Today, 32*(2), 1–7. **A**

Ibarra, H., & K. Lineback. (2005). What's your story? *Harvard Business Review, 83*(1), 64–71. **A**

Ideus, K. (2005). The leader as coach. *Industrial & Commercial Training, 37*(4), 189–192. **A**

Jayne, V. (2005). Take it from the top. *New Zealand Management, 52*(1), 59–60. **A**

Kandrup, S. (2005). On systems coaching. *IEEE Software, 22*(1), 52–54. **A**

Kenrick, R. (2005). The Wild West of executive coaching. *Harvard Business Review, 83*, 142. **A**

Kets de Vries, M. F. R. (2005). Leadership group coaching in action: The zen of creating high performance teams. *Academy of Management Executive, 19*(1), 61–76. **A**

Khosh, M. (2005). The confidence game. *Harvard Business Review, 83*(7), 45–46. **A**

Korthagen, F. A. J. (2005). The organization in balance: Reflection and intuition as complementary processes. *Management Learning, 36*(3), 371–387. **A**

Latham, G. P., J. Almost, et al. (2005). New developments in performance management. *Organizational Dynamics, 34*(1), 77–87. **A**

Lloyd, J. (2005). Coaching employees to handle peer-to-peer issues. *Receivables Report for America's Health Care Financial Managers, 20*(5), 4–6. **A**

Lowman, R. L. (2005). Executive coaching: The road to Dodoville needs paving with more than good assumptions. *Consulting Psychology Journal: Practice & Research, 57*(1), 90–96. **A**

McLean, G. N., B. Yang, et al. (2005). Development and initial validation of an instrument measuring managerial coaching skill. *Human Resource Development Quarterly, 16*(2), 157–178. **E**

Newman, K. (2005). Delivering the mail: General Physics (UK) Ltd. *Industrial & Commercial Training, 37*(6/7), 361–364. **A**

Orenstein, E. (2005). Ask Ferf about . . . diversity training resources. *Financial Executive, 21*(4), 62. **A**

Peterson, D. B., & B. Little. (2005). Invited reaction: Development and initial validation of an instrument measuring managerial coaching skill. *Human Resource Development Quarterly, 16*(2), 179–184. **A**

Peterson, D. B., & J. Millier. (2005). The alchemy of coaching: "You're good, Jennifer, but you could be really good." *Consulting Psychology Journal: Practice & Research, 57*(1), 14–40. **Ecase**

Roche, T., C. Wick, et al. (2005). Innovation in learning: Agilent Technologies thinks outside the box. *Journal of Organizational Excellence, 24*(4), 45–53. **A**

Rossi, J. (2005). Growing strong leaders. *T+D, 59*(2), 53–55. **E**

Schnell, E. R. (2005). A case study of executive coaching as a support mechanism during organizational growth and evolution. *Consulting Psychology Journal: Practice & Research, 57*(1), 41–56. **Ecase**

Seligman, M. (2005). The corporate chill pill. *New Zealand Management, 52*(6), 64–66. **A**

Stone, F. (2005). You can mentor a team, too. *Employment Relations Today, 32*(1), 35–40. **A**

Trinka, J. A. (2005). What's a manager to do? *Industrial & Commercial Training, 37*(3), 154–159. **A**

Vloeberghs, D., R. Pepermans, et al. (2005). High-potential development policies: An empirical study among Belgian companies. *Journal of Management Development, 24*(6), 546–558. **E**

Volckmann, R. (2005). Assessing executive leadership: An integral approach. *Journal of Organizational Change Management, 18*(3), 289–302. **A**

Wasylyshyn, K. M. (2005). The reluctant president. *Consulting Psychology Journal: Practice & Research, 57*(1), 57–70. **Ecase**

Weiss, J., & J. Hughes. (2005). Want collaboration? *Harvard Business Review, 83*(3), 93–101. **A**

Winum, P. C. (2005). Effectiveness of a high-potential African American executive: The anatomy of a coaching engagement. *Consulting Psychology Journal: Practice & Research, 57*(1), 71–89. **Ecase**

Wright, J. (2005). Coaching mid-life, baby boomer women in the workplace. *Work, 25*(2), 179–183. **A**

Wright, J. (2005). Workplace coaching: What's it all about? *Work, 24*(3), 325–328. **A**

Yemm, G. (2005). Who do you talk to? *Management Services, 49*(1), 20–21. **A**

Zweibel, B. (2005). A strategic coach. *T+D, 59*(4), 62–64. **A**

2004

Anon. (2004). Coaching comes to stay. *New Zealand Management, 51*(10), 7–8. **A**

Anon. (2004). Firms turn to scripts to handle investor questions. *Operations Management, 10*(49), 3. **A**

Anon. (2004). New CIPD evidence proves front line leaders make the difference between low-performing and high-performing firms. *Management Services, 48*(3), 6. **E**

Anon. (2004). New standards help coaches and mentors to meet workplace challenges. *Industrial & Commercial Training, 36*(5), 220. **A**

Armandi, B. (2004). Special topic: Coaching. *Academy of Management Learning & Education, 3*(4), 457. **A**

Arond-Thomas, M. (2004). Resilient leadership for challenging times. *Physician Executive, 30*(4), 18–21. **A**

Barrett, F. (2004). Coaching for resilience. *Organization Development Journal, 22*(1), 93–96. **A**

Blackman-Sheppard, G. (2004). Executive coaching. *Industrial & Commercial Training, 36*(1), 5–8. **A**

Blitman, B., & J. Maes (2004). Visioning & coaching techniques in mediation. *Dispute Resolution Journal, 59*(2), 20–23. **A**

Bluckert, P. (2004). The state of play in corporate coaching: Current and future trends. *Industrial & Commercial Training, 36*(2), 53–56. **A**

Bossé-Smith, L. (2004). What tennis has taught me about business. *T+D, 58*(11), 26. **A**

Brecher, N. D. (2004). Better, not bitter. *Journal of Property Management, 69*(3), 52–55. **A**

Brooks, A. K. (2004). Transformational learning theory and implications for human resource development. *Advances in Developing Human Resources, 6*(2), 211–225. **A**

Burton, C. (2004). Do you "work to live" or "live to work"? *Journal for Quality & Participation, 27*(3), 14–16. **A**

Burton, C. (2004). What does work-life balance mean anyway? *Journal for Quality & Participation, 27*(3), 12–13. **A**

Cocivera, T., & S. Cronshaw. (2004). Action frame theory as a practical framework for the executive coaching process. *Consulting Psychology Journal: Practice & Research, 56*(4), 234–245. **A**

Ditze, A., P. Schmidt, et al. (2004). The human side of innovation. *Journal of Business Chemistry, 1*(2), 48–53. **A**

Dubouloy, M. (2004). The transitional space and self-recovery: A psychoanalytical approach to high-potential managers' training. *Human Relations, 57*(4), 467–496. **A**

Ducharme, M. J. (2004). The cognitive-behavioral approach to executive coaching. *Consulting Psychology Journal: Practice & Research, 56*(4), 214–224. **A**

Dumaine, D. (2004). Leadership in writing. *T+D, 58*(12), 52–54. **A**

Edwards, C. C. (2004). Redundancy: An opportunity in disguise. *Management Services, 48*(3), 34. **A**

Ellis, C. (2004). Leaders who inspire commitment. *MIT Sloan Management Review, 45*(3), 5. **A**

Frame, D., & A. Hendren. (2004). Digging out of the leadership hole. *Nursing Management, 35*(4), 80–81. **A**

Frigo, M. L. (2004). Strategy and execution: A continual process. *Strategic Finance, 85*(10), 7–21. **A**

Fryer, B., J. Goodnight, et al. (2004). The micromanager. *Harvard Business Review, 82*, 31–40. **A**

Fuimano, J. (2004). Add coaching to your leadership repertoire. *Nursing Management, 35*(1), 16–17. **A**

Gaillour, F. R. (2004). Want to be CEO? Focus on finesse. *Physician Executive, 30*(4), 14–16. **A**

Geller, S., S. R. Perdue, et al. (2004). Behavior-based safety coaching. *Professional Safety, 49*(7), 42–49. **Ecase**

Greenfield, D. P., & W. K. Hengen Jr. (2004). Confidentiality in coaching. *Consulting to Management—C2M, 15*(1), 9–14. **A**

Griffiths, M. (2004). Nurturing community coaching at Bt. *KM Review, 7*(5), 20–23. **A**

Hazard, P. (2004). Tackling performance management barriers. *Strategic HR Review, 3*(4), 3. **A**

Herzog, C. (2004). Enabling managers at JP Morgan. *Strategic Communication Management, 8*(6), 9. **A**

Jayne, V. (2004). Coaching pays. *New Zealand Management, 51*(1), 47–52. **A**

Khoury, G. C., & F. Analoui. (2004). Innovative management model for performance appraisal: The case of the Palestinian public universities. *Management Research News, 27*(1/2), 56–73. **A**

004). Trudging toward Dodoville: Conceptual approaches and in executive coaching. *Consulting Psychology Journal: Practice &* (4), 203–213. **A**

2004). When shadows fall: Using psychodynamic approaches in coaching. *Consulting Psychology Journal: Practice & Research, 56*(4),

Kirby, , lisold, et al. (2004). Left on a mountainside. *Harvard Business Review, 82,* 15–25. **A**

Koonce, R. (2004). Today consulting. *T+D, 58*(7), 48–51. **A**

Landale, A. (2004). Sales training bags the results for Cleanaway. *Industrial & Commercial Training, 36*(5), 216–218. **Ecase**

Lubitsh, G., & R. J. Shaw. (2004). The learning contract: A behavioural approach to managing poor performance by consultants and preventing disciplinary action. *Clinician in Management, 12*(4), 181–186. **Ecase**

Ludeman, K., & E. Erlandson. (2004). Coaching the alpha male. *Harvard Business Review, 82*(5), 58–67. **A**

Martin, C. A. (2004). Turn on the staying power. *Nursing Management, 35*(3), 21–27. **A**

Morsman, E. M., Jr. (2004). Up in profits or up in smoke? *RMA Journal, 86*(6), 66–68. **A**

Murray, E. (2004). Intuitive coaching—summary. *Industrial & Commercial Training, 36*(5), 203–206. **A3**

Naveh, E., & M. Erez. (2004). Innovation and attention to detail in the quality improvement paradigm. *Management Science, 50*(11), 1576–1586. **E**

Norman, C., & A. Powell. (2004). Transforming HR to deliver innovation at Accenture. *Strategic HR Review, 3*(3), 32–35. **A**

Offermann, L. R. (2004). When followers become toxic. *Harvard Business Review, 82*(1), 54–60. **A**

Parmenter, E. M. (2004). Health care benefits crisis: Cost drivers and strategic solutions. *Journal of Financial Service Professionals, 58*(4), 63–78. **A**

Perrewé, P. L., & D. L. Nelson. (2004). Gender and career success: The facilitative role of political skill. *Organizational Dynamics, 33*(4), 366–378. **A**

Quick, J. C., & M. Macik-Frey. (2004). Behind the mask: Coaching through deep interpersonal communication. *Consulting Psychology Journal: Practice & Research, 56*(2), 67–74. **A**

Ralph, E. C. (2004). Developing managers' effectiveness: A model with potential. *Journal of Management Inquiry, 13*(2), 152–163. **A**

Selmer, J. (2004). Motivating western business expatriates in China to localize. *Journal of Asian Business, 20*(1), 49–68. **E**

Sherin, J., & L. Caiger. (2004). Rational-emotive behavior therapy: A behavioral change model for executive coaching? *Consulting Psychology Journal: Practice & Research, 56*(4), 225–233. **E**

Sherman, S., & A. Freas (2004). The Wild West of executive coaching. *Harvard Business Review, 82*(11), 82–90.**A**

Steege, T. (2004). I know, I'll be a coach! *T+D, 58*(6), 0. **A**

Steelman, L. A., P. E. Levy, et al. (2004). The feedback environment scale: Construct definition, measurement, and validation. *Educational & Psychological Measurement, 64*(1), 143–164. **E**

Stern, L. R. (2004). Executive coaching: A working definition. *Consulting Psychology Journal: Practice & Research, 56*(3), 154–162. **E**

Stewart, T. A. (2004). Alpha bets. *Harvard Business Review, 82*, 10. **A**

Sue-Chan, C., & G. P. Latham. (2004). The relative effectiveness of external, peer, and self-coaches. *Applied Psychology: An International Review, 53*(2), 260–278. **E**

Summers, G. J. (2004). Today's business simulation industry. *Simulation & Gaming, 35*(2), 208–241. **A**

Thilo, J. L. (2004). More coaches needed to advise physician executives. *Physician Executive, 30*(6), 58–61. **A**

Van Velzen, J. H., & H. H. Tillema. (2004). Students' use of self-reflective thinking: When teaching becomes coaching. *Psychological Reports, 95*(3), 1229–1238. **E**

Wade, H. (2004). Managerial growth: A coaching case study. *Industrial & Commercial Training, 36*(2), 73–78. **Ecase**

Walker, L. J. (2004). A letter from camp. *Journal of Financial Planning, 17*(1), 24–27. **A**

Wasylyshyn, K. M., B. Gronsky, et al. (2004). Current practices. *Human Resource Planning, 27*(4), 7–12. **A**

Watkins, T. (2004). Two easy steps. *New Zealand Management, 51*(3), 42–44. **E**

Whitmore, J. (2004). Something really has to change: "Change management" as an imperative rather than a topic. *Journal of Change Management, 4*(1), 5–14. **A**

Wilson, C. (2004). Coaching and coach training in the workplace. *Industrial & Commercial Training, 36*(3), 96–98. **A**

Yapp, M. (2004). How can "role transition management" transform your company? *Industrial & Commercial Training, 36*(3), 110–112. **A**

2003

Anon. (2003). Lessons learned: How executive education is unique. *T+D, 57*(12), 51. **A**

Anon. (2003). Personal development for VW apprentices. *Journal of European Industrial Training, 27*(8), 436. **A**

Archer, E., & R. Morgan. (2003). Cultivate finance talent from bottom to top. *Strategic Finance, 84*(7), 30. **A**

Arnaud, G. (2003). A coach or a couch? A Lacanian perspective on executive coaching and consulting. *Human Relations, 56*(9), 1131–1154. **A**

Bacon, T. R. (2003). Helping people change. *Industrial & Commercial Training, 35*(2/3), 73. **A**

Bakker, A. B., E. Demerouti, et al. (2003). Dual processes at work in a call centre: An application of the job demands resources model. *European Journal of Work & Organizational Psychology, 12*(4), 393–417. **E**

Bannon, J. (2003). Anger at work. *T+D, 57*(10), 64–65. **A**

Bersin, J. (2003). Admiral leadership. *T+D, 57*(12), 44–51. **A**

Biggs, B. (2003). Indelible impressions of an authentic coach. *Team Performance Management, 9*(7/8), 205–206. **A**

Birchfield, R. (2003). World-class performance. *New Zealand Management, 50*(1), 7. **A**

Bonfield, H. (2003). Executive coaching is not just for big companies. *British Journal of Administrative Management, 36*, 18–19. **A**

Brooke, J., & A. Ham. (2003). Coaching managers to become better team leaders. *Strategic Communication Management, 7*(2), 4. **A**

Chung, Y. B., & M. C. Allen Gfroerer. (2003). Career coaching: Practice, training, professional, and ethical issues. *Career Development Quarterly, 52*(2), 141–152. **A**

Crosby, L. A., & S. L. Johnson. (2003). Watch what I do. *Marketing Management, 12*(6), 10–11. **A**

Eales-White, R. (2003). Creating growth for yourself as leader. *Industrial & Commercial Training, 35*(6), 247–250. **A**

Edmondson, A. C. (2003). Speaking up in the operating room: How team leaders promote learning in interdisciplinary action teams. *Journal of Management Studies, 40*(6), 1419–1452. **E**

Edwards, K., L. Chisholm, et al. (2003). Craving for coaching: A case study from Kwik-Fit Insurance Services. *Journal of Financial Services Marketing, 8*, 167–173. **Ecase**

Edwards, L. (2003). Coaching—the latest buzzword or a truly effective management tool? *Industrial & Commercial Training, 35*(7), 298–300. **A**

Ellingeic, A. D., A. F. Ellinger, et al. (2003). Supervisory coaching behavior, employee satisfaction, and warehouse employee performance: A dyadic perspective in the distribution industry. *Human Resource Development Quarterly, 14*(4), 435–458. **E**

Goldberg, S. (2003). Team effectiveness coaching: An innovative approach for supporting teams in complex systems. *Leadership & Management in Engineering, 3*(1), 15. **Ecase**

Goldsmith, M. (2003). Upfront research: Coaching for behavioural change. *Business Strategy Review, 14*(3), 7. **A**

Goldsmiths, M. (2003). Helping successful people get even better. *Business Strategy Review, 14*(1), 9–16. **A**

Gordon, P. J. (2003). Advising to avoid or to cope with dissertation hang-ups. *Academy of Management Learning & Education, 2*(2), 181–187. **A**

Hakim, C. (2003). We are all self-employed: Coaching for success and satisfaction. *Journal for Quality & Participation, 26*(1), 23–25. **A**

Hawkins, L. (2003). Solutions coaching? No problem!—Part 1. *Industrial & Commercial Training, 35*(7), 285–289. **A**

Hughes, J. E. (2003). A reflection on the art and practice of mentorship. *Journal of Wealth Management, 5*(4), 8. **A**

Jayne, V. (2003). Coaches, mentors and you. *New Zealand Management, 50*(1), 34. **A**

Martone, D. (2003). A guide to developing a competency-based performance-management system. *Employment Relations Today, 30*(3), 23–32. **A**

Mike, B., & J. W. Slocum Jr. (2003). Slice of reality: Changing culture at Pizza Hut and Yum! Brands, Inc. *Organizational Dynamics, 32*(4), 319. **A**

Neil, M. (2003). Someone to watch over you. *ABA Journal, 89*(10), 32. **A**

O'Neill, T., & B. Broadbent (2003). Personal coaching. *T+D, 57*(11), 77–79. **A**

Palmer, B. (2003). Maximizing value from executive coaching. *Strategic HR Review, 2*(6), 26. **A**

Palus, C. J., D. M. Horth, et al. (2003). Exploration for development: Developing leadership by making shared sense of complex challenges. *Consulting Psychology Journal: Practice & Research, 55*(1), 26–40. **A**

Pastore, D. L. (2003). A different lens to view mentoring in sport management. *Journal of Sport Management, 17*(1), 1. **A**

Quirke, B., & D. Walters. (2003). What every manager should know about communication. *Strategic Communication Management, 7*(5), 26. **Ecase**

Richard, J. T. (2003). Ideas on fostering creative problem solving in executive coaching. *Consulting Psychology Journal: Practice & Research, 55*(4), 249–256. **E**

Richards, B. (2003). Intelligent coaching: Unleashing human potential. *Journal for Quality & Participation, 26*(1), 13–16. **A**

Smither, J. W., M. London, et al. (2003). Can working with an executive coach improve multisource feedback ratings over time? A quasi-experimental field study. *Personnel Psychology, 56*(1), 23–44. **E**

Sung, J. (2003). Developing the next generation. *T+D, 57*(4), 14. **A**

Sung, T. (2003). Coaching better leaders. *T+D, 57*(3), 14. **A**

Vinnicombe, S., & V. Singh. (2003). Women-only management training: An essential part of women's leadership development. *Journal of Change Management, 3*(4), 294. **A**

Vloeberghs, D., & L. Berghman. (2003). Towards an effectiveness model of development centres. *Journal of Managerial Psychology, 18*(6), 511. **A**

Wales, S. (2003). Why coaching? *Journal of Change Management, 3*(3), 275. **Ecase**

Wasylyshyn, K. M. (2003). Executive coaching: An outcome study. *Consulting Psychology Journal: Practice & Research, 55*(2), 94–106. **Ecase**

Wycoff, J. (2003). The "Big 10" innovation killers: How to keep your innovation system alive and well. *Journal for Quality & Participation, 26*(2), 17. **A**

2002

Anon. (2002). Coaching finds favour among senior managers. *Journal of European Industrial Training, 26*(8), 404. **E**

Anon. (2002). Firms "failing to evaluate the results of coaching." *Industrial & Commercial Training, 34*(5), 203–204. **E**

Anon. (2002). Managers urge wider use of coaching. *Industrial & Commercial Training, 34*(7), 294. **A**

Bagshaw, M., & C. Bagshaw. (2002). Radical self-development—a bottom up perspective. *Industrial & Commercial Training, 34*(5), 194–197. **A**

Barrett, D. J., R. B. Worley, et al. (2002). Achieving results in MBA communication. *Business Communication Quarterly, 65*(3), 93–98. **A**

Berglas, S. (2002). The very real dangers of executive coaching. *Harvard Business Review, 80*(6), 86. **A**

Dyer, T. J. (2002). Executive development: Outer goals and inner coaching. *Employment Relations Today, 29*(1), 55–61. **A**

Elder, E., & M. L. Skinner. (2002). Managing executive coaching consultants effectively. *Employment Relations Today, 29*(2), 1–8. **A**

Ellinger, A. D., & R. P. Bostrom. (2002). An examination of managers' beliefs about their roles as facilitators of learning. *Management Learning, 33*(2), 147. **E**

Feldman, D. A. (2002). Distance coaching. *T+D, 56*(9), 54. **E**

Goski, J., G. Blackstone, et al. (2002). A model of leadership development. *Public Personnel Management, 31*(4), 517. **E**

Graziano, C. d. M. (2002). Ask an FEI researcher about . . . succession planning. *Financial Executive, 18*(6), 71. **A**

Green, M. E. (2002). Internal human resources consulting: Why doesn't your staff get it? *Public Personnel Management, 31*(1), 111. **A**

Homan, M., & L. Miller. (2002). Ace coaching alliances. *T+D, 56*(1), 40. **E**

Hunt, J. M., & J. Weintraub. (2002). How coaching can enhance your brand as a manager. *Journal of Organizational Excellence, 21*(2), 39–44. **A**

Hunter, L., P. Beaumont, et al. (2002). Knowledge management practice in Scottish law firms. *Human Resource Management Journal, 12*(2), 4–21. **A**

Kirkland, J. (2002). Executive coaching making strides in relatively untapped Czech market. *Prague Business Journal, 7*(10), 4. **A**

Lam Detzler, M., & S. M. Machuga. (2002). Earnings management surrounding top executive turnover in Japanese firms. *Review of Pacific Basin Financial Markets & Policies, 5*(3), 343. **E**

Levy, P. E., R. T. Cober, et al. (2002). The effect of transformational and transactional leadership perceptions on feedback-seeking intentions. *Journal of Applied Social Psychology, 32*(8), 1703–1720. **E**

Lyons, D. M. (2002). Executive commentary. *Academy of Management Executive, 16*(2), 120–121. **A**

Masciarelli, J. P. (2002). Meet Don Fabio, supercoach. *Consulting to Management—C2M, 13*(1), 38. **A**

Neghabat, A. R. (2002). Private matters. *Marketing Health Services, 22*(4), 25–27. **A**

Niemes, J. (2002). Discovering the value of executive coaching as a business transformation tool. *Journal of Organizational Excellence, 21*(4), 61–69. **A**

Orenstein, R. L. (2002). Executive coaching. *Journal of Applied Behavioral Science, 38*(3), 355. **A**

Rider, L. (2002). Coaching as a strategic intervention. *Industrial & Commercial Training, 34*(6), 233–236. **Ecase**

Rogers, E., C. W. Rogers, et al. (2002). Improving the payoff from 360-degree feedback. *Human Resource Planning, 25*(3), 44–54. **E**

Stratford, D. (2002). Coaching the chief executives. *Far Eastern Economic Review, 165*(19), 56. **A**

Walker, C. A. (2002). Saving your rookie managers from themselves. *Harvard Business Review, 80*(4), 97. **A**

Wilson, J. (2002). Wilson warns of hi-tech avalanche. *Journal of Accountancy, 193*(4), 18. **A**

Wright, P., W. F. Szeto, et al. (2002). *Guanxi* and professional conduct in China: A management development perspective. *International Journal of Human Resource Management, 13*(1), 156–182. **E**

Yoon, S.-K. (2002). A friend in need. *Far Eastern Economic Review, 165*(44), 60. **A**

2001

Anon. (2001). Executive coaching promises to address senior management "skills gap." *Industrial & Commercial Training, 33*(7), 275. **A**

Anon. (2001). Part I—How professionals learn—the theory! *Journal of European Industrial Training, 25*(5), 250–269. **A**

Bennett, J. L., & D. J. Martin. (2001). The next professional wave. *Consulting to Management— C2M, 12*(3), 6. **A**

Berry, J. (2001). New doors for professional development. *Consulting to Management—C2M, 12*(1), 13. **A**

David, M. (2001). When to call in "the coach." *Consulting to Management—C2M, 12*(1), 16. **A**

Deane, R. (2001). Coaching—a winning strategy. *British Journal of Administrative Management, 25,* 22. **Ecase**

Dikken, L. v. d. S.-d., & L. H. Hoeksema. (2001). The palette of management development. *Journal of Management Development, 20*(2), 168. **A**

Feldman, D. C. (2001). Career coaching: What HR professionals and managers need to know. *Human Resource Planning, 24*(2), 26. **A**

Fitzpatrick, M. A. (2001). Coaching champions. *Nursing Management, 32,* 7. **A**

Gilley, J. W. (2001). Taming the organization. *Human Resource Development International, 4*(2), 217–233. **A**

Gittell, J. H. (2001). Supervisory span, relational coordination and flight departure performance: A reassessment of postbureaucracy theory. *Organization Science: A Journal of the Institute of Management Sciences, 12*(4), 468. **E**

Greco, J. (2001). Hey, Coach! *Journal of Business Strategy, 22*(2), 28. **A**

Isley, K. M. (2001). Coaching for success. *Strategic Communication Management, 5*(2), 8. **A**

Kraines, G. A. (2001). Are you L.E.A.D.ing your troops? *Strategy & Leadership, 29*(2), 29. **A**

Maurer, T. J., K. D. Andrews, et al. (2001). Interviewee coaching, preparation strategies, and response strategies in relation to performance in situational employment interviews: An extension of Maurer, Solamon, and Troxel (1998). *Journal of Applied Psychology, 86*(4), 709–717. **E**

McDermott, L. C. (2001). Developing the new young managers. *T+D, 55*(10), 42. **A**

Miller, A. (2001). Two interviews, two perspectives. *IEEE Software, 18,* 56. **A**

Mintzer, B. (2001). The manager as coach . . . maximizing people potential. *Information Executive, 5*(10), 3. **A**

Newton, C. (2001). When planners are coached. *Journal of Financial Planning, 14,* 78. **A**

Oermann, M. H., & M. F. Garvin. (2001). When coaching new grads . . . *Nursing Management, 32*(1), 26. **A**

Piasecka, A. (2001). Creating champions. *Industrial & Commercial Training, 33*(2), 69. **A**

Pullen, C. (2001). Appreciative inquiry in financial planning and life. *Journal of Financial Planning, 14*(10), 52. **A**

Scott, G. (2001). Creating a learning environment: A win-win approach. *Journal of Healthcare Management, 46*(6), 361. **A**

Wageman, R. (2001). How leaders foster self-managing team effectiveness: Design choices versus hands-on coaching. *Organization Science: A Journal of the Institute of Management Sciences, 12*(5), 559. **E**

Zunitch, V. M. (2001). Put me in, Coach. *Journal of Accountancy, 192*(5), 55. **A**

1996–2000 N = 87

2000

Adkins, J. A. (2000). Ceridian Performance Partners' President Linda Hall Whitman on navigating work and life. *Academy of Management Executive, 14,* 28. **A**

Antonioni, D. (2000). Leading, managing, and coaching. *Industrial Management, 42*(5), 27. **A**

Arnold, J. A., S. Arad, et al. (2000). The empowering leadership questionnaire: The construction and validation of a new scale for . . . *Journal of Organizational Behavior, 21*(3), 249. **E**

Bernhardt, S. A., & G. A. McCulley. (2000). Knowledge management and pharmaceutical development teams: Using writing to guide science. *IEEE Transactions on Professional Communication, 43*(1), 22. **A**

Piasecka, A. (2000). Not leadership but leadership. *Industrial & Commercial Training, 32*(7), 253. **A**

Porter, S. (2000). Building business success: A case study of small business coaching. *Industrial & Commercial Training, 32*(7), 241. **Ecase**

Redshaw, B. (2000). Do we really understand coaching? How can we make it work better? *Industrial & Commercial Training, 32*(3), 106. **A**

Skinner, M. (2000). Training managers to be better communicators. *Employment Relations Today, 27*(1), 73–81. **A**

Solomon, P. (2000). Colloquium on change in accounting education: A report on the 2000 colloquium and a look forward to 2001. *Accounting Education, 9*(4), 417–418. **A**

Strickland, K. G., & S. Spanier (2000). I think you've got it! *Strategic Finance, 81*(7), 44. **A**

Young, A. M., & P. L. Perrewe. (2000). What did you expect? An examination of career-related support and social support among mentors and proteges. *Journal of Management, 26*(4), 611–632. **E**

1999

Burke, L. A., & T. T. Baldwin. (1999). Workforce training transfer: A study of the effect of relapse prevention training and transfer . . . *Human Resource Management, 38*(3), 227. **E**

De Jong, J. A., & B. Versloot. (1999). Structuring on-the-job training: Report of a multiple case study. *International Journal of Training & Development, 3*(3), 186. **A**

Douglas, C. A., & C. D. McCauley. (1999). Formal developmental relationships: A survey of organizational practices. *Human Resource Development Quarterly, 10*(3), 203–220. **E**

Edmondson, A. (1999). Psychological safety and learning behavior in work teams. *Administrative Science Quarterly, 44*(2), 350–383. **E**

Ellinger, A. D., & R. P. Bostrom. (1999). Managerial coaching behaviors in learning organizations. *Journal of Management Development, 18*(9), 752. **E**

Gurkov, I. (1999). Training needs in Russian industrial companies: Assessment by CEOs. *Post-Communist Economies, 11*(4), 541–549. **E**

Hall, D. T., K. L. Otaz , et al. (1999). Behind closed doors: What really happens in executive coaching. *Organizational Dynamics, 27*(3), 39. **A**

Hohmann, L., & R. Pressman. (1999). Coaching the rookie manager. *IEEE Software, 16*(1), 16. **A**

Kellett, P. (1999). Organisational leadership: Lessons from professional coaches. *Sport Management Review, 2*(2), 150–171. **E**

King, P., & J. Eaton. (1999). Coaching for results. *Industrial & Commercial Training, 31*(4), 145. **A**

Lewis, B. J. (1999). The case for management coaching. *Journal of Management in Engineering, 15*(3), 7. **A**

Masciarelli, J. P. (1999). Less lonely at the top. *Management Review, 88*(4), 58. **A**

Mobley, S. A. (1999). Judge not: How coaches create healthy organizations. *Journal for Quality & Participation, 22*(4), 57. **A**

Opiela, N. (1999). Professional coaches: Planners seek help in making dreams reality. *Journal of Financial Planning, 12*(9), 62–71. **A**

Roffe, I. (1999). Innovation and creativity in organisations: A review of the implications for training and development. *Journal of European Industrial Training, 23*(4/5), 224. **A**

Rohlander, D. G. (1999). How to effectively coach. *Journal of Management in Engineering, 15*(2), 16. **A**

Ryska, T. A., & D. Cooley. (1999). Developing team cohesion: A comparison of cognitive-behavioral strategies of U.S. and Australian sport coaches. *Journal of Psychology, 133*(5), 523. **E**

Sauerberg, S. K., & K. Prunty. (1999). Executive coaching: An Rx for MDs. *Physician Executive, 25*(2), 23. **A**

Smith, L., & J. Sandstrom. (1999). Executive leader coaching as a strategic activity. *Strategy & Leadership, 27*(6), 33. **A**

Tapsell, S. (1999). With a little help from my friend. *New Zealand Management, 46*(2), 45. **A**

Thach, L., & T. Heinselman. (1999). Executive coaching defined. *Training & Development, 53*(3), 34. **A**

Tulgan, B. (1999). Fast feedback. *Employment Relations Today, 26*(2), 73–83. **A**

1998

Bagshaw, M. (1998). Coaching, mentoring and the sibling organization. *Industrial & Commercial Training, 30*(3), 87. **A**

Bassi, L., S. Cheney, et al. (1998). Trends in workplace learning: Supply and demand in interesting times. *Training & Development, 52*(11), 51. **A**

Brunner, R. (1998). Psychoanalysis and coaching. *Journal of Managerial Psychology, 13*(7), 515. **A**

Burdett, J. O. (1998). Forty things every manager should know about coaching. *Journal of Management Development, 17*(2/3), 142. **A**

Fine, L. M., & E. B. Pullins. (1998). Peer mentoring in the industrial sales force: An exploratory investigation of men and women in developmental relationships. *Journal of Personal Selling & Sales Management, 18*(4), 89. **A**

Giglio, L., T. Diamante, et al. (1998). Coaching a leader: Leveraging change at the top. *Journal of Management Development, 17*(2/3), 93. **A**

Johnson, R. (1998). Get ahead, get a coach. *British Journal of Administrative Management, 8*, 8. **A**

Koonce, R. (1998). How to be high-tech and high-touch. *Training & Development, 52*(10), 22. **A**

Lester, M. (1998). Real-time coaching cuts training downtime. *Journal of Management in Engineering, 14*(4), 22. **A**

Liu, J., A. Srivastava, et al. (1998). Transference of skills between sports and business. *Journal of European Industrial Training, 22*(2/3), 93. **A**

Maccoby, M. (1998). Coaching technology leaders. *Research Technology Management, 41*(1), 57. **A**

Maurer, T., T. Jerry Solamon, et al. (1998). Relationship of coaching with performance in situational employment interviews. *Journal of Applied Psychology, 83*(1), 128–136. **E**

McManus, G. (1998). Up, up and away. *New Zealand Management, 45*(10), 60. **E**

Merritt, E. A., & F. Berger. (1998). The value of setting goals. *Cornell Hotel & Restaurant Administration Quarterly, 39*(1), 40. **A**

Norvell, T. L. (1998). From goal-setting to goal-getting: With a little help from . . . *Journal of Property Management, 63*(1), 14.

Phillips, K. R. (1998). The Achilles' heel of coaching. *Training & Development, 52*(3), 41. **A**

Rich, G. A. (1998). The constructs of sales coaching: Supervisory feedback, role modeling and trust. *Journal of Personal Selling & Sales Management, 18*(1), 53. **A**

Richardson, L. (1998). Five-minute sales coaching. *Training & Development, 52*(9), 53. **A**

Salopek, J. J. (1998). Arrested development. *Training & Development, 52*(9), 65. **E**

Sussman, L., & R. Finnegan. (1998). Coaching the star: Rationale and strategies. *Business Horizons, 41*(2), 47. **A**

Valkeavaara, T. (1998). Exploring the nature of human resource developers' expertise. *European Journal of Work & Organizational Psychology, 7*(4), 533–547. **E**

Wright, A. (1998). Counselling skills: Part II—Making sense of performance appraisal, coaching and mentoring. *Industrial & Commercial Training, 30*(5), 176. **A**

1997

Bagshaw, M. (1997). Coaching—Not new but newly relevant. *Industrial & Commercial Training, 29*(5), 166. **A**

Bagshaw, M. (1997). Employability—Creating a contract of mutual investment. *Industrial & Commercial Training, 29*(6), 187–189. **A**

Benson, G. (1997). Battle of the buzzwords. *Training & Development, 51*(7), 51. **A**

Chanen, J. S. (1997). Turning game plans into reality. *ABA Journal, 83*(8), 84. **A**

Dutton, G. (1997). Executive coaches call the plays. *Management Review, 86*(2), 39. **A**

Gould, D. (1997). Developing directors through personal coaching. *Long Range Planning, 30*(1), 29–37. **A**

Judge, W. Q., & J. Cowell. (1997). The brave new world of executive coaching. *Business Horizons, 40*(4), 71. **A**

Krug, J. (1997). Coaching engineers. *Journal of Management in Engineering, 13*(3), 13. **A**

Linde, K. V., & N. Horney. (1997). Seven ways to make your training department one of the best. *Training & Development, 51*(8), 20. **A**

Messmer, M. (1997). Coaching tips for accounting managers. *Government Accountants Journal, 45*(4), 50. **A**

Nowack, K. M., & S. Wimer. (1997). Coaching for human performance. *Training & Development, 51*(10), 28. **A**

Olivero, G., K. D. Bane, et al. (1997). Executive coaching as a transfer of training tool: Effects on productivity in a public agency. *Public Personnel Management, 26*(4), 461. **E**

Salters, L. (1997). Coaching and counseling for peak performance. *Business & Economic Review, 44*(1), 26. **A**

Waugh, T. A. (1997). Coaching for success. *CPA Journal, 67*(8), 75. **A**

1996

Adler, G. (1996). When a new manager stumbles, who's at fault? *Harvard Business Review, 74*, 22. **A**

Allerton, H. (1996). Reality check. *Training & Development, 50*(4), 8. **E**

Ashton, J. T., & J. Wilkerson. (1996). Establishing a team-based coaching process. *Nursing Management, 27*(3), 48N–48Q. **A**

Barner, R. (1996). The new millennium workplace: Seven changes that will challenge managers—and workers. *Futurist, 30*(2), 14. **A**

Bivens, B. (1996). Coaching for results. *Journal for Quality & Participation, 19*(3), 50. **A**

Blair, E. H. (1996). Achieving a total safety paradigm through authentic caring . . . *Professional Safety, 41*(5), 24. **A**

Good, D. J., & C. O. Swift. (1996). A coaching exercise in the sales management class. *Marketing Education Review, 6*(3), 73–83. **A**

Harari, O. (1996). The magic consultant's report. *Management Review, 85*(10), 9. **A**

Leeds, D. (1996). Training one-on-one. *Training & Development, 50*(9), 42. **A**

McDermott, L. (1996). Wanted: Chief executive coach. *Training & Development, 50*(5), 67. **A**

Olesen, M. (1996). Coaching today's executives. *Training & Development, 50*(3), 22. **A**

Peters, H. (1996). Peer coaching for executives. *Training & Development, 50*(3), 39. **A**

Rayman, J. R. (1996). Apples and oranges in the career center: Reaction to R. Reardon. *Journal of Counseling & Development, 74*(3), 286. **A**

Rubens, A. J., & M. A. Halperin. (1996). Mentoring in health care organizations. *Hospital Topics, 74*(4), 23. **A**

Sanders, D. L. (1996). Eight things you should know about business coaching before contracting for service. *Employment Relations Today, 23*(2), 67–75. **A**

Waldroop, J., & T. Butler. (1996). The executive as coach. *Harvard Business Review, 74*(6), 111. **A**

White, D. (1996). Stimulating innovative thinking. *Research Technology Management, 39*(5), 30. **A**

Witherspoon, R., & R. P. White. (1996). Executive coaching: What's in it for you? *Training & Development, 50*(3), 14. **A**

1991–1995 N = 28

1995

Allard, L. A. C. (1995). The new international manager. *Management Review,* *84*(8), 6. **A**

Ashburn, S. A. (1995). Coaching the client: Another role for management consultants. *Journal of Management Consulting, 8,* 2. **A**

Boyd, S. D. (1995). Executive speech coaching: An on-site, individualized, abbreviated course in public speaking. *Business Communication Quarterly,* *58*(3), 58–60. **A**

Clemmons, K. (1995). A practical approach to breaking the glass ceiling. *Management Review, 84*(2), 62. **A**

Geller, E. S. (1995). Safety coaching. *Professional Safety, 40*(7), 16. **A**

Gilsdorf, J. W. (1995). The evolving professional identity of the association for business communication. *Business Communication Quarterly, 58*(2), 47–50. **A**

Greeley, P. J. (1995). Energizing boards, commissions, task forces and volunteer groups. *Economic Development Review, 13*(3), 24. **A**

Kennedy, M. M. (1995). Personal trainer, personal coach. *Physician Executive,* *21*(3), 14. **A**

Rancourt, K. L. (1995). Real-time coaching boosts performance. *Training & Development, 49*(4), 53. **A**

Rheem, H. (1995). Performance management. *Harvard Business Review, 73*(3), 11–12. **E**

Snyder, A. (1995). Executive coaching: The new solution. *Management Review,* *84*(3), 29. **A**

Stoltz, P. G., & R. E. Major. (1995). Coaching windows. *Management Review,* *84*(9), 2. **A**

1994

Burch, J. C., & B. E. Smith. (1994). Nondirective counseling for managers: A triadic role-play preceded by cognitive structuring. *Simulation & Gaming,* *25*(1), 27. **A**

Johann, B. (1994). The meeting as a lever for organizational improvement. *National Productivity Review, 13*(3), 369. **A**

Koonce, R. (1994). One on one. *Training & Development, 48*(2), 34. **A**

Sorohan, E. G. (1994). Coaching Executives. *Training & Development, 48*(4), 14. **A**

1993

Good, D. J. (1993). Managerial coaching as a sales performance moderator. *Journal of Marketing Theory & Practice, 1*(3), 74. **A**

Haverkamp, B. E., & D. Moore. (1993). The career-personal dichotomy: Perceptual reality, practical illusion, and workplace integration. *Career Development Quarterly, 42,* 154. **Ecase**

Hendrickson, J. M., & N. Gardner. (1993). Evaluation of a social interaction coaching program in an integrated day-care setting. *Journal of Applied Behavior Analysis, 26*(2), 213. **E**

Kroeger, L. (1993). Coaching the internal audit team to writing success. *Internal Auditor, 50*(4), 59. **A**

Le Blanc, P. M., R. D. De Jong, et al. (1993). Leader member exchanges: Distinction between two factors. *European Work & Organizational Psychologist, 3*(4), 297. **E**

Rosenblatt, Z., K. S. Rogers, et al. (1993). Toward a political framework for flexible management of decline. *Organization Science: A Journal of the Institute of Management Sciences, 4*(1), 76. **ECase**

Thomas, D. A. (1993). Racial dynamics in cross-race developmental relationships. *Administrative Science Quarterly, 38*(2), 169–194. **E**

1992

Ambler, T., A. Roberts, et al. (1992). Developing international marketing managers: Getting out of the boxes. *European Business Journal, 4*(2), 40. **A**

Barry, T. (1992). The manager as coach. *Industrial & Commercial Training, 24*(2), 14. **A**

Hodes, B. (1992). A new foundation in business culture: Managerial coaching. *Industrial Management, 34*(5), 27. **A**

Marsh, L. (1992). Good manager: Good coach? *Industrial & Commercial Training, 24*(9), 3. **A**

1991

Burdett, J. O. (1991). To coach, or not to coach—that is the question! *Industrial & Commercial Training, 23*(6), 17. **A**

1986–1990 N = 11

1989

Bell, C. (1989). Coaching for distinctive service. *Management Review, 78*(5), 27. **A**

Clement, R. C., & R. E. McCormick (1989). Coaching team production. *Economic Inquiry, 27*(2), 287. **A**

Evered, R. D., & J. C. Selman (1989). Coaching and the art of management. *Organizational Dynamics, 18*(2), 16. **A**

1988

Kirkpatrick, D. L. (1988). Supervisory management development: Update from an expert. *Training & Development Journal, 42*(8), 59. **A**

Lawler, E. E., III. (1988). Substitutes for hierarchy. *Organizational Dynamics, 17*(1), 5–15. **A**

Stowell, S. J. (1988). Coaching: A commitment to leadership. *Training & Development Journal, 42*(6), 34. **A**

1987

Bell, C. R. (1987). Coaching for high performance. *SAM Advanced Management Journal (1984)*, 52(4), 26. **A**

Orth, C. D., H. E. Wilkinson, et al. (1987). The manager's role as coach and mentor. *Organizational Dynamics*, 15(4), 66–74. **A**

Webber, A. M. (1987). Red Auerbach on management. *Harvard Business Review*, 65, 84. **A**

Williams, T. (1987). Repertory grid combined with learning styles: A pilot study. *Industrial & Commercial Training*, 19(2), 3. **E**

1986

Kanter, R. M., & J. P. Zolner. (1986). What the "new" coaches can teach managers. *Management Review*, 75(11), 10. **A**

1981–1985 N = 13

1985

Kelly, P. J. (1985). Coach the coach. *Training & Development Journal*, 39(11), 54. **A**

1984

Finn, W. T. (1984). Keep your eye on the sales training manager. *Training & Development Journal*, 38(7), 65. **A**

Richardson, J., & B. Bennett. (1984). Applying learning techniques to on-the-job development part II. *Journal of European Industrial Training*, 8(3), 5. **Ecase**

Robison, W. L. (1984). Management and ethical decision-making. *Journal of Business Ethics*, 3(4), 287. **A**

1983

Allenbaugh, G. E. (1983). Coaching . . . a management tool for a more effective work performance. *Management Review*, 72(5), 21. **A**

Donarski, J., R. W. Heath, et al. (1983). Training through consultancy to improve maintenance management. *Journal of European Industrial Training*, 7(3), 10. **A**

Fox, D. (1983). Coaching: The way to protect your sales training investment. *Training & Development Journal*, 37(11), 37. **A**

Tyson, L., & H. Birnbrauer. (1983). Coaching: A tool for success. *Training & Development Journal*, 37(9), 30. **A**

1982

Kurecka, P. M., J. M. Austin Jr., et al. (1982). Full and errant coaching effects on assigned role leaderless group discussion performance. *Personnel Psychology*, 35(4), 805–812. **E**

1981

McBrien, R. J. (1981). Coaching clients to manage depression. *Personnel & Guidance Journal, 59*(7), 429. **A**

Randolph, A. B. (1981). Managerial career coaching. *Training & Development Journal, 35*(7), 54. **A**

Sashkin, M. (1981). Appraising appraisal: Ten lessons from research for practice. *Organizational Dynamics, 9*(3), 37-50. **A**

Wolf, J. F., & F. P. Sherwood. (1981). Coaching: Supporting public executives on the job. *Public Administration Review, 41*(1), 73–76. **A**

1976–1980 N = 12

1980

Kondrasuk, J. (1980). The coaching controversy . . . revisited. *Training & Development Journal, 34*(2), 70. **A**

Weissman, S., & G. Montgomery. (1980). Techniques for group family enrichment. *Personnel & Guidance Journal, 59*(2), 113. **A**

1979

Hague, H. (1979). Tools for helping self-development, part 3: On-the-job coaching by the tutor. *Journal of European Industrial Training, 3*(1), 25. **A**

Joyce, L. (1979). Management training: Developments and trends. *Journal of European Industrial Training, 3*(6), 15. **A**

Kondrasuk, J. (1979). The best method to train managers . . . *Training & Development Journal, 33*(8), 46. **A**

Rackham, N. (1979). The coaching controversy. *Training & Development Journal, 33*(11), 12–16. **A**

1978

Hague, H. (1978). Tools for helping self-development—part 1. *Journal of European Industrial Training, 2*(3), 13. **A**

Hague, H. (1978). Tools for helping self-development—part 2. *Journal of European Industrial Training, 2*(5), 18. **A**

Odiorne, G. S. (1978). MBO: A backward glance. *Business Horizons, 21*(5), 14. **A**

1977

Buzzotta, V. R., R. E. Lefton, et al. (1977). Coaching and counseling: How you can improve the way it's done. *Training & Development Journal, 31*(11), 50. **A**

Kessler, B. M. (1977). New selling skills for today's changing marketplace. *Training & Development Journal, 31*(11), 38. **A**

Linnet, L. J. (1976). Planned coaching. *Management Services, 20*(5), 10–13. **A**

1971–1975 N = 2

1971

Clarke, M. (1971). Why managers don't coach. *Industrial & Commercial Training,* 3(7), 308. **A**

Kastens, M. L. (1971). A management coach concept for management development. *Training & Development Journal,* 25(8), 8. **A**

1966–1970 N = 7

1970

Utgaard, S. B., & R. V. Dawis. (1970). The most frequently used training techniques. *Training & Development Journal,* 24(2), 40. **E**

Wohlking, W. (1970). Attitude change, behavior change: The role of the training department. *California Management Review,* 13(2), 45. **A**

1969

Burke, R. J., & D. S. Wilcox. (1969). Characteristics of effective employee performance review and development Interviews. *Personnel Psychology,* 22(3), 291–305. **A**

Scharinger, D. H. (1969). Performance appraisal—a means or an end. *Training & Development Journal,* 23(4), 52. **A**

1967

Banaka, W. H. (1967). Invention: A key to effective coaching. *Training & Development Journal,* 21(11), 44. **A**

1966

Huse, E. F. (1966). Putting in a management development program that works. *California Management Review,* 9(2), 73. **E**

Manske, F. A., Jr. (1966). Supervisory training. *Training & Development Journal,* 20(9), 44. **A**

1955–1965 N = 2

1958

Davis, R. T. (1958). Sales management in the field. *Harvard Business Review,* 36(1), 91. **A**

1955

Given, W. B., Jr. (1955). The engineer goes into management. *Harvard Business Review,* 33(1), 43. **A**

Author Index

Subject Index